Nanotechnology in Drug Delivery: Fundamentals, Design, and Applications

Nanotechnology in Drug Delivery: Fundamentals, Design, and Applications

Editor

Lino Messana

scitus
academics

Nanotechnology in Drug Delivery: Fundamentals, Design, and Applications

Edited by **Lino Messana**

ISBN: 978-1-68117-691-8
Library of Congress Control Number: 2016958862

SCITUS Academics LLC,
616, Corporate Way, Suite 2, 4766,
Valley Cottage, NY 10989

www.scitusacademics.com

Notice

Printed in United States of America on Acid Free Paper

Preface

The use of nanotechnology in medicine and more specifically drug delivery is set to spread rapidly. Currently many substances are under investigation for drug delivery and more specifically for cancer therapy. Nanotechnology is the study, design, creation, synthesis, manipulation, and application of materials, devices, and systems at the nanometre scale. Recent years have witnessed unprecedented growth of research and applications in the area of nanoscience and nanotechnology. There is increasing optimism that nanotechnology, as applied to medicine, will bring significant advances in the diagnosis and treatment of disease. Anticipated applications in medicine include drug delivery, both in vitro and in vivo diagnostics, nutraceuticals and production of improved biocompatible materials. Engineered nanoparticles are an important tool to realize a number of these applications.

Nanotechnology in Drug Delivery: Fundamentals, Design, and Applications presents reviews and original matter from renowned experts working in the interdisciplinary field of nanotechnology use in drug delivery. From their direct and current practice, the readers can realize a wide vision on the new and enduring potentialities of nanotechnology application of drug delivery.

Nanotechnology is expected to have a revolutionary impact on medicine. Nanoparticles can play a major role in medicine and especially in diagnosis and therapy of cancer, cardiovascular diseases and infectious diseases. To further the application of nanoparticles in pharmacy, it is important that the systems are stable, capable of being functionalized, biocompatible and directed to specific target sites in the body after systemic administration. Nanotechnology is on its way to make a big impact in Pharmaceutical and Medical diagnostics sciences. A dynamic collaboration is observed within the Researchers, Government, Pharmaceutical - Biomedical companies and educational institutions all over the world in developing the nanotechnology applications in advanced medicine and patient care. It is expected that the forthcoming generations of nano products will have target specificity, may carry multiple drugs and could potentially release the payloads at varying time intervals. Pharmaceutical education in India is also taking significant steps in incorporating courses as well as offering specialization in nanotechnology and its applications in Pharmaceutical scenario.

Table of Contents

Chapter 1

Nanotechnology in drug delivery: the need for more cell culture based studies in screening

Aminu Umar Kura[1], Sharida Fakurazi[1,2*], Mohd Zobir Hussein[3] and Palanisamy Arulselvan[1]

[1]*Laboratory of Vaccine and Immunotherapeutics, Institute of Bioscience, Universiti Putra Malaysia, 43400 Selangor, Malaysia*

[2]*Faculty of Medicine and Health Science, Pharmacology Unit, Universiti Putra Malaysia, Selangor, Malaysia*

ABSTRACT

Advances in biomedical science are leading to upsurge synthesis of nanodelivery systems for drug delivery. The systems were characterized by controlled, targeted and sustained drug delivery ability. Humans are the target of these systems, hence, animals whose systems resembles humans were used to predict outcome.

Thus, increasing costs in money and time, plus ethical concerns over animal usage. However, with consideration and planning in experimental conditions, *in vitro* pharmacological studies of the nanodelivery can mimic the *in vivo*system. This can function as a simple method to investigate the effect of such materials without endangering animals especially at screening phase.

Keywords: *In vitro* Animal studies Nanodelivery system Toxicity and bio distribution

INTRODUCTION

Nanodelivery system (NDS) is a branch of Nanomedicine characterized by controlled, targeted and sustained drug delivery ability, a limitation and drawback that is currently limiting conventional drug delivery system especially in drug delivery to tight areas like the brain [1]. NDS, due to their small sizes usually below 100 nm and unique physico-chemical and biological properties, are now becoming the favourable system in drug delivery and imaging system covering wider ailments including cancers and central nervous pathologies [2, 3]. Drugs susceptible to enzymatic degradation and/or pH destabilization can be incorporated into this delivery system, it also offer them with additional possibilities of targeted and controlled release potential [4]. However to achieve these foreseeable advantages offered by nanodelivery systems, challenges which include developing toxic-free system, improved biocompatibility, effective drug loading, proper targeting, transport and release ability must be ascertained [1]. Biocompatibility and bio-distribution are part of the key to success for drug development in achieving its aim, consequently more *in vitro* and *in vivo* study needed to achieve the desired characteristics.

However, with changes and improvement in drug delivery via NDS comes a price (possible toxic effect), the evaluation of which is important before any biological application can be introduce. In 2004, the term nanotoxicity was coined; referring to the study of the potential toxic impacts of nanoparticles on biological and ecological systems [5]. The field arose due to concern over the growing field of nanotechnology and the potential health effects of nano-materials, especially to humans. The low soluble or insoluble type nano-material capable of passing through various defence systems because of their tiny size are of the greatest concern [6]. The toxicity and bio-distribution of these delivery systems could be influenced by the synthetic process; coating materials; particle sizes and or route of administration [7, 8]. Hence, toxicity and distribution studies should target these to evaluate the potential of NDS in drug delivery.

Animals have been in the forefront of chemical toxicity test, including drugs intended for human consumption [9]. In 2005, 20% of the over 10 billion euro spent on animal experiments worldwide and 100million animals used were in toxicity studies [9]. Although, animal usage is a part of the legislation before chemical usage is allowed for both life and environmental protections [10]. The values of the obtained results are sometimes challenged with respect to transfer to humans, extreme doses application during the studies and a time a false positive correlation are made with respect to the low toxicity of most of the tested chemicals [10]. Animal based-studies are generally costly in term of money and time, plus ethical issues associated with it, these reasons make tissue and cell-based exposure studies very useful for toxicity screening of new compounds (nanoparticles inclusive). Therefore, human as well as other animal tissue/cells will continue to serve as an alternative (*in-vitro*) test methods. The application of which may provide endpoints result, which are directly associated with specific organs. Nevertheless, it is well acknowledged, especially in the European community that cell and tissue cultures will not be able to replace animal tests completely [11]. This is mainly due to the complexity of the human and the short lifetime of culture, negating for the assessment of chronic toxicity needed before human application [11].

In the past, cytotoxicity study used few survival mechanisms following exposure to the chosen chemicals, mechanism like mitochondrial activity, membrane damage and enzymes leakages into the culture media were studied. However, advances were made over the years, which resulted in cell usage for gene analysis in toxicity, microscopic changes in cell cytoskeleton due to toxicity among others [12, 13, 14, 15]. This review aimed at reviewing some of those methods used in assessing nanomaterial toxicity using cell/tissue culture technique, with emphasis on their advantage over entire animal usage, especially during screening processes.

REVIEW

Nanodelivery systems effects in relationship to dose and time

Among the barrage of methods used in the NDS toxicity assessment is the whole cell quantification following exposure to certain concentration of the expected toxic nanomaterial as compared to the untreated cell [2, 3]. These methods have the advantage of conveying the actual number of viable cells, an increase (cell proliferation) or decrease (cytotoxicity) in comparison to control (untreated cells). In some instances, they measure the activity of viable cells in the treated sample and the control, indirectly counting live and dead cells [2, 3].

Trypan blue is an example of quantitative dye exclusion assay. In this experiment, cells are treated with NDS or any chemical/drug for a desired period, then stained with trypan blue to observe for cell proliferation or cell's dead [16]. The dye is called an exclusion diazo dye, which is taken up by dead cells only, but excluded, by viable cells [16]. The cells are viewed at higher magnification using a light microscope, where unstained cells reflect the total number of viable cells recovered from a given treatment. The toxicity potential of zinc-layered hydroxide (ZLH) and its corresponding cetirizine nanocomposite (CETN) were tested on normal Chang liver cells after 24 hours of treatment using the trypan blue stain; it was done to show dose-dependent toxic effects of the nano-carrier (ZLH) as compared to the corresponding intercalated counterpart (CETN) [17]. Other nanomaterial tested using this method included but not limited to zinc oxide (ZnO), copper oxide (CuO) and multi wall carbon nanotubes (MWCNT) [12].

Stress exposure in the form nutrient deprivation or drugs induced toxicity, could lead to necrotic or apoptotic death at the cellular level [18]. Propidium iodide and acridine (AOPI) are examples of double dye stain; they can be used to study the apoptotic and necrotic cell death. Viable cells stain green, while apoptotic cells stain green and shrunken with condensation of the nucleus, the necrotic cells stain red [18]. These morphological changes will appear under fluorescence microscope with AOPI stain. Propidium iodide (PI) intercalates into double-stranded nucleic acids of dying or dead cells as it can penetrate damaged cell membranes. It is excluded by viable cells, but acridine orange (AO) can penetrate intact membrane to stain viable cells [18]. Copper oxide nanoparticles were shown to induce apoptosis and subsequent cell death, in human skin keratinocytes, utilizing the AOPI staining technique [13]. Apoptosis is generally regarded as an active or programmed form of cell death. It is the preferred cell death; it allows the normal immune system to get rid of the demise cells and tissues from the system [14]. In contrast to this method of cell death is the necrotic method, also referred to as uncontrolled or pathological cell death. The two systems, are not exclusively separated as they may happen at the same time on the same tissue, especially where different concentrations were used [14].

As stated earlier apoptotic cells stands the chances of being engulfed by neighbouring immune cells, but necrosis may lead to a secondary effect especially where immunity has weakened and or inefficient. These and other double dye studies are capable of screening NDS and other compounds at the cellular level for a possible cell death method before endangering animal or human lives. Using this technique, silver nanoparticle was shown to have both apoptotic and necrotic effects on breast cancer cells (MCF-7) in a dose dependent fashion [19]. Doses below 50 μg/mL demonstrated apoptotic death and above 80 μg/mL caused more of necrotic cell death. Not just killing the cancer cell is important, but also what happen after cancer cell death. The proceeding secondary reaction due to the toxic substances release to the surrounding normal cells by the dying cancer cells could be more deadly than cancer itself [20]. A clinical syndrome called tumour lysis syndrome seen in the case cancer cells lysis, could be reduce if apoptosis is induce more in cancer treatment rather than necrosis. Thus, results like this one could be handy in deciding doses to be use during animal and subsequent clinical trials.

Cell functions and membrane integrity

Cellular metabolism and cell membrane integrity as functions of living cells were used in the past to assess drug and other chemical's toxicity. Now they are in use for NDS screening [21]. Proliferation assay like MTT (3-(4,5-dimethylthiazol-2-yl)-2,5-diphenyltetrazolium bromide) and neutral assay are typical examples of functional assessment used in toxicity and or efficacy studies. They are rapid and convenient in determining viable cell number in proliferation or cytotoxicity studies. While lactate dehydrogenase (LDH) assay is, an example of cell membrane integrity study commonly applied in the study of nanoparticle toxicity, as well as other drugs and chemicals intended for human or environmental uses [21]. LDH is a cellular enzyme that is release into the cytoplasm upon cell lysis. The assay, therefore, can be used to measure membrane integrity. Principally the assay work by converting lactate to pyruvate through oxidation by the LDH, subsequently Pyruvate reacts with the tetrazolium salt to form formazan, water-soluble formazan dye that can be detected by a spectrophotometer [21].

In the case of MTT, the assay is dependent on the reduction of tetrazolium salt MTT (3-(4,5-dimethylthazol-2-yl)-2,5-diphenyl tetrazolium bromide) by mitochondrial dehydrogenase of only viable cells to form a blue formazan product [15]. Neutral red on the other hand is an uptake viability assay [22]. Principally it works by the accumulation of the dye in the lysosomes of uninjured cells.

Utilizing some of the above-described assays, doses and time-dependent effect of different types of nanomaterial was evaluated to stimulate and estimate possible *in vivo* effect [12, 13, 17]. In most instances, 24-72h period was employed to determine these effects, which will have been days to weeks if similar effects were to be determined in animals. For example, eighty experimental animals of both sexes were used to study the possible toxicity of a synthesized titanium oxide nanoparticle of different sizes and over three weeks period used [23]. The tissues collected from these animals undergoes several days of processing before a decision emerged as to either the titanium oxide nanoparticle used where toxic or not [23]. Above stated assays will have been a better choice in screening these nanoparticles for their likely toxicity, and where toxicity exists, modification can be made at the level of synthesis with the view to address what causes the toxicity. Satisfactory results obtained from these *in vitro*assays will help in designing a successful *in vivo* study, limiting wastage in lives, money and time.

Oxidative stress studies of nanodelivery systems

In vitro assays such as nitric oxide (NO) assay (Greiss reaction) are used as a measure of free radical production following exposure to NDS or any oxidative stress inducing drugs [24]. This measurement provides a surrogate marker and quantitative indicator of nitric oxide production due to a nano-delivery treatment of particular cell line or tissue. Other oxidative stress assays such as glutathione reductase (GR), reactive oxygen species (ROS) are also valuable in assessing oxidative stress potential of nano-delivery systems. Cytotoxicity and free radical assessment via nitric oxide analysis is becoming very curial [25]. This is so due to the growing evidence, that high concentrations of nitric oxide (NO) in the brain might be involve in a variety of neurodegenerative diseases, of which Parkinson disease is one of them. Others are Alzheimer's, cerebral ischemia and epilepsy [25]. These and other related oxidative stress markers associated with different diseases, including cancers could be predicted with ease using cell culture techniques [26]. The timing of which could be considered relatively short when compared to animal studies of similar aim. Within 24h of exposure, titanium oxide nanoparticle demonstrated a dose related increase in reactive oxygen species from normal human bronchial epithelium (BEAS-2B) [27]. In the same study, a relationship was established between production of ROS and glutathione reductive enzymes (GSH) depletion. Recently, an important development was demonstrated in the treatment of cardiomyopathy with cerium oxide (CeO2) nanoparticles [28]. This group of nanoparticles were shown to modulate oxidative stress in transgenic mice with cardiomyopathy through free radical scavenging activity. The promising result was generated from animal model study, but the pre-requisite and preliminary findings were obtained from cell culture models (29. 30). Where, CeO2 nanoparticles was shown to rescued HT22 cells from oxidative stress-induced cell death [29], in another related study it was demonstrated to protect normal human breast cells from radiation-induced apoptotic cell death [30]. Here, *in vitro* studies predicted an outstanding animal result, negating the need for excessive animal usage. Thus, proper screening and designing of preliminary cell culture work will likely limit the number of animal to be use, indirectly cutting down cost and preserving ecological balance.

Uptake mechanism and blood brain barrier delivery of drugs

The cellular uptake and delivery of nanoparticles across the blood brain barrier is another aspect of pharmacology where cell culture technology is of essence. With proper usage of available *in vitro* techniques, tedious procedure like micro dialysis, used in evaluating delivery of nanoparticles and other drugs to the brain can be minimize. Other molecular details like the receptor involve in nanoparticle transport across the BBB could also be explore using these models [31]. A group of scientist demonstrated the role of temperature and alternative receptor in transporting poly (methoxypolyethyleneglycol cyanoacrylate-co-hexadecylcyanoacrylate nanoparticle (PEG-PHDCA) to the brain [31, 32]. These researchers used a relatively simple and cheap *in vitro* BBB model [31, 32]. These cell culture models are becoming important tools in investigating drug delivery to the brain without necessarily torturing animals, especially during the initial screening phase [33, 34]. Unlike the animal models, cell culture technology has the advantage of rapid evaluation in nanoparticle uptake mechanism, toxicity potentials and other related molecular mechanism needed in achieving drug delivery to the CNS.

The uptake and internalization of drugs intercalated into NDS can be studied with relative ease using *in vitro* cell models. An optical microscope and electron spin resonance (ESR) spectroscopic studies exemplifies this [15]. Where, the mechanism of uptake and internalization of iron oxide nanoparticles (IONs) into a brain tumour cell were shown [15]. A water dispersible iron oxide nanoparticle based formulation that was loaded with an anticancer agent also showed good cell penetration via an *in vitro* modelling [35]. The NDS (IONs) get internalize into the cell through cell membrane invagination, forming an early endosome that transformed into a late endosome within five minutes, then later a lysosome containing the particle and drug [18, 36, 37]. Entrance and uptake of paclitaxel-LDH nanoparticles bounded with FITC into cervical cancer was also studied using fluorescence and transmission electron microscope (TEM). The two demonstrated endocytosis as a means of cell entrance by the nanoparticles [9]. Demonstrating these, effects in animals require many lives to be sacrifice at intervals, added to which is a long and a lacklustre process needed before the result is acquired in most cases [38].

In the near future, thousands of these drug delivery vehicles may be synthesized for the treatment and diagnosis of CNS disease. Consequently, a BBB *in-vitro* cell culture models that closely resembles the *in-vivo* system, reflecting at least the characteristics "barrier", are in high demand. This is to minimise cost and other ethical issues attributed with *in-vivo* test systems. The *In vitro* BBB models are usually made-up of cerebral capillary endothelial or choroid plexus epithelial cells mostly of porcine in origin that closely resembles the animal brain system [33]. Interestingly, a reasonable correlation between, these *in vitro* models and the animal models existed [39]. Thus, strengthen further the importance of alternative to animal in BBB drug delivery studies.

Live cells imaging in nanoparticle studies

Live cell imaging studies are other emerging *in vitro* techniques used in the study of nanoparticles and other related drugs [34]. With the live cell imaging systems, cellular activity like mode of death, proliferation and inhibition as a result nanoparticle or other compounds exposure can be studied. This method observe living cells; images are acquired from microscopes and other high content screening systems. The system gives a better view of cellular dynamics as it relates to any form of treatment and the researcher sees changes, as they are unfolding.

Cancer diagnosis and its therapy are among the areas that benefited from nanoparticles and live cell imaging systems studies [40]. Huge advances emerged through studying the dynamic biological processes taking place during cancer treatment [41, 42]. This technique enabled researchers to follow the movement of individually labelled nanoparticles to specific parts of the cell. In some instances they are able to look at the receptor mediated transport and entrance of the particles into the chosen cells [34, 40]. Two different types of nanoparticles (polystyrene and silica nanoparticles) were quantitatively analysed and localised in the cytoplasm and nucleus of Hep-2 cells about one hour after treatment using the live cell imaging [40]. Quantification was done through the fluorescence intensities of the tagged nanoparticles in the cytoplasm and nucleus of the cells. This observation has added to the list of nanoparticles with the capability of gene transfer into the nucleus.

Nanoparticles in cancer screening

Over the last six decades or so more than 85,000 compounds were screened against cancers, most of which using short-term assays [43]. Cell and tissue culture (*in vitro*) studies were used as a baseline test in screening these compounds for their anti-cancer activity [43]. Significant number of the compounds were initially considered effective and promising, but failed clinical test in treating cancer [43]. By far the number of compounds that failed outweighs those that succeed to clinical usage [43]. The lost in time, money and more importantly lives, would likely wither if proper screening of intending anti-cancer agent were maximally utilized. One way of screening nanoparticles for possible anti-cancer activity is through *in vitro* methods using cells or tissues.

Cancer nanotechnology is emerging as result of interdisciplinary research and has great potential application in diagnosis and treating cancers [44]. As such, synthesis of hundreds of nano-biotechnology base cancer treatment/diagnostic tools is on the increase, this is to cater for cancer, a major public health problem [44, 45]. Targeted drug deliveries in cancer treatment with reduce toxicity to surrounding normal cells and increase efficiency is but a few advantages explored while using this nanodelivery system [45]. Crossing the blood brain barrier to diagnose and treat CNS tumours, control release and increase solubility are also additional advantages of NDS [45]. Achieving these involves synthesizing and re-synthesizing several nanodelivery systems using nanotechnology, each time adjusting for a particular parameter to achieve the desired character. With each adjustment came the need for testing a peculiar property, doing this on animal's means a lot in terms of time and money.

Nanoparticle in cancer treatment was studied using an *in vitro* model, where uptake of the polylactic-co-glycolic acid (PLGA) nanoparticles coated with polyvinyl alcohol (PVA) was shown to be 1.4 times less than that coated with vitamin E TPGS on a colorectal cancer cell line [45]. Recently our team demonstrated the effect of coating on iron oxide nanoparticle intercalated with Gallic acid in a cell culture-base study [46]. The magnetic nanoparticles with average size of 11.4 nm and coated with Polyethylene glycol (PEG) showed enhanced anti-cancer effect on breast cancer but not lung cancer compared to pure Gallic acid [46]. However, the same nanodelivery system containing Gallic acid coated with chitosan demonstrated lesser anti-cancer activity on both breast and colon cancer compare to the pristine Gallic acid [3]. Thus, cell culture studies allowed for the choice of better polymer on this nanoparticle containing Gallic acid in cancer treatment. It also helps in the screening of different cancer for which the delivery system will likely have better effect on.

The size-dependent quantum effect of nanoparticle is providing them unique physico-chemical and biological properties that makes them fundamentally different from their corresponding bulk counterpart, especially in cancer diagnosis and treatment [47]. *In vitro* cell proliferation assays were selected to show time and dose dependent the cytotoxicity of zinc oxide nanoparticles on colon cancer cells [47]. The same technique demonstrated the effect of particles sizes on the chosen cancer cells, where sizes below 30 nm showed higher toxicity compared to 90 nm size particles. The above-mentioned experiments look, sound relatively simple and cheap. However, the information generated could serve as a reasonable baseline in predicting possible *in vivo* outcome.

Limitation of cell culture technique

Absence of immune effect, blood proteins, the endocrine system and the general lack of complex interaction of the whole animal in most *in vitro* system is limiting the potential transfer of some cell culture-based results of nanoparticle studies to animals/humans [48]. Tissue-specific differentiation functions of many cells and their physiological context of the primary cell cultures in *in vitro* systems are lost, like the loss of bio-transformational enzymes in primary liver cell cultures [49]. This lost in bio-transformational enzymes of liver cells will hinder the usage of primary liver cells in assessing nanoparticle for metabolism and toxicity potentials.

The assumption of neurotoxic potential of a compound if tested on neuronal cell line without considering the effect of blood brain barrier in animal model may lead to erroneous conclusion [48]. Recently, a group of researchers tried to evaluate the toxicity potential of zinc oxide nanoparticle on both cell and animal based models [50]. The two models showed a dose-dependent toxicity potential by the nanoparticle. However, in animal-based study, additional information emerged that relate route of administration and toxicity by the same delivery system. Another disturbing conclusion made from *in vitro* studies are that of glass fibre's ability in generating reactive oxygen species and causing oxidant stress leading to DNA damage, but a low pathogenic potential was reported when tested in animal models [51]. *In vitro* study also reported kaolin to be as cytotoxic as quartz, and purified single-walled carbon nanotubes not inducing oxidative stress in cell studies but resulted in progressive interstitial fibrosis in mice [51]. In general, animal systems are extremely complicated, and the closer a proposed nanoparticle is for human use, the more it requires animal model research. However, properly planned *in vitro* technique will likely serve as a good screening mechanism for NDS. This will likely reduce cost, time and more importantly preserve more lives of animal in the future.

CONCLUSION

There are many variables to consider when working with nanomaterial and these include type of material, their size, shape, surface, charge, coating, dispersion, agglomeration, aggregation, concentration and matrix. By carefully considering the experimental conditions, *in vitro* toxicity, bio-distribution, BBB deliveries, mechanism of cellular uptake and other related studies of nanoparticles can minimise the usage of *in vivo* system to assess these. This can play a role as a simple method to investigate the effect of such materials. However, animal systems are extremely complicated with unique bio-distribution, clearance, immune response, and metabolism. Therefore, *in vitro* study can only complement animal studies in assessing NDS. However, adequate and meaningful screening using cell culture technique will ensure reduction in the number of animal usage significantly.

ACKNOWLEDGEMENTS

We would like to thank the Ministry of Science, Technology, and Innovation Malaysia for project funding under nanofund NND/NA/(I) TD11-010. VOT No 5489101.

COMPETING INTERESTS

The authors declare that they have no competing interest.

AUTHORS' CONTRIBUTIONS

AUK performed the data gathering and the initial write-up, SF, MZH and AP were involved drafting the manuscript, intellectual revision and gave approval for the final manuscript. All authors read and approved the final manuscript.

REFERENCES

1. Wilczewska AZ, Niemirowicz K, Markiewicz KH, Car H: Nanoparticles as drug delivery systems. Pharmacol Rep. 2012, 64: 1020-1037.

2. Aminu Umar K, Samer Hasan Hussein Al A, Mohd Zobir H, Sharida F, Palanisamy A: Development of a controlled-release anti-parkinsonian nanodelivery system using levodopa as the active agent. Int J Nanomedicine. 2013, 8: 1103-1110.

3. Dorniani D, Hussein MZB, Aminu Umar K, Sharida F, Abdul Halim S, Zalinah A: Preparation of Fe3O4 magnetic nanoparticles coated with gallic acid for drug delivery. Int J Nanomedicine. 2012, 7: 5745-5756.

4. Li P, Dai YN, Zhang JP, Wang AQ, Wei Q: Chitosan-alginate nanoparticles as a novel drug delivery system for nifedipine. Int J Biomed Sci. 2008, 4 (3): 221-228.

5. Donaldson K, Stone V, Tran CL, Kreyling W, Borm PJA: Nanotoxicology. Occup Environ Med. 2004, 61: 727-728.

6. Ostiguy C, Soucy B, Lapointe G, Woods C, Ménard L, Trottier M: Studies and Research Projects Health Effects of Nanoparticles. 2008, 114-REPORT R-589, 2

7. Katrien L, Dorota N, Ben N, Peter H, Hoet M: How physico-chemical characteristics of nanoparticles cause their toxicity: complex and unresolved interrelations. Environ Sci: Process Impacts. 2013, 15: 23-38.

8. Kasemets K, Ivask A, Dubourguier HC, Kahru A: Toxicity of nanoparticles of ZnO, CuO and TiO2 to yeast Saccharomyces cerevisiae. Toxicol in Vitro. 2009, 23 (6): 1116-1122.

9. Taylor K, Gordon N, Langley G, Higgins W: Estimates for Worldwide Laboratory Animal Use in 2005. ATLA. 2008, 36: 327-342.

10. Hartung T: Toxicology for the twenty-first century. Nature. 2009, 460: 208-212.

11. Festing S, Wilkinson R: The ethics of animal research: talking point on the use of animals in scientific research. EMBO Rep. 2007, 8 (6): 526-530.

12. Hillegass JM, Arti S, Lathrop SA, MacPherson MB, Fukagawa NK, Mossman BT: Assessing nanotoxicity in cells in vitro. WIREs Nanomed Nanobiotechnol. 2010, 2 (3): 219-231.

13. Alarifi S, Ali D, Verma A, Alakhtani S, Ali BA: Cytotoxicity and genotoxicity of copper oxide nanoparticles in human skin keratinocytes cells. Int J Toxicol. 2013, 32 (4): 296-307.

14. Zong WX, Thompson CB: Necrotic death as a cell fate. Genes Dev. 2006, 20: 1-15.

15. Mosmann T: Rapid colorimetric assay for cellular growth and survival: application to proliferation and cytotoxicity assays. J Immunol Methods. 1983, 65 (1–2): 55-63.

16. Louis KS, Siegel AC: Cell viability analysis using trypan blue: manual and automated methods. Mamm Cell Viability. 2011, 740: 7-12.

17. Samer Hasan Hussein Al A, Al-Qubaisi M, Mohd Zobir H, Maznah I, Zulkarnain Z, Muhammad Nazrul H: Controlled-release formulation of antihistamine based on cetirizine zinc-layered hydroxide nanocomposite and its effect on histamine release from basophilic leukaemia (RBL-2H3) cells. Int J Nanomedicine. 2012, 7: 3351-3363.

18. Siti Aishah Abu B, Madihah Z, Abdul Manaf A, Aini I: Induction of apoptosis by newcastle disease virus strains AF220 and V4-UPM in human promyelocytic leukemia (HL60) and human tlymphoblastic leukemia (CEM-SS) cells. World Academy of Science, Engineering & Technology. 2012, 64: 395-

19. Hakan ÇİFTÇİ, Mustafa T, Uğur T, Siyami K, Yusuf M: Silver nanoparticles: cytotoxic, apoptotic, and necrotic effects on MCF-7 cells. Turk J Biol. 2013, 37: 573-581.

20. Jessica H, Mitchell S: Cairo: tumor lysis syndrome: current perspective. Haematologica. 2008, 93 (1): 9-13.

21. Decker T, Lohmann-Matthes ML: A quick and simple method for the quantitation of lactate dehydrogenase release in measurements of cellular cytotoxicity and tumor necrosis factor (TNF) activity. J Immunol Methods. 1988, 115 (1): 61-69.

22. Hamley IW: Nanotechnology with soft materials. Angew Chem Int Ed. 2003, 42: 1692-1712.

23. Jiangxue Wang AB, Guoqiang Z, Chunying C, Hongwei Y, Tiancheng W, Yongmei M, Guang J, Yuxi G, Bai L, Jin S, Yufeng L, Fang J, Yuliang Z, Zhifang C: Acute toxicity and biodistribution of different sized titanium dioxide particles in mice after oral administration. Toxicol Lett. 2007, 168: 176-185.

24. Tsikas D: Analysis of nitrite and nitrate in biological fluids by assays based on the Griess reaction: appraisal of the Griess reaction in the L-arginine/nitric oxide area of research. J Chromatogr B Anal Technol Biomed Life Sci. 2007, 851 (1-2): 51-70.

25. Alessandra R, Francesca B, Agata C, Rosaria A, Giuseppina R, Angelo V: Nitric oxide-related toxicity in cultured astrocytes: effect of Bacopa monniera. Life Sci. 2003, 73 (12): 1517-1526.

26. Reuter S, Gupta SC, Chaturvedi MM, Aggarwal BB: Oxidative stress, inflammation, and cancer: how are they linked?. Free Radic Biol Med. 2010, 49 (11): 1603-1616.

27. Park EJ, Yi J, Chung KH, Ryu DY, Choi J, Park K: Oxidative stress and apoptosis induced by titanium dioxide nanoparticles in cultured BEAS-2B cells. Toxicol Lett. 2008, 180: 222-22941.

28. Niu J, Azfer A, Rogers LM, Wang X, Kolattukudy PE: Cardioprotective effects of cerium oxide nanoparticles in a transgenic murine model of cardiomyopathy. Cardiovasc Res. 2007, 73 (3): 549-559.

29. Schubert D, Dargusch R, Raitano J, Chan SW: Cerium and yttrium oxide nanoparticles are neuroprotective. Biochem Biophys Res Commun. 2006, 342: 86-91.

30. Tarnuzzer RW, Colon J, Patil S, Seal S: Vacancy engineered ceria nanostructures for protection from radiation-induced cellular damage. Nano Lett. 2005, 5: 2573-2577.

31. Wohlfart S, Gelperina S, Kreuter J: Transport of drugs across the blood-brain barrier by nanoparticles. J Control Release. 2012, 161 (2): 264-73.

32. Naik P, Cucullo L: In vitro blood–brain barrier models: current and perspective technologies. J Pharm Pharm Sci. 2012, 101 (4): 1337-1354.

33. Ambikanandan M, Ganesh S, Ganesh S, Ganesh S, Ganesh S, Ganesh S, Ganesh S, Ganesh S, Aliasgar S, Shah SP: Drug delivery to the central nervous system: a review. J Pharm Pharm Sci. 2003, 6 (2): 252-273.

34. Yung-Chu C, Wen-Yuan H, Wen-Fu L, Ding-Tai Z: Effects of surface modification of PLGAPEG-PLGA nanoparticles on loperamide delivery efficiency across the blood–brain barrier. J Biomater Appl. 2013, 27 (7): 909-922.

35. Jain TK, Morales MA, Sahoo SK, Leslie-Pelecky DL, Labhasetwar V: Iron oxide nanoparticles for sustained delivery of anticancer agents. Mol Pharm. 2005, 2 (3): 194-205.

36. Lee PW, Hsu SH, Wang JJ, Tsai JS, Lin KJ, Wey SP, Chen FR, Lai CH, Yen TC, Sung HW: The characteristics, biodistribution, magnetic resonance imaging and biodegradability of superparamagnetic core–shell nanoparticles. Biomaterials. 2010, 31 (6): 1316-1324.

37. Vijayaraghavan R, Kulkarni A, Pant SC, Kumar P, Rao PV, Gupta N, Gautam A, Ganesan K: Differential toxicity of sulfur mustard administered through percutaneous, subcutaneous, and oral routes. Toxicol Appl Pharmacol. 2005, 202 (2): 180-188.

38. Batrakova EV, Li S, Brynskikh AM, Sharma AK, Li Y, Boska M, Gong N, Mosley RL, Alakhov VY, Gendelman HE, Kabanov AV: Effects of pluronic and doxorubicin on drug uptake, cellular metabolism, apoptosis and tumor inhibition in animal models of MDR cancers. J Control Release. 2010, 143 (3): 290-301.

39. Garberg P, Ball M, Borg N, Cecchelli R, Fenart L, Hurst RD, Lindmark T, Mabondzo A, Nilsson JE, Raub TJ, Stanimirovic D, Terasaki T, Oberg JO, Osterberg T: In vitro models for the blood-brain barrier. Toxicol In vitro. 2005, 19 (3): 299-334.

40. Hemmerich PH, Von Mikecz AH: Defining the subcellular interface of nanoparticles by live-cell imaging. PLoS One. 2013, 8 (4): e62018-

41. Orth JD, Tang Y, Shi J, Loy CT, Amendt C, Wilm C, Zenke FT, Mitchison TJ: Quantitative live imaging of cancer and normal cells treated with Kinesin-5 inhibitors indicates significant differences in phenotypic responses and cell fate. Mol Cancer Ther. 2008, 7: 3480-

42. Pockwinse SM, Kota KP, Quaresma AJC, Imbalzano AN, Lian JB, Van Wijnen AJ, Stein JL, Stein GS, Nickerson JA: Live cell imaging of the cancer-related transcription factor RUNX2 during mitotic progression. J Cell Physiol. 2011, 226 (5): 1383-1389.

43. Marie S, Bibby MC: 50 years of preclinical anticancer drug screening: empirical to target-driven approaches. Clin Cancer Res. 2005, 11: 971-981.

44. Shuming N, Yun X, Kim GJ, Simons JW: Nanotechnology applications in cancer. Annu Rev Biomed Eng. 2007, 9: 257-288.

45. Khin E, Yin W, Fenga SS: Effects of particle size and surface coating on cellular uptake of polymeric nanoparticles for oral delivery of anticancer drugs. Biomaterials. 2005, 26: 2713-2722.

46. Dorniani D, Kura AU, Hussein-Al-Ali SH, Hussein MZB, Fakurazi S, Shaari AH, Ahmad Z: In vitro sustained release study of gallic acid coated with magnetite-PEG and magnetite-PVA for drug delivery system. Sci World J. 2014, 416354: 11-

47. Kang T, Rongfa G, Xiaoqiang C, Yijuan S, Han J, Jin Z: In vitro toxicity of different-sized ZnO nanoparticles in Caco-2 cells. Nanoscale Res Lett. 2013, 8: 496-

48. Blaauboer BJ: The contribution of in vitro toxicity data in hazard and risk assessment: current limitations and future perspectives. Toxicol Lett. 2008, 180: 81-84.

49. Worth AP, Balls M: Alternative (non-animal) methods for chemicals testing: current status and future prospects. Altern Lab Anim. 2002, 30 (Suppl. 1): 125-

50. Hong TK, Tripathy N, Son HJ, Ha KT, Jeong HS, Hahn YB: A comprehensive in vitro and in vivo study of ZnO nanoparticles toxicity. J Mat Chem B. 2013, 1: 2985-2992.

51. Ken D, Borm PJA, Vincent C, Mary G: The limits of testing particle-mediated oxidative stress in vitro in predicting diverse pathologies; relevance for testing of nanoparticles. Parti Fibre Toxicol. 2009, 6: 13-

Chapter 2

Application of Nanotechnology in Drug Delivery

Joana Silva[1], Alexandra R. Fernandes[1,2] and Pedro V. Baptista[1,3]

[1] *Department of Life Sciences, Faculdade de Ciências e Tecnologia, Universidade Nova de Lisboa, Portugal*

[2] *Centro de Química Estrutural, Instituto Superior Técnico, Lisboa, Portugal*

[3] *CIGMH, Departamento de Ciências da Vida, Faculdade de Ciências e Tecnologia, Universidade Nova de Lisboa, Campus de Caparica, Portugal*

1. INTRODUCTION

1.1. NANOMEDICINE FOR CANCER

Cancer is one of the leading causes of death worldwide, occupying the second place in developing countries, and showing a growing incidence over time [1]. Current cancer therapy strategies are based in surgery, radiotherapy and chemotherapy, being the chemotherapy the one that shows the greater efficiency for cancer treatment, mainly in more advanced stages [2, 3]. Despite of this great response, anticancer agents are administrated at higher amounts in order to provide a final suitable concentration to the target tissues or organs, and this procedure is repeated in each cycle of chemotherapy [4]. Introduction of new agents to cancer therapy has greatly improved patient survival but still there are several biological barriers that antagonize drug delivery to target cells and tissues, namely unfavorable blood half-life and physiologic behavior with high off-target effects and effective clearance from the human organism [2, 5, 6]. Moreover, in cancer, there is a small subset of cancer cells-cancer stem cells (CSC)-that, like normal stem cells, can self-renew, give rise to heterogeneous populations of daughter cells, and proliferate extensively [7, 8]. Standard chemotherapy is directed against rapidly dividing cells, the bulk of non-stem cells of a tumor, and thus CSC often appear relatively refractory to those agents [7-9]. The development of side effects in normal tissues (e.g. nephrotoxicity, neurotoxicity, cardiotoxicity, etc) and multidrug resistance (MDR) mechanisms by cancer cells leads to a reduction in drug concentration at target location, a poor accumulation in the tumor with consequent reduction of efficacy that may associate to patient relapse [9-13]. To overcome these issues and still improve the efficiency of chemotherapeutic agents there is a demand for less toxic and more target specific therapies towards cancer cells, i.e. novel drugs, drug delivery systems (DDSs) and also gene delivery systems [3, 4, 14-17].

Nanotechnology is the manipulation of matter on an atomic, molecular, and supramolecular scale involving the design, production, characterization and application of different nanoscale materials in several key areas providing novel technological advances mainly in the field of medicine (so called Nanomedicine) [6, 18-20]. The development and optimization of drug delivery approaches based in nanoparticles concerns the early detection of cancer cells and/or specific tumor biomarkers, and the enhancement of the efficacy of the treatments applied [21]. The most important biomedical applications of nanoscale materials can be organized as shown in Figure 1.

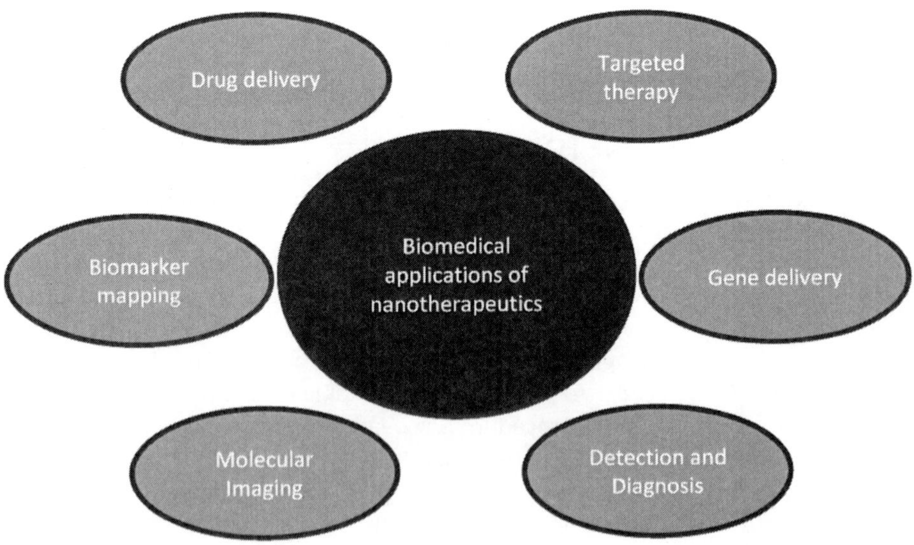

FIGURE 1. Biomedical application of nanotherapeutics (adapted from [6]).

These nanotherapeutics' potential in cancer relies on i) passive targeting due to the enhance of the permeability and retention (EPR) effect promoted by angiogenic vessels with defective vasculature and improper lymphatic flow surrounding the tumor [18] that can be reinforced by ii) specific targeting based on multifunctional nanomaterials that bypass the biological barriers and reach cancer cells [4]. Nanotechnology for drug vectorization provides for new and more specific drug targeting and delivery platforms that can reduce toxicity and other side effects and also maintain or improve the therapeutic index [9, 22, 23]. In fact, the development of targeting delivery systems is the ultimate goal in cancer therapy, which has been taking the lead in what concerns overcoming the MDR problem [9, 13, 24,25].

Here, we will discuss recent applications on AuNPs as platforms for anticancer therapy, emphasizing strategies for targeted delivery for gene silencing focusing on the optimal pathways to test these therapeutics *in vitro* and *in vivo*. Also, an overview of the toxicological aspects of these materials will be provided.

2. NANOPARTICLES AS DELIVERY SYSTEMS

Nanoparticles have been developed as effective target specific strategies for cancer treatment, acting as nanocarriers and also as active agents [4, 6, 5, 26]. Over the last decades, different types of nanoparticles have been developed based on various components, including carbon, silica oxides, metal oxides, nanocrystals, lipids, polymers, dendrimers, and quantum dots, together with increasing variety of newly developed materials [4, 27-34]. These nanomaterials are capable to provide a high degree of biocompatibility before and after conjugation to biomolecules for specific function so as to translate into nanomedicines and clinical practice. Nanomaterials provide for a favorable blood half-life and physiologic behavior with minimal off-target effects, effective clearance from the human organism, and minimal or no toxicity to healthy tissues in living organisms [35, 36].

In fact, the protection from adsorption to plasma proteins and/or degradation by circulating nucleases allows for an increased availability of effector molecule at site of interest. This is further enhanced by the considerable decrease to clearance from the organism that conjugation to nanoparticles confers. The modulation of pharmacokinetic and pharmacodynamics parameter constitutes a key factor when modifying the mode of administration (and vehicle and route of administration associated) that is usually neglected when compared to the ability of therapeutic nanoconjugates to offer the possibility of enhanced targeting (active and/or passive) and cell uptake. When considering nanoparticles for therapeutics one should also evaluate the effect on cellular metabolism and fate that can be attained via optimal conjugation with (bio)molecules of interest.

DDSs can improve the properties of free drugs by increase their *in vivo* stability and biodistribution, solubility and even by modulation of pharmacokinetics, promoting the transport and even more important the release of higher doses of the drug in the target site in order to be efficient [18, 22, 37,38].

DDSs can be constructed by direct conjugation with the drugs and further surface modifications can lead to a better delivery for such systems, promoting a targeted delivery to specific types of cells and reaching cell compartments such as nucleus and mitochondria [15, 39]. As far as drug delivery is concerned, the most important nanoparticle platforms are liposomes, polymer conjugates, metallic nanoparticles (for example AuNPs), polymeric micelles, dendrimers, nanoshells, and protein and nucleic acid-based nanoparticles (for a more complete review see [40-42].

Among a wide variety of nanosystems, only a few nanomedicines, such as Doxil® (Janssen Biotech Inc., Horsham, PA, USA), DaunoXome® (Galen US Inc., Souderton, PA, USA), Depocyt® (Pacira Pharmaceuticals Inc., San Diego, CA, USA), Genexol-PM® (Samyang Biopharmaceuticals Corporation, Jongno-gu, Seoul, Korea), Abraxane® (Celgene Corporation, Inc., Berkeley Heights, NJ, USA), Myocet® (Sopherion Therapeutics Inc., Princeton, NJ, USA) and Oncaspar® (Enzon Pharmaceuticals Inc., Bridgewater, NJ, USA), are approved for use in the treatment of cancer (for a review see [6]).

The implementation of nanoparticles towards cancer treatment can be based in certain characteristics as their size, surface properties and the possibility of a variety of specific ligands in their surface [18]. The high surface properties and other physicochemical features of nanoparticles can be modulated for the development of valuable systems that detect tumor cells either qualitatively or quantitatively [10,19].

Targeting the cancer cells occurs via two different strategies: passive targeting and active targeting [4,43, 44]. The passive targeting of tumor cells by nanoparticles depends upon an EPR effect promoted by angiogenic vessels with defective vasculature and improper lymphatic flow, reaching a higher accumulation in tumor cells compared to normal cells [15]. The increased accumulation of a drug in the tumor *interstitium* achieved by nanoparticles can be more than ten times higher compared to the drug alone [4]. This type of deliver is based in nanoparticle's half-time of circulation on the bloodstream, size and surface properties, and even depends on the degree of angiogenesis [45]. Despite the increased drug accumulation inside the tumor, this strategy rise some concerns about the targeting specificity of such mechanism based in the controversial influence of the EPR effect on drug externalization, which promotes a widespread distribution all over the tumor [4, 46]. The lack of specificity of such targeting led to further innovation with the implementation of an active targeting, which is achieved by the functionalization of nanoparticle's surface with a plethora of functional moieties such as antibodies and other biomolecules that recognized the specific surface antigens or specific biomarker of tumor cells [4, 44]. The targets choice depends on its high abundance in cell surface and its unique expression, and consequently the capacity of internalization of the nanoconjugate [4, 47, 48]. Although it is considered that active targeting does not have a direct association to the total nanoparticles accumulated within the tumor, it will influence the uptake of nanoparticles via receptor-mediated internalization and improve the efficiency of anti-tumor agents that have intracellular targets [49, 50]. Active targeting can be the potential way of polymeric nanoparticles to deliver chemotherapeutic drugs to cancer cells and is, therefore, one of the main vectors of DDS development at present involving tailoring of nanoparticles to deliver the effective cargo without compromising the selective targeting.

3. GOLD NANOPARTICLES (AUNPS)

Metallic nanostructures are more flexible particles compared to other nanomaterials owed to the possibility of controlling the size, shape, structure, composition, assembly, encapsulation and tunable optical properties [51, 52]. Between the metallic nanostructures possible applied, AuNPs appears of great interest in the medical field, 3showing great efficiency towards cancer therapy [51-54]. The continuous interest in AuNPs is based in their tunable optical properties that can be controlled and modulated for the treatment and diagnosis of diseases [9, 54, 52].

3.1. SYNTHESIS, FUNCTIONALIZATION, CHARACTERIZATION AND PROPERTIES OF AUNPS

The synthesis of nanoparticles follows some aspects relying in a high homogeneity of the materials in physical properties that greatly influence the size, shape and surface characteristics. The main process for nanoparticles development requires chemical administration of capping agents that adsorb in the surface of nanoparticles ([55] and references therein). AuNPs can be synthesized with different sizes through the reduction of gold with different agents such molecules bearing a thiol group, an aliphatic chain and a charged end group, and that can avoid particle aggregation [37]. Furthermore, this dense layer of stabilizing agent promotes a general change in the surface charge of AuNPs allowing ligand exchange with several molecules, promoting AuNPs functionalisation and then an increase in particle stability in physiological environments [55, 56]. AuNPs deliver systems can be formulated based in their capacity to bearing different functional groups, once it can be involved in covalent and non-covalent bindings by a thiol-linker [37, 55]. In fact, robust AuNPs appear by the stabilization with thiolates once the bond between Au and the thiol (S) is very strong [57]. This process enhances the affinity of the AuNPs surface for several types of ligands such as polyethylene glycol (PEG) molecules, nucleic acids (DNA and RNA), peptides, antibodies, and also small drug molecules (Figure 2) [9, 13, 37, 47, 52, 56, 57].

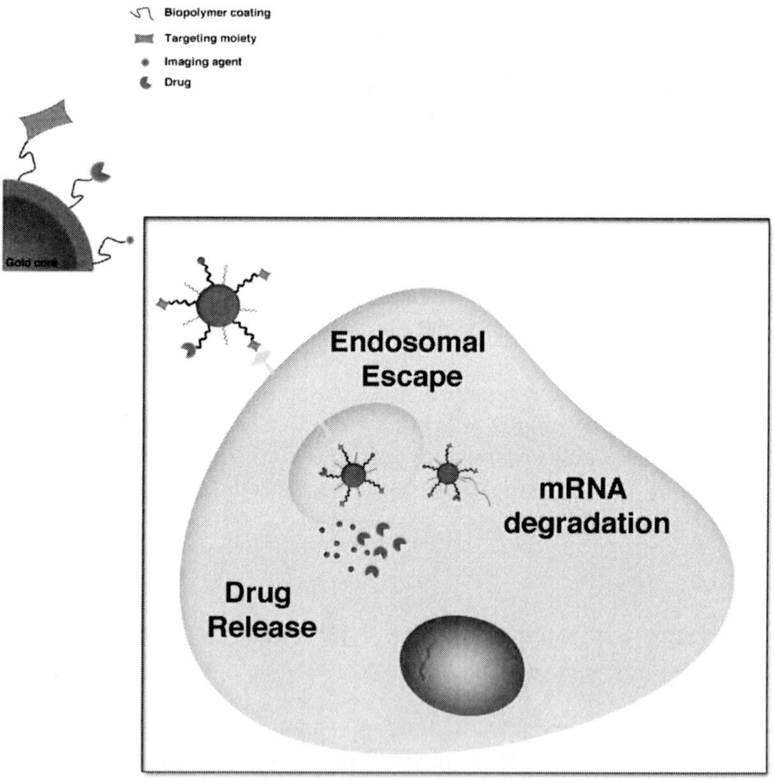

FIGURE 2. Multifunctional NP-based systems for tumor targeting, delivery and imaging. These innovative NPs comprise a targeting moiety, a silencing moiety and anticancer drug molecules for delivery to the target tissue. Depending on the targeting mechanism, they can be on the surface or inside the NPs. Multifunctional systems can carry reporter molecules tethered to the particle surface and employed as tracking and/or contrast agents.

Most passive targeting AuNPs have a surface coated with PEG for biocompatibility and "stealth" purposes [58]. Importantly, it should be noted that increased hydrophilicity on the AuNPs surface can impede its uptake by cancer cells, thereby hampering efficient drug delivery to tumors by passive targeting nanoparticles [58, 59].

As far as the targeting approach is concerned, one key issue relies on the choice of optimal targeting ligands, possibly by balancing their stoichiometry in comparison with the antibiofouling surface of AuNPs. More specifically, two important ligand properties, ie, affinity and density, can have a key role in effective targeting of nanoparticles to the cell surface membrane. Again, the ligand binding affinity is the result of the equilibrium between enthalpic advantages (for ligand-receptor interaction) and entropic losses (stretching, flexibility, or compressibility of the nanosystem). For example, greater ligand density does not necessarily lead to a higher intracellular concentration, given the decrease in "stealth" surface characteristics. Moreover, although the uptake of AuNPs usually increases with an increasing+/− charge ratio of nanoparticles (in terms of zeta potential values), an excess positive charge can induce toxicity and promote an immunologic reaction. Therefore, the optimal ligand density and charge on the AuNPs surface should be investigated on a case-by-case basis. AuNPs can be incorporated into larger structures such as polymeric nanoparticles or liposomes that deliver large payloads for enhanced diagnostic applications, efficiently encapsulate drugs for concurrent therapy or add additional imaging labels. This array of features has led to their application in biomedical fields, but more recently in approaches where multifunctional gold nanoparticles are used for multiple methods, such as concurrent diagnosis and therapy, so-called theranostics [53, 60-63].

AuNPs characterization is based on UV-Vis spectroscopy for the determination of the surface plasmon resonance (SPR) of the metallic gold, Transmission Electron Microscopy (TEM) for the determination of the average size of the particles, Scanning Electron Microscopy (SEM) for the characterization of the morphological features and Atomic Absorption Spectrometry that quantify the amount of gold [64]. AuNPs biodistribution can be monitored before the delivery of its payload which allows the establishment of treatment plan [65].

The application of AuNPs for *in vitro* diagnosis, *in vivo* imaging, therapy and also as DDSs relies in their chemical stability, high solubility in water, suitable morphology and limited dispersiiity, high surface-to-volume ratio, non-toxicity in biologic systems and an easy synthesis and functionalisation with a plethora of biomolecules (targeting and also silencing moieties) and drugs (Figure 2) [19, 21,55, 56, 66-68].

3.2. AUNPS IN CANCER THERAPY

3.2.1. PHOTOTHERMAL THERAPY

AuNPs formulations gain a major impact in cancer therapy in different contexts based in their properties that gain particular interest given some cancer specificities. AuNPs presents tunable optical properties that allow the absorption of light at near UV to near infrared, being the last one a characteristic that allows nanoparticles to enter cells, constituting a major breakthrough for its application in photothermal therapy or hyperthermia [57, 69]. This is thought due to the fact that increasing temperature of the cells above 42ºC lead to a loss of cell viability [5]. Thus, nanoparticles heat up after irradiation of the body or local area with a magnetic field or another source of energy and consequently induce an increase in cancer cells temperature until cell death [5]. Several gold nanostructures are being referred as successful candidates as photothermal agents, such as the case described by Sirotkina and coworkers where AuNPs reach a high concentration in the skin tumor tissue and lead to an apoptotic response [70]. AuNPs compared to the simple irradiation method, the laser hyperthermia (a methodology though to circumvent the side effects associated to the current cancer therapies), has an advantageous of needing less irradiation energy to promote tumor ablation [57].

3.2.2. RADIOTHERAPY

AuNPs have been review in radiotherapy experiments in order to overcome the problems associated to the healthy tissue damage imposed by radiotherapy [5, 57]. This strategy is based in the well-known accumulation of AuNPs in the tumor that will be acting as a decoy to focus the radiation in the tumor and limit its action in normal tumor vicinity, being able to decrease the initial quantity of radiation administrated [5, 71, 72]. A long term study using AuNPs and irradiation in mices bearing implanted tumors in order to eliminate the possibility of tumor regression, results in a reduction of the tumor size until not be detected and 86% long term cure, i.e. for more than a year, which was much higher than the 20% survival for the implementation of just radiotherapy [65].

3.2.3. ANGIOGENESIS INHIBITION

The inhibition of angiogenesis, i.e. the formation process of new blood vessels, is also a potent mechanism by which AuNPs can operate for cancer therapy [57, 73]. AuNPs have the ability to prevent phosphorylation of the proteins involved in this process of angiogenesis, by their binding to the cysteine residues in heparin-binding growth factors [73]. Complementary, the AuNPs intravenously administrated can be irradiated which leads to endothelium damage and then a break in the oxygen and nutrient supply to the tumors involved, another way of angiogenic therapy [65]. Radiotherapy, once have a major impact in rapidly divided cells, presents reduced activity towards the niche of central cells that become independent of blood supply and then hypoxic and with reduced proliferation capacity, leading to a continuous survival of such cells, which is the main cause of tumor relapse [65]. So the complete abolish of angiogenesis is a potential strategy to eradicate these cancer cells and then eradicate cancer [65].

3.3. AUNPS AS DELIVERY SYSTEMS

The well-known application of AuNPs in cancer therapy described above, lead to further investigation of new potential therapeutic strategies and was verified that AuNPs can be used in the design of delivery systems [74, 75]. The motivation for the implementation of AuNPs as drug delivery platforms is built in their easy to synthesis, functionalisation and also great biocompatibility, demonstrating that functionalisation with specific payloads have a great potential to destroy cancer cells [15, 76]. As described above, AuNPs as a potential nanocarrier have the possibility to carry different payloads, such as small drug molecules for drug delivery or biomolecules like DNA, proteins and RNA (siRNAs), being recognized as an attractive gene delivery system (Figure 2) [37]. The conjugation of the two types of therapeutic functions in nanoparticles, i.e. a cytotoxic drug and a specific cancer cell target moiety, act as a single platform in a synergetic way to promote a higher affinity to cancer cells in order to signaling them to the efficiently release of the anticancer agent, circumventing the biological and biophysical barriers [23, 5, 77].

3.3.1. SPECIFIC TARGETING

Nanoconjugates for drug delivery can accommodate a myriad of anti-cancer molecules that will be release and have its therapeutic effects in cancer cells, however healthy tissues can also be affected and to avoid this problem a targeting strategy is an important feature for combined therapy [78]. Taking advantage of tumor molecular markers as docking sites to concentrate the therapeutic effect at tumors, it is possible to increase therapeutic efficacy while reducing systemic exposure and off-target effects. Several of these tumor molecular markers are surface proteins/receptors present in cancer cells and in tumor vasculature that are not expressed or are expressed at much lower levels in normal cells, thereby distinguishing tumor masses from the surrounding normal tissues [79]. For a selective and with great potential delivery systems based in nanoparticles it is needed an efficient targeting to uniquely overexpressed receptors in cancer cells [76]. The potency of such systems is achieved by the enhancement of cellular accumulation of AuNPs by an active targeting to cancer cells compared to a free drug that passively enters the cells, which simultaneously avoid the biological response and biophysical barriers *in vivo* [5, 80]. In fact, nanoparticles need to continue in the bloodstream for enough time and cannot be eliminated in order to target the tumor site in the body, and surface modifications can be a useful property to avoid the mononuclear phagocytic system [4].

Based in this specificity, this platform can be a potential methodology for cancer therapy once it can differentiate with high certainty between cancer cells and non-cancer cells, one major concern related to the current cancer therapies [5, 81]. The increase of the surface area of AuNPs associated with other features such as distance-and refractive index-spectroscopic properties appears important for the construction of relevant biodetection molecules [55]. This capacity of AuNPs can be exploited for the improving of the therapeutic capacity of such systems, once the application of diagnostic and therapeutic strategies at the same time, Theranostics, can lead to a greater release at a specific tumor site, the targeting moiety or the drug, and it can be tracking in the whole body [82].

There are several types of tumor-targeting biomolecules such as peptides like RGD [47], proteins (transferrin, epidermal growth factor (EGF)) and carbohydrates [5], oligonucleotides such as aptamers [83], and monoclonal antibodies [85-87]. For example, the anti-epithelial growth factor receptor (EGFR) monoclonal antibody has been used as an active targeting agent, since EGFR and its ligands are commonly overexpressed in a variety of solid tumors [86-88].

Functionalization of AuNPs with specific ssDNA molecules (Au-nanoprobes) concerns a great detection system for specific DNA targets, being a rapid, sensitive, specific and inexpensive system [19]. For example, cancer cells overexpressing the folate receptors can be specifically targeted by AuNPs functionalized with folate ligands, and then the chemotherapeutic agent Doxorubicin (DOX) can be release into them and induce a higher toxicity compared to the one in healthy cells (do not express these receptors) and when compared to the DOX alone [89]. Additionally, the cell-surface specific markers that characterize the CSC pool constitute a way for targeting those cells in the whole tumor [7, 8]. Therapeutic strategies need to be focused in this specific CSC niche instead of the rapidly divided in order to prevent tumor regression [7, 8].

The targeting of tumor angiogenic vessels is also gaining increased attention, as it may improve therapeutic efficiency in cases where tumor cells are less accessible [79]. In combination with passive targeting strategies, active targeting may enhance receptor-mediated endocytosis of the AuNP conjugates in target cells [80, 90]. The intracellular localization of effector molecules can be further directed with the use of cell-penetrating peptides, which are short peptides that facilitate the delivery of various cargoes to cells, or with nuclear localization sequences, which direct cargos to the nucleus [91,92]. Decorating AuNPs with proton sponge groups or using photothermal heating can further assist escape from endosomal sequestration/degradation [93]. Active targeting by AuNPs [94-96] has been shown to result in greater tumor accumulation than passive targeting, when AuNPs are administered systemically in vivo (6-13% versus 2-5%) [94, 95].

3.3.2. AUNPS FOR DRUG/CARGO DELIVERY

The construction of DDSs depends on size, charge and surface functionalities of the AuNPs, once they dictate the uptake capacity of such nanovectorization systems as well as its intracellular fate [5, 75]. The possibility to functionalize AuNPs with a plethora of different cargos allows the development of several distinct approaches for drug delivery [76]. Moreover, stable nanovectorization systems in the blood-stream, drug release rate and clearance of the vector are two other important properties for the use of nanoparticles as DDSs [5, 57]. The use of vectorisation systems based in nanoparticles reveal the capacity to transpose the biological barriers imposed, with the release of low molecular-weight molecules that rapidly diffuse into the body, promoting a selective distribution towards cancer cells [5].

The active release of the drug into cells depends on the interaction between the drug and AuNPs (covalent or non-covalent binding) and even on methods of release after reaching the cells [76]. Non-covalent binding, such as the one used for hydrophobic drugs, does not need further alterations to the drug in order to be released [97] while for covalent interactions, establish for prodrugs, it implies the application of an internal or external mechanisms [98, 99]. The tunable optical properties of AuNPs surface is a prominent feature for the release of a drug either by internal or external stimuli [5]. External stimuli can be administrated by a photo-regulated release, which depends on the administration of light to photo-cleavage of nanoparticles-drug interaction to activate the drug once free [100-102], like was demonstrated with AuNPs functionalized with 5-fluorouracil [103]. You and collaborators [104] reported that up to 60% of a doxorubicin payload could be loaded onto hollow gold nanospheres because the drug molecules were adsorbed to both the inner and the outer surfaces of the hollow gold nanospheres via electrostatic attraction.

Owing to the strong SPR absorption of novel gold nanostructures, drug release can be activated by NIR light [104, 105]. Glutathione can be a good internal stimulus of release for covalent interactions, by exchange reactions between disulfide of AuNPs and the intracellular glutathione [75]. AuNPs loaded with doxorubicin have been shown to be able to reverse cancer cells' resistance to the drug [106].

AuNPs with a high surface area attractive to establish interactions to a plethora of platinum drugs have been described [107]. Brown and coworkers designed a platinum-tethered AuNP system bearing the active compound of oxalipatin as its platinum molecule, and tested its platform in lung and colorectal cancer cell lines, demonstrating a more cytotoxic effect compared to oxaliplatin alone and also a higher accumulation of the active compound in those cancer cells reaching the nucleus for possible DNA interaction, what constitute a good delivery system [107].

3.3.3. AUNPS FOR GENE THERAPY

Gene therapy is though as a hopeful strategy in cancer therapy being considered as a powerful treatment like chemotherapy and radiotherapy, however the implementation of such systems is based in viral vectors that raise cytotoxic and immune response problems [57, 108]. When conjugated to AuNPs, siRNAs have been shown to exhibit increased stability, cellular uptake and efficacy in physiological conditions, retaining the ability to act through the RNAi pathway [109, 110]. The first demonstration that DNA-AuNP conjugates could be easily internalized into cells, without the need for transfection agents, and induced gene silencing by an antisense mechanism was reported by Rosi and co-workers in 2006 [111]. AuNPs as gene-delivery vectors emerged initially with cationic ligands that appears a good gene delivery system once protects the DNA molecule from degradation by DNAse I [112]. Han and coworkers have identified that cationic AuNPs can trigger DNA release into cells by glutathione intracellular concentrations [113].These remarkable studies prompted others to use AuNPs as siRNA delivery systems and contributed to the development of many strategies to improve intracellular siRNA delivery in vitro and in vivo. These strategies can be grouped into two major categories that are currently used for tethering siRNAs to AuNPs, namely (1) the gold-thiol bond and (2) electrostatic interactions. Both categories involve, in some way, the use of poly(ethylene glycol (PEG) or other passivating agents for stabilization and to promote endosomal escape of the AuNP conjugates into the cell cytoplasm [114].

The silencing of cancer-related molecules can be addressed by this delivery platform, being of major concern the oncogenes that have specific involvement in cell survival and proliferation [115]. siRNAs can be pointed as potential therapeutic molecules once its function relies in the suppression of gene expression [78]. siRNA molecules present limitations when administrated alone: do not cross the cell membrane, are rapidly degradable by endo-and exo-nucleases, have low stability in the blood and induces systemic toxicity [116]. Nanoparticles functionalized with siRNAs that have been tested for targeting reporter genes in *in vitro* cell cultures and recently AuNPs functionalized with siRNAs were investigated for *in vitro* and *in vivo* targeting genes [67, 116]. AuNPs can in fact be a good system for antisense and siRNA delivery since they can protect these molecules from degradation [109]. Thus, in order to improve cytoplasmatic translocation of siRNAs and promoting a complete gene silencing, is of utmost important the formulation of these nanoconjugates with siRNAs once its smaller size can potentiate and improve the interactions between biomolecules in the surface or into a cell [4, 116].

In vivo studies using this system are still scarce, alerting us for the need to overcome remaining barriers that prevent its translation into the clinics. Some recent studies are highlighted. Zhang and co-workers have developed an anti-metastasis therapy consisting of gold nanorods (AuNRs) conjugated electrostatically with siRNAs, which targeted the protease-activated receptor 1 (PAR-1) [117]. These conjugates were then delivered to highly metastatic human breast cancer cells. The authors observed efficient downregulation of PAR-1 mRNA and protein levels and decreased metastatic ability of the cancer cells [117]. By allowing any short nucleic acid to be hybridized to the cargo DNA covalently linked to the AuNP, the former can be designed for a specific purpose, such as gene knockdown, redirection of alternative splicing, and modulation of signal transduction pathways, Ryou and collaborators delivered shRNAs targeting the Mcl-1L mRNA to a xenografted tumor in a mouse model, and showed a ~5% reduction in protein expression which was sufficient to induce apoptosis of the xenograft tumor cells [118]. These studies did not include a targeting strategy because they were performed either in vitro or in vivo by directly injecting the conjugates into tumors. However, for systemic delivery, an additional targeting moiety is generally required to improve treatment efficacy and reduce off-target effects. Lu and co-workers [93] used Au nanocages targeted to folate receptors (overexpressed in many types of cancer) and carrying a siRNA against the NFkBp65, which encodes a transcription factor highly involved in tumor formation and progression. They injected these constructs intravenously into in nude mice bearing HeLa cervical cancer xenografts and observed a significantly higher tumor uptake of the targeted conjugates compared to the non-targeted ones. They additionally took advantage of the photothermal properties of the Au nanocages to achieve a controlled cytoplasmic delivery of siRNA upon NIR light irradiation and observed efficient NF-kappaB p65 downregulation only when tumors were irradiated with NIR light [93].

AuNPs functionalized with c-myc siRNAs were studied in a cervix adenocarcinoma cell line and demonstrate a great accumulation in the cytoplasm of the tumor cells and an evident ability to silencing the *c-myc* oncogene [67]. They functionalized AuNPs with PEG, cell penetration (TAT) and cell adhesion peptides (RGD, which binds to the integrin αVβ3 receptor family) [119], and c-myc targeting-siRNAs [5]. They have also shown in a more recent study that these same nanoconjugates are capable of targeting tumor cells in a lung cancer murine model and of inducing significant downregulation of the c-myc oncogene, followed by tumor growth inhibition and prolonged survival of lung tumor bearing mice [116].

Furthermore, miRNAs can appear with aberrant patterns of expression in tumors and then be related to its development, progression and tumor differentiation [47]. miRNAs can act as oncogenes or tumor suppressor genes accounting to its deregulation in cells, then it's down-regulation or up-regulation respectively, can be a major breakthrough for cancer therapy [120]. Conde and coworkers revealed a platform based in Au-nanobeacons to targeting and efficiently silencing miR-21, an oncogenic miRNA commonly up-regulated in almost all types of cancers [47, 121].

This targeting approached can also become a potential strategy to overcome the problem of multidrug resistance of cancer cells to the application of several drugs (Fernandes and Baptista, 2014). One of the major mechanisms of multidrug resistance in cancer is associated to ATP-binding cassette (ABC) membrane transporters, such as P-glycoprotein (P-gp), and others efflux pumps such as BCRP, which imply these as potential targets of silencing for cancer therapy [122, 123]. Cancer stem cells (CSCs) can also express these membrane proteins which confer to this subpopulation resistance to the current chemotherapeutic agents [123, 124]. Thus, the implication of a silencing strategy towards these cancer related genes evolve in order to minimize cancer resistance barriers to the actual therapy and then obtain an efficient response towards the chemotherapeutic agents applied [115, 125]. It was demonstrated by a system of lipid-modified dextran nanoparticles bearing siRNAs towards *ABCB1*gene (P-gp), that this approach can efficiently deliver the siRNA molecule and reduces the expression of P-gp although at the same order of greatness as the siRNA alone [126]. This reveals the necessity to continuously develop nanoparticles systems that can target and silencing these genes and proteins.

Another multidrug resistance mechanism is associated to the capacity of cancer cells to evade apoptotic response, when resistance induced by efflux pumps is not seen [127]. Apoptosis is the major cellular process induced by chemotherapeutic agents, so cancers bearing apoptosis defects cannot be efficiently treated by those agents, then discovery of the molecular basis of such system can formulate novel therapeutic approaches [127, 128]. For example, the anti-apoptotic protein Bcl2 is considered a proto-oncogene, and nano-based vector delivery systems has been establish with great efficacy towards this molecule [127, 129].

4. TOXICITY OF AUNPS

One major concern regarding AuNPs application in medical field relies in its toxicity in the biological systems, i.e. the production of a general toxicity response not only in cancer cells but also reaching healthy cells at the vicinity [78]. Taken into account the size, surface modifications and solubility in promoting biocompatibility of the nanovectorization systems, they can be safer to apply in the medical field to the treatment of cancer [130]. In fact, nanoparticles size is an important feature because it turns possible to circumvent the immune response and renal clearance, which maintains the therapeutic capacity of such systems [5].

Toxicity of AuNPs is generally accepted to be dependent on particle size, shape, and surface charge and chemistry [131-134]. However, it is thought that once AuNPs have a smaller size, approximately the size of biomolecules, it can be taken like one and then evade cellular barriers, with access to different tissues, and in the end can lead to the disruption of cell biological processes [75, 135]. A control of the size dependent cytotoxicity of AuNPs, revealed that AuNPs with a 1-2 nm size represents more toxicity towards four cancer cells lines compared to AuNPs with 15 nm that do not display any toxicity (Pan *et al.*, 2007). Additionally, the main organs affected by AuNPs are the liver and the spleen (Sun *et al.*, 2011). Also, very small particles (1.4 and 5 nm in diameter) seem to be capable to enter the nucleus, where they can interact with DNA and cause molecular disturbance [136,137]. Larger particles (16 nm and 33 nm) are retained in endosomes and accumulate in the periphery of the nuclear region [138, 139]. At least three different studies reported that cellular uptake of AuNPs reach maximum levels for a particle size of about 50 nm [140-142]. Also, surface functionalisation seem to be capable of inducing higher level of apoptotic cell death, probably related to increased cell uptake when compared to unmodified 40 nm AuNPs [141]. According to data from in vitro studies, AuNPs' toxicity is believed to result mainly from the induction of oxidative stress [143-145]. Indeed, up-regulation of stress related genes was found to result from cell exposure to AuNPs, which also promoted the down-regulation of cell cycle related genes [145-147]. Nevertheless, most of these studies paid little attention to genome damage, such as DNA strand breaks and nuclear abnormalities, or characterization of protein markers for toxicity. An integrated toxicology evaluation encompassing DNA damage, stress related enzymes and a proteome profiling approach showed no significant cytotoxicity of PEGylated AuNPs and no up-regulation of proteins related to oxidative damage [148].

Nevertheless, previous studies using metallic nanoparticles showed acute toxicity, mainly by the introduction of damages to the DNA molecule and also by oxidative damage [146, 149, 150].

AuNPs are however generally considered a system that do not cause acute or adverse toxicity, and then are been taken as safer systems for therapeutic use [135]. AuNPs demonstrate to be a safe system due to their easy of functionalization [151]. This ideal is based in the assumption that gold nanoparticles do not lead to any effect in the cell, and instead, the function moiety in its surface promote the cytotoxic effect expected [139]. In the other way, expression studies revealed an overexpression of stress and inflammation related genes after AuNPs treatment, being associated to the action of AuNPs in oxidative stress induction [75]. A decrease in cell cycle genes expression was simultaneously observed, which symbolizes an irreversible damage that leads to cell death by necrosis [75].

Nanoparticles surface composition is another relevant point when talking about toxicity of nanoparticles systems [5]. The ligands and surface capping agents of AuNPs as the first line of contact with the different actors in the cell pathways can promote toxicity that in the end represents the overall toxicity associated to these nanoconjugates [5]

Also, both positive and negatively charged AuNPs were found to be similarly more cytotoxic against human keratinocytes (HaCaT cells) when compared to neutral AuNPs, with LD50 values of roughly half of those determined for the latter [152]. Despite the disruption in cell morphology and the dose-dependent toxicity observed for all three types of AuNPs, both anionic and cationic AuNPs induce mitochondrial stress and apoptosis in opposition to the necrotic cell death caused by neutral particles [152]. Another in vitro study comparing positive and negatively charged AuNPs reported that cationic NPs were far more toxic to Cos-1 cells, human red blood cells and E. coli than anionic NPs, possibly as a result of cell lysis, as shown by a dye leakage technique [133]. However, Alkilany and co-workers clearly showed that serum proteins become readily adsorbed to the surface of charged NPs, inducing an inversion of surface charge in particles that were originally cationic [153]. This would reduce electrostatic interaction between the original positive NPs and the negative cell membrane, the first step towards cell lysis mediated toxicity of cationic NPs [133].

Regarding in vivo experiments, several studies have demonstrated that AuNPs of 50 nm and larger were non-toxic to mice, conversely to what has been observed for AuNPs <40 nm [54, 55]. In fact, there are concordant data from different studies on the biodistribution and accumulation of AuNPs in mice showing that most of the intravenously injected nanoparticles are retained in the liver, regardless of their size [156-158]. There is also an agreement in that

AuNPs have the ability to transpose the blood-brain barrier and thus reach the brain, with a cut-off limit in diameter of around 20 nm [159], and that smaller particles have the most widespread organ distribution [156-158]. Organ distribution seems to be ruled by a more or less complex relationship with nanoparticle size. For instance, it is known that renal excretion of AuNPs is maximized for a narrow size range of 6-8 nm, resulting in an accelerated clearance rate [160]. Despite the valuable use of animal models, the effect of size on the toxicity of AuNPs in humans is difficult to predict since the size of endothelial cells' fenestrae is highly variable between individuals, thereby affecting nanoparticle clearance [75]. Therefore, more consistent data on the toxicological profile of AuNPs in vivo is necessary. For a more complete review on biodistribution, encompassing earlier studies and administration routes other than intravenous injection, see Khlebtsov and Dykman [159]. Furthermore, core size, charge and surface chemistry of AuNPs seems to correlate to toxicity on the development of zebrafish embryos, with positive and negatively charged AuNPs causing mortality and malfunctions to the embryos, respectively [161]. Adverse effects were also found in the model system Drosophila melanogaster after exposure to citrate-capped AuNPs, which were shown to reduce fertility in a dose-dependent manner and also the life span [144, 162].

Nonetheless, long-term studies in higher organisms are necessary to further characterise the safety of AuNPs as therapeutic agents, so they can be safely administrated to humans without concerns about late toxicity symptoms.

5. CONCLUSIONS & FUTURE

Cancer is a complex disease with a plethora of cell types and differentiation stages that trigger standard molecular mechanisms towards recruitment of cells and nutrients to enhance survival and proliferation. Cancer complexity is also dependent from the specific and multifaceted umor microenvironment. All these different molecular pathways, mechanism and markers can be used as potential targets for therapeutics. However, current therapeutics (drugs and molecules) show serious cell toxicity that is not merely directed at the cancer cells but instead promote off-target cellular disarray and cell death, usually reported ad undesirable side effects and systemic toxicity.

Nanomedicine has been putting forward several therapeutic concepts that disrupt the way we have been dealing with cancer therapy, i.e. nanoparticles as drug delivery agents, minimising side effects and toxicity of the drugs. Furthermore, these nanoparticle platforms allow for selective targeting of cancer cells or tumor vessels either by incorporating novel or standard anticancer drugs and/or the delivery of therapeutic genetic modulators. These approaches, often based on the robustness and chemical properties of AuNPs, have shown great promise in preclinical models. Some recent advances in ligand-targeted NPs have begun to demonstrate improvement in cancer therapy.

What is more, many tumors become resistant to drugs, requiring that novel strategies involving drug targeting vehicles that deliver high concentrations of combinatorial therapeutics to the selected targets. For this to happen, it is crucial that these nanoconjugates are capable to withstand the body's clearance and reaction to non-self particulates. The robustness of AuNPs as target delivery platforms will be achieved when reticuloendothelial system clearance is avoid and occur an enhance of the endothelial penetration, once the first one can lead to a longer time in circulation and the second leads to an increase of targeting and drug accumulation (Kumar *et al.*, 2013).

The use of multiple nanoparticles that can be used together may overcome current limitations of each individual nanoformulation alone. For example, AuNPs have proven to be outstanding vectorisation systems for gene delivery and can be used to target molecular pathways, including those involved in drug resistance and in survival of cancer cells. These NPs may be used in combination with any other polymeric and/or metallic nanoparticles in therapeutic approaches that include drug and thermal ablation, selective delivery via out of the boy triggering (light source).

All of these applications of AuNPs in therapeutics still lack enough toxicology and pharmacology studies and data that can support the effective translation into the clinics. However, the efficacy in fighting cancer cells shows that the effort to push forward with the needed regulatory requirements and compliance is worth pursuing since the enhanced properties allow for outstanding improvements to biocompatibility, circulation and therapeutic response.

6. ACKNOWLEDGEMENTS

The authors acknowledge Fundação para a Ciência e Tecnologia (FCT/MEC) for funding: CIGMH (PEst-OE/SAU/UI0009/2011); PTDC/BBB-NAN/1812/2012.

REFERENCES

1. Jemal A, Bray F, Center MM, Ferlay J, Ward E, Forman D. Global cancer statistics. CA: A Cancer Journal for Clinicians 2011;61(2): 69-90.

2. Blanco E, Hsiao A, Mann AP, Landry MG, Meric-Bernstam F, Ferrari M. Nanomedicine in cancer therapy: Innovative trends and prospects. Cancer Science 2011;102(7): 1247-1252.

3. Peer D, Karp JM, Hong S, Farokhzad OC, Margalit R, Langer R. Nanocarriers as an emerging platform for cancer therapy. Nature Nanotechnology 2007;2(12): 751-760.

4. Baptista PV. Cancer nanotechnology—prospects for cancer diagnostics and therapy. Current Cancer Therapy Reviews 2009;5(2): 80-88.

5. Conde J, Doria G, Baptista P. Noble Metal Nanoparticles Applications in Cancer. Journal of Drug Delivery 2012;2012(2012): 1-12.

6. Sanna A, Pala N, Sechi M. Targeted therapy using nanotechnology: focus on cancer. International Journal of Nanomedicine 2014;9: 467-483.

7. Clarke MF, Dick JE, Dirks PB, Eaves CJ, Jamieson CHM, Jones DL, Visvader J, Weissman IL, Wahl GM. Cancer Stem Cells-Perspectives on Current Status and Future Directions: AACR Workshop on Cancer Stem Cells. Cancer Research 2006;66(19): 9339-9344.

8. Jordan CT, Guzman ML, Noble M. Mechanisms of Disease: Cancer Stem Cells. The New England Journal of Medicine 2006;355(12): 1253-1261.

9. Fernandes AR, Baptista PV. Nanotechnology for Cancer Diagnostics and Therapy – An Update on Novel Molecular Players. Current Cancer Therapy Reviews 2014;9(3): 1-9.

10. Brigger I, Dubernet C, Couvreur P. Nanoparticles in cancer therapy and diagnosis. Advanced Drug Delivery Reviews 2012;64: 24-36.

11. Oerlemans C, Bult W, Bos M, Storm G, Nijsen JFW, Hennink WE. Polymeric Micelles in Anticancer Therapy: Targeting, Imaging and Triggered Release. Pharmaceutical Research 2010;27(12): 2569-2589.

12. Larsen AK, Escargueil AE, Skladanowski A. Resistance mechanisms associated with altered intracellular distribution of anticancer agents. Pharmacology & Therapeutics 2000;85(3): 217-229.

13. Conde J, de la Fuente JM, Baptista PV. Nanomaterials for reversion of multidrug resistance in cancer: a new hope for an old idea?. Frontiers and Pharmacology 2013;4(134): 1-5.

14. Brannon-Peppas L, Blanchette JO. Nanoparticle and targeted systems for cancer therapy. Advanced Drug Delivery Reviews 2012;64: 206-212.

15. Tiwari G, Tiwari R, Sriwastawa B, Bhati L, Pandey S, Pandey P, Barnnerjee SK. Drug delivery systems: An updated review. International Journal of Pharmaceutical Investigation 2012;2(1): 2-11.

16. Ganta S, Devalapally H, Shahiwala A, Amiji M. A review of stimuli-responsive nanocarriers for drug and gene delivery. Journal of Controlled Release 2008;126(3): 187-204.

17. Koo OM, Rubinstein I, Onyuksel H. Role of nanotechnology in targeted drug delivery and imaging: a concise review. Nanomedicine 2005;1(3): 193-212.

18. Drbohlavova J, Chomoucka J, Adam V, Ryvolova M, Eckschlager T, Hubalek J, Kizek R. Nanocarriers for Anticancer Drugs-New Trends in Nanomedicine. Current Drug Metabolism 2013;14(5): 547-564.

19. Baptista PV, Pereira E, Eaton P, Doria G, Miranda A, Gomes I, Quaresma P, Franco R. Gold nanoparticles for the development of clinical diagnosis methods. Analytical Bioanalalytical Chemistry 2008;391(3): 943-950.

20. Silva GA. Introduction to Nanotechnology and Its Applications to Medicine. Surgical Neurology 2004;61(3): 216-220.

21. Baptista PV. Could gold nanoprobes be an important tool in cancer diagnostics?. Expert Reviews of Molecular Diagnostics 2012; 12(6): 541-543.

22. De Jong WH, Borm PJA. Drug delivery and nanoparticles: Applications and hazards. International Journal of Nanomedicine 2008;3(2): 133-149.

23. Ganesh T. Improved Biochemical Strategies for Targeted Delivery of Taxoids. Bioorganic & Medicinal Chemistry 2007;15(11): 3597-3623.

24. Hu CMJ, Zhang LF. Therapeutic Nanoparticles to Combat Cancer Drug Resistance. Current Drug Metabolism 2009;10(8): 836-841.

25. Nakanishi T, Fukushima S, Okamoto K, Suzuki M, Matsumura Y, Yokoyama M, Okano T, Sakurai Y, Kataoka K. Development of the polymer micelle carrier system for doxorubicin. Journal of Controlled Release 2001;74(1-3): 295-302.

26. Ferrari M. Cancer nanotechnology: Opportunities and challenges. Nature Reviews Cancer 2005;5(3): 161-171.

27. Kim BY, Rutka JT, Chan WC. Nanomedicine. The New England Journal of Medicine 2010;363(25): 2434–2443.

28. Riehemann K, Schneider SW, Luger TA, Godin B, Ferrari M, Fuchs H. Nanomedicine – challenge and perspectives. Angewandte Chemie International Edition England 2009;48(5): 872-897.

29. Petros RA, DeSimone JM. Strategies in the design of nanoparticles for therapeutic applications. Nature Reviews Drug Discovery 2010;9(8): 615-627.

30. Bae KH, Chung HJ, Park TG. Nanomaterials for cancer therapy and imaging. Moleculles and Cells 2011;31(4): 295-302.

31. Taylor A, Wilson KM, Murray P, Fernig DG, Levy R. Long-term tracking of cells using inorganic nanoparticles as contrast agents: are we there yet? Chemical Society Reviews 2012;41(7):2707-2717.

32. Villalonga-Barber C, Micha-Screttas M, Steele BR, Georgopoulos A, Demetzos C. Dendrimers as biopharmaceuticals: synthesis and properties. Current Topics in Medicinal Chemistry 2008;8(14): 1294-1309.

33. Clift MJ, Stone V. Quantum dots: an insight and perspective of their biological interaction and how this relates to their relevance for clinical use. Theranostics 2012;2(7): 668-680.

34. Yamashita T, Yamashita K, Nabeshi H, Yoshikawa T, Yoshioka Y, Tsunoda S, Tsutsumi Y. Carbon nanomaterials: efficacy and safety for nanomedicine. Materials 2012;5(2): 350-363.

35. Lammers T, Kiessling F, Hennink WE, Storm G. Drug targeting to tumors: principles, pitfalls and (pre-) clinical progress. Journal of Controlled Release 2012;161(2): 175-187.

36. Walkey CD, Chan WC. Understanding and controlling the interaction of nanomaterials with proteins in a physiological environment. Chemical Society Reviews 2012;41(7): 2780-2799.

37. Ghosh P, Han G, De M, Kim CK, Rotello VM. Gold nanoparticles in delivery applications. Advanced Drug Delivery Reviews 2008;60(11): 1307-1315.

38. Cai W, Gao T, Hong H, Sun J. Applications of gold nanoparticles in cancer nanotechnology. Nanotechnology, Science and Applications 2008;1: 17-32.

39. Pissuwan D, Niidome T, Cortie MB. The forthcoming applications of gold nanoparticles in drug and gene delivery systems. Journal of Controlled Release 2011;149(1): 65-71.

40. Pathak Y, Thassu D. Drug Delivery Nanoparticles Formulation and Characterization. Rijeka: PharmaceuTech Inc.; 2009. p1-393.

41. Zhang L, Gu FX, Chan JM, Wang AZ, Langer RS, Farokhzad OC. Nanoparticles in medicine: therapeutic applications and developments. Clinical Pharmacology & Therapeutics 2008;83(5): 761-769.

42. Davis ME, Chen ZG, Shin DM. Nanoparticle therapeutics: an emerging treatment modality for cancer. Nature Reviews Drug Discovery 2008;7(9): 771-782.

43. Dinarvand R, de Morais PC, D'Emanuele A. Nanoparticles for Targeted Delivery of Active Agents against Tumor Cells. Journal of Drug Delivery 2012; 2012(2012): 1-2.

44. Nie S. Understanding and overcoming major barriers in cancer nanomedicine. Nanomedicine 2010;5(4): 523-528.

45. Allen TM, Cullis PR. Drug delivery systems: entering the mainstream. Science 2004;303(5665): 1818-1822.

46. Stohrer M, Boucher Y, Stangassinger M, Jain RK. Oncotic pressure in solid tumors is elevated. Cancer Research 2000;60(15): 4251-4255.

47. Conde J, Rosa J, de la Fuente JM, Baptista PV. Gold-nanobeacons for simultaneous gene specific silencing and intracellular tracking of the silencing events. Biomaterials 2013;34(10): 2516-2523.

48. Gao H Yang Z, Zhang S, Cao S, Shen S, Pang Z, Jiang X. Ligand modified nanoparticles increases cell uptake, alters endocytosis and elevates glioma distribution and internalization. Scientific Reports 2013;3(2534): 1-8.

49. Bartlett DW, Su H, Hildebrandt IJ, Weber WA, Davis ME. Impact of tumor-specific targeting on the biodistribution and efficacy of siRNA nanoparticles measured by multimodality in vivo imaging. PNAS 2007;104(39): 15549-15554.

50. Kirpotin DB, Drummond DC, Shao Y, Shalaby MR, Hong K, Nielsen UB, Marks JD, Benz CC, Park JW. Antibody Targeting of Long-Circulating Lipidic Nanoparticles Does Not Increase Tumor Localization but Does Increase Internalization in Animal Models. Cancer Research 2006;66(13): 6732-6740.

51. Huang X, Jain PK, El-Sayed IH, El-Sayed MA. Gold nanoparticles: interesting optical properties and recent applications in cancer diagnostics and therapy. Nanomedicine 2007;2(5): 681-693.

52. Figueiredo S, Cabral R, Luís D, Fernandes AR, Baptista PV. 2014. Integration of Gold nanoparticles and liposomes for combined anti-cancer drug delivery. In: Seifalian A. (ed.) Nanomedicine; University College London (UK); 2014. Chapter 3; available from http://www.onecentralpress.com/nanomedicine/#.

53. Cobley CM, Chen J, Cho EC, Wang LV, Xia Y. Gold nanostructures: a class of multifunctional materials for biomedical applications. Chemical Society Reviews 2011;40(1): 44-56.

54. Kumar A, Boruah BM, Liang XJ. Gold nanoparticles: Promising nanomaterials for the diagnosis of cancer and HIV/AIDS. Journal of Nanomaterials 2011;2011(2011): 1-17.

55. Baptista PV, Doria G, Quaresma P, Cavadas M, Neves CS, Gomes I, Eaton P, Pereira E, Franco R. Nanoparticles in Molecular Diagnostics. In: Villaverde A. (ed.) Progress in Molecular Biology and Translational Science Elsevier Inc.; 2011. p427-488.

56. Dreaden EC, Austin LA, Mackey MA, El-Sayed MA. Size matters: gold nanoparticles in targeted cancer drug delivery. Therapeutic Delivery 2012;3(4): 457-478.

57. Boisselier E, Astruc D. Gold nanoparticles in nanomedicine: preparations, imaging, diagnostics, therapies and toxicity. Chemical Society Reviews 2009;38(6): 1759-1782.

58. Alexis F, Pridgen E, Molnar LK, Farokhzad OC. Factors affecting the clearance and biodistribution of polymeric nanoparticles. Molecular Pharmaceutics 2008;5(4): 505-515.

59. Knop K, Hoogenboom R, Fischer D, Schubert US. Poly(ethylene glycol) in drug delivery: pros and cons as well as potential alternatives. Angewandte Chemie International Edition England 2010;49(36): 6288-6308.

60. Mieszawska AJ, Mulder WJ, Fayad ZA, Cormode DP. Multifunctional gold nanoparticles for diagnosis and therapy of disease. Molecular Pharmaceutics 2013;10(3): 831-47.

61. Makadia HK, Siegel SJ. Poly lactic-co-glycolic acid (PLGA) as biodegradable controlled drug delivery carrier. Polymers (Basel) 2011;3(3): 1377-1397.

62. Elsabahy M, Wooley KL. Design of polymeric nanoparticles for biomedical delivery applications. Chemical Society Reviews 2012;41(7): 2545-2561.

63. Nicolas J, Mura S, Brambilla D, Mackiewicz N, Couvreur P. Design, functionalisation strategies and biomedical applications of targeted biodegradable/biocompatible polymer-based nanocarriers for drug delivery. Chemical Society Reviews 2013;42(3): 1147-1235.

64. Yazid H, Adnan R, Hamid SA, Farrukh MA. Synthesis and characterization of gold nanoparticles supported on zinc oxide via the deposition-precipitation method. Turkish Journal of Chemistry 2010;34: 639-650.

65. Hainfeld JF, Dilmanian FA, Slatkin DN, Smilowitz HM. Radiotherapy enhancement with gold nanoparticles. Journal of Pharmacy and Pharmacology 2008;60(8): 977-985.

66. Cabral R, Baptista PV. The chemistry and biology of gold nanoparticle-mediated photothermal therapy: promises and challenges. Nano LIFE 2013;3(3): 1330001.

67. Conde J, Ambrosone A, Sanz V, Hernandez Y, Marchesano V, Tian F, Child H, Berry CC, Ibarra MR, Baptista PV, Tortiglione C, de la Fuente JM. Design of Multifunctional Gold Nanoparticles for *In Vitro* and *In Vivo* Gene Silencing. ACSNANO 2012;6(9): 8316-8324.

68. Murphy CJ, Gole AM, Hunyadi SE, Stone JW, Sisco PN, Alkilany A, Kinard BE, Hankins P. Chemical sensing and imaging with metallic nanorods. Chemical Communications 2008;5: 544-557.

69. Huang CW, Hao YW, Nyagilo J, Dave DP, Xu LF, Sun XK. Porous Hollow Gold Nanoparticles for Cancer SERS Imaging. Journal of Nano Research 2010;10: 137-148.

70. Sirotkina MA, Elagin VV, Shirmanova MV, Bugrova ML, Snopova LB, Kamensky VA, Nadtochenko VA, Denisov NN, Zagaynova EV. OCT-guided laser hyperthermia with passively tumor-targeted gold nanoparticles. Journal of Biophotonics 2010;3(10-11): 718-727.

71. Cardinal J, Klune JR, Chory E, Jeyabalan G, Kanzius JS, Nalesnik M, Geller DA. Non-invasive Radiofrequency Ablation of Cancer Targeted by Gold Nanoparticles. Surgery 2008;144(2): 125-132.

72. Gannon CJ, Patra CR, Bhattacharya R, Mukherjee P, Curley SA. Intracellular gold nanoparticles enhance non-invasive radiofrequency thermal destruction of human gastrointestinal cancer cells. Journal of Nanobiotechnology 2008;6(2): 1-9.

73. Bhattacharya R, Mukherjee P. Biological properties of “naked” metal nanoparticles. Advanced Drug Delivery Reviews 2008;60(11): 1289-1306.

74. Wang J, Yao K, Wang C, Tang C, Jiang X. Synthesis and drug delivery of novel amphiphilic block copolymers containing hydrophobic dehydroabietic moiety. Journal of Materials Chemistry B 2013;1(17): 2324-2332.

75. Lim ZZJ, Li JEJ, Ng CT, Yung LYL, Bay BH. Gold nanoparticles in cancer therapy. Acta Pharmacologica Sinica 2011;32(8): 983-990.

76. Duncan B, Kim C, Rotello VM. Gold nanoparticle platforms as drug and biomacromolecule delivery systems. Journal of Controlled Release 2010;148(1): 122-127.

77. Schroeder A, Heller DA, Winslow MM, Dahlman JE, Pratt GW, Langer R, Jacks T, Anderson DG. Treating metastatic cancer with nanotechnology. Nature Reviews Cancer 2012;12(1): 39-50.

78. Hu CMJ, Aryal S, Zhang L. Nanoparticle-assisted combination therapies for effective cancer treatment. Therapeutic Delivery 2010;1(2): 323-334.

79. Ruoslahti E, Bhatia SN, Sailor MJ. Targeting of drugs and nanoparticles to tumors. Journal of Cell Biology 2010;188(6): 759-768.

80. Dreaden EC, Mwakwari SC, Sodji QH, Oyelere AK, El-Sayed MA. Tamoxifen-Poly(ethylene glycol)-Thiol Gold Nanoparticle Conjugates: Enhanced Potency and Selective Delivery for Breast Cancer Treatment. Bioconjugate Chemistry 2009;20(12): 2247-2253.

81. Liu Y, Miyoshi H, Nakamura M. Nanomedicine for drug delivery and imaging: a promising avenue for cancer therapy and diagnosis using targeted functional nanoparticles. International Journal of Cancer 2007;120(12): 2527-2537.

82. Xie J, Lee S, Chen X. Nanoparticle-based theranostic agents. Advanced Drug Delivery Reviews 2010;62(11): 1064-1079.

83. Farokhzad OC, Cheng J, Teply BA, Sherifi I, Jon S, Kantoff PW, Richie JP, Langer R. Targeted nanoparticle-aptamer bioconjugates for cancer chemotherapy *in vivo*. PNAS 2006;103(16): 6315-6320.

84. Sapra P, Allen TM. Internalizing Antibodies are Necessary for Improved Therapeutic Efficacy of Antibody-targeted Liposomal Drugs. Cancer Research 2002;62(24): 7190-7194.

85. Park JW, Kirpotin DB, Hong K, Shalaby R, Shao Y, Nielsen UB, Marks JD, Papahadjopoulos D, Benz CC. Tumor targeting using anti-her2 immunoliposomes. Journal of Controlled Release 2001;74(1-3): 95-113.

86. Chattopadhyay N, Fonge H, Cai Z, Scollard D, Lechtman E, Done SJ, Pignol JP, Reilly RM. Role of antibody-mediated tumor targeting and route of administration in nanoparticle tumor accumulation in vivo. Molecular Pharmaceutics 2012;9(8): 2168-2179.

87. Kao HW, Lin YY, Chen CC, Chi KH, Tien DC, Hsia CC, Lin MH, Wang HE. Evaluation of EGFR-targeted radioimmuno-gold-nanoparticles as a theranostic agent in a tumor animal model. Bioorganic & Medicinal Chemistry Letters 2013;23(11): 3180-3185.

88. Ang KK, Berkey BA, Tu X, Zhang HZ, Katz R, Hammond EH, Fu KK, Milas L. Impact of epidermal growth factor receptor expression on survival and pattern of relapse in patients with advanced head and neck carcinoma. Cancer Research 2002;62(24): 7350-7356.

89. Asadishad B, Vossoughi M, Alemzadeh I. Folate-Receptor-Targeted Delivery of Doxorubicin Using Polyethylene Glycol-Functionalized Gold Nnanoparticles. Industrial & Engineering Chemistry Research 2010;49(4): 1958-1963.

90. Chithrani BD, Chan WC. Elucidating the mechanism of cellular uptake and removal of protein-coated gold nanoparticles of different sizes and shapes. Nano Letters 2007;7(6): 1542-1550.

91. Kang B, Mackey MA, El-Sayed MA. Nuclear targeting of gold nanoparticles in cancer cells induces DNA damage, causing cytokinesis

arrest and apoptosis. Journal of the American Chemical Society 2010;132(5): 1517-1519.

92. de la Fuente JM, Berry CC. Tat Peptide as an Efficient Molecule To Translocate Gold Nanoparticles into the Cell Nucleus. Bioconjugate Chemistry 2005;16(5): 1176-1180.

93. Lu W, Zhang G, Zhang R, Flores LG, 2nd, Huang Q, Gelovani JG, Li C. Tumor site-specific silencing of NF-kappaB p65 by targeted hollow gold nanosphere-mediated photothermal transfection. Cancer Research 2010;70(8): 3177-3188.

94. Lu W, Xiong C, Zhang G, Huang Q, Zhang R, Zhang JZ, Li C. Targeted photothermal ablation of murine melanomas with melanocyte-stimulating hormone analog-conjugated hollow gold nanospheres. Clinical Cancer Research 2009; 15(3): 876-886.

95. Choi CH, Alabi CA, Webster P, Davis ME. Mechanism of active targeting in solid tumors with transferrin-containing gold nanoparticles. Proceedings of the National Academy of Sciences of the United States of America 2010;107(3): 1235-1240.

96. Melancon MP, Lu W, Yang Z, Zhang R, Cheng Z, Elliot AM, Stafford J, Olson T, Zhang JZ, Li C. In vitro and in vivo targeting of hollow gold nanoshells directed at epidermal growth factor receptor for photothermal ablation therapy. Molecular Cancer Therapeutics 2008;7(6): 1730-1739.

97. Park C, Youn H, Kim H, Noh T, Kook YH, Oh ET, Park HJ, Kim C. Cyclodextrin-covered gold nanoparticles for targeted delivery of an anti-cancer drug. Journal of Materials Chemistry 2009;19(16): 2310-2315.

98. Han G, You CC, Kim BJ, Turingan RS, Forbes NS, Martin CT, Rotello VM. Light-Regulated Release of DNA and Its Delivery to Nuclei by Means of Photolabile Gold Nanoparticles. Angewandte Chemie International Edition England 2006;45(19): 3165-3169.

99. Hong R, Han G, Fernández JM, Kim BJ, Forbes NS, Rotello VM. Glutathione-Mediated Delivery and Release Using Monolayer Protected Nanoparticle Carriers. Journal of the American Chemical Society 2006;128(4): 1078-1079.

100. Mayer G, Heckel A. Biologically Active Molecules with a "Light Switch". Angewandte Chemie International Edition England 2006;45(30): 4900-4921.

101. McCoy CP, Rooney C, Edwards CR, Jones DS, Gorman SP. Light-Triggered Molecule-Scale Drug Dosing Devices. Journal of the American Chemical Society 2007;129(31): 9572-9573.

102. Li J, Gupta S, Li C. Research perspectives: gold nanoparticles in cancer theranostics. Quantitative Imaging in Medicine and Surgery. 2013;3(6): 284-291.

103. Agasti SS, Chompoosor A, You C-C, Ghosh P, Kim CK, Rotello VM. Photoregulated Release of Caged Anticancer Drugs from Gold Nanoparticles. Journal of the American Chemical Society 2009;131(16): 5728-5729.

104. You J, Zhang G, Li C. Exceptionally high payload of doxorubicin in hollow gold nanospheres for near-infrared light-triggered drug release. ACS Nano 2010;4(2): 1033-1041.

105. Yavuz MS, Cheng Y, Chen J, Cobley CM, Zhang Q, Rycenga M, Xie J, Kim C, Song KH, Schwartz AG, Wang LV, Xia Y. Gold nanocages covered by smart polymers for controlled release with near-infrared light. Nature Materials 2009;8: 935-939.

106. Gu YJ, Cheng J, Man CW, Wong WT, Cheng SH. Gold-doxorubicin nanoconjugates for overcoming multidrug resistance. Nanomedicine 2012;8(2): 204-211.

107. Brown SD, Nativo P, Smith J-A, Stirling D, Edwards PR, Venugopal B, Flint DJ, Plumb JA, Graham D, Wheate NJ. Gold Nanoparticles for the Improved Anticancer Drug Delivery of the Active Component of Oxaliplatin. Journal of the American Chemical Society 2010;132(13): 4678-4684.

108. Hunt KK, Vorburguer SA. Hurdles and Hopes for Cancer Therapy. Science 2002;297(5580): 415-416.

109. Whitehead KA, Langer R, Anderson DG. Knocking down barriers: advances in siRNA delivery. Nature Reviews Drug Discovery 2009;8(2): 129-138.

110. Giljohann DA, Seferos DS, Prigodich AE, Patel PC, Mirkin CA. Gene regulation with polyvalent siRNA-nanoparticle conjugates. Journal of the American Chemical Society 2009;131(6): 2072-2073.

111. Rosi NL, Giljohann DA, Thaxton CS, Lytton-Jean AK, Han MS, Mirkin CA. Oligonucleotide-modified gold nanoparticles for intracellular gene regulation. Science 2006;312(5776): 1027-1030.

112. Han G, Martin CT, Rotello VM. Stability of Gold Nanoparticle-Bound DNA toward Biological, Physical, and Chemical Agents. Chemical Biology & Drug Design 2006;67(1): 78-82.

113. Han G, Chari NS, Verma A, Hong R, Martin CT, Rotello VM. Controlled Recovery of the Transcription of Nanoparticle-Bound DNA by Intracellular Concentrations of Glutathione. Bioconjugate Chem. 2005;16(6): 1356-1359.

114. Lytton-Jean AK, Langer R, Anderson DG. Five years of siRNA delivery: spotlight on gold nanoparticles. Small 2011;7(14): 1932-1937.

115. Gowda R, Jones NR, Banerjee S, Robertson GP. Use of Nanotechnology to Develop Multi-Drug Inhibitors for Cancer Therapy. Journal of Nanomedicine and Nanotechnology 2013;4(6): 1-16.

116. Conde J, Tian F, Hernández Y, Bao C, Cui D, Janssen K-P, Ibarra MR, Baptista PV, Stoeger T, de la Fuente JM. *In vivo* tumor targeting via nanoparticle-mediated therapeutic siRNA coupled to inflammatory response in lung cancer mouse models. Biomaterials 2013;34(31): 7744-7753.

117. Zhang W, Meng J, Ji Y, Li X, Kong H, Wu X, Xu H. Inhibiting metastasis of breast cancer cells in vitro using gold nanorod-siRNA delivery system. Nanoscale 2011;3(9): 3923-3932.

118. Ryou SM, Park M, Kim JM, Jeon CO, Yun CH, Han SH, Kim SW, Lee Y, Kim S, Han MS, Bae J, Lee K. Inhibition of xenograft tumor growth in mice by gold nanoparticle-assisted delivery of short hairpin RNAs against Mcl-1L. Journal of Biotechnology 2011;156(2): 89-94.

119. Brooks PC, Montgomery AM, Rosenfeld M, Reisfeld RA, Hu T, Klier G, Cheresh DA. Integrin alpha v beta 3 antagonists promote tumor regression by inducing apoptosis of angiogenic blood vessels. Cell 1994;79(7): 1157-1164.

120. Wahid F, Shehzad A, Khan T, Kim YY. MicroRNAs: synthesis, mechanism, function, and recent clinical trials. Biochimica et Biophysica Acta 2010;1803(11): 1231-1243.

121. Yu Y, Sarkar FH, Majumdar APN. Down-regulation of miR-21 Induces Differentiation of Chemoresistant Colon Cancer Cells and Enhances Susceptibility to Therapeutic egimens. Translational Oncology 2013;6(2):180-186.

122. Baguley BC. Multiple Drug Resistance Mechanisms in Cancer. Molecular Biotechnology 2010;46(3): 308-316.

123. Huls M, Russel FGM, Masereeuw R. The Role of ATP Binding Cassette Transporters in Tissue Defense and Organ Regeneration. The Journal of Pharmacology and Experimental Therapeutics 2009;328(1): 3-9.

124. Wang K, Wu X, Wang J, Huang J. Cancer stem cell theory: therapeutic implications for nanomedicine. International Journal of Nanomedicine 2013;8(1): 899-908.

125. Ganesh S, Iyer AK, Weiler J, Morrissey DV, Amiji MM. Combination of siRNA-directed Gene Silencing With Cisplatin Reverses Drug Resistance in Human Non-small Cell Lung Cancer. Molecular Therapy-Nucleic Acids 2013;2(7): 1-11.

126. Susa M, Iyer AK, Ryu K, Choy E, Hornicek FJ, Mankin H, Milane L, Amiji MM, Duan Z. Inhibition of ABCB1 (MDR1) Expression by an siRNA Nanoparticulate Delivery System to Overcome Drug Resistance in Osteosarcoma. PLoS ONE 2010; 5(5): 1-12.

127. Chaabane W, User SD, El-Gazzah M, Jaksik R, Sajjadi E, Rzeszowska-Wolny J, Los M. Autophagy, Apoptosis, Mitoptosis and Necrosis: Interdependence Between Those Pathways and Effects on Cancer. Archivum Immunologiae et Therapiae Experimentalis 2013;61(1): 43-58.

128. Amaravadi RK, Thompson CB. The Roles of Therapy-Induced Autophagy and Necrosis in Cancer Treatment. Clinical Cancer Research 2007;13(24): 7271-7279.

129. Saad M, Garbuzenko OB, Minko T. Co-delivery of siRNA and an anticancer drug for treatment of multidrug-resistant cancer. Nanomedicine 2008;3(6): 761-776.

130. Kim D, Yu MK, Lee TS, Park JJ, Jeong YY, Jon S. Amphiphilic polymer-coated hybrid nanoparticles as CT/MRI dual contrast agents. Nanotechnology 2011;22(15): 1-7.

131. Pan Y, Neuss S, Leifert A, Fischler M, Wen F, Simon U, Schmid G, Brandau W, Jahnen-Dechent W. Size-dependent cytotoxicity of gold nanoparticles. Small 2007;3(11): 1941-1949.

132. Yildirimer L, Thanh NTK, Loizidou M, Seifalian AM. Toxicology and clinical potential of nanoparticles. Nano Today 2011;6(6): 585-607.

133. Goodman CM, McCusker CD, Yilmaz T, Rotello VM. Toxicity of gold nanoparticles functionalized with cationic and anionic side chains. Bioconjugate Chemistry 2004;15(4): 897-900.

134. Chen YS, Hung YC, Liau I, Huang GS. Assessment of the In Vivo Toxicity of Gold Nanoparticles. Nanoscale Research Letters 2009;4(8): 858-864.

135. Connor EE, Mwamuka J, Gole A, Murphy CJ, Wyatt MD. Gold nanoparticles are taken up by human cells but do not cause acute cytotoxicity. Small 2005;1(3): 325-327.

136. Tsoli M, Kuhn H, Brandau W, Esche H, Schmid G. Cellular uptake and toxicity of Au55 clusters. Small 2005;1(8-9): 841-844.

137. Ryan JA, Overton KW, Speight ME, Oldenburg CN, Loo L, Robarge W, Franzen S, Feldheim DL. Cellular uptake of gold nanoparticles passivated with BSA-SV40 large T antigen conjugates. Analytical Chemistry 2007;79(23): 9150-9159.

138. Nativo P, Prior IA, Brust M. Uptake and intracellular fate of surface-modified gold nanoparticles. ACS Nano 2008;2(8): 1639-1644.

139. Patra HK, Banerjee S, Chaudhuri U, Lahiri P, Dasgupta AK. Cell selective response to gold nanoparticles, Nanomedice: Nanotechnology, Biology, and Medicine 2007;3(2): 111-119.

140. Chithrani BD, Ghazani AA, Chan WC. Determining the size and shape dependence of gold nanoparticle uptake into mammalian cells. Nano Letters 2006;6(4): 662-668.

141. Jiang W, Kim BY, Rutka JT, Chan WC. Nanoparticle-mediated cellular response is size-dependent. Nature Nanotechnology 2008;3(3): 145-50.

142. Arnida, Malugin A, Ghandehari H. Cellular uptake and toxicity of gold nanoparticles in prostate cancer cells: a comparative study of rods and spheres. Journal of Applied Toxicology 2010;30(3): 212-217.

143. Hauck TS, Ghazani AA, Chan WC. Assessing the effect of surface chemistry on gold nanorod uptake, toxicity, and gene expression in mammalian cells. Small 2008;4(1): 153-159.

144. Sabella S, Brunetti V, Vecchio G, Galeone A, Maiorano G, Cingolani R, Pompa P. Toxicity of citrate-capped AuNPs: an *in vitro* and *in vivo*assessment. Journal of Nanoparticle Research 2011;13(12): 6821-6835.

145. Pan Y, Leifert A, Ruau D, Neuss S, Bornemann J, Schmid G, Brandau W, Simon U, Jahnen-Dechent W. Gold nanoparticles of diameter 1.4 nm trigger necrosis by oxidative stress and mitochondrial damage. Small 2009;5(18): 2067-2076.

146. Li JJ, Hartono D, Ong CN, Bay BH, Yung LYL. Autophagy and oxidative stress associated with gold nanoparticles. Biomaterials 2010;31(23): 5996-6003.

147. Li JJ, Zou L, Hartono D, Ong CN, Bay BH, Lanry Yung LY. Gold Nanoparticles Induce Oxidative Damage in Lung Fibroblasts In Vitro. Advanced Materials 2008;20(1): 138-142.

148. Conde J, Larguinho M, Cordeiro A, Raposo LR, Costa PM, Santos S, Diniz MS, Fernandes AR, Baptista PV. Gold-nanobeacons for gene therapy: evaluation of genotoxicity, cell toxicity and proteome profiling analysis. Nanotoxicology 2014;8(5): 521-532.

149. Hackenberg S, Scherzed A, Kessler M, Hummel S, Technau A, Froelich K, Ginzkey C, Koehler C, Hagen R, Kleinsasser N. Silver nanoparticles: evaluation of DNA damage, toxicity and functional impairment in human mesenchymal stem cells. Toxicology Letters 2011;201(1): 27-33.

150. Asharani PV, Xinyi N, Hande MP, Valiyaveettil S. DNA damage and p53-mediated growth arrest in human cells treated with platinum nanoparticles. Nanomedicine 2010;5(1): 51-64.

151. El-Sayed I, Huang X, El-Sayed MA. Selective laser photo-thermal therapy of epithelial carcinoma using anti-EGFR antibody conjugated gold nanoparticles. Cancer Letters 2006;239(1): 129-135.

152. Schaeublin NM, Braydich-Stolle LK, Schrand AM, Miller JM, Hutchison J, Schlager JJ, Hussain SM. Surface charge of gold nanoparticles mediates mechanism of toxicity. Nanoscale 2011;3(2): 410-420.

153. Alkilany AM, Nagaria PK, Hexel CR, Shaw TJ, Murphy CJ, Wyatt MD. Cellular uptake and cytotoxicity of gold nanorods: molecular origin of cytotoxicity and surface effects. Small 2009;5(6): 701-708.

154. Cho WS, Cho M, Jeong J, Choi M, Cho HY, Han BS, Kim SH, Kim HO, Lim YT, Chung BH, Jeong J. Acute toxicity and pharmacokinetics of 13 nm-sized PEG-coated gold nanoparticles. Toxicology and Applied Pharmacology 2009;236(1): 16-24.

155. Chen YS, Hung YC, Liau I, Huang GS. Assessment of the In Vivo Toxicity of Gold Nanoparticles. Nanoscale Research Letters 2009;4(8): 858-864.

156. De Jong WH, Hagens WI, Krystek P, Burger MC, Sips AJ, Geertsma RE. Particle size-dependent organ distribution of gold nanoparticles after intravenous administration. Biomaterials 2008;29(12): 1912-1919.

157. Sonavane G, Tomoda K, Makino K. Biodistribution of colloidal gold nanoparticles after intravenous administration: effect of particle size. Colloids and Surfaces B: Biointerfaces 2008;66(2): 274-280.

158. Hirn S, Semmler-Behnke M, Schleh C, Wenk A, Lipka J, Schaffler M, Takenaka S, Moller W, Schmid G, Simon U, Kreyling WG. Particle size-dependent and surface charge-dependent biodistribution of gold nanoparticles after intravenous administration. European Journal of Pharmaceutics and Biopharmaceutics 2011;77(3): 407-416.

159. Khlebtsov N, Dykman L. Biodistribution and toxicity of engineered gold nanoparticles: a review of in vitro and in vivo studies. Chemical Society Reviews 2011;40(3): 1647-1671.

160. Longmire M, Choyke PL, Kobayashi H. Clearance properties of nano-sized particles and molecules as imaging agents: considerations and caveats. Nanomedicine (Lond) 2008;3(5): 703-717.

161. Harper SL, Carriere JL, Miller JM, Hutchison JE, Maddux BL, Tanguay RL. Systematic evaluation of nanomaterial toxicity: utility of standardized materials and rapid assays. ACS Nano 2011;5(6): 4688-4697.

162. Pompa P, Vecchio G, Galeone A, Brunetti V, Sabella S, Maiorano G, Falqui A, Bertoni G, Cingolani R. In Vivo toxicity assessment of gold nanoparticles in Drosophila melanogaster. Nano Research 2011;4(4): 405-413.

Chapter 3

Scope of Nanotechnology in Drug Delivery

Kashif Maroof[1], Farya Zafar[1], Huma Ali[1], Safila Naveed[2] and Sidra Tanwir[1]

[1]*Ziauddin University Karachi, Pakistan*

[2]*Jinnah University for Women Karachi, Pakistan*

ABSTRACT

Today more than 70% of newly discovered drugs (independent from the therapeutic class) showed poor water solubility which may results a serious challenge to the development of new compounds. There are several drug formulation strategies are available to further improve the solubility and / or dissolution rate i.e. solid dispersion technique, self-emulsifying systems or complex formation. These strategies have been successfully used in the past but today nanotechnology has produced a massive impact to meet the needs. Various factors particularly economic, social, public health and environmental benefits have together made nanotechnology based drug delivery systems a very popular one. In this article we have discussed the scope of nanotechnology in the designing of new drug delivery systems.

Keywords: Nanotechnology; Self-emulsifying systems; Bioavailability

INTRODUCTION

Nanotechnology is characterized as the science, engineering and technology carried out at the nano scale [1]. It is a revolutionary technique which utilizes devices and molecules in the range of 1-100 nanometers. The use of particles in very diminutive range helps to facilitate the features and overall quality of the system. Particles exposed to nanotechnology exhibits superior characteristics including resistance to settling, higher saturation solubility state and protection from decomposition, enhanced drug release, increased adhesion to biological membranes, improved strength and reduced weight, enhanced absorption and improved chemical reactivity as compared to their larger scale corresponding item [2]. Nanotechnology tailors drugs at a molecular level which results in reducing side effects and produced rapid onset of therapeutic action and much improved bioavailability [3].

History of Nanotechnology in Drug Delivery

The idea of nanotechnology was initially proposed by Feynman in 1959. The term nanotechnology was first devised by Norio Taniguchi in the year 1974 [4] whereas the term nano-medicine was coined by Drexler and colleagues in 1980's [5]. The first development in the field was reported in early 70s at the ETH Zurich, when the first controlled released system was developed along with other several drugs that showed the capability to cross the blood brain barrier with much improved pharmacokinetics [6]. However, it wasn't until 2006 when the first international journal in nano-medicine was introduced called 'International Journal of Nano-medicine' to cater to the emerging needs of nanotechnology in medicine [7].

Advances in Drug Delivery System through Nanotechnology

This new innovative technique has had revolutionary impact on the management of prevalent diseases.

Cancer

According to a report published in 2013 an average of 1,660,290 fresh cancer cases were reported to occur in the United States alone in that year [8]. Another report published in the same year [9], segregated the types of cancer according to the most prevalent one in accordance to the geographical region. Cervix cancer was highly reported in Africa and prostate cancer in North America, whereas stomach cancer was highly recognized in Eastern Asia [9]. The staggering numbers of patients suffering from cancer only emphasized the need for development of a novel drug delivery system with enhanced specificity, improved therapeutic efficacy and decreased side effects.

The ability of the drug to reach their objective location and minimum action at non-specific sites determines the superiority of anti-cancer treatments [10]. This could only be achieved by modification at the surface of the nano particles carriers. Incorporation of nano particles with Poly Ethylene Glycol (PEG)/ Poly Ethylene Oxide (PEO) not only reduces non-specific uptake but also enhances specific tumor-targeting ability by preventing white blood cells from identifying the nano particles as foreign objects and allowing them to flow in the blood stream extended enough to attach to tumors [11]. The prime example of this avant-garde technology was the introduction of hydro gel, which when administered by subcutaneous route allows drug delivery for weeks with a single dose [12]. Herceptin, which is presently accepted as an intravenous therapy with a loading dose followed by 6 mg.kg-1 or 2 mg.kg-1 every 3 weeks or every week respectively. It acts by targetingcancer cells that display HER2+ (human epidermal growth factor receptor 2), which exists in about one of every four breast cancer patients and makes this type of breast cancer more aggressive than any other type of breast cancer [13,14]. After the formulation of hydro gel a team of researchers have succeeded in designing a vitamin E-based hydrogel that can release Herceptin under the skin for several weeks [15]. It has been observed that this hydrogel possesses greater antitumor ability in comparison to conventional intravenous and subcutaneous delivery of Herceptin, due to better reservation of compound within the tumor [15].

Another approach to improve the capability of drug to enter tumors is the use of photosensitizing agents, where the photosensitizing agent is caused to gather in the tumor, and then the tumor is irradiated with light of suitable wavelength. The photosensitizing agent facilitates the blood vessels in the tumor to become highly permeable, therefore allowing more drug carrying nano particles to enter the tumor. Novel ceramic-based nanoparticles known as Ultrafine has been reported which is a modified silica-based nanoparticles. It exhibits its action by entrapping water-insoluble photosensitizing anticancer drug 2-devinyl- 2-(1-hexyloxyethyl) pyropheophorbide. in vitro studies have confirmed the active uptake of drug-doped nanoparticles into the cytosol of tumor cells produces significant destruction [16].

Nano disks (NDs) are nano scale, disk-shaped phosphor lipid bi-layers whose edge is stabilized by apolipoproteins [17] and can be developed in vitro by combining recombinant apoA-I proteins with different phospholipids [18]. A study showed that by using laponite (LAP) nanodisks effective transport of doxorubicin (DOX) to cancer cells can take place [19]. Ion exchange process was used to encapsulate DOX into the interlayer space of LAP, in this study the results showed a greater therapeutic efficacy in hindering the growth of a model cancer cell line than free DOX drug at the similar concentration [19].

Super-para-magnetic iron oxide nano particles (SPION) have been widely used experimentally for drug delivery. Magnetic nanoparticles can bind to drugs and can be directed towards tumor using an external magnetic field. Absorption, distribution, metabolism and excretion of the drug are dictated by the nature of surface coating, surface chemistry and size of nanoparticles [20]. A group of researchers have formulated water-dispersible oleic acid (OA)-Pluronic-coated iron oxide magnetic nanoparticle product that not only provides an advantage of loading high doses of water-insoluble anticancer agents but can also be employed as a general drug carrier system for systemic administration of class II drugs while simultaneously allowing magnetic targeting and/ or imaging [21]. The nano particles showed an additional advantage of sustained release and a sustained intracellular drug withholding as compared to drug in solution while exhibiting an anti-proliferative effect in different types of tumors [21].

Another approach to target cancer cells is conveying conjugated gold nano particles with specific peptides to the nuclei of cancer cells. The gold nano particles confine at the nucleus of a cancer cell and impair the DNA due to the failure to thorough cell division resulting in apoptosis [22].

Carbon nanotubes have found great importance in drug delivery of chemotherapeutic agents since 2004 because of their potential to minimize the side effects [23]. Detailed research was performed to calculate approximately the opposite radius of the nano tube that will provide the maximum uptake of the drug molecule [24]. Cisplastin was used as a model drug, which is the first platinum based drug approved to be used in clinics about 40 years ago [25]. Cisplatin acts as a DNAdamaging agent and brings about cells to arrest at either the G1-, S- or G2-phase of the cell cycle in an effort to heal the damage. Weakening satisfactory repair, the cells ultimately experience an abnormal mitosis followed by apoptosis [26]. Three orientations of cisplatin were examined for nano tubes. It was revealed that, for all three orientations of cisplatin to be recognized into the carbon nanotube, the least radius must be at least 4.785 Å. This research laid the foundation for an essential pilot design which might offer cancer researchers complete guiding principle to ensure the efficient working of these nano tubes [24]. Another study [27] premeditated the effects of using carbon nano tubes immersed in poly ethylene glycol (PEG). Paclitexal (PTX) was used as a model drug here. The samples showed greater effectiveness to destroy HeLa cells and MCF-7 cells, than free PTX. Hence, these showed great capability to be employed for cancer therapeutics [27].

Carbon nano fibers (CNF's) were formed and discovered in the course of catalytic transformation of carbon-containing gases. These days CNF's are used for various biomedical applications [28]. Polyurethane (PU) is a multipurpose elastomer that is usually employed in biomedicine [29]. A group of scientists examined the dispersion of CNFs in PU with varying PU and CNF weight ratio to make an ideal bladder prosthetic material that should not only encourage usual chief human urothelial cell (HUC) purpose, but also hinder the reappearance of bladder cancerous cell action. The results were promising and delivered a new nano composite comprising of CNF and PU that should be considered for preventing the reoccurrence of cancerous bladder tissue and for encouraging usual non-cancerous bladder tissue development [30-36].

Number of studies have been reported in past few years related to the efficacy and safety of various nanoparticles like cholesteroltethered platinum II-based supramolecular nanoparticle [37-41], polymeric-ceramic nanocarriers (NCs) in order to achieve oral delivery of the anticancer neutraceutical iron-saturated bovine lactoferrin (Fe-bLf) protein) [42,43], novel alginate-enclosed chitosan–calcium phosphate-loaded iron-saturated bovine lactoferrin nanocarriers for oral delivery in colon cancer therapy etc. [44-50]. Another targeting systems for cancer treatment was also investigated with microRNAdirected oncology approach using MRX34 (a liposome-containing miRNA carrier), for usefulness in metastatic liver cancer [51,52]. The amalgamation of various targeted and control release polymeric nano particles have also been illustrated with different programmable approaches and applications. One of them is nanotherapeutic product of docetaxel (BIND-014), which is tested for its effectiveness in solid tumors [53].

Cardiovascular Disease

Cardiovascular diseases may produce a negative impact not only on economy but also on the quality of life, hence there is an urgent need to develop more effective approaches for the prevention and management of CHF [31]. The burden of stroke is high and is expected to further upturn in forth coming years as a consequence of demographic and epidemiological changes in populations [32]. Hypertension is an imperative community health challenge [33]. Blockade of standard blood movement, is one of the foremost cause of death and prolonged disability [34].

A new nano therapeutic approach has the potential to advance both the effectiveness and efficacy of thrombolytic drugs. It involves the mechanical activation within blood vessels by high-fluid shear strains to selectively aim drugs to locations of vascular hindrance. in vitro andin vivo readings have revealed that this methodology can be employed competently to lyse clots by means of a significantly lesser quantity of thrombolytic drug than is a prerequisite when given in a soluble preparation [34]. The prime example of this is seen in application ofdendrimers. Dendrimers are circular designed nanoparticles that have been considered as a mean to administer medicinal agents for a variety of diseases [35]. A group of researchers developed a technique to attach tissue plasminogen activator (tPA) to dendrimers creating a drug delivery system which would necessitate lesser doses with reduced side effects. The results revealed that this drug delivery system produced an advanced concentration of tPA- dendrimer complex during the course of a varied proportion of dilutions [36].

Nanoburrs technique has also been utilized by the researchers to combat cardiovascular diseases. These are the nanoparticles covered with an adhesive protein that makes them adhere to arterial walls while they gradually discharge medications [37].

Opthamology

Even though eye drops and drug-saturated lenses ensure local effect but their use is rendered inadequate due to loss of drug by eruption from eye and also due to absence of prolonged therapeutic delivery. A group of scientists formulated a nanodiamond (ND)-embedded contact lens having the ability of lysozyme-triggered release of drugs for persistent therapy [38], here Timolol maleate was used as a model drug and the results showed that ND-embedded lenses provided prolonged delivery of TM making them promising tools for ocular drug delivery [38]. Ibrahim et al. in 2015 formulated and tested the biodegradable nanoparticles with natural bioadhesives for ophthalmic application of Brimonidine in glaucoma management. Nanoparticles were illustrated with respect to particle size, morphology, zeta potential & content of drug [54-56]. Nano particles of Celecoxib-loaded drug were developed using different biodegradable polymers like poly(L-lactide) (PLA), poly-ε-caprolactone (PCL) and poly(D,L-lactide-co-glycolide) (PLGA) by impulsive solvent emulsification of diffusion process. Release of drug from these formulations was exhibited in sustained way with no bursting effect. Non-fickian diffusion with suitable fitting to Higuchi model was observed. Toxicity potential of these products was in acceptable level, when determined by cytotoxic examination [57].

Orthodontology and Orthopedics

Research has proved that nanotechnology has a great scope in the field of onthrodontology and orthopedics. Investigators are refining dental implants by the addition of nano tubes to the outward of the implant. It increases the capability to load the nanotubes with antiinflammatorydrugs that can be applied directly to the area around the implant [39]. Silver nanoparticles have gained an ever increasing attention in orthopaedics due to their promising antimicrobial features. They are utilized in tumour prostheses, trauma implants and also as bone cement [58]. In another study novel defensive salivary peptides & the chitosan based nanoparticles as delivery system were studied extensively in orthodontic field [59].

Diabetes

Scientists reported that nanoparticles illustrate distinctive biophysical features which are estimated by their size and shape [60]. Nanoparticles depend upon the characteristics of the active compound and as carriers for vaccine delivery with the development of microand nano-technologies; several micro-engineering methods have been developed to fabricate three-dimensional (3D) islet models in vitro which can better mimic the islet of pancreases in vivo. These in vitro islet models have shown better cell function than monolayer cells, indicating their great potential as better experimental platforms to elucidate islet behaviors under both physiological and pathological conditions, such as the molecular mechanisms of diabetes and clinical islet transplantation.

The use of chitosan in drug delivery has two-fold purpose. Scientists demonstrated the usage of chitosan reduced gold nanoparticles as carriers for drug delivery of insulin and the outcomes showed that oral and nasal administration of insulin loaded chitosan reduced gold nanoparticles has resulted in improved pharmacodynamic effect encompassing the ability to manage the postprandial hyperglycemia [40].

Another novel approach utilizing nanotechnology to treat hyperglycemia is a self-regulating glucose-responsive closed-loop insulin delivery system. Scientists reported that microgels with enzyme nanocapsules enables insulin discharge and causes a decrease in blood glucose levels in a mouse model of Type I diabetes. The microgel system expanded when exposed to hyperglycemic environments acting as a regulator and releasing insulin as a consequence of the enzymatic transformation of glucose into gluconic acid and protonation of the chitosan network [41]. Scientists developed various micro-engineering techniques which is utilized to fabricate in vitro 3D (three-dimensional) islet models which can facilitate islet of pancreases in vivo under different physiological and pathological conditions i.e., clinical islet transplantation and different molecular mechanisms of diabetes [61]. Lee and Kim [62] construct biomimetic nano-sized polymers with bioreducible poly (disulfide amine)s for the management of anemia, cancer, cardiovascular disease and diabetes.

Lung Diseases

Another potential application of nanoparticles is in investigative and therapeutic aiming of diagnostic material's transport to the lungs. It has been reported that nanoparticles have established an extraordinary retaining power in lung airspaces and alveolar macrophages [42]. Confocal microscopy was applied in one study to display the ardent intake of mesoporous silica nanoparticles labeled as RITC and loaded with isoniazid (anti-tubercular drug) by macrophages of human [54]. These macrophages are infected with Mycobacterium tuberculosisGFP-expression. Mohseni et al. in 2015 also assessed the probability of rifampin loading into mesoporous nanoparticles of silica such nanoparticles were found to be proficient in releasing drug contents about 95% in 24 hours [55].

Inflammation

Nanoparticles-mediated delivery of antimicrobial agent(s) into macrophages is probable therapeutic objectives in many human ailments [43,44]. Polyalkylcyanoacrylates (PACA) nanoparticles were employed as a transporter for directing anti-leishmanial drugs into macrophages. This nano material did not encourage interleukin-1 discharge by macrophages [45]. Another group of scientists add the antifungal and anti-leishmanial agent amphotericin B (AmB) and complexed with nanotubes to develop a less toxic formulation in trilaurin based nanosize lipid particles (emulsomes) stabilized by soya phosphatidylcholine as a new intravenous drug delivery system for macrophage targeting [46]. Nanoemulsions of anti-inflammatory agent Flurbiprofen have also been stated in literature [47]. Also, nanoaAPC stimulation enhanced by magnetic field can develop massive numbers of activated antigen-specific T cells which can be used for adoptive immunotherapy [63]. Various categories of nanomaterials i.e., nanoporous scaffolds, nanoparticles, carbon nanotubes and nanofibers are widely utilized for various processing techniques. These nanomaterials are efficiently used in the field of tissue engineering to enhance the manufacturing of biomimetic alternates to substitute damaged organs and tissues. Applications of nanomaterials in tissue engineering are dependent upon the inflammatory conditions they elicit in vivo [64].

CONCLUSION

The current advancement in the delivery of water-insoluble drugs and biopharmaceuticals are expected to notably influence the pharmaceutical and biotechnological industries. Furthermore, the relentless advancement in the current drug delivery nanotechnology which scientists could use to develop formulations has had a remarkable impact on reducing cost and improving the efficiency and productivity.

REFERENCES

1. Ochekpe NA, Olorunfemi PO, Ngwuluka NC (2009) Nanotechnology and Drug DeliveryPart 1: Background and Applications. Trop J Pharm Res 8: 265-274.

2. Jain N, Jain R, Thakur N, Gupta BP, Jain DK, et al. (2010) Nanotechnology: A Safe and effective drug delivery system. Asian J Pharm Clin Res 3: 159-165.

3. Kakade T, Kadam V, Dhanavade K, Salunkhe V (2013) A review on pharmaceutical nanotechnology: dendrimers. WJPPS 2: 4815-4830.

4. Webster TJ (2007) IJN's second year is now a part of nanomedicine history! Int J Nanomedicine 2: 1-2.

5. Tibbals HF (2011) Medical Nanotechnology and Nanomedicine. CRC press Taylor and Francis group 31

6. Najlah M, Freeman S, Attwood D, D'Emanuele A (2007) in vitro evaluation of dendrimerprodrugs for oral drug delivery. Int J Pharm 336: 183-190.

7. Cevc G (2004) Lipid vesicles and other colloids as drug carriers on the skin. Adv Drug Deliv Rev 56: 675-711.

8. Siegel R, Naishadham D, Jemal A (2013) Cancer statistics, 2013. CA Cancer J Clin 63: 11-30.

9. Bray F, Ren JS, Masuyer E, Ferlay J (2013) Global estimates of cancer prevalence for 27 sites in the adult population in 2008. Int J Cancer 132: 1133-1145.

10. van Vlerken LE, Vyas TK, Amiji MM (2007) Poly(ethylene glycol)-modified nanocarriers for tumor-targeted and intracellular delivery. Pharm Res 24: 1405-1414.

11. Biswas AK, Islam R, Choudhury ZS, Mostafa A and Kadir MF (2014) Nanotechnology based approaches in cancer therapeutics. Adv Nat Sci: NanosciNanotechnol 5: 2043-6262.

12. Gupta P, Vermani K, Garg S (2002) Hydrogels: from controlled release to pH-responsive drug delivery. Drug Discov Today 7: 569-579.

13. McKeage K, Lyseng-Williamson KA (2008) Trastuzumab: a pharmacoeconomic review of its use in early breast cancer. Pharmacoeconomics 26: 699-719.

14. Baselga J (2000) Current and planned clinical trials with trastuzumab (Herceptin). Seminoncol 27-32.

15. Steinbach OC (2014) Industry Update: the latest developments in therapeutic delivery. TherDeliv 5: 505-509.

16. Roy I, Ohulchanskyy TY, Pudavar HE, Bergey EJ, Oseroff AR, et al. (2003) Ceramic-based nanoparticles entrapping water-insoluble photosensitizing anticancer drugs: a novel drug-carrier system for photodynamic therapy. J Am ChemSoc 125: 7860-7865.

17. Ghosh M, Singh AT, Xu W, Sulchek T, Gordon LI, et al. (2011) Curcuminnanodisks: formulation and characterization. Nanomedicine 7: 162-167.

18. Murakami T (2012) Phospholipid nanodisc engineering for drug delivery systems. Biotechnol J 7: 762-767.

19. Wang S, Wu Y, Guo R, Huang Y, Wen S, et al. (2013) Laponitenanodisks as an efficient platform for Doxorubicin delivery to cancer cells. Langmuir 29: 5030-5036.

20. Gupta AK, Gupta M (2005) Synthesis and surface engineering of iron oxide nanoparticles for biomedical applications. Biomaterials 26: 3995-4021.

21. Jain TK, Morales MA, Sahoo SK, Leslie-Pelecky DL, Labhasetwar V (2005) Iron oxide nanoparticles for sustained delivery of anticancer agents. Mol Pharm 2: 194-205.

22. Kang B, Mackey MA, El-Sayed MA (2010) Nuclear targeting of gold nanoparticles in cancer cells induces DNA damage, causing cytokinesis arrest and apoptosis. J Am ChemSoc 132: 1517-1519.

23. Chen J, Chen S, Zhao X, Kuznetsova LV, Wong SS, et al. (2008) Functionalized single-walled carbon nanotubes as rationally designed vehicles for tumor-targeted drug delivery. J Am ChemSoc 130: 16778-16785.

24. Hilder TA, Hill JM (2008) Theoretical comparison of nanotubes materials for drug delivery. Micro Nano Lett 3:18-24.

25. Desoize B, Madoulet C (2002) Particular aspects of platinum compounds used at present in cancer treatment. Crit Rev OncolHematol 42: 317-325.

26. Eastman A (1991) Mechanisms of resistance to cisplatin. Cancer Treat Res 57: 233-249.

27. Liu Z, Sun X, Nakayama-Ratchford N, Dai H (2007) Supramolecular chemistry on water-soluble carbon nanotubes for drug loading and delivery. ACS Nano 1: 50-56.

28. Serp P, Corrias M, Kalck P (2003) Carbon nanotubes and nanofibers in catalysis. Applied Catalysis A: General 253: 337–358.

29. Romaškevic T, Budriene S, Pielichowski K and Pielichowski J (2006) Application of polyurethane-based materials for immobilization of enzymes and cells: a review. Chemija 17: 74-89.

30. Tsang M, Chun YW, Im YM, Khang D, Webster TJ (2011) Effects of increasing carbon nanofiber density in polyurethane composites for inhibiting bladder cancer cell functions. Tissue Eng Part A 17:1879-1889.

31. Rich MW (1997) Epidemiology, pathophysiology, and etiology of congestive heart failure in older adults. J Am GeriatrSoc 45: 968-974.

32. Heidenreich PA, McClellan M (2001) Trends in treatment and outcomes for acute myocardial infarction: 1975-1995. Am J Med 110: 165-174.

33. Kearney PM, Whelton M, Reynolds K, Whelton PK, He J (2004) Worldwide prevalence of hypertension: a systematic review. J Hypertens 22: 11-19.

34. Korin N, Gounis MJ, Wakhloo AK, Ingber DE (2015) Targeted drug delivery to flow-obstructed blood vessels using mechanically activated nanotherapeutics. JAMA Neurol 72: 119-122.

35. Wolinsky JB, Grinstaff MW (2008) Therapeutic and diagnostic applications of dendrimers for cancer treatment. Adv Drug Deliv Rev 60: 1037-1055.

36. D'Emanuele A, Attwood D (2005) Dendrimer-drug interactions. Adv Drug Deliv Rev 57: 2147-2162.

37. Lee L, Horowitz J, Frenneaux M (2004) Metabolic manipulation in ischaemic heart disease, a novel approach to treatment. Eur Heart J 25: 634-641.

38. Hiratani H, Fujiwara A, Tamiya Y, Mizutani Y, Alvarez-Lorenzo C (2005) Ocular release of timolol from molecularly imprinted soft contact lenses. Biomaterials 26: 1293-1298.

39. Bjursten LM, Rasmusson L, Oh S, Smith GC, Brammer KS, et al. (2010) Titanium dioxide nanotubes enhance bone bonding in vivo. J Biomed Mater Res A 92: 1218-1224.

40. Bhumkar DR, Joshi HM, Sastry M, Pokharkar VB (2007) Chitosan reduced gold nanoparticles as novel carriers for transmucosal delivery of insulin. Pharm Res 24: 1415-1426.

41. Gu Z, Dang TT, Ma M, Tang BC, Cheng H, et al. (2013) Glucose-responsive microgels integrated with enzyme nanocapsules for closed-loop insulin delivery. ACS Nano 7: 6758-6766.

42. Sajja HK, East MP, Mao H, Wang YA, Nie S, et al. (2009) Development of multifunctional nanoparticles for targeted drug delivery and noninvasive imaging of therapeutic effect. Curr Drug DiscovTechnol 6: 43-51.

43. Singh RK, Srivastava A, Gour JK, Tiwari VK (2012) Targeting Leishmania Species: Nanotechnological Prospects. AdvSciLett 5: 11-20.

44. Gaspar R, Préat V, Opperdoes FR, Roland M (1992) Macrophage activation by polymeric nanoparticles of polyalkylcyanoacrylates: activity against intracellular Leishmaniadonovani associated with hydrogen peroxide production. Pharm Res 9: 782-787.

45. Balland O, Pinto-Alphandary H, Viron A, Puvion E, Andremont A, et al. (1996) Intracellular distribution of ampicillin in murine macrophages infected with Salmonella typhimurium and treated with (3H) ampicillin-loaded nanoparticles. J AntimicrobChemother 37:105-115.

46. Gupta S, Vyas SP (2007) Development and characterization of amphotericin B bearing emulsomes for passive and active macrophage targeting. J Drug Target 15: 206-217.

47. Maroof K, Zafar F, Ali H and Naveed S (2015) Flurbiprofen: A Potent Pain Reliever. J BioequivAvailab 7: 56-58.

48. Sengupta P, Basu S, Soni S, Pandey A, Roy B, et al. (2012) Cholesterol-tethered platinum II-based supramolecular nanoparticle increases antitumor efficacy and reduces nephrotoxicity. Proc. NatlAcadSci 109: 11294-11299 .

49. Kanwar JR, Mahidhara G, Kanwar RK (2013) Novel alginate-enclosed chitosan–calcium phosphate-loaded iron-saturated bovine lactoferrinnanocarriers for oral delivery in colon cancer therapy. Nanomedicine 7: 1521-1550.

50. Lee JM, Yoon TJ, Cho YS (2013) Recent developments in nanoparticle-based siRNA delivery for cancer therapy. Biomed Res Int 2013: 782041.

51. (2013) A Multicenter Phase I Study of MRX34, MicroRNA miR-RX34 Liposome Injectable Suspension.

52. Bader AG (2012) miR-34 - a microRNA replacement therapy is headed to the clinic. Front Genet 3: 120.

53. Sanna V, Pala N, Sechi M (2014) Targeted therapy using nanotechnology: focus on cancer. Int J Nanomedicine 9: 467-483.

54. Hwang AA, Lee BY, Clemens DL, Dillon BJ, Zink JI, et al. (2015) Tuberculosis: pH-Responsive Isoniazid-Loaded Nanoparticles Markedly Improve Tuberculosis Treatment in Mice. Small 11: 50-65.

55. Mohseni M, Gilani K, Mortazavi SA (2015) Preparation and characterization of rifampin loaded mesoporous silica nanoparticles as a potential system for pulmonary drug delivery. Iran J Pharm Res 14: 27-34.

56. Ibrahim MM, Abd-Elgawad AH, Soliman OA, Jablonski MM (2015) Natural Bioadhesive Biodegradable Nanoparticle-Based Topical Ophthalmic Formulations for Management of Glaucoma. Transl Vis SciTechnol 4:12.

57. Ibrahim MM, Abd-Elgawad AE, Soliman OA, Jablonski MM (2013) Nanoparticle-based topical ophthalmic formulations for sustained celecoxib release. J Pharm Sci 102: 1036-1053.

58. Brennan SA, NÃ¬FhoghlÃº C, Devitt BM, O'Mahony FJ, Brabazon D, et al. (2015) Silver nanoparticles and their orthopaedic applications. Bone Joint J 97-97B: 582-9.

59. Zaidan CSF (2015) Novel protective salivary peptides and the chitosan nanoparticles delivery system.Electronic Thesis and Dissertation Repository.Paper 3159.

60. Jeevanandam J, DanquahMK, Debnath S, Meka VS, Chan YS (2015) Opportunities for Nano-Formulations in Type 2 Diabetes Mellitus Treatments. Curr Pharm Biotechnol 16: 853-870.

61. Gao B, Wang L, Han S, Pingguan-Murphy B, Zhang X, et al. (2015) Engineering of microscale three-dimensional pancreatic islet models in vitro and their biomedical applications. Crit Rev Biotechnol 15:1-11.

62. Lee YS, Kim SW (2014) Bioreducible polymers for therapeutic gene delivery. J Control Release 190: 424-439.

63. Perica K, Tu A, Richter A, Bieler JG, Edidin M, et al. (2014) Magnetic field-induced T cell receptor clustering by nanoparticles enhances T cell activation and stimulates antitumor activity. ACS Nano 8: 2252-2260.

64. Padmanabhan J, Kyriakides TR (2015) Nanomaterials, inflammation, and tissue engineering. Wiley Interdiscip Rev NanomedNanobiotechnol 7: 355-370.

Chapter 4

Nanoparticles in Drug Delivery and Cancer Therapy: The Giant Rats Tail

Vinod Prabhu, Siddik Uzzaman, Viswanathan Mariammal Berlin Grace, Chandrasekharan Guruvayoorappan*

[1]*Department of Biotechnology, Karunya University, Karunya Nagar, Coimbatore, Tamil Nadu, India.*

ABSTRACT

Nanotechnology has the potential to offer solutions to these current obstacles in cancer therapies, because of its unique size and large surface-to-volume ratios. Nanoparticles may have properties of self-assembly, stability, specificity, drug encapsulation and biocompatibility as a result of their material composition. Nanoscale devices have impacted cancer biology at three levels: early detection, tumour imaging using radiocontrast nanoparticles or quantum dots; and drug delivery using nanovectors and hybrid nanoparticles. Other role of nanotechnology, in management of various diseases and also in drug resistance in leukemia by blocking drug efflux from cancer cells and induce efficient delivery of si RNA into lymphocytes to block apoptosis in sepsis and targeting tumors also. Nanocrystals labeling with immune cells can act as a platform technology for nanoimmunotherapy. This review addresses the advancement of nanoparticles in drug delivery and in cancer therapy.

Keywords: Nanoparticles, Cancer Therapy, Drug Delivery, Drug Targeting, Quantum Dots

1. INTRODUCTION

Nanotechnology deals with the design, production and characterization on ultra small particles which is extended to broad area in pharmaceutical, medical, chemical and engineering application due to its unique properties [1]. The development of technology occurs at the atomic, molecular or macromolecular range of approximately 1 nm - 100 nanometers (nm) to create and use structures that have novel properties [2]. Nanoparticles (NPs) are defined as a small object that behaves as a whole unit in term of its transport and properties. They can be further classified according to the size and diameter. Fine particles have the range of 100 to 2500 nm or ultrafine particles having the size of 1 to 100 nm [3]. Nanoclusters have one dimension between 1 and 10 nm and narrow size distribution and nanopowders which are agglomerates of ultrafine particles [4]. NPs research is currently an area of passionate scientific interest due to its wide variety of potential application in therapeutic and biomedical interest. The field of nanotechnology holds the promise of significant improvements in the health and well being of patients as well in manufacturing technologies [5]. Specialized nanotechnological approaches like dendrimers, quantum dots, monoclonal antibodies and intergrins which are extensively researched for diagnostic and targeted delivery of therapeutic agents [6]. Nanorobotics centers on self sufficient machines of some functionally operating at the nanoscale. These are hopes for applying nanorobots in medicine [7-9]. The advance of contemporary materials and methodologies have to be manifested with some patients granted about new nano devices which will help in establishing NPs with the use of embedded nanobioelectronics concept in future [10,11]. Nanomedicine access to drug delivery on development of nanoscale molecules which can improve drug bioavailability [12,13]. It was disclosed that this can potentially be achieved by molecules targeting by nanoengineering devices. This new method will be effective in treating a variety of illness such as neurological disorders, diabetes, osteoporosis, Alzheimer's, Parkinson's, amyotrophic lateral sclerosis, multiple sclerosis, HIV-1 associated neuro cognitive disorders, cardio vascular disorders, tuberculosis and cancer [14-22]. NPs such as lipid or polymer can be designed to improve the pharmacological and therapeutical properties of drugs [21]. Cells take up these NPs because of their size and also the ability of the drug to get into the cell cytoplasm through cell membrane. NPs have a very high surface area to volume ratio and it allows many functional group to be attached to a NPs which can bind to certain tumor cells [22]. The smaller size of the NPs facilitates them to accumulate in tumor micro environment thus facilitating newer therapeutic strategies which may replace radiation and chemotherapy.

Recent research has developed a number of NPs such as metals, semiconductor and polymeric particles used in imaging probes and delivery vehicles [23-25]. The use of NPs based drug delivery systems such as polyethleneimine liposomes (PEI), silica NPs, micelles and chitosan have effective role in drug delivery with reduced drug side effects [26,27]. Recent technology have developed many multifunctional NPs for targeting, imaging, drug delivery, sensing of anticancer agents and small interference RNA (si RNA) delivery [28,29]. Nanotechnology promises construction of artificial cells, enzymes and genes that helps in the replacement therapy of many disorders which are due to deficiency of enzymes, mutation of genes or repair in the synthesis of protein [30]. In this review, we discuss the recent emerging trends of NPs in drug delivery system and in cancer therapy.

2. MULTIFUNCTIONAL NANOPARTICLES

Liposome comprises lipid bilayer membrane surrounding an aqueous interior and it can be used as nanoparticles that have similarities with biological membrane that improves the efficacy and safety of drugs [31]. Liposomes are classified into three categories such as small unilamellar vesicles, large unilamellar vesicles and multilamellar vesicles on the basis of their size and lamellarity. The active compound can be located either in the aqueous spaces, if it is water-soluble, or in the lipid membrane, if it is lipid-soluble. The new generation of liposome called 'stealth liposomes' have the ability to evade the interception by the immune system, and have longer half-life [32]. The emulsions comprise of oil in water-type mixtures that are stabilized with surfactants to maintain size and shape. The lipophilic material can be dissolved in water organic solvent that is emulsified in an aqueous phase. Like liposomes, emulsions have been used for improving the efficacy and safety of diverse compounds [33]. Polymers such as polysaccharide chitosan NPs have been used for some time as drug delivery systems [34]. Water-soluble polymer hybrid constructs polymer–protein conjugation that reduces immunogenicity, prolongs plasma half-life and enhances protein stability. Polymer–drug conjugation promotes tumor targeting through the enhanced permeability and retention effect and at the cellular level following endocytic capture, allows lysosomotropic drug delivery [35]. Ceramic NPs are inorganic systems with porous characteristics that have emerged as drug vehicles [36]. These vehicles are biocompatible ceramic NPs such as silica, titania and alumina that can be used in cancer therapy. Gold shell NPs and other metal-based agents can serve as novel category of spherical NPs consisting of a dielectric core covered by a thin metallic shell which is typically gold. These particles possess highly favorable optical and chemical properties for biomedical imaging and therapeutic applications [37]. Carbon nanomaterials include fullerenes and nanotubes. Fullerenes are novel carbon allotropes with a polygonal structure made up exclusively by 60 carbon atoms. These NPs are characterized by having numerous points of attachment whose surfaces also can be functionalized for tissue binding [38]. Nanotubes have been one of the most extensively used types of NPs because of their high electrical conductivity and excellent strength. Carbon nanotubes can be structurally visualized as a single sheet of graphite rolled to form a seamless cylinder. There are two classes of carbon nanotubes that are single-walled (SWCNT) and multi-walled (MWCNT). MWCNT are larger and consist of many single-walled tubes stacked one inside the other compared to SWCNT. Functionalized carbon nanotubes are emerging as novel components in nanoformulations for the delivery of therapeutic molecules [39]. Quantum dots are NPs made of semiconductor materials with fluorescent properties which are mostly used in biological applications and quantum dots must be covered with other materials allowing dispersion and preventing leaking of the toxic heavy metals [40].

2.1. Synthesis of Nanoparticles

Size of the nanoparticle is very important for efficient drug delivery. Generally, 10 nm - 100 nm is considered as the optimal size for nanoparticle drug carriers. If the particle size is less than 10 nm, the NPs will be quickly eliminated by renal clearance (threshold < 6 nm) and at sizes greater than 100 nm, will have chances to be captured by the reticuloendothelial system (RES) [41]. Surface coating is essential for the stability and circulation time of NPs delivery system. For example a sodium citrate-stabilized gold particle aggregates in phosphatebuffered saline (PBS) within several minutes but once coated with thiol-terminated polyethylene glycol (PEG) polymer provides stability not only in PBS but also under low or high pH conditions [42]. Neutral charged NPs exhibits longer circulation time and reduce the chance of nanoparticle capture by the immune system.

2.2. Gold Nanoparticles

Nanoparticles synthesis and the study of their size and its properties are fundamental importance in the advancement of recent research [43]. It is exposed that optical, electronic, magnetic and catalytic properties of metal NPs depends on their size, shape and chemical surroundings. In NP synthesis it is important to control not only particles size but also the particle shape and morphology. Colloidal gold also known as nanogold is a suspension or colloid of sub-micrometer sizes particles of gold in a fluid—usually water [44]. Gold NPs can be produced in liquid chemical method by reduction of chloroauric acid ($HAuCl_4$). After dissolving HAuCl4 the solution is then rapidly stirred followed by the addition of reducing agents. This enhanced the production of Au^{3+}ions which gets reduced to neutral gold atoms. More and more of these gold atoms from the solution turns to precipitate in the form of sub nanometer particles. Vigorously stirring of this solution results in the production of particles of uniform size [44].

2.3. Silver Nanoparticles

The uniform silver NPs can be obtained by the reduction of silver ions by ethanol at 800°C to 1000°C under atmospheric condition [45]. In this synthesis process 20 ml of aqueous solution containing silver nitrate (0.5 g of $AgNO_3$) can be treated with sodium linoleate ($C_{18}H_{32}O_2$) (1.5 g) in tubes under continuous agitation. The aqueous solution containing silver ions and sodium linoleate can be further treated with a mixture of linoleic acid and ethanol resulting in the formation of an ethanol solution phase containing silver ions. The ethanol in the liquid and solution phase reduces the silver ions into silver NPs. Linoleic acid will be absorbed on the surface of the silver NPs with alkyl chains on the outer side in a circular shape. Wang [46] demonstrated that on changing the concentration of the electrolyte a reddish brown color developed on addition of linoleic acid their by indicating 100% conversion of silver ions into silver NPs.

2.4. Copper Nanoparticles

A novel method for the preparation of copper NPs is by reducing the copper sulphate ($CuSO_4$) with hydrazine in ethylene glycol under microwave irradiation. The heating method and reaction temperature on the particle size and composition of powder have been investigated by X-ray diffractometry (XRD) and transmission electron microscopy (TEM). Well-dispersed copper nanopowder with a diameter of 15 nm can be obtained in the absence of a protective polymer [47]. In order to obtain pure-phase copper NPs using water, the reaction time of 8 hr is essential. Owing to the reduction property of ethylene glycol, the reaction rate using ethylene glycol is higher. In addition, the amount of reduction agent can be reduced largely. Polyvinylpyrrolidone (PVP) plays greater role on the size of copper particles, and increase in the (PVP) concentration that attributes to the smaller dimension particles. The mean diameter is about 4 nm when the concentration of PVP is 0.5 mmol/L. PVP acts as the polymeric capping agents in the reaction preventing the agglomeration of the copper NPs. When water is the reaction medium, the Cu^{2+} complex is reduced to Cu^{+} complex and further reduction of Cu^{+} will form the pure copper NPs [48].

2.5. Microencapsulation of Nanoparticles

There are various methods available for the microencapsulation but most useable methods are as follow: The particles are tumbled in a pan or other device while the coating material is applied slowly. Air-suspension coating of particles by solutions gives better control and flexibility. The particles are coated while suspended in an upward-moving air stream. They are supported by a perforated plate having different patterns of holes inside and outside a cylindrical insert. Just sufficient air is permitted to rise through the outer annular space to fluidize the settling particles. Most of the rising air (usually heated) flows inside the cylinder, causing the particles to rise rapidly. At the top, as the air stream diverges and slows, they settle back onto the outer bed and move downward to repeat the cycle. The particles pass through the inner cylinder many times in a few minutes. Spray drying serves as a microencapsulation technique when an active material is dissolved or suspended in a melt or polymersolution and becomes trapped in the dried particle. The main advantage is the ability to handle labile materials because of the short contact time in the dryer. In addition, the operation is economical. In modern spray dryers the viscosity of the solutions to be sprayed can be as high as 300 mPa·s. In chemical method the two reactants in a polycondensation meet at an interface and react rapidly. The basis of this method is the classical SchottenBaumann reaction between an acid chloride and a compound containing an active hydrogen atom, such as an amine or alcohol, polyesters, polyurea, polyurethane. Under the right conditions, thin flexible walls form rapidly at the interface. A solution of the pesticide and a diacid chloride are emulsified in water and an aqueous solution containing an amine and a polyfunctional isocyanate is added. To neutralize the acid formed during the reaction base may be added. Condensed polymer walls form instantaneously at the interface of the emulsion droplets. In a number of processes, a core material is imbedded in a polymeric matrix during formation of the particles. A simple method of this type is spray-drying, in which the particle is formed by evaporation of the solvent from the matrix material. However, the solidification of the matrix also can be caused by a chemical change [49].

2.6. Advancement of Nanoparticle Based Drug Delivery System

The important technological advantages of NPs used on drug carrier are high stability, high carrier capacity, feasibility of incorporation of both hydrophilic, hydrophobic substances and feasibility of variable routes of administration including oral application and inhalation [50]. The NPs can also be designed to allow controlled sustained drug release from the matrix. These properties will enhance to improve the drug bioavailability and reduces of dosing frequency and prevent non adherence to prescribed therapy. Micelles so called core shell structure in which the core of the micelles which is either the hydrophobic part or the ionic part of the NPs can contains small or bigger therapeutic drug [51]. The novel intracellular pH sensitive polymeric micelles drug carrier which control the systemic and sub cellular distribution of pharmacologically active drug. The micelles can be prepared from self assembling amphiphilic block copolymers, poly (ethylene glycol), poly (aspirate hydrazone adriamycin) to which the adriamycin (anticancer drug) is conjugated to the hydrophobic segments by acid sensitive hydrazone linkers. Therefore micelles can preserve drug under pH 7.4 and can release them by sensing the intracellular pH of the endosomes and lysosomes when they decreases to pH 5-6.

Nanomater sized semiconductor particles can be covalently linked with biorecognition molecules such as peptides, antibodies, nucleic acid, and small molecules ligand as biological labels [52]. The new approach of quantum dots technology with anticancer drug therapy called ZnQ Quantum dots which is loaded with anti cancer agents and encapsulated with biocompatible polymer represent a potential platform to deliver tumor targeted drugs and document the delivery process [53]. The non toxic water dispersed ZnQ quantum dots with long term fluorescence stability can be synthesized by a chemical hydrolysis method encapsulated with chitoson and loaded with anticancer drug. Chitosan enhanced the stability of quantum dots for its hydrophilicity and cationic charge of chitoson [45]. NPs are being developed as delivery vehicles for therapeutic pharmaceuticals such as liposomal NPs (LNPs), encapsulated therapeutic agents for cancer therapy, pegylated form of liposomal encapsulated doxorubicin for breast cancer, layered double hydroxide (LDHs), nanoscale polymer carrier therapy for targeting tumor cells, water soluble polymers drug conjugate to increases half life with potent antitumor effect, 5-flurorouracil loaded iron/ethylcellulose NPs for active targeting of cancer cells can be used in nanomedicine [54-58]. NPs play a vital role in developing new drugs to neural disorders [15]. It is more challenging for delivery of drugs to central nervous system (CNS) and brain but NPs and neuropeptides can over comes these problems and the drug can be delivered in the brain successfully through the carrier such as hexapeptide dalargin, dipeptide kyotorphin across blood brain barriers (BBB) through endocytosis by endothelical cell lining of the brain blood capillaries. Nimje [59] impart that NPs can be used as carrier such as mannose conjugated solid lipid NPs (SLNPs) that can be exploited for effective and targeted delivery of rifabutin. [60]. The nanosized carriers like micro nanosuspension, liposome, dendrimer, ocular inserts, hydrogels are useful in ocular drug delivery which improves the release profile and reduced toxicity. This method of approach will also increase the efficiency of drug delivery than conventional delivery system. Ladewing [61] reveals that using of layered double hydroxides (LDHs) NPs can be used as carriers for nucleic acids and drug against the general background of bottlenecks that are encountered by cellular delivery system. Nanogels have hydrophilic or amphiphilic polymer chain which can also be used as carriers of drugs and designed spontaneously incorporated biologically active molecules by formation of salt bond, hydrogen bond or hydrophobic interaction [62]. In addition Poly electrolyte nanogels can readily incorporate oppositely changed low molecular mass drug and biomacromolecules such as oligo and polynucleotides (si RNA, DNA) and protein. A general comparison of untargeted and targeted drug delivery by using encapsulated drug system is shown in **Figure 1**.

2.7. Role of Nanoparticles as Medicine

Nanotechnology contributes in management of lung, blood disease and also it counters multiple drug resistance in leukemia by blocking drug efflux from cancer cells and induce efficient delivery of si RNA in to lymphocytes to block apoptosis in sepsis [63]. NPs based thrombocytic agent have potential to improve effectiveness of clot removal and also used in nanodentistry in treatment like dention re-naturalization, permanent hyper sensitivity, complete orthodontic realignments and convalently bonded diamondized enamel [64]. Nanosilver which is a nanoproduct of 100 nm contains 20-15:000 silver atoms that have strong antibacterial activity which used in wounds and burn healing [65]. Nanocrysalin silver have the property of inhibiting antibiotic resistance and anti septic resistance microbes. Dendrimers is a novel polymers with well defined structure, high molecular uniformity and low polydispersity property that makes them more attractive in development of nanomedicine [66]. Dendrimers based delivery system transports drug across cellular barrier efficiently. Mesoporous silica particle (MSP), layered double hydroxide (LDHS) are used for efficient drug delivery [67,68]. NPs based drug deliveries can target intracellular infection like tuberculosis and also polymeric NPs employing polylactide co-glycolide have more potent anti-tubercular activity [22]. These NPs can be used for site specific delivery by avoiding the unwanted toxicity due to non specific distribution and improve the quality of the patients [69]. NPs can act as potent free radical scavenger and they may have anti-inflammatory activity [20]. These NP antioxidants may provide opportunities to counteract the pathogencity of Pseudonomas aeruginosa and its biofilm formation. These advances in nanotechnology research provide new set of research tools, materials, structures and application in nanomedicine in nanotherapy.

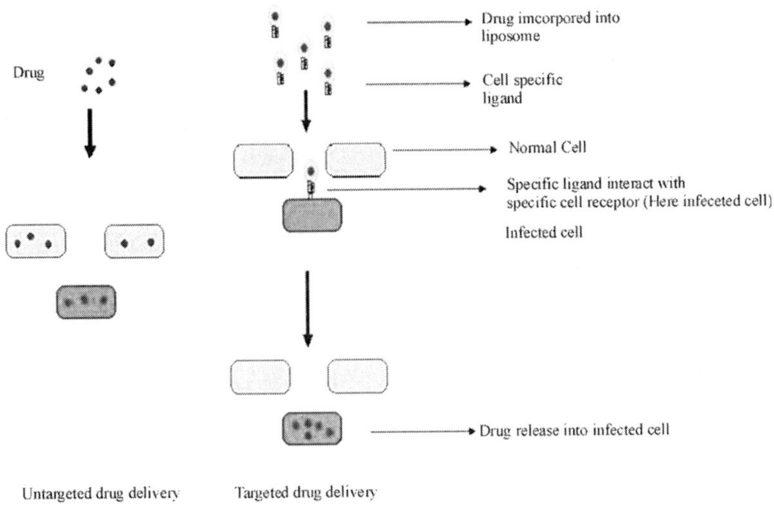

Figure 1. Drug delivery system using nanotechnology.

2.8. Nanoparticles Based Diagnostic in Cancer Therapy

Nanotechnology has provided an advance biomedical research tool in diagnostic imaging, therapy and targeting of NPs to individual cells and sub cellular compartment [70]. The gold NPs in cellular uptake depend upon their size and surface properties which is transported at 300 - 500 nm diameter within the cytoplasm. In advances, NPs is also used in mediating thermal therapy indicating absorption of infrared light, radiofrequency ablation and magnetically induced heating [71]. The use of radio labeled NPs tagged with radio nuclides and fluorescent NPs such as organic dye doped NPs, Quantum dots and multi function NPs which can be conjugated with several functional molecules that may promote new diagnostic tool in cancer therapy [28,72]. Nanotechnology enabled drug delivery approaches usually to reduce the systemic distribution and associated side effects typically observed with conventional chemotherapeutic molecules [73]. Recent research has developed number of NPs such as metal, semiconductor and polymeric particles to be use as imaging probes, diagnosis and as delivery vehicles in cancer therapy [28]. NPs play an important role in cancer diagnosis. The particles such as organic dye, doped polymer, liposomes, and quantum dots are used in cancer diagnosis [74-77]. Multi functional NPs have the capability to simultaneously carry therapeutic agents, squares imaging contrast agent, diamonds and targeting moieties (circle) that can be used as anti cancer agents [28]. Drug loaded NPs can also be used in treating cancer in animal model. Multi functional miscelle has been developed for in vitro cancer cell targeting, distribution imaging and anti cancer delivery [78]. Doxorubicin (DOX) drugs released from micelles have strong effects on the viability of human liver carcinoma cell line (Hep G2). In addition to DOX drugs loaded NPs have greater anti cancer activity in HER -2 over expressing human breast adenocarcinoma cell line (SK-BR-3) [79,80]. Among inorganic nanomaterials, silica or mesoporous silica materials can be used as potential delivery vehicles and imaging probes for their effective biocompatibility and easy surface fictionalization [78,81-85]. NPs play an important role by delivering drug in a targeted manner to the malignant tumor cells by reducing the systemic toxicity of the anti cancer drugs [86]. Rapamycin loaded polymeric (poly (lactide-co-gyycolide) (PLGA) NPs conjugate with antibodies to epidermal growth factor receptor (EGFR) that have efficient and targeted delivery of anticancer drugs.

2.9. Nanoparticles Mediated Targeting Tumors

Nanoparticles can deliver anti cancer agent to tumor site by two strategies such as active and passive that offers significant benefits to cancer patients [85,23]. Passive targeting of tumor site will depend upon the nanoparticle size and tumor vasculature in order to enhance the efficacy of drugs. The solid tumor increase their surrounding vasculature through angiogenesis in order to grow beyond 1 mm - 2 mm diameter but during the development of blood vessels they have several abnormalities like deficiency in pericytes, aberrant basement membrane formation. These abnormalities result in leaky vessels with gap size of 200 nm to 1.2 μm between adjacent endothelial cells that allow extravasations of NPs through these gaps in to extra vascular space [87-89]. These NPs gain access to the tumor that has higher retention times than normal tissues [90]. The leaky vasculature with non effective lymphatic drainage induces the enhanced permeability and retention (EPR) effect lead to accumulation of NPs at tumor site [91-93]. Active targeting of tumor cells by conjugate targeting moieties to NPs lead to accumulation of NPs in tumor sites. The antibodies bind to an antigen on the tumor cell surface and assist NPs drug delivery system to tumor sites [94-97].

Lyp-1 nanoparticles target specific peptide of (PEG -PLGA) NPs to tumor lymph metastasis is a promising carrier to target specific drug delivery to lymphatic metastasis tumor [98]. The nanocarrier allows accumulation of melittin in murine tumor growth without toxicity. In a direct assay the molecularly targeted nanocarriers selectively delivered melittin to multiple tumor targets such as endothelial and cancer cells through a hemifusion mechanism. In animals it may causes regression of precancerous dysplastic lesions and this provides an innovative molecular design for chemotherapy with broad spectrum cytolytic peptides treated for cancer at multiple stages. Silver NPs can act as anti-angiogenic molecules by targeting the activation of P13K/AKT signaling pathway [99]. These silver (Ag) NPs have ability to inhibit angiogenesis, invasiveness, metastasis, vascular endothelial growth factor (VEGF) induced cell proliferation, migration and capillary like tube formation of bovine retinal endothelial cells. In addition silver NPs also have the property of inhibiting the formation of new blood micro vessels induced by VEGF in the mouse matrigel plug assay [99]. In addition NPs mediated targeting of phosphatidylinositol -3-kinase signaling inhibits angiogenesis [100]. NPs enabled targeting the p13K pathway result in inhibition of proliferation and induction of apoptosis of B16F-10 melanoma. Therefore NPs enabled targeting of p13K pathway resulted in inhibition of endothelial cell proliferation and tumor angiogenesis [100]. Singh [101] demonstrated that canine parvovirus NPs (CPVNPs) can be used for targeting tumor cells. The viral particles are nanostructures with nanocontainer for cellular delivery as they have naturally evolved mechanisms for binding to an entering to cells. Canine parvovirus have natural affinity for transferrin receptor (TIRs) canine and human origin and this property could be harnessed as (TIRs) are over expressed by a variety of human tumor cells. CPV based VLPs for TIRs which provides a novel nanomaterial for delivery of a therapy. Labeling nanocrystals with immune cells act as platform technology for nanoimmunotherapy. The combination of plasmid DNA encoding a multimeric soluble form of CD40L (Psp d-CD40L) can reduced tumor growth which can be established through B16F-10 melanoma tumor [102]. The combination of Toll-like Receptor (TLR) agonists, -C-phosphate-G- (CpG) and poly (i:c) reduces the tumor growth and increase the survival rate. It is also associated with reduction of intra tumoral CD11c+ dendritic cells and an influx of CD8 T cells. The intra tumoral injection of Psp-d-Cb40L containing NPs formed form poly ethylenimine (PEI) in combination with CpG +poly (i:c) may have dramatic anti-tumor effect and it can also treat B16F-10 tumor bearing mice.

3. CONCLUSIONS

The multidisciplinary field of nanotechnology's application for discovering new molecules and manipulating those available naturally could be excited in its potential to improve health care. Nanotechnology is definitely a medical boon for diagnosis, treatment and prevention of various diseases including cancer. It supports and expands the scientific advances in genomic and proteomics and builds on our understanding of the molecular underpinnings of cancer and its treatment. We then review the current state of the art of nanoparticle-based therapeutics that have reached the clinic for its efficient advantage as drug carrier which are high stability, high carrier capacity, feasibility of incorporation of both hydrophilic and hydrophobic substances of variable routes of administration including oral application and inhalation. Multi functional NPs also have the capability to concurrently carry therapeutic agents, squares imaging contrast agent, diamonds and targeting moieties which can be used as anti-cancer agents. Interestingly pharmaceutical sciences are using NPs to reduce toxicity and side effects of drugs. The kind of hazards that are introduced by using NPs for drug delivery are beyond that posed by conventional hazards imposed by chemicals in classical delivery matrices. Predicting the future of nanotechnology in drug delivery system is not simple due to its fast developing technology and changing rapidly. Additional research is required in multifunctional NPs based drug delivery systems to overcome the problems for effective therapy without side effects which can improve the quality of life in cancer patients.

4. ACKNOWLEDGEMENTS

The valuable help and support of Dr. Patrick Gomez, Director, School of Biotechnology and Health Sciences, Karunya University is gratefully acknowledged.

REFERENCES

1. S. Majuru and O. Oyewumi, "Nanotechnology in Drug Development and Life Cycle Management," Nanotechnology in Drug Delivery, Vol. 10, No. 4, 2009, pp. 597-619.

2. K. K. Jain, "The Role of Nanobiotechnology in Drug Discovery," Drug Discover Today, Vol. 10, No. 21, 2005, pp. 1435-1442.

3. C. Buzea,I. I. Pacheco and K. Robbie, "Nanomaterials and Nanoparticles: Sources and Toxicity," Biointerphases, Vol. 2, No. 4, 2007, pp. 17-71.

4. B. D. Fahlman, "Materials Chemistry," Springer, Berlin, 2007, pp. 282-283.

5. W. Yang, J. I. Peters, R. O. and Williams, Eds., "Inhaled Nanoparticles—A Current Review," International Journal of Pharmceutical, Vol. 22, No. 356, 2008, pp. 239-247.

6. B. Mishra, B. B Patel and S. Tiwari, "Colloidal Nanocarriers: A Review on Formulation Technology, Types and Applications toward Targeted Drug Delivery," Nanomedicine, Vol. 6, No. 1, 2010, pp. 9-24.

7. Z. Ghalanbor, S. A. Marashi and B. Ranjbar, "Nanotechnology Helps Medicine: Nanoscale Swimmers and Their Future Applications," Medical Hypotheses, Vol. 65, No. 1, 2005, pp. 198-199.

8. T. Kubik, K. Bogunia-Kubik and M. Sugisaka, "Nanotechnology on Duty in Medical Applications," Current Pharmaceutical Biotechnology, Vol. 6, No. 1, 2005, pp. 17-33.

9. S. N. Kundra, "Toward the Emergence of Nanoneurosurgery: Part III-Nanomedicine: Targeted Nanotherapy, Nanosurgery and Progress toward the Realization of Nanoneurosurgery," Neurosurgery, Vol. 62, No. 6, 2008, p. 1384.

10. A. Cavalcanti, B. Shirinzadeh and R. A. Freitas, "Medical Nanorobot Architecture Based on Nanobioelectronics," Recent Patents on Nanotechnology, Vol. 1 No. 1, 2007, pp. 1-10.

11. M. Boukallel, M. Gauthier, M. Dauge, E. Piat and J. Abadie, "Smart Microrobots for Mechanical Cell Characterization and Cell Convoying," IEE Transaction on Biomedical Engneering, Vol. 54, No. 8, 2007, pp. 1536-1540.

12. D. A. La Van, T. McGuire and R. Langer, "Small-Scale Systems for in vivo Drug Delivery," Nature Biotechnology, Vol. 21, No. 10, 2003, pp. 1184-1191.

13. A. Cavalcanti and B. Shirinzadeh, "Nanorobot Architecture for Medical Target Identification," Nanotechnology, Vol. 19, 2008, p. 015103.

14. R. R. Zhu, L. L. Qin, M. Wang, S. L. Wang, R.Zhang, Z. X. Liu, X. Y. Sun and S. D. Yao, "Preparation, Characterization, and Anti-tumor Property of PodophyllotoxinLoaded Solid Lipid Nanoparticles," Nanotechnology, Vol. 20, No. 5, 2009, p. 55702.

15. K. K. Jain, "Role of Nanotechnology in Development of New Therapies for Diseases of the Nervous System," Nanomedicine, Vol. 1, No. 1, 2006, pp. 9-12.

16. J. C. Pickup, Z. L. Zhi, F. Khan, T. Saxl and D. J. Birch, "Nanomedicine and Its Potential in Diabetes Research and Practice," Diabetes/Metabolism Research and Reviews, Vol. 24, No. 8, 2008, pp. 604-610.

17. L. Jianguo, Z. Li, Z. Yi, W. Huanan, L. Jidong,Z. Qin and L. Yubao, "Development of Nanohydroxyapatite/ Polycarbonate Composite for Bone Repair," Journal of Biomaterials Applications, Vol. 24, No. 1, 2009, pp. 31-45.

18. A. Nowacek, L. M. Kosloski and H. E. Gendelman, "Neurodegenerative Disorders and Nanoformulated Drug Development," Nanomedicine, Vol. 4, No. 5, 2009, pp. 541-555.

19. D. N. Patel and S. R. Bailey, "Nanotechnology in Cardiovascular Medicine," Catheterization and Cardiovascular Interventions, Vol. 69, No. 5, 2007, pp. 643-654.

20. S. F.Elswaifi, J. R. Palmieri, K. S. Hockey and B. A. Rzigalinski, "Antioxidant Nanoparticles for Control of Infectious Diseases," Infect Disorder Drug Target, Vol. 9, No. 4, 2009, pp. 445-452. [Paper reference:1]

21. M. Smola, T. Vandamme and A. Sokolowski, "Nanocarriers as Pulmonary Drug Delivery Systems to Treat and to Diagnose Respiratory and Non Respiratory Diseases," International Journal of Nanomedicine, Vol. 3, No. 1, 2008, pp. 1-19. [Paper reference:1]

22. R. Pandey and G. K. Khuller, "Nanotechnology Based Drug Delivery System(s) for the Management of Tuberculosis," Indian Journal of Experimental Biology, Vol. 44, No. 5, 2006, pp. 357-366. [Paper reference:2]

23. Y. Y. Liu, H. Miyoshi and M. Nakamura, "Nanomedicine for Drug Delivery and Imaging: A Promising Avenue for Cancer Therapy and Diagnosis Using Targeted Functional Nanoparticles," International Journal of Cancer, Vol. 120, No. 12, 2007, pp. 2527-2537.

24. X. Wang, L. L. Yang, Z. Chen and D. M. Shin, "Application of Nanotechnology in Cancer Therapy and Imaging," A Cancer Journal for Clinicians, Vol. 58, 2008, pp. 97-110.

25. K. Riehemann, S. W. Schneider, T. A. Luger, B. Godin, M. Ferrari and H. Fuchs, "Nanomedicine-Challenge and Perspectives," Angewandte Chemie International Edition, Vol. 48. No. 5, 2009, pp. 872-897.

26. R. Sinha, G. J. Kim, S. Nie and D. M. Shin, "Nanotechnology in Cancer Therapeutics: Bioconjugated Nanoparticles for Drug Delivery," Molecular Cancer Therapeutics, Vol. 5, No. 8, 2006, pp. 1909-1917.

27. K. J. Cho, X. Wang, S. M. Nie and D. H. Shin, "Therapeutic Nanoparticles for Drug Delivery in Cancer," Clinical Cancer Research, Vol. 14, 2008, pp. 1310-1316.

28. S. Jiang, M. K. Ganesammandhan and Y. Zhang, "Optical Imaging Guided Cancer Therapy with Fluorescent Nanoparticles," Journal of the Royal Society Interface, Vol. 7, No. 42, 2010, pp. 3-18.

29. D. Castanotto and J. J. Rossi, "The Promises and Pitfalls of RNA-Interference-Based Therapeutics," Nature, Vol. 457, No. 7228, 2009, pp. 426-433.

30. S. Sandhiya, S. A. Dkhar and A. Surendiran, "Emerging Trends of Nanomedicine—An Overview," Fundamental & Clinical Pharmacology, Vol. 23, No. 3, 2009, pp. 263-269.

31. R. D. Hofheinz, S. U. Gnad-Vogt, U. Beyer and A. Hochhaus, "Liposomal Encapsulated Anti-cancer Drug," Anticancer Drugs, Vol. 16, No. 7, 2005, pp. 691-707.

32. S. M. Moghimi and J. Szebeni, "Stealth Liposomes and Long Circulating Nanoparticles: Critical Issues in Pharmacokinetics, Opsonization and Protein-Binding Properties," Progress in Lipid Research, Vol. 42, No. 6, 2003, pp. 463-478.

33. D. K. Sarker, "Engineering of Nanoemulsions for Drug Delivery," Current Drug Delivery, Vol. 2, 2005, pp. 297-310.

34. S. A. Agnihotri, N. N. Mallikarjuna and T. M. Aminabhavi, "Recent Advances on Chitosan-Based Microand Nanoparticles in Drug Delivery," Journal of Controlled Release, Vol. 100, No. 1, 2004, pp. 5-28.

35. L. J. Lee, "Polymer Nano-Engineering for Biomedical Applications," Annals of Biomedical Engineering, Vol. 34, No. 1, 2006, pp. 75-88.

36. A. K. Cherian, A. C. Rana and S. K. Jain, "Self-Assembled Carbohydratestabilized Ceramic Nano-particles for the Parenteral Delivery of Insulin," Drug Development and Industrial Pharmacy, Vol. 26, No. 4, 2000, pp. 459-463.

37. L. R. Hirsch, A. M. Gobin, A. R. Lowery, F. Tam, R. A. Drezek, N. J. Halas and J. L. West, "Metal Nanoshells," Annals of Biomedical Engineering, Vol. 34, No. 1, 2006, pp. 15-22.

38. S. Bosi, T. Da Ros, G. Spalluto and M. Prato, "Fullerene Derivatives: An Attractive Tool for Biological Applications," European Journal of Medicinal Chemistry, Vol. 38, No. 11-12, 2003, pp. 913-923.

39. G. Pagona and N. Tagmatarchis, "Carbon Nanotubes: Materials for Medicinal Chemistry and Biotechnological Applications," European Journal of Medicinal Chemistry, Vol. 13, 2006, pp. 1789-1798.

40. J. Weng and J. Ren, "Luminescent Quantum Dots: A Very Attractive and Promising Tool in Biomedicine," Current Medicinal Chemistry, Vol. 13, 2006, pp. 97-909.

41. M. E. Davis, Z. G. Chen and D. M. Shin, "Nanoparticle Therapeutics: An Emerging Treatmentmodality for Cancer," Nature Reviews Drug Discovery, Vol. 7, 2008, pp. 771-782.

42. H. Pelicano, D. S. Martin, R. H, Xu and P. Huang, "Glycolysis Inhibition for Anticancer Treatment," Oncogene, Vol. 25, 2006, pp. 4633-4646. S. S. Nath, D. Chakdar, G. Gope and D. K. Avasthi, "Characterizations of CdS and ZnS Quantum Dots Prepared by Chemical Method on SBR Latex," AZojono Journal of Nanotechnology Online, 2008. doi:10.2008, 2240.

43. V. R. Reddy, "Gold Nanoparticles: Synthesis and Applications," Thieme eJournals, Vol. 2006, No. 11, 2006, pp. 1791-1792.

44. R. Das, S. S. Nath, D. Chakdar, G. Gope and R. Bhattacharjee, "Preparation of Silver Nanoparticles and Their Characterization," AZojono Journal of Nanotechnology Online, Vol. 5, No. 10, 2009, p. 2240.

45. X. Wang, J. Zhuang, Q. Peng and Y. Li, "General Strategy for Nanocrystal Synthesis," Nature, Vol. 437, No. 7055, 2005, pp. 121-124.

46. H. Zhu, C. Zhang and Y. Yin, "Novel Synthesis of Copper Nanoparticles: Influence of the Synthesis Conditions on the Particle Size," Nanotechnology, Vol. 16, No. 12, 2005, p. 3079.

47. Y. Wei, H. Xie, L. Chen, Y. Li and C. Zhang, "Controlled Synthesis of Narrow-Dispersed Copper Nanoparticles," Journal of Dispersion Science and Technology, Vol. 31, No. 3, 2010, pp. 364-367.

48. L. S. Jackson and K. Lee, "Microencapsulation and the Food Industry," Lebensmittel—Wissenschaft Technologie, 1991.

49. S. Gelperina, K. Kisich, M. D. Iseman and L. Heifets, "The Potential Advantages of Nanoparticle Drug Delivery Systems in Chemotherapy of Tuberculosis," American Journal of Respiratory and Critical Care Medicine, Vol. 172, No. 12, 2005, pp. 1487-1490.

50. Y. Bae, N. Nishiyama, S. Fukushima, H. Koyama, M. Yasuhiro and K. Kataoka, "Preparation and Biological Characterization of Polymeric Micelle Drug Carriers with Intracellular pH-Triggered Drug Release Property: Tumor Permeability, Controlled Subcellular Drug

Distribution, and Enhanced in vivo Antitumor Efficacy," Bioconjugate Chemistry, Vol. 16, No. 1, 2005, pp. 122-130.

51. E. Physica, "Quantum Dots in Biology and Medicine," Low-Dimensional Systems and Nanostructures, Vol. 25, No. 1, 2004, pp. 1-12.

52. Q. Yuan, S. Hein and R. D. Misra, "New Generation of Chitosan-Encapsulated ZnO Quantum Dots Loaded with Drug: Synthesis, Characterization and in vitro Drug Delivery Response," Acta Biomaterialia, Vol. 6, No. 7, 2010, pp. 2732-2739.

53. D. B. Fenske, A. Chonn and P. R. Cullis, "Liposomal Nanomedicines: An Emerging Field," Toxicology Pathology, Vol. 36, No. 1, 2008, pp. 21-29.

54. S. Praveen and S. K. Sahoo, "Polylymeric Nanoparticles for Cancer Therapy," Journal of Drug Targeting, Vol. 16, No. 2, 2008, pp. 108-123.

55. Y. Luo and G. D. Prestwich, "Cancer Targeted Polymeri Drug," Current Cancer Drug Targets, Vol. 2, No. 3, 2002, pp. 209-226.

56. J. L Arias, M. López-Viota, A. V. Delgado and M. A. Ruiz, "5-Fluorouracil-Loaded Iron/Ethylcellulose (Core/ Shell) Nanoparticles for Active Targeting of Cancer," Journal of Drug Targeting, Vol. 17, No. 10, 2009, p. 813.

57. T. Tanaka, P. Decuzzi , M.Cristofanilli, J. H. Sakamoto, E.Tasciotti, F. M. Robertson and M. Ferrari, "Nanotechnology for Breast Cancer Therapy," Biomedical Microdevices, Vol. 11, No. 1, 2009, pp. 49-63.

58. N. Nimje, A. Agarwal, G. K. Saraogi, N. Lariya, G. Rai, H. Agrawal and G. P. Agrawal, "Nanoparticulate Carriers of Rifabutin for Alveolar Targeting, Journal of Drug Targeting, Vol. 17, No. 10, 2009. pp. 777-787.

59. S. Wadhwa, R. Paliwal, S. R. Paliwal and S. P. Vyas, "Nanocarriers in Ocular Drug Delivery," Current Pharmceutical Design, Vol. 15, No. 23, 2009, pp. 2724-2750.

60. K. Ladewing, Z. P. Xu and G. C. Lu, "Layered Double Hydroxide Nanoparticle in Gene and Drug Delivery," Expert Opinion on Drug Delivery, Vol. 6, No. 9, 2009, pp. 907-922.

61. A. V. Kabanov and S. K. Vinogradov, "Nanogels as Pharmaceutical Carriers: Finite Network of Infinite Capabilities," Angewandte Chemie International Edition, Vol. 48, No. 30, 2009, pp. 5418-5429.

62. D. B.Buxton, "Nanomedicine for the Management of Lung and Blood Diseases," Nanomedicine, Vol. 4, No. 3. 2009, pp. 331-339.

63. R. A. Freitas, "Nanodentistry," Journal of American Dental Association, Vol. 131, No. 11, 2000, pp. 1559-1565. [Paper reference:1]

64. J. B. Lyczak and P. J. Schechter, "Nanocrystalline Silver Inhibits Antibiotic, Antiseptic-Resistant Bacteria," Clinical Pharmacology Therapeutics, Vol. 77, 2005, p. 60.

65. A. Samad, M. I. Alam and K. Saxena, "Dendrimers: A Class Of Polymers in the Nanotechnology for the Delivery of Active Pharmaceuticals," Current Pharmceutical Design, Vol. 15, No. 25, 2009, pp. 2958-2969.

66. L. Pasqua, S. Cundari, C. Ceresa and G. Cavaletti, "Recent Development, Applications, and Perspectives of Mesoporous Silica Particles in Medicine and Biotechnology," Current Medical Chemistry, Vol. 16, No. 23, 2009, pp. 3054-3063.

67. K. Ladewig, Z. P. Xu and G. C. Lu, "Layered Double Hydroxide Nanoparticles in Gene and Drug Delivery," Expert Opinion on Drug Delivery, Vol. 6, No. 9. 2009, pp. 907-922.

68. H. Devalapally, A. Chakilam and M. M. Amiji, "Role of Nanothechnology in Pharmaceutical Product Development," Journal of Pharmaceutical Sciences, Vol. 96, No. 10, 2007, pp. 2547-2567.

69. B. D. Chithrani, J. Stewart, C. Allen and D. A. Jaffray, "Intracellullar Uptake, Transport, and Processing of Nanostructures in Cancer Cells," Nanomedicine, Vol. 5, No. 2, 2009, pp. 118-127.

70. E. S. Day, J. G. Morton and J. L. West, "Nanoparticles for Thermal Cancer Therapy," Journal of Biomechanical Engneering, Vol. 131, No. 7, 2009, p. 74001.

71. G. Ting, C. H. Chang and H. E. Wang, "Cancer Nanotargeted Radiopharmaceutical for Tumor Imaging and Therapy," Anticancer Research, Vol. 29, No. 10, 2009, pp. 4107-4108.

72. B. Thierry, "Drug Nanocarriers and Functional Nanoparticles Application in Cancer Therapy," Current Drug Delivery, Vol. 6, No. 4, 2009, pp. 391-403.

73. S. Santra, D. Dutta, G. A.Walter and B. M. Moudgil, "Fluorescent Nanoparticle Probes for Cancer Imaging," Technology in Cancer Research and Treatment, Vol. 4, No. 6, 2005, pp. 593-602.

74. K. Licha and C. Olbrich, "Optical Imaging in Drug Discovery and Diagnostic Applications," Advanced Drug Delivery Reviews, Vol. 57, No. 8, 2005, pp. 1087-1108.

75. P. Grodzinski, M. Silver and L. K. Molnar, "Nano-Technology for Cancer Diagnostics: Promises and Challenges," Expert Review of Molecular Diagnostics, Vol. 6. No. 3, 2006, pp. 307-318.

76. J. Rao, A. Dragulescu-Andrasi and H. Yao, "Fluorescence Imaging in vivo: Recent Advances," Current Opinion in Biotechnology, Vol. 18, No. 1, 2007, pp. 17-25.

77. D. M. Huang, Y. Hung, B. S. Ko, S. C. Chien, C. P. Tsai, C. T. Kuo, J. C. Kang, C. S. Yang, C. Y. Mou and Y. C. Chen, "Highly Efficient Cellular Labeling of Mesoporous Nanoparticles in Human Mesenchymal Stem Cells: Implication for Stem Cell Tracking," Journal of the Federation of American Societies for Experimental Biology, Vol. 19, No. 14, 2005, pp. 2014-2016. [Paper reference:1]

78. J. Kim, J. E. Lee, S. H. Lee, J. H. Yu, J. H. Lee, T. G. Park and T. Hyecon. "Designed Fabrication of a Multifunctional Polymer Nanomedical Platform for Simultaneous Cancer-Targeted Imaging and Magnetically Guided Drug Delivery," Advanced Materials, Vol. 20, 2008, pp. 478-483.

79. K. Shah, A. Jacobs, X. O. Breakefield and R. Weissleder, "Molecular Imaging of Gene Therapy for Cancer," Gene Therapy, Vol. 11, No. 15, pp. 1175-1187.

80. Y. S. Lin, S. H. Wu, Y. Hung, Y. H. Chou, C. Chang, M. L. Lin, C. P. Tsai and C. Y. Mou, "Multifunctional Composite Nanoparticles: Magnetic, Luminescent, and Mesoporous," Chemistry of Materials, Vol. 18, No. 22, 2006, pp. 5170-5172.

81. S. T. Selvan, P. K. Patra, C. Y. Ang and J. Y. Ying, "Synthesis of Silica-Coated Semiconductor and Magnetic Quantum Dots and Their Use in the Imaging of Live Cells," Angewandte Chemie International Edition, Vol. 46, No. 14, 2007, pp. 2448-2452.

82. S. H. Wu, Y. S. Lin, Y. Hung, Y. H. Chou, Y. H. Hsu, C. Chang and C. Y. Mou, "Multifunctional Mesoporous Silica Nanoparticles for Intracellular Labeling and Animal Magnetic Resonance Imaging Studies," Chembiochem, Vol. 9, No. 1, 2008, pp. 53-57.

83. C. H. Lee, S. H. Cheng, Y. J. Wang, Y. C. Chen, N. T. Chen, J. Souris, C. T. Chen, C. Y. Mou, C. H. Yang and L. W. Lo, "Near-Infrared Mesoporous Silica Nanoparticles for Optical Imaging: Characterization and in vivo

Biodistribution," Advanced Functional Materials, Vol. 19, No. 2, 2009, pp. 215-222.

84. J. D. Byrne, T. Betancourt and L. Brannon-Peppas, "Active Targeting Schemes for Nanoparticle Systems in cancer Therapeutics," Advanced Drug Delivery Reviews, Vol. 60, No. 15, 2008, pp. 1615-1626.

85. S. Acharya, F. Dilnawaz and S. K. Sahoo, "Targeted Epidermal Growth Factor Receptor Nanoparticle Bioconjugates for Breast Cancer Therapy," Biomaterials, Vol. 30, No. 29, 2009, pp. 5737-5750.

86. J. Folkman, "What Is the Evidence that Tumors are Angiogenesis Dependent?" Journal of naternational Cancer Insititution, Vol. 82, No. 1, 1990, pp. 4-6.

87. J. Folkman and Y. Shing, "Angiogenesis," Journal of Biology Chemistry, Vol. 267, No. 10, 1992, pp. 931-934.

88. D. F. Baban and L. W. Seymour, "Control of Tumour Vascular Permeability," Advanced Drug Delivery Reviews, Vol. 34, No. 1, 1998, pp. 109-119.

89. J. W. Baish, Y. Gazit, D. A. Berk, M. Nozue, L. T. Baxter and R. K. Jain, "Role of Tumor Vascular Architecture in Nutrient and Drug Delivery: An Invasion Percolation-Based Network Model," Microvascular Research, Vol. 51, No. 3, 1996, pp. 327-346.

90. R. K. Jain, "Delivery of Molecular Medicine to Solid Tumors: Lessons from in vivo Imaging of Gene Expression and Function," Journal of Controlled Release, Vol. 74, No. 1-3, 2001, pp. 7-25.

91. R. Duncan, "The Dawning Era of Polymer Therapeutics," Nature Reviews Drug Discovery, Vol. 2, No. 5, 2003, pp. 347-360.

92. L. Brannon-Peppas and J. O. Blanchette, "Nanoparticle and Targeted Systems for Cancer Therapy," Advanced Drug Delivery Reviews, Vol. 56, No. 11, 2004, pp. 1649-1659.

93. K. Ulbrich, T. Etrych, P. Chytil, M. Jelínková and B. Ríhová, "Antibody-Targeted Polymer-Doxorubicin Conjugates with pH-Controlled Activation," Journal of Drug Targeting, Vol. 12, No. 8, 2004, pp. 477-489.

94. Z. Xu, W. Gu, J. Huang, H. Sui, Z. Zhou, Y. Yang, Z, Yan and Y. I. Li, "In vitro and in vivo Evaluation of Actively Targetable Nanoparticles for Paclitaxel Delivery," International Journal of Pharmaceutics, Vol. 288, No. 2, 2005, pp. 361-368.

95. J. Cheng, B. A. Teply, I. Sherifi, J. Sung, G. Luther, F. X. Gu, E. Levy-Nissenbaum, A. F. Radovic-Moreno, R. Langer and O. C. Farokhzad, "Formulation of Functionalized PLGA-PEG Nanoparticles for in vivo Targeted Drug Delivery," Biomaterials, Vol. 28, No. 5, 2007, pp. 869-876.

96. S. Díez, G. Navarro and C. T. de ILarduya, "In vivo Targeted Gene Delivery by Cationic Nanoparticles for Treatment of Hepatocellular Carcinoma," The Journal of Gene Medicine, Vol. 11, No. 1, 2009, pp. 38-45.

97. G.Luo, X. Yu, C. Jin, F. Yang, D. Fu, J.Long, J.Xu, C.Zhan and W. Lu, "Lyp-1 Conjugated Nanoparticles for Targeting Drug Delivery to Lymphatic Metastatic Tumours," International Journal of Pharmaceutics, Vol. 385, No.1-2, 2010, pp. 150-156.

98. S. Gurunathan, K. J. Lee, K. Kalishwaralal, S. Sheikpranbabu, R. Vaidyanathan and S. H. Eom, "Antiangiogenic Properties of Silver Nanoparticles," Biomaterials, Vol. 30, No. 31, 2009, pp. 6341-6350.

99. R. Harfouche, S. Basu, S. Soni, D. M. Hentschel, R. A. Mashelkar and S. Sengupta, "Nanoparticles Mediated Targeting of Phosphatidylinositol-3-Kinase Signaling Inhibits Angiogenesis,"Angiogenesis, Vol. 12, No. 4, 2009, pp. 325-338.

100. P. Singh, "Tumour Targeting Using Canine Parvovirus Nanoparticles," Current Topics in Microbiology and Immunology, Vol. 327, 2009, pp. 123-141.

101. G.W. Stone, S. Barzee, V. Snarsky, C. Santucci, B. Tran, R. Langer, G. T. Zugates, D. G. Anderson and R. S. Kornbluth, "Nanoparticle Delivered Multimeric Soluble CD40 LDNA Combined with Like Receptor Agonists as a Treatment for Melanoma," PLOS One, Vol. 4, No. 10, 2009, p. 7334.

Chapter 5

Nanotechnology-Based Drug Delivery Systems for Photodynamic Therapy of Cancer: A Review

Giovana Maria Fioramonti Calixto [1,*,†], Jéssica Bernegossi [1], Laura Marise de Freitas [2,†], Carla Raquel Fontana [2,*] and Marlus Chorilli [1,*]

[1]*Faculdade de Ciências Farmacêuticas, UNESP—Univ. Estadual Paulista, Campus Araraquara, Departamento de Fármacos e Medicamentos, Araraquara 14800-903 SP, Brazil*

[2]*Faculdade de Ciências Farmacêuticas, UNESP—Univ. Estadual Paulista, Campus Araraquara, Departamento de Análises Clínicas, Araraquara 14800-903 SP, Brazil*

ABSTRACT

Photodynamic therapy (PDT) is a promising alternative approach for improved cancer treatment. In PDT, a photosensitizer (PS) is administered that can be activated by light of a specific wavelength, which causes selective damage to the tumor and its surrounding vasculature. The success of PDT is limited by the difficulty in administering photosensitizers (PSs) with low water solubility, which compromises the clinical use of several molecules. Incorporation of PSs in nanostructured drug delivery systems, such as polymeric nanoparticles (PNPs), solid lipid nanoparticles (SLNs), nanostructured lipid carriers (NLCs), gold nanoparticles (AuNPs), hydrogels, liposomes, liquid crystals, dendrimers, and cyclodextrin is a potential strategy to overcome this difficulty. Additionally, nanotechnology-based drug delivery systems may improve the transcytosis of a PS across epithelial and endothelial barriers and afford the simultaneous co-delivery of two or more drugs. Based on this, the application of nanotechnology in medicine may offer numerous exciting possibilities in cancer treatment and improve the efficacy of available therapeutics. Therefore, the aim of this paper is to review nanotechnology-based drug delivery systems for photodynamic therapy of cancer.

Keywords: photodynamic therapy; cancer; nanotechnology; drug delivery systems

1. INTRODUCTION

The combination of dyes and light for treatment of diseases dates back to ancient Egypt, where conditions such as psoriasis and vitiligo were treated with vegetal-derived substances and sunlight [1]. However, it was only in the beginning of 20th century that modern PDT (photodynamic therapy) began with the discoveries of O. Raab [2] and H. von Tappeiner and A. Jesionek [3]. O. Raab observed the deleterious effect of treating *Paramecium caudatum* with acridine orange and accidentally exposing it to sunlight [2]. In 1903, von Tappeiner and Jesionek reported the tumoricidal effect of eosin associated with exposure to the white light on skin tumors. They conceived the term "photodynamic action" [3].

PDT is considered a promising alternative treatment modality to current treatments against several types of cancers. A non-toxic dye (capable of transferring light energy to other molecules, *i.e.*, a photosensitizing agent) is administered to the patients with subsequent exposure to a light source of specific wavelength that leads to the death of the target cell via oxidative damage [4].

Three components act simultaneously in PDT: a photosensitizer (PS), a light source, and oxygen. The PS and light source must be harmless to the target cell [5]. When the PS is excited by light of a specific wavelength, its interactions with the surroundings can follow two pathways. These pathways are named Type I and Type II reactions, as illustrated in Figure 1. In type I reactions, the PS in its excited triplet state reacts with biomolecules (*i.e.*, lipids, proteins, and nucleic acids), transferring hydrogen atoms via the radical mechanism. It generates free radicals and radical ions (radical type depends on the target molecule, *i.e.*, lipids, proteins, or nucleic acids) that then react with oxygen resulting in reactive oxygen species (ROS) generation [6,7,8,9].

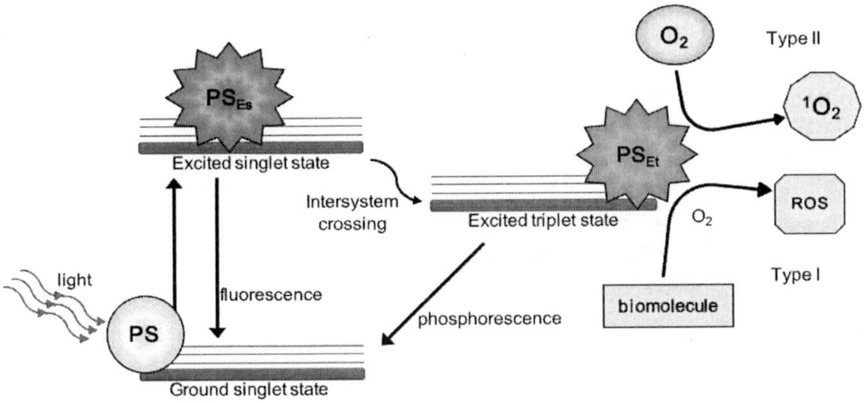

Figure 1. Type I and Type II reactions in PDT (photodynamic therapy). Schematic Jablonski's diagram showing PDT's mechanism of action. Following light absorption, the PS reaches an excited singlet state. After an intersystem crossing, the PS, now in a triplet excited state, can react in two ways: react with biomolecules through a hydrogen atom (electron) transfer to form radicals, which react with molecular oxygen to generate ROS (type I reaction); or, the PS in its triplet state can react directly with oxygen through energy transfer, generating singlet oxygen (Type II reaction). PS: photosensitizer; PS_{Es}: PS excited singlet state; PS_{Et}: PS excited triplet state; ROS: reactive oxygen species; $^1O_2$: singlet oxygen.

Type II reactions are based on a phenomenon called triplet–triplet annihilation. In these reactions, the PS in its excited triplet state reacts with oxygen in its triplet ground state. This yields singlet oxygen that is highly reactive and cytotoxic. Both types of reactions take place at the same time. The balance between these two processes depends on the PS being used, the concentrations of oxygen and substrate, and affinity of the PS with the substrate [6,7,8,9]. However, singlet oxygen generation pathway *i.e.*, Type II reactions are considered the principal mechanism of [10].

ROS and singlet oxygen have high reactivity and short half-life. Due to this, PDT directly affects only those biological substrates that are close to the region where these species are generated, usually within a 20 nanometers radius [11]. Therefore, PS localization is a primary factor in drug release studies to target tissues because it selectivity promotes localized sensitization.

2. CLINICAL PDT AGAINST CANCER

Although the discovery of photodynamic effect was based in the field of microbiology, the use of PDT against microbial infections was severely cutback after the introduction of antibiotics in the 1940s. However, it is being revisited in the last few decades as an alternative therapy due to the increasing bacterial resistance to existing antibiotics [6]. PDT advancements occurred primarily for the treatment of cancer and non-infectious diseases, such as vitiligo, macular degeneration, and psoriasis [12]. Various clinical protocols have been approved for the treatment of pre-malignant and malignant lesions since its introduction in clinical practice in the 1980s [7,8]. The cancer types treated using PDT include cancers of the digestive tract [13,14] and esophagus [15,16], lesions of the head and neck [17], lung and malignant pleural mesothelioma [18], cervix, bladder, and non-melanoma skin cancer, and basocellular carcinoma [8], among others.

Clinical PDT protocol usually includes a standard dose of the drug, a dose from a light source, and a drug-light interval. However, the clinical outcomes may vary enormously. This is probably due to poor light delivery to the target tissue, resistance to the drugs (e.g., in tumors), or metabolism of the PS in individual patients [19].

Light delivery can be enhanced by using deeper wavelengths (from 600 to 800 nm, the "therapeutic window") [20,21] or a different illumination approach, such as interstitial instead of superficial light delivery [22]. PDT-resistant tumor cells were isolated *in vitro*. The mechanisms of resistance to PS are similar to those described for general drugs, including increased drug inactivation, decreased uptake, drug efflux, and altered intracellular trafficking [23]. The combination of at least two different treatment modalities is one of the strategies to overcome tumor resistance. For example, combination of PDT and chemotherapy was extremely efficient in eliminating cancer cells as shown by our group [21] and others [24,25,26].

PDT has several advantages over conventional cancer treatment approaches. First generation PSs cause minor self-limited photosensitivity to the eyes and skin; however, PDT has no long-term side effects when properly used [27]. It is less invasive than surgical procedures and the side effects usually last for a shorter period than chemotherapy or radiotherapy. Furthermore, PDT procedures are most often performed on an outpatient basis. Moreover, it also destroys the vasculature associated with the tumor besides the tumor itself, which contributes greatly to tumor death [11]. Furthermore, PDT can be directed to a target tissue very precisely due to its dual selectivity (only the irradiated area receives the PS and the light simultaneously). It can be repeated several times at one location if necessary, unlike radiation. There is little or no scarring after healing. Lastly, it generally costs less than other cancer treatments [28].

However, like every therapy, PDT has some limitations. The photodynamic effect takes place selectively at the irradiated site, which makes it impossible for PDT to be used in disseminated metastases with currently available technology, and this does not allow for a whole body irradiation with the appropriate light intensity [28]. Tissue and tumor oxygenation is crucial for the photodynamic effect to take place; therefore, tumors surrounded by necrotic tissue or dense tumor masses lead to impaired PDT. Finally, the likelihood of the precise light delivery to the target tissues is the most important point when considering PDT as a treatment option. Therefore, deep tumors (not easily accessible without surgical intervention) are hard to treat due to low tissue penetration of visible light [29]. The advantages and disadvantages of PDT are summarized in Table 1.

Table 1. Advantages and disadvantages of Photodynamic Therapy.

	Advantages	Disadvantages
PDT for cancer	-Fewer adverse effects -Little invasiveness -Short treatment time -Usable in outpatient settings -Double selectivity -Can be applied at the same location several times -Little or no scar after healing -Lower costs than other treatments	-Photosensitivity after treatment -Treatment efficacy depends on accurate light delivery to the tumor -Tissue oxygenation is crucial to the photodynamic effect -Impossible to treat metastatic cancers with current technology

2.1. Photosensitizers

The choice of PS is critical for successful treatment with PDT. The PS should be preferably excited by light of a wavelength in the therapeutic window (600–700 nm), which has greater capacity for tissue penetration. It must be non-toxic to the cells in the dark (*i.e.*, it should not cause cell death in the absence of light). Furthermore, it must be selectively captured and/or retained by the target cells. Lastly, it should be able to induce immunogenic cell death (characterized by changes in the composition of the cell surface to release soluble mediators that activate dendritic and T cells) that promotes the development of a specific immune response against malignant tumors [4,7,30]. In this section, a few photosensitizers that generally meet the above-mentioned principles have been described. Furthermore, some *in vitro* and/or *in vivo*applications are also described.

2.1.1. Methylene Blue (Phenothiazine Derivative)

Methylene blue (MB) is an organic dye with both fluorescent and photosensitizing properties [31,32,33]. This PS effectively inactivates virus and bacteria (*in vitro*), and kills malignant cells (*in vivo*) [34,35,36]. The positive charge and its low molecular weight promote an enhanced interaction with bacteria and mammalian cells. This makes it a suitable option for PDT of infections and cancer [36,37].

Hydrophilic/lipophilic balance and net positive charge on MB allows it to easily penetrate biological membrane [36]. It is most commonly used as a PS in antimicrobial PDT, for the treatment of *Candida albicans*, *Enterococcus faecalis*, and *Escherichia coli* infections. MB application as a PS in anticancer PDT is increasing. It has shown promising results as evidenced by several studies including from our group [38], Tardivo and colleagues [36], and Wagner and colleagues [39], among others. MB application in anticancer PDT is especially interesting because of its lower cost and easier availability compared to conventional PSs. Samy *et al.* [40] used MB–PDT to treat basal cell carcinoma in 17 patients. Out of the 17 patients, 11 achieved a complete response with good cosmetic outcome and minimal side effects. Currently, MB–PDT is limited to clinical studies, with no approved clinical protocol.

Although MB has substantial water solubility, its solutions are rapidly eliminated after intravenous administration due to reduction into leucoMB in erythrocytes and peripheral tissues [41]. Since leucoMB has no photosensitizing action, protecting MB from blood and peripheral reduction is essential when considering IV administration. Nanoparticles prepared from PGLA and chitosan, two biocompatible polymers, can be used to improve MB stability.

2.1.2. Photogem® (Hematoporphyrin Derivative, HpD)

Photogem® is a hematoporphyrin derivative from Russia (Moscow). It is a first generation PS produced from animal blood. Its chemical, photophysical, diagnostic, and therapeutic characteristics are identical to Photofrin®. It has been approved for human use by the Pharmacology State Committee of the Russian Federation and by the Brazilian Health Surveillance Agency (ANVISA). It consists of a mixture of monomers and oligomers with an absorption spectrum between 500 and 630 nm [42].

Photogem® is usually administered systemically and its main adverse reaction is photosensitivity for a few weeks after administration. The adverse reaction can be limited by incorporating Photogem® into drug delivery systems or targeting systems, which allows for a slow release of the PS to the body or its specific delivery to the tumor. However, it has low light absorption within the therapeutic window (from 600 to 700 nm) and induces prolonged photosensitivity. Therefore, second generation photosensitizers with better absorption features and fewer adverse reactions were developed, including 5-aminolevulinic acid (ALA, Levulan®) and chlorins [9].

2.1.3. Chlorins

Chlorins and bacteriochlorins have a strong light absorption between 640 and 700 nm and are found in natural products. For example, chlorins are found in chlorophyll-a (present in some species of *Spirulina*) and bacteriochlorins are found in *Rhodobacter capsulatus* bacteria [43]. Chlorins are hydrophilic reduced porphyrins; therefore, their basic structure is similar to porphyrins [44,45]. Several chlorin derivatives have been studied for use as PSs, including mono-L-aspartyl chlorin e6 (NPe6). It has two important properties: a high quantum yield of singlet oxygen (0.70) and an intense light absorption in wavelengths within 650 and 680 nm (therapeutic window) [46]. Some synthetic chlorins, such as meso-tetrakis (m-hydroxyphenyl) chlorin (m-THPC) and the benzoporphyrin derivative BPDMA, show promising biological activity [47].

Photodithazine® (PDZ) is another PS drug (also from Russia) from the chlorins family. It is obtained from cyanobacteria *Spirulina platensis* and its structure is modified by the addition of 0.5% *N*-methyl-D-glucosamine as a solubilizing and stabilizing agent [48]. It is a second-generation PS which induces little or no skin photosensitivity [49].

Chlorins have been extensively investigated for their potential to treat oral cancer [50,51]. For example, Parihar *et al.* [50] studied the potential of chlorin-PDT to treat oral squamous cell carcinoma, both *in vitro* and *in vivo*. They reported extensive cellular damage and complete tumor regression within a week after chlorin-PDT.

Although chlorins exhibit good water solubility and stability, aqueous solutions are not always the preferred delivery system to administer a PS for treating lesions of the oral cavity. Incorporation of the chlorins into a mucoadhesive delivery system is a better choice in such cases. It increases the residence time of the dosage form at the site of absorption and improves the overall outcome [52]. For example, chlorin e6 (the most commonly used chlorin) has been incorporated into a variety of nano-vehicles prepared from chitosan, human serum albumin, silica, iron oxide, hyaluronic acid, and various polymeric nanoparticles [53].

2.1.4. Curcumin

Curcumin is a polyphenolic compound isolated from *Curcuma longa* L. that has been used for centuries as a medicine, dye, and spice. It can also be used as a PS. Curcumin has a variety of pharmaceutical applications in wound treatment, liver diseases, blood purification, joint inflammation, and for antimicrobial effects [54].

Curcumin has a wide light absorption range from 300 to 500 nm (maximum peak at 430 nm) and exerts its biological activity in micromolar concentrations [55]. It presents a strong potential as a PS for the treatment of localized superficial infections caused by either fungi or bacteria [56] and for the treatment of superficial tumors, especially skin and oral cavity cancers [57]. Curcumin is more efficacious to treat "superficial" infections because it absorbs blue light, which has poorer tissue penetration than red light (therapeutic window), which is not suitable for deeper lesions [58]. The main limitation of using curcumin in PDT is its poor water solubility (<0.1 mg/mL), which leads to poor bioavailability and suboptimal pharmacokinetics. This limitation can be overcome by using nanotechnology-based drug delivery systems to improve curcumin solubility. For instance, Yallapu *et al.* [59] designed curcumin-loaded cellulose nanoparticles to treat prostate cancer, *in vitro*. They demonstrated that curcumin-loaded cellulose nanoparticles showed improved efficacy compared to free curcumin.

2.1.5. Phthalocyanines

Phthalocyanines are second-generation PSs similar to porphyrins. They have superior photophysical and photochemical properties [60], including: simple synthesis and possibility of modification to alter hydrophilicity; high photo- and chemical-stability; long-wavelength absorption with high extinction coefficients (much more intense absorption in the 650–750 nm region); and high singlet oxygen quantum yields [61].

Like porphyrins, phthalocyanines coordinate metal ions within their core, which offers numerous options to control their physical properties by synthetic modifications. However, phthalocyanines lack tumor cell specificity [62]. To address this drawback, phthalocyanines have been conjugated to tumor-targeting peptides [61] or incorporated in liposomes [62]. For example, Muehlmann *et al.* [63] conjugated aluminum-phthalocyanine chloride (AlPc, a highly hydrophobic phthalocyanine derivative) with poly (methyl vinyl ether-co-maleic anhydride) nanoparticles, which increased the singlet oxygen generation capacity of

AlPc by 10-fold compared to its free form, thus significantly improving its photodynamic activity.

Furthermore, systems combining a PS and metal nanoparticles (hybrid nanostructures) are also highly attractive for cancer treatment due to the extended PDT capabilities [64]. The hybrid nanostructures containing phthalocyanines and metal nanoparticles enhance the therapeutic effects by: increasing the singlet oxygen quantum yield; the synergetic effect by means of metal nanostructures and singlet oxygen generated by phthalocyanine; and facilitating in phthalocyanine cellular uptake [65].

2.1.6. Hypericin

Hypericin (HYP) is a naturally occurring red plant pigment extracted from *Hypericum perforatum* L. (St John's Wort) [66,67], which has been used for centuries in traditional medicine. Extensive biochemical research in the last three decades showed that HYP is a multifunctional agent and has medicinal applications, such as antidepressant, antineoplastic, antitumor, and antiviral (human immunodeficiency and hepatitis C virus) agent [68]. It has drawn increased interest as a PS due to its photochemical properties, such as high quantum yields of singlet oxygen, light absorption close to the therapeutic window (590 nm), tumor selectivity, and low production costs. Additionally, it shows low photobleaching, low cytotoxicity in the absence of light, and no mutagenicity. Several *in vitro* and *in vivo* studies have shown its anticancer potential in PDT [67].

For example, Kleeman *et al.* [66] showed that HYP-PDT is effective in eliminating melanoma cells *in vitro*. Similarly, Barathan *et al.* [69] found that HYP-PDT could eliminate hepatocellular carcinoma cells. Furthermore, antitumor properties of HYP-PDT have also been demonstrated *in vivo* and in clinical studies. These studies highlighted the potential of HYP-PDT to treat recurrent mesothelioma, basal-, and squamous-cell carcinoma [68,70,71,72]. However, clinical applications of HYP-PDT for other types of cancer are still lacking.

HYP is highly hydrophobic. It is soluble in alkaline aqueous solutions, organic bases, polar organic substances, and biological media. However, it is insoluble in water and non-polar solvents [67], which means it readily aggregates in water. This impairs the administration of the PS (HYP) *in vivo*, and leads to a drastic loss of its photodynamic activity [63,73,74].

Lima *et al.* [75] demonstrated that nanotechnology has an important role in photodynamic therapy. They entrapped HYP in solid lipid nanoparticles. It increased cell uptake of the PS by 30% and improved the photodynamic effect.

Therefore, nanotechnology-based PS delivery represents an emerging approach to improve the outcome of cancer PDT. Development of the nanotechnology-based drug delivery systems, such as illustrated in the Figure 2, can facilitate precise PS intracellular delivery.

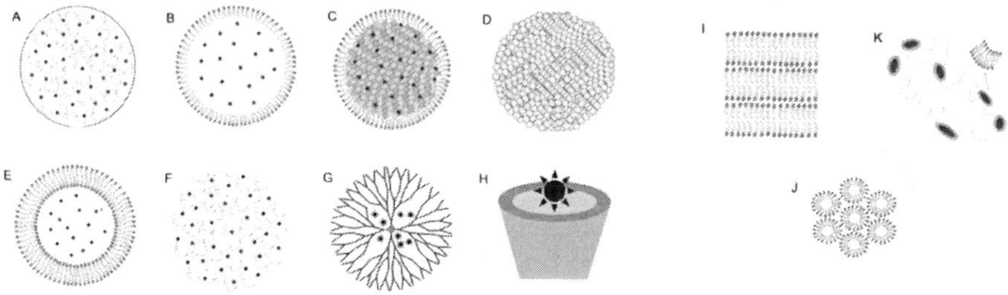

Figure 2. Schematic representation of nanotechnology-based drug delivery systems such as (**A**) polymeric nanoparticles (PNPs); (**B**) nanostructured lipid carriers (NLCs); (**C**) solid lipid nanoparticles (SLNs); (**D**) gold nanoparticles (AuNPs); (**E**) liposomes; (**F**) hydrogels; (**G**) dendrimers; (**H**) cyclodextrin; and (**I**) lamellar; (**J**) hexagonal; or (**K**) cubic mesophases liquid crystallines for photodynamic therapy of cancer.

Additionally, nanotechnology-based drug delivery systems have advantages such as: (1) improved delivery of poorly water-soluble PS; (2) facilitating transcytosis of PS across tight epithelial and endothelial barriers; (3) delivery of large macromolecular PS to intracellular sites of action; and (4) co-delivery of two or more drugs (including chemotherapeutics) for combination therapy [76].

The following section presents the efforts of researchers to create novel strategies to develop nanotechnology-based drug delivery systems in cancer–PDT.

3. NANOTECHNOLOGY-BASED DRUG DELIVERY SYSTEMS

3.1. Nanoparticle Systems

Nanoparticles (NPs) are sub-micrometer size particles. They have numerous advantages as a PS delivery system, such as (i) protection of the PS against enzymatic degradation; (ii) the control of PS release allowing a constant and uniform concentration into target cells; (iii) the ability to penetrate target cells due to their submicron size; (iv) biocompatibility and resorbability through natural pathways; and (v) photostability [77].

NPs can be classified as polymeric nanoparticles (PNPs), solid lipid nanoparticles (SLNs), nanostructured lipid carriers (NLCs), and metallic nanoparticles (MNs), depending on the material of which they are made [78].

PNPs are prepared from natural or synthetic polymers such as PLGA (poly-D,L-lactide-co-glycolide), PLA (polylactic acid), PCL (poly-caprolactone), PAC (Poly-alkyl-cyano-acrylates), chitosan, and gelatin, among others [79,80]. Ohulchanskyy *et al.* [80] developed PNPs for the treatment of colon cancer. They synthesized ultralow size organically modified silica nanoparticles (SiNPs) that were covalently linked with iodobenzylpyropheophorbide PS by the alkaline hydrolysis and polycondensation of the organotrialkoxysilane precursors within the nonpolar core of Tween-80/water micro-emulsion. They showed that the prepared SiNPs had a great affinity for cancer cells, evidencing their great potential for cancer treatment and diagnosis by PDT.

Dioctyl sodium sulfosuccinate and sodium alginate PNPs were fabricated using a multiple-emulsion cross-linking process by Khdair *et al.* [81]. They investigated the ability of these PNPs to enhance the therapeutic efficacy of the PS MB in two cancer cell lines, MCF-7 and 4T1. NP-encapsulated MB enhanced the accumulation of MB in the nucleus and increased the ROS production, which improved its anticancer photodynamic efficacy *in vitro.* They suggested that this NP system proved to be a promising MB delivery system for anticancer PDT.

Similarly, Yu *et al.* [82] developed Photosan PS-loaded NPs from a amphiphilic sodium alginate derivative conjugated with cholesteryl residues using a simple self-assembly method in an aqueous solution. They showed that the PNPs improved the phototoxicity of Photosan against human pancreatic cancer cells and induced the cell death by apoptosis.

Yuan and Liu fabricated paclitaxel-loaded PNPs based on a poly (ethylene glycol) (PEG)-grafted conjugated polyelectrolyte (CPE), which itself serves as a photosensitizer. This strategy to combine both chemo and photodynamic cancer therapy against U87-MG and MCF-7 cells resulted in higher toxicity than each treatment alone. It showed that this novel PNP system offers a potential alternative for the cancer treatment [83]. Jin *et al.* [84] developed hypocrellin A (HA) PS-loaded blue-emitting upconversion nanoparticles (UCNPs). The assessment of anticancer activity of HA-loaded NPs against human epithelial lung cancer cells (A549) and human cervical cancer cells (HeLa) showed an efficient cancer cell killing ability.

Photonic explorers for biomedical use by biologically localized embedding (PEBBLE) is an interesting technology for development of NPs. El-Daly *et al.* [85] developed NPs based on PEBBLE using organically modified silicate (ormosil) as the matrix to entrap indocyanine green (ICG) PS. They investigated the photodynamic effect of ICG-loaded NPs and free ICG on human breast adenocarcinoma cells (MCF-7) and hepatocellular carcinoma cells (HepG2). They found that the NPs increased the stability of ICG while maintaining the ICG phototoxic power, and suggested that PDT with ICG-loaded NPs causes lesser oxidative damage to DNA than in PDT with free ICG.

In the early 1990s, SLNs made from solid lipids and particles were introduced as an alternative to the PNP. SLNs do not present the disadvantages that some PNPs present, such as cytotoxicity and difficult large-scale manufacturing. Moreover, the solid lipids are better tolerated and SLNs are cost-effective than PNPs [86]. However, the SLNs also have some limitations, such as low encapsulation efficiency, drug expulsion during storage, and crystallization. Therefore, NLCs were developed to overcome these problems. NLCs are formed by solid lipid and liquid lipid phases, which creates a disorganized matrix, preventing the solid lipid crystallization and increasing the drug payload in the NLC. Both SLNs and NLCs can be prepared by hot or cold high-pressure homogenization, by microemulsion or by the precipitation method [86].

Youssef *et al.* [87] prepared and physicochemically characterized SLNs using the microemulsion-based technique to deliver HYP. HYP-loaded SLNs showed good compatibility between HYP and lipids (forming the cores of SLN). Moreover, HYP encapsulation in SLNs improved its photostability. Interestingly, phototoxicity of HYP was decreased by encapsulation in SLNs, which might be due to the quenching-induced deactivation of HYP resulting from the compactness and thickness of the SLN structure. Using the ultrasonication technique, Lima *et al.* [75] prepared HYP-SLNs with high entrapment efficiency and drug loading capacity. In contrast to Youssef *et al.* [87], they showed that HYP-loaded SLNs increased the cell uptake by 30% and improved the cytotoxicity by 26%. This improvement was most likely due to the smaller size of SLNs (153 nm) in this study and the preparation technique that led to an increase in cellular internalization mediated by the SLN vehicle and increased the concentration of HYP inside the cells [75].

Another type of NP that excelled greatly as a drug delivery system is the metallic nanoparticles (MNs). MNs are NPs functionalized mainly by gold (AuNPs). Due to monolayer tunability, the AuNPs can be loaded with the drug by different mechanisms, such as by covalent and non-covalent conjugation. Furthermore, it is easy to control the target, stability, and release of the drug from AuNPs. There are several ways to synthesize these NPs with varying core sizes. For example, the reduction of AuCl (PPh3) with diborane of sodium borohydride is usually used to prepare AuNPs with up to 2 mm core size. NPs from 1.5 nm to 6 nm core sizes can be fabricated by biphasic reduction of thiol capping agents. Similarly, NPs with up to 150 nm diameter can be formed by citrate reduction of gold salts or ripening approaches [88]. Shi *et al.* [89] prepared and PEGylated iron oxide NPs (IONPs) decorated onto the surface of fullerene (C60) obtaining a multifunctional C60-IONP-PEG nanocomposite. Subsequently, they conjugated hematoporphyrin-monomethyl-ether (HMME) PS to the C60-IONP-PEG and tested it against B16-F10 cells *in vitro* and in an *in vivo* murine tumor model. The results demonstrated that C60-IONP-PEG/HMME markedly enhanced the photodynamic cancer cell killing effect compared to free HMME.

3.1.1. Liposomes

Liposomes are unilamellar or multilamellar nanometer scale systems spontaneously formed when phospholipids are dispersed in an aqueous medium. Clinically, they are the most established controlled drug delivery system due to their structural flexibility and their ability to incorporate a variety of hydrophilic and hydrophobic drugs, besides being biocompatible and biodegradable. Therefore, liposomes can be used to incorporate lipophilic and hydrophilic PSs used in cancer PDT [90,91].

For instance, Bovis *et al.* [92] investigated the efficacy of the clinical PDT PS m-THPC incorporated in liposomes following intravenous administration to normal and tumor-bearing rats. Liposomes were prepared as a 9:1 mixture of dipalmitoylphosphatidylcholine and dipalmitoylphosphatidylglycerol with 2% and 8% (molar equivalent ratio) pegylation using 1,2-distearoyl-sn-glycero-3-phosphoethanolamine-*N*-[amino(polyethylene glycol)-2000]. The results showed that m-THPC-loaded liposomes improved tumor selectivity in comparison to the commercial formulation. It was attributed to the higher tumor uptake and blood plasma concentrations, which was suggested to reduce the damage to healthy cells. Furthermore, it was also suggested that the cost of treatment could be reduced by using liposomes because a lower dosage of m-THPC was required when loaded in liposomes.

Derycke *et al.* [93] evaluated the potential of aluminum phthalocyanine tetrasulfonate (AlPcS4)-loaded liposomes as an effective and safe strategy for PDT of superficial bladder cancer. They incorporated AlPcS4 in unconjugated liposomes (Lip-AlPcS4) or transferrin-conjugated liposomes (Tf-Lip-AlPcS4) and observed the accumulation of free AlPcS4, Lip-AlPcS4, and Tf-Lip-AlPcS4 in human AY-27 transitional-cell carcinoma cells and in an orthotopic rat bladder tumor model by fluorescence microscopy. They found that Tf-Lip-AlPcS4 accumulated substantially in AY-27 cells. Furthermore, *in vivo*results showed that Tf-Lip-AlPcS4 selectively accumulated in tumors. Based on this, this formulation can be a promising vehicle to selectively deliver PSs to bladder tumor cells.

The efficacy of the PDT treatment performed by an intravenous injection of benzoporphyrin derivative monoacid ring A (BPD-MA)-entrapped liposomes and polycation liposomes (PCLs) followed by exposure to a laser light (689 nm with 150 J/cm^2 fluence 15 min post injection) was investigated by Takeuchi *et al.* [94]. They evaluated the efficiency of uptake in tumor-derived angiogenic vascular endothelial cells. The results showed that BPD–MA entrapped in PCLs induced a higher destruction of angiogenic vessels and subsequent tumor suppression by vessel occlusion than the other liposome type. This was probably due to the strong electrostatic adhesion between the polycation and the plasma membrane, improving the phototherapeutic efficacy.

Pierre *et al.* [95] developed a novel liposome formulation composed of mammalian stratum corneum lipids (stratum corneum lipid liposomes; SCLLs) to study 5-aminolevulinic acid (5-ALA) skin delivery intended for skin cancer PDT. SCLLs improved the delivery of 5-ALA into viable epidermis and dermis compared to 5-ALA aqueous solution. The authors suggested that the similarity in structure of this liposome and a human cell could have favored the interaction of SCLLs with the skin. Therefore, SCLLs can be a suitable system for the topical delivery of 5-ALA.

Nombona evaluated the photodynamic efficiency of 1,6-hexanedithiol tetra-substituted zinc phthalocyanine PS-loaded liposomes or gold nanoparticles on MCF-7 cells. The results demonstrated that PS-loaded liposomes caused more damage to the breast cancer cells than gold nanoparticles. It again suggests that liposomes can be a potential formulation for cancer PDT [96].

Barbugli *et al.* [97] studied the uptake of chloroaluminium phthalocyanine (ClAlPc) liposomes in metastatic melanoma cells as well as its PDT efficiency in 3D cell culture models using metastatic melanoma cells WM1617 (s1–s13). They found that the ClAlPc molecule was taken up and present in the cytoplasm. Furthermore, it inhibited the growth of spheroids and colonies in 3D cell cultures, suggesting that this liposome efficiently targets the melanoma cells.

3.1.2. Hydrogels

Hydrogels are systems comprised of polymeric materials that are capable of absorbing water and present a three-dimensional mesh structure [98].

These systems are widely used for the controlled release of hydrophilic drugs [99], mainly due to the ease of dispersing the drug in the matrix. Additionally, they are biocompatible and have physical properties that are similar with living tissues [100]. In addition, hydrogels can possibly be used for applications delivery of hydrophilic PSs for PDT, including PAD-S31 (13,17-bis(1-carboxypropion)carbamoylethyl-3-ethenyl-8-ethoxyiminoethylidene-7-hydroxy-2,7,12,18-tetramethyl-porphyrin sodium), Mono-L-aspartyl chlorin, FA-PEG-PheoA, and aluminum (III) phthalocyanine chloride tetrasulfonic acid (Al-4), among others [101,102,103].

For example, Saboktakin *et al.* [104] investigated biodegradable NP hydrogels loaded with the PS temoporfin (mTHPP) for cancer-PDT. Chitosan hydrogels were prepared from lyophilized conjugates of chitosan standards (stored at −80 °C). The mTHPP-loaded nanoparticles were prepared from 0.2% chitosan hydrogel plus 0.04% mTHPP dispersed in deionized water by stirring. After approximately 3 h, the sample was sprayed into a liquid nitrogen bath cooled down to 77 K. The formed frozen droplets which were dried by sublimation. The NP analysis showed that mTHPP has interesting features, which remained stable during the analyzed period. They concluded that these NPs are suitable as carriers for PDT.

Recently, porphyrin-loaded hydrogels were studied for controlled chemotherapeutics release and PDT. Poly-(ε-caprolactone)-b-poly-(ethylene glycol) (SPPCL-b-PEG) copolymer was synthesized and used as a building block for constructing supramolecular hydrogels. The hydrogel was prepared by mixing an aqueous solution of amphiphilic SPPCL-b-PEG copolymer and α-CD at 37 °C. The authors found that the new hydrogel system was more stable and showed significantly improved sustained release compared to copolymer micelles. Rheologic characterization showed that it was a reversible thixotropic system. Moreover, they also found that hydrogels exhibited efficient singlet oxygen generation upon irradiation by visible light (650 nm), proving to have the potential for the treatment of cancer [105].

3.1.3. Liquid Crystalline Systems

Lyotropic liquid crystal systems have attributes of both liquids (because they are fluids) and solids (as they present an organized structure). They are formed by surfactants, more precisely by their solvates or hydrates

[106]. They are briefly characterized as mesophases lamellar, hexagonal or cubic, and have been extensively investigated by researchers [107] because they are non-toxic, biodegradable, and have bioadhesive properties which also contribute to their applications in drug delivery of PSs [108]. The lamellar liquid crystals exhibit low interfacial tensions with oil despite their minimal oil solubilization and they have low viscosities [109]. They are formed by parallel layers of surfactant bilayers separated by layers of solvent [106]. Hexagonal mesophase can be visualized under polarized light microscopy as long cylinders arranged in a two-dimensional array [99]. Finally, the cubic mesophase presents further complicated structures to be visualized, usually presenting a cubic symmetry. Additionally, the tetragonal and rhombohedral phases were also detected in some systems [110].

Researchers recently investigated nanoparticles of lyotropic liquid crystals loaded with a chlorine derivative, a PS used for PDT of skin cancer. They prepared the hexagonal phase nanodispersion by mixing monoolein, oleic acid, poloxamer, and water at a temperature of 45 °C. They found that the particle of size was 161 ± 4 nm and the polydispersity index was 0.175 ± 0.027, and that the hexagonal liquid crystalline phase remained stable even after the drug addition. Based on the penetration studies, they suggested that the absorption of the PS loaded in the hexagonal system was significantly higher than in the control (PS in polyethylene glycol). They showed that the PS incorporated in the hexagonal liquid crystalline phase nanodispersion had deeper distribution among the skin layers when compared to the control. Finally, they concluded that the nanodispersion showed potential for the delivery of the PS into the skin, which is the crucial condition for successful topical PDT [111,112].

3.1.4. Dendrimers

Dendrimers are highly branched polymers and have a very precisely defined diameter, usually about 1–10 nm. Their main advantage is the predictability and control of size and number of functional groups available for modifications. This provides greater certainty in predicting the amount of incorporated drug. Therefore, it enables reproducible pharmacokinetics, which makes dendrimers an interesting drug delivery system for PDT [113].

There are three ways to conjugate PS in dendrimers: (i) PS is trapped in the voids of a dendrimer; (ii) PS is covalently bound to the dendrimer; (iii) PS is used as a scaffold to form a dendrimer [114].

The second approach to conjugate PS with a dendrimer was used by Narsireddy *et al.* [115] who conjugated 5,10,15,20-tetrakis(4-hydroxyphenyl)-21*H*,23*H*-porphine (PS) and nitrilotriacetic acid (NTA) group in a dendrimer. They conjugated a peptide (specific to human epidermal growth factor 2) to the NTA group on the dendrimer to act as a tumor-targeting peptide for targeted *in vitro* and *in vivo* PDT. They found that PS-dendrimers were efficient in PDT-mediated cell death assays in human epidermal growth factor receptor 2 (HER2) positive SKOV-3 cells, and PS-dendrimers significantly suppressed the tumors in a xenograft animal tumor model.

Similarly, Rodriguez *et al.* [116] reported that the conjugation of ALA dendrimers enhances porphyrin synthesis. Therefore, they evaluated the ability of ALA dendrimers carrying 6 and 9 ALA residues (6m-ALA and 9m-ALA) to photosensitize carcinoma cells. They found that at low concentrations porphyrin synthesis from dendrimers was higher than from ALA. However, porphyrin synthesis was similar from both compounds at high concentrations. Furthermore, skin application of ALA dendrimers showed no diffusion to distant skin sites, indicating a promising use of the ALA macromolecules in superficial cancer models.

Kojima *et al.* [117] synthesized poly (ethylene glycol) (PEG)-attached dendrimers derived from poly (amido amine) (PAMAM) and poly (propylene imine) (PPI) dendrimers (PEG-PAMAM and PEG-PPI) using rose bengal (RB) and protoporphyrin IX (PpIX) as PSs. They showed that PEG-PPI kept the PSs more stable than PEG-PAMAM due to its inner hydrophobicity. Moreover, PpIX loaded-PEG-PPI exhibited more cytotoxicity, which may have been caused by the high level of singlet oxygen production and the efficient delivery to mitochondria. Hence, it can be suggested that this dendrimer is a promising vehicle for PDT.

Nishiyama *et al.* [118] showed that porphyrin-loaded dendrimers with ionic peripheral groups (DPs) spontaneously generated polyion complex (PIC) micelles through electrostatic interactions with oppositely charged block copolymers. Moreover, there was no self-quenching of the dye molecule inside the micellar core due to a unique DP structure that lead to a remarkable *in vitro* photocytotoxicity. This dendrimer also showed potential in treatment of choroidal neovascularization (CNV) in rats without any sign of side effects.

Karthikeyan *et al.* [119] investigated the potential of Rose Bengal (RB)-loaded polyamidoamine dendrimers as well as their phototoxic efficiency on Dalton's Lymphoma Ascite (DLA) cancer cell lines. They showed that this dendrimer acted as a suitable PS drug delivery system releasing above 80% of RB in 72 h. Furthermore, RB-loaded dendrimer exhibited minimized dark toxicity and enhanced phototoxicity to DLA cells compared to the dark phototoxicity of free RB; therefore, dendrimers can be a promising drug delivery system for PDT.

3.1.5. Cyclodextrin

Natural cyclodextrins (CDs) are cyclic oligosaccharides obtained by action of cyclodextrin-α-glycosyl transferase enzyme (CGTase). They have six, seven, or eight glucose units connected by α-1,4 bonds named, respectively, α-, β-, and γ-CD [120]. Several modified CDs have been synthesized in order to improve the structures of natural CDs, making them suitable for pharmaceutical applications. They have a shape similar to a cone, therefore, a nonpolar internal cavity is formed, allowing the formation of inclusion complexes of lipophilic drugs [121].

Making use of this, Conte *et al.* [122] developed biodegradable nanoassemblies based on heptakis (2-oligo(ethyleneoxide)-6-hexadecylthio-)-β-CD (SC16OH) and zinc-phthalocyanine (ZnPc) to overcome poor aqueous solubility of phthalocyanines. They found potential photodynamic anticancer effects in HeLa cancer cells, suggesting a promising Zn-Pc delivery system.

Similarly, Lourenço *et al.* [123] prepared phthalocyanines conjugated with α-, β-, and γ-CDs. They found that both Pc-α-CD and Pc-γ-CD showed a potential photoactivity against UM-UC-3 human bladder cancer cells.

4. NEW APPROACHES AND CHALLENGES

The greatest challenge in oncology is selectively killing the tumor cells without harming healthy cells. In this regard, PDT offers clear advantages over other therapeutic modalities, such as chemotherapy and radiotherapy. It requires a concomitant presence of PS and light for the photodynamic effect to take place. Therefore, the photodynamic action can be preferentially localized in malignant tissues resulting in irreversible destruction of tumor cells. Nonetheless, the systemic administration of PS can result in photosensitivity of skin and eyes, forcing the patient to avoid direct light exposure for a period of up to 30 days after each administration. Furthermore, there is a major difficulty in establishing an appropriate interval between PS administration and light irradiation (drug–light interval), which is crucial for the success of PDT. If light irradiation is too early, it will only affect the tumor vasculature. Accordingly, if the light irradiation is too late, it will have a diminished effect due to PS clearance [8]. Therefore, these challenges motivate researchers to improve PDT using nanotechnology-based drug delivery systems.

These NP drug delivery systems offer benefits for PSs, such as: targeting only tumor tissues; enhancing its permeability and retention (EPR effect);

and increasing its retention time in the malignant tissue, which improves the drug–light interval and offers the clinicians a wider window of time in which they can irradiate the patient. Furthermore, a tumor-targeted delivery system diminishes the accumulation of PS in healthy tissues and, hence, decreases any adverse effects of photosensitivity. Tumor-targeting delivery systems of PS can help improve PDT by targeting specific tumor types, reaching inner organs more efficiently.

Much remains to be learned about PDT in cancer treatment. Therefore, further research is required for PDT to become the mainstream therapy preferred by oncologists and to ensure a hopeful future for the treatment of cancer.

ACKNOWLEDGMENTS

This work was financially supported by Grant #2013/01565-1 and Grant #2014/24581-5 from Fundação de Amparo à Pesquisa do Estado de São Paulo (FAPESP), Conselho Nacional de Desenvolvimento Científico e Tecnológico (CNPq), and Programa de Apoio ao Desenvolvimento Científico—Faculdade de Ciências Farmacêuticas—UNESP (PADC-FCF).

AUTHOR CONTRIBUTIONS

Giovana Maria Fioramonti Calixto, Jéssica Bernegossi, and Marlus Chorilli did the literature search and wrote the nanotechnology section. Laura Marise de Freitas and Carla Raquel Fontana did the literature search and wrote the photodynamic therapy section. Marlus Chorilli coordinated the manuscript. All authors read and approved the final manuscript.

CONFLICTS OF INTEREST

The authors confirm that this article content has no conflicts of interest.

REFERENCES

1. Spikes, J.D. The historical development of ideas on applications of photosensitized reactions in the health sciences. InPrimary Photo-Processes in Biology and Medicine; Bensasson, R.V., Jori, G., Land, E.J., Truscott, T.G., Eds.; Springer: Boston, MA, USA, 1985; pp. 209–227.

2. Rabb, O. Über die wirkung fluoreszierender stoffe auf infusoren. Z. Biol. 1900, 39, 524–526.

3. Von Tappeiner, H.; Jesionek, A. Therapeutische versuche mit fluoreszierenden stoffen. Münch. Med. Wochenschr. 1903,47, 2042–2044.

4. Mroz, P.; Hashmi, J.T.; Huang, Y.-Y.; Lange, N.; Hamblin, M.R. Stimulation of anti-tumor immunity by photodynamic therapy. Expert Rev. Clin. Immunol. 2011, 7, 75–91.

5. Lim, M.E.; Lee, Y.-L.; Zhang, Y.; Chu, J.J.H. Photodynamic inactivation of viruses using upconversion nanoparticles.Biomaterials 2012, 33, 1912–1920.

6. Kharkwal, G.B.; Sharma, S.K.; Huang, Y.-Y.; Dai, T.; Hamblin, M.R. Photodynamic therapy for infections: Clinical applications. Lasers Surg. Med. 2011, 43, 755–767.

7. Ribeiro, M.S.; da Silva, D.d.F.T.; Cristina Nunez, S.; Zezell, M.D. Laser em baixa intensidade. In Técnicas e Procedimentos Terapêuticos; Quintessense Editora: São Paulo, SP, Brazil, 2004; pp. 945–953.

8. Dolmans, D.E.J.G.J.; Fukumura, D.; Jain, R.K. Photodynamic therapy for cancer. Nat. Rev. Cancer 2003, 3, 380–387.

9. Machado, A.E.d.H. Terapia fotodinâmica: Princípios, potencial de aplicação e perspectivas. Quim. Nova 2000, 23, 237–243.

10. Macdonald, I.J.; Dougherty, T.J. Basic principles of photodynamic therapy. J. Porphyr. Phthalocyanines 2001, 5, 105–129.

11. Allison, R.R.; Moghissi, K. Photodynamic therapy (pdt): Pdt mechanisms. Clin. Endosc. 2013, 46, 24–29.

12. Epstein, J.H. Phototoxicity and photoallergy. Semin. Cutan. Med. Surg. 1999, 18, 274–284.

13. Shah, P.M.; Gerdes, H. Endoscopic options for early stage esophageal cancer. J. Gastrointest. Oncol. 2014, 6, 20–30.

14. Nanashima, A.; Nagayasu, T. Current status of photodynamic therapy in digestive tract carcinoma in Japan. Int. J. Mol. Sci. 2015, 16, 3434–3440.

15. Yano, T.; Muto, M.; Yoshimura, K.; Niimi, M.; Ezoe, Y.; Yoda, Y.; Yamamoto, Y.; Nishisaki, H.; Higashino, K.; Iishi, H. Phase i study of photodynamic therapy using talaporfin sodium and diode laser for

local failure after chemoradiotherapy for esophageal cancer. Radiat. Oncol. 2012, 7.

16. Yano, T.; Muto, M.; Minashi, K.; Iwasaki, J.; Kojima, T.; Fuse, N.; Doi, T.; Kaneko, K.; Ohtsu, A. Photodynamic therapy as salvage treatment for local failure after chemoradiotherapy in patients with esophageal squamous cell carcinoma: A phase ii study. Int. J. Cancer 2012, 131, 1228–1234.

17. Green, B.; Cobb, A.R.M.; Hopper, C. Photodynamic therapy in the management of lesions of the head and neck. Br. J. Oral Maxillofac. Surg. 2013, 51, 283–287.

18. Simone, C.B., II; Cengel, K.A. Photodynamic therapy for lung cancer and malignant pleural mesothelioma. Semin. Oncol. 2014, 41, 820–830.

19. Allison, R.R.; Moghissi, K. Oncologic photodynamic therapy: Clinical strategies that modulate mechanisms of action.Photodiagn. Photodyn. Ther. 2013, 10, 331–341.

20. Yoon, I.; Li, J.Z.; Shim, Y.K. Advance in photosensitizers and light delivery for photodynamic therapy. Clin. Endosc.2013, 46, 7–23.

21. Szaciłowski, K.; Macyk, W.; Drzewiecka-Matuszek, A.; Brindell, M.; Stochel, G. Bioinorganic photochemistry: Frontiers and mechanisms. Chem. Rev. 2005, 105, 2647–2694.

22. Baran, T.M.; Foster, T.H. Comparison of flat cleaved and cylindrical diffusing fibers as treatment sources for interstitial photodynamic therapy. Med. Phys. 2014, 41.

23. Casas, A.; Venosa, G.D.; Hasan, T.; Al, B. Mechanisms of resistance to photodynamic therapy. Curr. Med. Chem. 2011,18, 2486–2515.

24. Zuluaga, M.F.; Lange, N. Combination of photodynamic therapy with anti-cancer agents. Curr. Med. Chem. 2008, 15, 1655–1673.

25. Ge, R.; Ahn, J.-C.; Shin, J.-I.; Bahk, C.W.; He, P.; Chung, P.-S. An in vitro and in vivo study of combination therapy with photogem®-mediated photodynamic therapy and cisplatin on mouse cancer cells (ct-26). Photomed. Laser Surg.2010, 29, 155–160.

26. Kawazoe, K.; Isomoto, H.; Yamaguchi, N.; Inoue, N.; Uehara, R.; Matsushima, K.; Ichikawa, T.; Takeshima, F.; Nonaka, T.; Nanashima, A.; et al. Effects of photodynamic therapy for superficial esophageal

squamous cell carcinoma in vivo and in vitro. Oncol. Lett. 2010, 1, 877–882. [PubMed]

27. O'Connor, A.E.; Gallagher, W.M.; Byrne, A.T. Porphyrin and nonporphyrin photosensitizers in oncology: Preclinical and clinical advances in photodynamic therapy. Photochem. Photobiol. 2009, 85, 1053–1074.

28. Brown, S.B.; Brown, E.A.; Walker, I. The present and future role of photodynamic therapy in cancer treatment. Lancet Oncol. 2004, 5, 497–508.

29. Dai, T.; Huang, Y.-Y.; Hamblin, M.R. Photodynamic therapy for localized infections—State of the art. Photodiagn. Photodyn. Ther. 2009, 6, 170–188.

30. Dougherty, T.J.; Marcus, S.L. Photodynamic therapy. Eur. J. Cancer 1992, 28, 1734–1742.

31. Jockusch, S.; Lee, D.; Turro, N.J.; Leonard, E.F. Photo-induced inactivation of viruses: Adsorption of methylene blue, thionine, and thiopyronine on qbeta bacteriophage. Proc. Natl. Acad. Sci. USA 1996, 93, 7446–7451.

32. Phoenix, D.A.; Harris, F. Phenothiazinium-based photosensitizers: Antibacterials of the future? Trends Mol. Med.2003, 9, 283–285.

33. Harris, F.; Chatfield, L.K.; Phoenix, D.A. Phenothiazinium based photosensitisers—Photodynamic agents with a multiplicity of cellular targets and clinical applications. Curr. Drug Targets 2005, 6, 615–627.

34. Tuite, E.M.; Kelly, J.M. New trends in photobiology. J. Photochem. Photobiol. B 1993, 21, 103–124.

35. Millson, C.E.; Wilson, M.; Macrobert, A.J.; Bedwell, J.; Bown, S.G. The killing of helicobacter pylori by low-power laser light in the presence of a photosensitiser. J. Med. Microbiol. 1996, 44, 245–252.

36. Tardivo, J.P.; del Giglio, A.; de Oliveira, C.S.; Gabrielli, D.S.; Junqueira, H.C.; Tada, D.B.; Severino, D.; de Fátima Turchiello, R.; Baptista, M.S. Methylene blue in photodynamic therapy: From basic mechanisms to clinical applications. Photodiagn. Photodyn. Ther. 2005, 2, 175–191.

37. Soukos, N.S.; Chen, P.S.-Y.; Morris, J.T.; Ruggiero, K.; Abernethy, A.D.; Som, S.; Foschi, F.; Doucette, S.; Luschke Bammann, L.; Fontana, C.R.; et al. Photodynamic therapy for endodontic disinfection. J. Endod. 2006, 32, 979–984.

38. De Freitas, L.M.; Soares, C.P.; Fontana, C.R. Synergistic effect of photodynamic therapy and cisplatin: A novel approach for cervical cancer. J. Photochem. Photobiol. B 2014, 140, 365–373.

39. Wagner, M.; Suarez, E.R.; Theodoro, T.R.; Machado Filho, C.D.A.S.; Gama, M.F.M.; Tardivo, J.P.; Paschoal, F.M.; Pinhal, M.A.S. Methylene blue photodynamic therapy in malignant melanoma decreases expression of proliferating cell nuclear antigen and heparanases. Clin. Exp. Dermatol. 2012, 37, 527–533.

40. Samy, N.A.; Salah, M.M.; Ali, M.F.; Sadek, A.M. Effect of methylene blue-mediated photodynamic therapy for treatment of basal cell carcinoma. Laser Med. Sci. 2014, 30, 109–115.

41. Disanto, A.R.; Wagner, J.G. Pharmacokinetics of highly ionized drugs ii: Methylene blue—Absorption, metabolism, and excretion in man and dog after oral administration. J. Pharm. Sci. 1972, 61, 1086–1090.

42. Kessel, D.; Thompson, P. Purification and analysis of hematoporphyrin and hematoporphyrin derivative by gel exclusion and reverse-phase chromatography. Photochem. Photobiol. 1987, 46, 1023–1025.

43. Bonnett, R.; Grahn, M.; Salgado, A.; Turkish, M.; Valles, M.; Williams, N. Amphiphilic chlorins derived from chlorophyll a for photodynamic therapy. Photodyn. Ther. Biomed. Lasers 1992, 10, 866–869.

44. Calvete, M.J.F.; Gomes, A.T.P.; Moura, N.M. Clorinas em terapia fotodinâmica-síntese e aplicações. Rev. Virtual Quím.2009, 1, 92–103.

45. Yano, S.; Hirohara, S.; Obata, M.; Hagiya, Y.; Ogura, S.-I.; Ikeda, A.; Kataoka, H.; Tanaka, M.; Joh, T. Current states and future views in photodynamic therapy. J. Photochem. Photobiol. C 2011, 12, 46–67.

46. Taber, S.W.; Fingar, V.H.; Coots, C.T.; Wieman, T.J. Photodynamic therapy using mono-L-aspartyl chlorin e6 (npe6) for the treatment of cutaneous disease: A phase i clinical study. Clin. Cancer Res. 1998, 4, 2741–2746. [PubMed]

47. Bonnett, R.; Charlesworth, P.; D. Djelal, B.; Foley, S.; J. McGarvey, D.; George Truscott, T. Photophysical properties of 5,10,15,20-tetrakis(m-hydroxyphenyl)porphyrin (m-thpp), 5,10,15,20-tetrakis(m-hydroxyphenyl)chlorin (m-thpc) and 5,10,15,20-tetrakis(m-hydroxyphenyl)bacteriochlorin (m-thpbc): A comparative study. J. Chem. Soc. Perkin Trans 21999, 325–328.

48. Correa, J.C.; Bagnato, V.S.; Imasato, H.; Perussi, J.R. Previous illumination of a water soluble chlorine photosensitizer increases its cytotoxicity. Laser Phys. 2012, 22, 1387–1394.

49. Ferreira, J.; Menezes, P.F.C.; Sibata, C.H.; Allison, R.R.; Zucoloto, S.; Castro e Silva, O.; Bagnato, V.S. Can efficiency of the photosensitizer be predicted by its photostability in solution? Laser Phys. 2009, 19, 1932–1938.

50. Parihar, A.; Dube, A.; Gupta, P.K. Conjugation of chlorin p 6 to histamine enhances its cellular uptake and phototoxicity in oral cancer cells. Cancer Chemother. Pharmacol. 2010, 68, 359–369.

51. Kobayashi, W.; Liu, Q.; Nakagawa, H.; Sakaki, H.; Teh, B.; Matsumiya, T.; Yoshida, H.; Imaizumi, T.; Satoh, K.; Kimura, H. Photodynamic therapy with mono-L-aspartyl chlorin e6 can cause necrosis of squamous cell carcinoma of tongue: Experimental study on an animal model of nude mouse. Oral Oncol. 2006, 42, 45–49.

52. Boddupalli, B.M.; Mohammed, Z.N.K.; Nath, R.A.; Banji, D. Mucoadhesive drug delivery system: An overview. J. Adv. Pharm. Technol. Res. 2010, 1, 381–387.

53. Master, A.; Livingston, M.; Sen Gupta, A. Photodynamic nanomedicine in the treatment of solid tumors: Perspectives and challenges. J. Control. Release 2013, 168, 88–102.

54. Aggarwal, B.B.; Sundaram, C.; Malani, N.; Ichikawa, H. Curcumin: The Indian solid gold. In The Molecular Targets and Therapeutic Uses of Curcumin in Health and Disease; Aggarwal, B.B., Surh, Y.-J., Shishodia, S., Eds.; Springer: Boston, MA, USA, 2007; pp. 1–75.

55. Lee, W.-H.; Loo, C.-Y.; Bebawy, M.; Luk, F.; Mason, R.S.; Rohanizadeh, R. Curcumin and its derivatives: Their application in neuropharmacology and neuroscience in the 21st century. Curr. Neuropharmacol. 2013, 11, 338–378.

56. Haukvik, T.; Bruzell, E.; Kristensen, S.; Tønnesen, H.H. Photokilling of bacteria by curcumin in selected polyethylene glycol 400 (peg 400) preparations. Studies on curcumin and curcuminoids, xli. Pharmazie 2010, 65, 600–606. [PubMed]

57. LoTempio, M.M.; Veena, M.S.; Steele, H.L.; Ramamurthy, B.; Ramalingam, T.S.; Cohen, A.N.; Chakrabarti, R.; Srivatsan, E.S.; Wang, M.B. Curcumin suppresses growth of head and neck squamous cell carcinoma. Clin. Cancer Res. 2005, 11, 6994–7002.

58. Fodor, L.; Elman, M.; Ullmann, Y. Aesthetic Applications of Intense Pulsed Light; Springer Science & Business Media: New York, NY, USA, 2010.

59. Murali Mohan, Y.; Mitch Ray, D.; Diane Michele, M.; Meena, J.; Subhash Chand, C. Design of curcumin loaded cellulose nanoparticles for prostate cancer. Curr. Drug Metab. 2012, 13, 120–128.

60. Allen, C.M.; Sharman, W.M.; van Lier, J.E. Current status of phthalocyanines in the photodynamic therapy of cancer.J. Porphyr. Phthalocyanines 2001, 5, 161–169.

61. Ranyuk, E.; Cauchon, N.; Klarskov, K.; Guérin, B.; van Lier, J.E. Phthalocyanine-peptide conjugates: Receptor-targeting bifunctional agents for imaging and photodynamic therapy. J. Med. Chem. 2013, 56, 1520–1534.

62. Swavey, S.; Tran, M. Porphyrin and phthalocyanine photosensitizers as pdt agents: A new modality for the treatment of melanoma. In Recent Advances in the Biology, Therapy and Management of Melanoma; Davids, L.M., Ed.; INTECH Open Access Publisher: Rijeka, Croatia, 2013; pp. 253–282.

63. Muehlmann, L.A.; Ma, B.C.; Longo, J.P.F.; Almeida Santos, M.d.F.M.; Azevedo, R.B. Aluminum-phthalocyanine chloride associated to poly(methyl vinyl ether-co-maleic anhydride) nanoparticles as a new third-generation photosensitizer for anticancer photodynamic therapy. Int. J. Nanomed. 2014, 9, 1199–1213.

64. Zasedatelev, A.V.; Dubinina, T.V.; Krichevsky, D.M.; Krasovskii, V.I.; Gak, V.Y.; Pushkarev, V.E.; Tomilova, L.G.; Chistyakov, A.A. Plasmon-induced light absorption of phthalocyanine layer in hybrid nanoparticles: Enhancement factor and effective spectra. J. Phys. Chem. C 2016, 120, 1816–1823.

65. Nombona, N.; Antunes, E.; Chidawanyika, W.; Kleyi, P.; Tshentu, Z.; Nyokong, T. Synthesis, photophysics and photochemistry of phthalocyanine-ε-polylysine conjugates in the presence of metal nanoparticles against staphylococcus aureus. J. Photochem. Photobiol. A 2012, 233, 24–33.

66. Kleemann, B.; Loos, B.; Scriba, T.J.; Lang, D.; Davids, L.M. St John's wort (hypericum perforatum l.) photomedicine: Hypericin-photodynamic therapy induces metastatic melanoma cell death. PLoS ONE 2014, 9, e103762.

67. Maduray, K.; Davids, L. The anticancer activity of hypericin in photodynamic therapy. J. Bioanal. Biomed. 2012, 2012.

68. Kubin, A.; Wierrani, F.; Burner, U.; Alth, G.; Grunberger, W. Hypericin—The facts about a controversial agent. Curr. Pharm. Des. 2005, 11, 233–253.

69. Barathan, M.; Mariappan, V.; Shankar, E.M.; Abdullah, B.J.; Goh, K.L.; Vadivelu, J. Hypericin-photodynamic therapy leads to interleukin-6 secretion by hepg2 cells and their apoptosis via recruitment of bh3 interacting-domain death agonist and caspases. Cell Death Dis. 2013, 4.

70. Guedes, R.C.; Eriksson, L.A. Theoretical study of hypericin. J. Photochem. Photobiol. A 2005, 172, 293–299.

71. Dets, S.M.; Buryi, A.N.; Melnik, I.S.; Joffe, A.Y.; Rusina, T.V. Laser-Induced Fluorescence Detection of Stomach Cancer Using Hypericin; Optical Biopsies and Microscopic Techniques: Vienna, Austria; The International Society for Optical Engineering, SPIE: Vienna, Austria, 1996; pp. 51–56.

72. Agostinis, P.; Vantieghem, A.; Merlevede, W.; de Witte, P.A.M. Hypericin in cancer treatment: More light on the way.Int. J. Biochem. Cell Biol. 2002, 34, 221–241.

73. Konan, Y.N.; Gurny, R.; Allémann, E. State of the art in the delivery of photosensitizers for photodynamic therapy. J. Photochem. Photobiol. B 2002, 66, 89–106.

74. Roozeboom, M.H.; Aardoom, M.A.; Nelemans, P.J.; Thissen, M.R.T.M.; Kelleners-Smeets, N.W.J.; Kuijpers, D.I.M.; Mosterd, K. Fractionated 5-aminolevulinic acid photodynamic therapy after partial debulking versus surgical excision for nodular basal cell carcinoma: A randomized controlled trial with at least 5-year follow-up. J. Am. Acad. Dermatol. 2013, 69, 280–287.

75. Lima, A.M.; Pizzol, C.D.; Monteiro, F.B.F.; Creczynski-Pasa, T.B.; Andrade, G.P.; Ribeiro, A.O.; Perussi, J.R. Hypericin encapsulated in solid lipid nanoparticles: Phototoxicity and photodynamic efficiency. J. Photochem. Photobiol. B 2013,125, 146–154.

76. Farokhzad, O.C.; Langer, R. Impact of nanotechnology on drug delivery. ACS Nano 2009, 3, 16–20.

77. Calixto, G.; Bernegossi, J.; Fonseca-Santos, B.; Chorilli, M. Nanotechnology-based drug delivery systems for treatment of oral cancer: A review. Int. J. Nanomed. 2014, 9, 3719–3735.

78. Bernegossi, J.; Calixto, G.; Santos, B.F.; Aida, K.L.; Negrini, T.C.; Duque, C.; Gremião, M.P.D.; Chorilli, M. Highlights in peptide nanoparticle carriers intended to oral diseases. Curr. Top. Med. Chem. 2015, 15, 345–355.

79. Manmode, A.S.; Sakarkar, D.M.; Mahajan, N.M. Nanoparticles-tremendous therapeutic potential: A review. Int. J. PharmTech Res. 2009, 1, 1020–1027.

80. Ohulchanskyy, T.Y.; Roy, I.; Goswami, L.N.; Chen, Y.; Bergey, E.J.; Pandey, R.K.; Oseroff, A.R.; Prasad, P.N. Organically modified silica nanoparticles with covalently incorporated photosensitizer for photodynamic therapy of cancer. Nano Lett. 2007, 7, 2835–2842.

81. Khdair, A.; Gerard, B.; Handa, H.; Mao, G.; Shekhar, M.P.V.; Panyam, J. Surfactant-polymer nanoparticles enhance the effectiveness of anticancer photodynamic therapy. Mol. Pharm. 2008, 5, 795–807.

82. Yu, Z.; Li, H.; Zhang, L.-M.; Zhu, Z.; Yang, L. Enhancement of phototoxicity against human pancreatic cancer cells with photosensitizer-encapsulated amphiphilic sodium alginate derivative nanoparticles. Int. J. Pharm. 2014, 473, 501–509.

83. Yuan, Y.; Liu, B. Self-Assembled Nanoparticles Based on PEGylated Conjugated Polyelectrolyte and Drug Molecules for Image-Guided Drug Delivery and Photodynamic Therapy. ACS Appl. Mater. Inter. 2014, 6, 14903–14910.

84. Jin, S.; Zhou, L.; Gu, Z.; Tian, G.; Yan, L.; Ren, W.; Yin, W.; Liu, X.; Zhang, X.; Hu, Z.; et al. A new near infrared photosensitizing nanoplatform containing blue-emitting up-conversion nanoparticles and hypocrellin a for photodynamic therapy of cancer cells. Nanoscale 2013, 5, 11910–11918.

85. El-Daly, S.M.; Gamal-Eldeen, A.M.; Abo-Zeid, M.A.; Borai, I.H.; Wafay, H.A.; Abdel-Ghaffar, A.R.B. Photodynamic therapeutic activity of indocyanine green entrapped in polymeric nanoparticles. Photodiagn. Photodyn. Ther. 2013, 10, 173–185.

86. Müller, R.H.; Mäder, K.; Gohla, S. Solid lipid nanoparticles (sln) for controlled drug delivery—A review of the state of the art. Eur. J. Pharm. Biopharm. 2000, 50, 161–177.

87. Youssef, T.; Fadel, M.; Fahmy, R.; Kassab, K. Evaluation of hypericin-loaded solid lipid nanoparticles: Physicochemical properties, photostability and phototoxicity. Pharm. Dev. Technol. 2012, 17, 177–186.

88. Duncan, B.; Kim, C.; Rotello, V.M. Gold nanoparticle platforms as drug and biomacromolecule delivery systems. J. Control. Release 2010, 148, 122–127.

89. Shi, J.; Yu, X.; Wang, L.; Liu, Y.; Gao, J.; Zhang, J.; Ma, R.; Liu, R.; Zhang, Z. Pegylated fullerene/iron oxide nanocomposites for photodynamic therapy, targeted drug delivery and mr imaging. Biomaterials 2013, 34, 9666–9677.

90. Andrade, C.A.S.; Correia, M.T.S.; Coelho, L.C.B.B.; Nascimento, S.C.; Santos-Magalhães, N.S. Antitumor activity of cratylia mollis lectin encapsulated into liposomes. Int. J. Pharm. 2004, 278, 435–445.

91. Chorilli, M.; Calixto, G.; Rimério, T.C.; Scarpa, M.V. Caffeine encapsulated in small unilamellar liposomes: Characerization and in vitro release profile. J. Dispers. Sci. Technol. 2013, 34, 1465–1470.

92. Bovis, M.J.; Woodhams, J.H.; Loizidou, M.; Scheglmann, D.; Bown, S.G.; MacRobert, A.J. Improved in vivo delivery of m-thpc via pegylated liposomes for use in photodynamic therapy. J. Control. Release 2012, 157, 196–205.

93. Derycke, A.S.; Kamuhabwa, A.; Gijsens, A.; Roskams, T.; de Vos, D.; Kasran, A.; Huwyler, J.; Missiaen, L.; de Witte, P.A. Transferrin-conjugated liposome targeting of photosensitizer alpcs4 to rat bladder carcinoma cells. J. Natl. Cancer Inst. 2004, 96, 1620–1630.

94. Takeuchi, Y.; Kurohane, K.; Ichikawa, K.; Yonezawa, S.; Nango, M.; Oku, N. Induction of intensive tumor suppression by antiangiogenic photodynamic therapy using polycation-modified liposomal photosensitizer. Cancer2003, 97, 2027–2034.

95. Pierre, M.B.R.; Tedesco, A.C.; Marchetti, J.M.; Bentley, M.V.L. Stratum corneum lipids liposomes for the topical delivery of 5-aminolevulinic acid in photodynamic therapy of skin cancer: Preparation and in vitro permeation study.BMC Dermatol. 2001, 1.

96. Nombona, N.; Maduray, K.; Antunes, E.; Karsten, A.; Nyokong, T. Synthesis of phthalocyanine conjugates with gold nanoparticles and liposomes for photodynamic therapy. J. Photochem. Photobiol. B 2012, 107, 35–44.

97. Barbugli, P.A.; Alves, C.P.; Espreafico, E.M.; Tedesco, A.C. Photodynamic therapy utilizing liposomal clalpc in human melanoma 3d cell cultures. Exp. Dermatol. 2015, 24, 970–972.

98. Eldin, M.S.M.; Kamoun, E.A.; Sofan, M.A.; Elbayomi, S.M. L-arginine grafted alginate hydrogel beads: A novel ph-sensitive system for specific protein delivery. Arab. J. Chem. 2015, 8, 355–365.

99. Lyra, M.A.M.d.; Soares-Sobrinho, J.L.; Brasileiro, M.T.; De la Roca, M.F.; Barraza, J.A.; Viana, O.d.S.; Rolim Neto, P.J. Sistemas matriciais hidrofílicos e mucoadesivos para liberação controlada de fármacos. Lat. Am. J. Pharm. 2007, 26, 784–793.

100. Barcellos, I.O.; Katime, I.A.; Soldi, V.; Pires, A.T.N. Influência do comonômero e do método de polimerização na cinética de liberação de fenobarbitona a partir de hidrogéis. Polímeros 2000, 10, 110–115.

101. Mori, K.; Yoneya, S.; Anzail, K.; Kabasawa, S.; Sodeyama, T.; Peyman, G.A.; Moshfeghi, D.M. Photodynamic therapy of experimental choroidal neovascularization with a hydrophilic photosensitizer: Mono-l-aspartyl chlorin e6. Retina2001, 21, 499–508.

102. Kim, J.; Kim, K.S.; Park, S.-J.; Na, K. Vitamin bc-bearing hydrophilic photosensitizer conjugate for photodynamic cancer theranostics. Macromol. Biosci. 2015, 15, 1081–1090.

103. Noiseux, I.; Mermut, O.; Bouchard, J.-P.; Cormier, J.-F.; Desroches, P.; Fortin, M.; Gallant, P.; Leclair, S.; Vernon, M.L.; Diamond, K.R.; et al. Effect of liposomal confinement on photochemical properties of photosensitizers with varying hydrophilicity. J. Biomed. Opt. 2008, 13.

104. Reza Saboktakin, M.; Tabatabaie, R.M.; Maharramov, A.; Ali Ramazanov, M. Synthesis and in vitro studies of biodegradable modified chitosan nanoparticles for photodynamic treatment of cancer. Int. J. Biol. Macromol. 2011, 49, 1059–1065.

105. Jin, H.; Dai, X.-H.; Wu, C.; Pan, J.-M.; Wang, X.-H.; Yan, Y.-S.; Liu, D.-M.; Sun, L. Rational design of shear-thinning supramolecular hydrogels with porphyrin for controlled chemotherapeutics release and photodynamic therapy. Eur. Polym. J. 2015, 66, 149–159.

106. Gosenca, M.; Bešter-Rogač, M.; Gašperlin, M. Lecithin based lamellar liquid crystals as a physiologically acceptable dermal delivery system for ascorbyl palmitate. Eur. J. Pharm. Sci. 2013, 50, 114–122.

107. Chorilli, M.; Prestes, P.S.; Rigon, R.B.; Leonardi, G.R.; Chiavacci, L.A.; Scarpa, M.V. Development of liquid-crystalline systems using silicon

glycol copolymer and polyether functional siloxane. Quim. Nova 2009, 32, 1036–1040.

108. Guo, C.; Wang, J.; Cao, F.; Lee, R.J.; Zhai, G. Lyotropic liquid crystal systems in drug delivery. Drug Discov. Today2010, 15, 1032–1040.

109. Ghosh, O.; Miller, C.A. Lamellar liquid crystals in equilibrium with excess oil in anionic surfactant-oil-brine systems.J. Colloid Interface Sci. 1987, 116, 593–597.

110. Garti, N.; Hoshen, G.; Aserin, A. Lipolysis and structure controlled drug release from reversed hexagonal mesophase. Colloids Surf. B 2012, 94, 36–43.

111. Lopes, L.B.; Ferreira, D.A.; Paula, D.; Garcia, M.T.J.; Thomazini, J.A.; Fantini, M.C.A.; Bentley, M.V.L.B. Reverse hexagonal phase nanodispersion of monoolein and oleic acid for topical delivery of peptides: In vitro and in vivo skin penetration of cyclosporin a. Pharm. Res. 2006, 23, 1332–1342.

112. Rossetti, F.C.; Depieri, L.V.; Praça, F.G.; del Ciampo, J.O.; Fantini, M.C.A.; Pierre, M.B.R.; Tedesco, A.C.; Bentley, M.V.L.B. Optimization of protoporphyrin ix skin delivery for topical photodynamic therapy: Nanodispersions of liquid-crystalline phase as nanocarriers. Eur. J. Pharm. Sci. 2016, 83, 99–108.

113. Tomalia, D.A.; Khanna, S.N. A systematic framework and nanoperiodic concept for unifying nanoscience: Hard/soft nanoelements, superatoms, meta-atoms, new emerging properties, periodic property patterns, and predictive mendeleev-like nanoperiodic tables. Chem. Rev. 2016, 116, 2705–2774.

114. Caminade, A.-M.; Turrin, C.-O.; Majoral, J.-P. Biological properties of water-soluble phosphorhydrazone dendrimers.Braz. J. Pharm. Sci. 2013, 49, 33–44.

115. Narsireddy, A.; Vijayashree, K.; Adimoolam, M.G.; Manorama, S.V.; Rao, N.M. Photosensitizer and peptide-conjugated pamam dendrimer for targeted in vivo photodynamic therapy. Int. J. Nanomed. 2015, 10, 6865–6878.

116. Rodriguez, L.; Vallecorsa, P.; Battah, S.; Di Venosa, G.; Calvo, G.; Mamone, L.; Saenz, D.; Gonzalez, M.C.; Batlle, A.; MacRobert, A.J.; et al. Aminolevulinic acid dendrimers in photodynamic treatment of cancer and atheromatous disease. Photochem. Photobiol. Sci. 2015, 14, 1617–1627.

117. Kojima, C.; Toi, Y.; Harada, A.; Kono, K. Preparation of poly(ethylene glycol)-attached dendrimers encapsulating photosensitizers for application to photodynamic therapy. Bioconjugate Chem. 2007, 18, 663–670.

118. Nishiyama, N.; Jang, W.-D.; Kataoka, K. Supramolecular nanocarriers integrated with dendrimers encapsulating photosensitizers for effective photodynamic therapy and photochemical gene delivery. New J. Chem. 2007, 31, 1074–1082.

119. Karthikeyan, K.; Babu, A.; Kim, S.-J.; Murugesan, R.; Jeyasubramanian, K. Enhanced photodynamic efficacy and efficient delivery of rose bengal using nanostructured poly(amidoamine) dendrimers: Potential application in photodynamic therapy of cancer. Cancer Nanotechnol. 2011, 2, 95–103.

120. Venturini, C.d.G.; Nicolini, J.; Machado, C.; Machado, V.G. Properties and recent applications of cyclodextrins. Quim. Nova 2008, 31, 360–368.

121. Saltão, R.; Veiga, F. Ciclodextrinas em novos sistemas terapêuticos. Braz. J. Pharm. Sci. 2001, 37, 1–17.

122. Conte, C.; Scala, A.; Siracusano, G.; Leone, N.; Patane, S.; Ungaro, F.; Miro, A.; Sciortino, M.T.; Quaglia, F.; Mazzaglia, A. Nanoassembly of an amphiphilic cyclodextrin and Zn(II)-phthalocyanine with the potential for photodynamic therapy of cancer. RSC Adv. 2014, 4, 43903–43911.

123. Lourenco, L.M.O.; Pereira, P.M.R.; Maciel, E.; Valega, M.; Domingues, F.M.J.; Domingues, M.R.M.; Neves, M.G.P.M.S.; Cavaleiro, J.A.S.; Fernandes, R.; Tome, J.P.C. Amphiphilic phthalocyanine-cyclodextrin conjugates for cancer photodynamic therapy. Chem. Commun. 2014, 50, 8363–8366.

Chapter 6

Nanotechnology Based Virosomal Drug Delivery Systems

Basavaraj K. Nanjwade Nagi F. Idris[1], Ramchandra N. Chilkawar[2], Basavaraj K. Nanjwade[3*], Teerapol Srichana[4] and Azam Sharif Md. Shafioul[5]

[1]Department of Pharmacology, Faculty of Pharmacy, Omer Al-Mukhtar University, Al-Bayda, P. O. Box 919, Libya.

[2]Department of Quality Assurance, Remidex Pharma Pvt Ltd., 2nd Stage, Peenya Industrial Area, Bengaluru-560058, Karnataka. India.

[3*]Department of Pharmaceutics, Faculty of Pharmacy, Omer Al-Mukhtar University, Tobruk, P. O. Box 919, Libya.

[4]Drug Delivery System Excellence Centre, Faculty of Pharmaceutical Sciences, Prince of Songkla University, Hat-Yai-90112, Songkla, Thailand.

[5]Chemical Kinomics Research Center, Future Convergence Research Division, Korea Institute of Science and Technology (KIST), Seoul 136-791, South Korea.

ABSTRACT

Over the years there has been a great revolution in drug delivery technologies. Virosomes delivery is an example of the various novel drug delivery systems available. Virosome is a drug or vaccine delivery mechanism which is spherical and consisting of unilamellar phospholipid bilayer vesicle with a mean diameter is in range of 120-180 nm. Virosomes represent reconstituted empty influenza virus envelopes, which contain 70% phosphatidylcholine and remaining 30% neuraminidase (NA) and haemagglutinin (HA) glycoproteins. Various techniques are used for the loading the drug, protein and peptide like package inside the IRIV (immunopotentiatin reconstituted influenza virosome), intrigrated into lipid bilayer also anchored into lipid bilayer, crosslinked with Hemaglutinin (HA) and adsorbed to the membrane. Various protein, peptide, and malarial drugs are loaded in virus to deliver at particular site to give the targeted drug delivery. The prospect of drug delivery and targeting using virosomes is an interesting field of research and development. Virosomes are biodegradable, biocompatible, nontoxic, and non-autoimmunogenic attempts were made to use them as a vaccines or pharmaceutical adjuvants as well as delivery systems for pharmaceutical drugs, nucleic acids, genes for therapeutic application. Virosomes could also be exploited as carriers for targeted drugs and for immunomodulating molecules particularly in cancer therapy. The success of virosomal drug delivery depends on the methods used to prepare the encapsulated bioactive materials and incorporate them into the virosomes, characterization and formulation of the finished preparation. This review article gives an insight of virosomes as a newer method of drug delivery and futuristic tool.

KEYWORDS: Virosomes; Biocompatible; Biodegradable; Drug delivery; Gene delivery.

INTRODUCTION

Virosome can use as a drug or vaccine delivery mechanism consisting of unilamellar phospholipid bilayer vesicle incorporating virus derived proteins to allow the virosomes to fuse with target cells and tissues. Virosomes are not able to replicate but are pure fusion-active macro and nano level vesicle. These are reconstituted viral envelopes that can serve as vaccines and as vehicles for cellular delivery of macromolecules and nanomolecules. The prospect of drug delivery system and targeting cells and tissues using virosomes is an interesting field of research and development. Virosomes are biodegradable, biocompatible, nontoxic and non- autoimmunogenic attempts were made to use them as a vaccines or adjuvant as well as delivery systems for drugs, nucleic acids, genes for therapeutic application. Influenza virus is the most common virus for choice of use. The success of virosomal drug delivery systems depends on the various methods used to prepare the encapsulated bioactive materials and incorporate them into the virosomes, characterization and formulation of the finished virosomal preparation. Virosomes protect pharmaceutically active substances from proteolytic degradation and low pH of endosomes and allowing their contents to remain intact when they reach the cytoplasm [1].

The transfer of genes to target cells by various delivery vehicles are mainly divided into viral and non-viral vectors systems. Viral vectors are obtained by replacement of one or more viral genes by a gene of interest and are considered to be the most efficient transducing system [2, 3]. Efficiency relates to properties of the viral capsid proteins or membrane glycoproteins, the ability to bind to cellular receptors and to pass through or fuse from/with cellular membranes. But the safety of viral vector system remains a matter of major problems and issues related to insertion mutagenesis as observed with retroviruses[4] and the induction of undesirable immune responses and inflammation still pose major challenges[5,6]. For non-viral gene delivery, chemical approaches (e.g. cationic polymers, cationic lipids and nanoparticles) and physical methods (e.g. gene gun and electroporation) are being employed[7]. Cationic liposomes are the most extensively studied vehicles[8-11]. In these systems, cationic lipids condense DNA through electrostatic interactions with the negatively charged phosphate groups of the nucleic acid, thereby forming so-called lipoplexes. With respect to in vivo use, liposomal delivery systems combining the characteristics of cellular interaction of viral vectors with the safety of liposomal delivery systems. Virosomes are the reconstitutes viral envelopes, having lipid membranes, viral spike glycoproteins, but absence of viral genetic material. Externally virosomes resemble that of a virus particle, with spiky proteins protruding from their membrane, and their interior compartment is empty. Almeida et al... Were the first to prepare virosomes, who inserted purified influenza spike proteins into preformed liposomes[12]. Virosome technology is developed in order to overcome the problem of incomplete delivery to targeting cells, tissues and organs of the body. The new generation of therapeutics against cancer or neurodegenerative disorders which require the delivery system that target drugs to specified cell types and host tissues by receptor-mediated uptake and controlled release.

Thus, the virosomal technique represents a novel sophisticated delivery system to meet all the above challenges and drawbacks. There after a wide range of viral envelopes have been reconstituted, including those of sendai virus and sindbis virus [13]. Virosomes display viral envelope of glycoproteins and their native conformation stimulate humoral responses. The receptor-binding and membrane-fusion properties of the viral envelope of glycoprotein can be preserved and virosomes can be used as transport vehicles for cellular delivery of biologically active macromolecules and nanomolecules.

Virosomes protect pharmaceutically active substances from proteolytic degradation and low pH of endosomes and allowing their contents to remain intact when they reach the cytoplasm. These are major advantage of virosomal carrier systems over other than drug-delivery vehicles and adjuvant including liposomal and proteoliposomal carrier systems.

What Is Virosomes

Virosomes are small spherical vesicles containing viral membrane proteins (fusion proteins of the influenza virus) embedded in their lipid membranes. Diameter is in range of 120-180 nm. Virosomes represent reconstituted empty influenza virus envelopes and devoid of the nucleocapsid including the genetic material of the source virus. Virosomes are not possible to replicate but are pure fusion-active vesicles. The main constituents of Immunostimulating Reconstituted Influenza Virosomes (IRIVs) consist of naturally occurring phospholipids (PL) and phosphatidylcholine (PC). Phosphatidylcholine forms approximately 70% of the virosomal structure. The remaining 30% of membrane components are the envelope phospholipids originating from the influenza virus that provide neuraminidase (NA) and haemagglutinin (HA) glycoproteins (Figure 1).

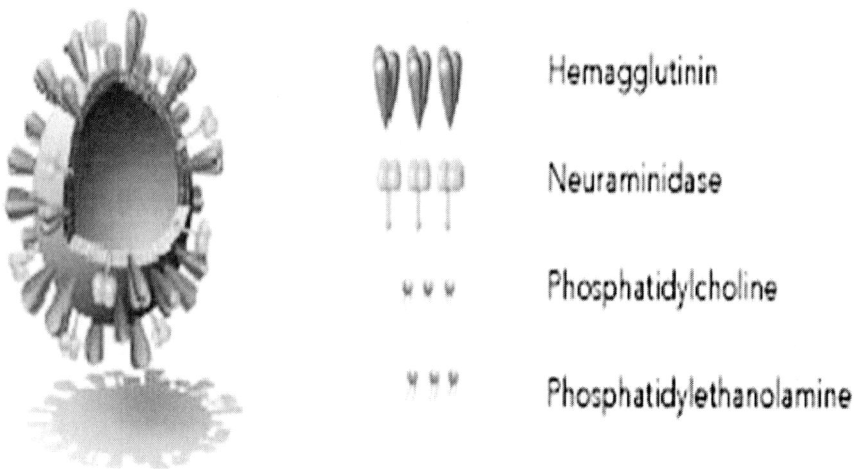

Figure 1: Ultrastructure of a Virosome: Influenza virus envelope with functional viral envelope of glycoprotein.

The neuraminidase (NA) is a tetramer composed in four equal spherical subunits hydrophobically embedded in the IRIV (Immunostimulating Reconstituted Influenza Virosomes) membrane by a central stalk and can readily intercalate into the phospholipid membrane. Neuraminidase (NA), present on the IRIV's (Immunostimulating Reconstituted Influenza Virosomes) surface and aids its action by the same mechanisms through which it enhances influenza virus pathogenicity, it catalyses the cleavage of N acetylneuraminic acid (sialic acid) from bound sugar residues resulting in a decreased viscosity of the host's mucus and allowing to the influenza virus an easier access to epithelial cells (Figure 2).

The different components of the virosome:

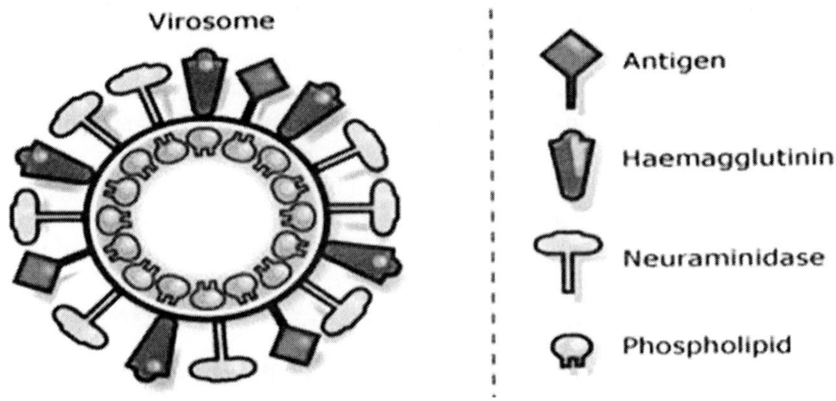

Figure 2: Showing different components of virosomes.

The same process leads to destruction of the HA (haemagglutinin) receptors within the cell membrane to which viruses and IRIVs bind. This allows the virus particles to avoid aggregation, as newly formed virus particles do not adhere to the infected host cell membrane after budding and allowing the influenza virus to retain its mobility. The mode of action of IRIVs is dependent on the influenza haemagglutinin. Haemagglutinin, intercalated into the phospholipid bilayer, stabilises the liposome base by preventing fusion with other liposomes. The HA (haemagglutinin), the major influenza antigen, is formed from two polypeptides, HA1 and HA2, that are responsible, upon conformational change, for the fusion of the virus with the endosomal membrane. The HA1 globular head contains a receptor site that has a high affinity towards sialic acid, present on the surface of antigen presenting cells (APCs), such as macrophages and lymphocytes and therefore facilitates the binding of IRIVs (Immunostimulating Reconstituted Influenza Virosomes). The actual fusion of IRIVs (Immunostimulating Reconstituted Influenza Virosomes) with the endosomal membranes is then mediated by the HA2 polypeptide[14-18].

Need Of Virosomal Technology

State-of-the-art-drugs must meet diverse medical, pharmacological and pharmaceutical demands. They have to be efficient, reliable and reduced severe side-effects. Market aspects also need to be considered. Due to the high number of competing products on the market, drugs should be cost effective. Stability is an issue as well, because drugs are often subject to unfavourable delivery and storage conditions. Moreover, the market potential of a drug also rises with its compliance and convenience. Apart from these requirements novel drug delivery system technologies should provide improved bioavailability, minimizing the quantities of the drug needed to be taken by the patient. Several drugs in clinical tests are discontinued at various stages in the development process because of the lack of suitable delivery technologies. Drug delivery system may rescue some of the products by overcoming these difficulties. The new generation of therapeutics against cancer or neurogenerative disorders needs drug delivery systems which guarantee targeted drug delivery to specified host tissues and cells, receptor-mediated uptake and controlled release into the lumen of the cells. This all requires vision and long-term, challenges meet with the development of a highly sophisticated carrier system based on its proprietary virosomal technology.

Effective vaccination against infectious agents or tumor antigens requires the induction of potent humoral and cellular immune responses based on antibodies and CD4+ T helper cells or cytotoxic T lymphocytes (CTLs). Depending on the targeting and the induction of neutralizing antibodies is also very important. There is a need for antigen delivery systems capable of directing nonreplicating exogenous antigen into the MHC class II and I presentation pathway Virosomes can be used as delivery system for unrelated molecules in vitro and in vivo and a list of so far tested applications of virosomes as carrier of different products (Table 1). The route of immunization is another important feature and which characterizes this system. Virosomes can be administered via nasal and vaginal mucosal, intradermal and intramuscular routes. Stimulation of local and systemic immune responses may improve the immunogenicity and efficacy of the vaccine. The first line of defence for the host is mucosal immunity, which is a major component of the immunological humoral and cell mediated response. Prevention and treatment of infectious diseases and active specific cancer immunotherapy frequently require the induction of a powerful cellular immune response, which can be achieved with virosomes carrying different types of antigens, such like peptides, proteins, virions or molecules such as an oligonucleotides or plasmids. An attractive feature of virosomes is that during the reconstitution process a variety of molecules can be incorporated either in the virosomal membrane or in the aqueous interior. Now days in drug delivery system Chimeric Virosomes (C-IRIV) can be used as a suitable carrier system for DNA and RNA since these fusogenic particles mimic like a virus. Virosomes can also be used as adjuvant, vehicle and this property has already been validated by three licensed vaccines against hepatitis A (Epaxal, Berna Biotech) and influenza (Inflexal, Berna Biotech and Invivac, Solvay Pharmaceuticals), which combine the superior safety of a subunit vaccine with the immunogenic potential and biological properties of a virus-like structure [19,20].

Table 1: Results of analysis of formulation and recovery studies

Molecules	Development Candidates, or Research Leads	References
Mumps F/HN DNA plasmid	Research	[43]
PTH-rP DNA plasmid	Research	[40]
CEA and CD40L DNA plasmid	Research	[44]
Antisense L-myc OPT	Research	[45]
Small interfering RNAs	Research	[38]
F RSV protein	Research	[46]
Fab' Her-2 Neu and doxorubicin	Research	[41]
mAb anti epithelial glycoprotein 2	Research	[47]
Plasmodium falciparum SPf66 peptide	Research	[14]
Plasmodium falciparum AMA-1 peptide	Phase I clinical trial (PEVION)	[42]
HCV peptides	Research	[48]
Amyloid Ab peptides	In development (PEVION)	[49]

Structure Of Virosomes

Virosomes are produced by dissolving the envelope of a virus by a detergent or short-chain phospholipids. Next viral genetic material and non-membrane proteins are removed. The subsequent removal of the detergent or short-chain phospholipids, the viral membrane is reconstituted and producing a virosome containing the viral membrane proteins and lipids. Viral proteins confirm to virosome based vaccine structural stability, homogeneity and increase the immunological properties of prepared virosomes (Figure 3 and Figure 4) [21].

Influenza virus shown in figure (Figure 3). The envelope made of influenza lipids constitute the membrane and proteins called Hemagglutinin (HA) and

Neuraminidase(NA) are intercalated on its envelope. Inside the envelope the Nucleocapsid and the genetic material of the source virus.

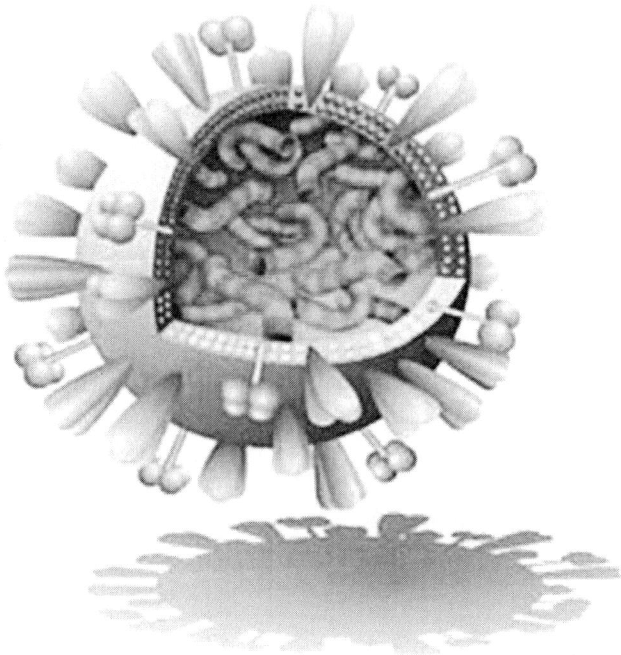

Figure 3: Influenza virus.

As shown in the (Figure 4), the virus is devoid of the nucleocapsid including the genetic material of the source virus and the virosome is created and devoid of its substance, it is not suitable to replicate, its cause an infection or a disease. Virosomes contain functional viral envelope glycoprotein's-influenza virus hemagglutinin and neuraminidase intercalated in the phospholipid bilayer membrane [22]. They have a typical mean diameter of 150 nm and essentially virosomes represent reconstituted empty influenza virus envelope devoid of the nucleocapsid including the genetic material of the source virus[23].

Figure 4: Lipid bilayer of virosomes.

Vehicle For Vaccines

Vaccine is a biological preparation that improves immunity to a particular infectious microorganism (microbe). A vaccine typically contains a small amount of an 'A' agent (immunogen) that resembles to a microorganisms. The immunogen stimulates to the body's immune system to recognize it as a oreign material, destroy it and "remember" it. The immune system can more easily recognize and destroy or neutralize the correspondent icroorganism that is its later encounters by avoiding severe infection and subsequently its pathologies. The immunogen is made up of some parts of the microbe, as like proteins, which are seen by the immune system as the microbe itself. This immunogen usually needs a vehicle and adjuvant to be delivered efficiently in the body and body parts[24].

Virosomes Adjuvant System

Virosomes are virus-like spherical particles with a average diameter of 150 nm (nanometrs), consisting of reconstituted influenza virus envelopes and lacking the genetic material of the native virus the cell binding and membrane fusion properties of the native virus also mediated by the viral envelope glycoprotein haemagglutinin. The functional characteristics of virosomes form the basis for their enhanced immunogenicity [25]. The Combination with combinatorial chemistry, this approach may have great potential for the rapid optimization of molecularly defined synthetic vaccine candidates against a wide variety of infectious agents.

Properties Of Virosomes

Virosomes are biodegradable; biocompatible, and non-toxic. An antigen can be incorporated into virosomes, adsorbed to the virosome surface and integrated in to the lipid membrane, either via hydrophobic domain or lipid moieties cross-linked to the antigen. They are also being considered for HIV-1 vaccine research. Virosomes were used as a drug carrier mechanism for experimental cancer therapies [26].

Delivery Through Viral Vector

Viral vectors can be utilized for epidermal transfer of the DNA or other suitable antigen. Viral vectors include adenovirus vector, RSVE and HSV amplicon vector. The epidermal gene transfer by means of HSV amplicon vector produces necrosis and cytotoxicity and hence, they cannot be applied repeatedly or for longer period of contact. Reconstituted viral vectors targeting of virosomes have also been utilized for intracellular targeting of encapsulated DNA/antigen. The RSVE can be applied topically for efficient gene or antigen transfer. RSVE constitute two types of proteins, namely haemagglutin (HN) and fusion (F) proteins, which determine the fusogenicity. The RSVE can be effective as cell microinjection vector to transfer immune response through topical route. They can serve as an efficient immunoadjuvant [27].

Pharmacokinetics Of Virosomes

Pharmacokinetics information can be used to interpret the differences in the pharmacological effect of liposomal-entrapped drug and free drug, subsequently can be exploited for dose designing. Pharmacokinetics deals with time course of absorption, distribution and degradation of the virosomal carriers in vivo. The pharmacokinetics of virosomes requires the knowledge of possible accessible sites after intravenous administration as this is the most accepted route for various virosomal formulations exploited for clinical therapeutics except topical formulations. Virosomes alters both the tissue distribution and the rate of clearance of a drug as they are affected by the pharmacokinetics parameters. Under optimal conditions the drug has been carried within the virosomal aqueous phase during circulation and it leaks at sufficient rate to become bioavailable on arrival at tissue or other specific sites. Bioavailability in case of virosomal carriers can be defined as the amount of free drug that is able to escape the confines of the carrier and thus become available for redistribution to neighboring tissue [28].

Mechanism Of Action Of Virosomes

Virosomes act both as a drug delivery carrier and also as an adjuvant with multiple functions during the induction of an immune response to body's. The carrier function comprises the positive effects of embedding the antigen into a higher structure, the virosome particle. The adjuvant function relates to immunestimulating properties of the virosomes and their components on the immune system. Most importantly, virosomes succeed in stimulating specific immunity without causing nonspecific inflammation [29]. By this mechanism, an antigen-specific helper immune response is induced, which potentiates both the cellular and humoral immune response (Figure 5).

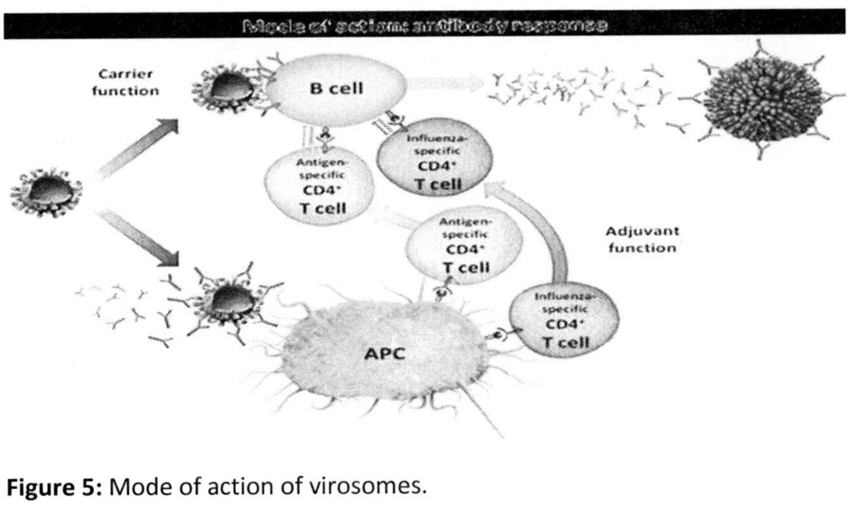

Figure 5: Mode of action of virosomes.

Carrier Function Response

The integration of the antigen into the higher structure of the virosome particle stabilizes the antigen to preserves the native status of B cell epitopes and protects the antigen from degradation. The antigen displayed on the surface virosomals which mimics the original pathogen or target cell and thereby favours the generation of antibodies relevant for protection. The presentation of he antigen as a repetitive surface structure enhances its recognition by antibody-producing B-cells. The size and surface structure of the virosome particles make them an attractive target for uptake and processing by immune cells and which is a crucial step in the initiation of an immune response [30].

Virosomes Adjuvant Function

The adjuvant function of virosomes relies on the presence of influenza-derived envelope proteins, in particular the predominant haemagglutinin (HA). Pre-existing antibodies against influenza bind to virosomes and tag them efficiently for rapid uptake and processing by antigen presenting cells (APC). The natural function of antibodies is to bind virus and block infection. Pre-existing influenza-specific helper T cells are activated by those antigen presenting cells (APC) displaying the processed fragments of the influenza proteins. Influenza proteins activated helper cells rapidly proliferate and secrete cytokines to support and enhance the induction of effect or immune cells, e.g. antibody-producing cells [31].

Difference Between Virosomes And Liposomes

Viral envelope glycoproteins with receptor-binding and membrane-fusion properties that enable the cellular liposomes have been considered promising vehicles for targeting and delivery of biologically active molecules to living cells both in vitro and in vivo. Liposomes have little potential to fuse with cells and generally fail to provide appreciable delivery of encapsulated molecules to the cell cytoplasm. Virosomes containing functional delivery of encapsulated molecules [32]

Virosome Uptake By Cells

Entry of virosomes into target cells divided into two different steps:

A. Attachment

This involves binding of the virosomes via HA to the cell receptors that are a membrane glycoprotein or glycolipid with terminal sialic acid. In case of specific virosomes, Fab fragments are coupled by a cross-linker with a spacer arm to the virosomal surface. Specific virosomes will additionally recognize antigenic structures on the targeting cell surface and resulting in an attachment to target cells by two different binding mechanisms. Thus, specific virosomes exert selectivity for special cell types.

B. Penetration

After attachment entry of virosomes occurs by receptor-mediated endocytosis. The virosomes are trapped in endosomes, acidic fusion of the virosomal membrane with endosomal membrane. The fusion is mediated by the viral spike glycoprotein hemagglutinin (HA). The membrane-fusion reaction in the endosome librates the virosomes from its lipid envelope and provides access for the encapsulated drugs to the cytosol.

Functions By The Carrier

The integration of the antigen into the higher structures of the virosomes particle stabilize the antigens, preserves the native status of B cell epitopes and protects the antigens from degradation. Moreover, the presentation of the antigen as a repetitive surface structure enhances its recognition by antibody-producing B cells.

Memory Support

The presence of influenza-derived hemagglutinin (HA) provokes a memory response as a vast majority of people have a degree of natural, pre- existing immunity against influenza. This comprises both humeral and cellular immunity: pre-existing influenza-specific antibodies tag virosomes efficiently for rapid uptake and processing by antigen presenting cells (APC). Memory T helper cells rapidly proliferate and secrete cytokines to support and enhances the induction of effector immune cells.

METHOD OF PREPARATION OF VIROSOME

A. Selection Of Virus For Virosomes

Virosomes are reconstituted viral envelope that can be derived from different virus. Influenza virus envelope is most often used to produce virosome but virosome can also be made from Sendai virus, Epstein-burr virus, HIV, sindbis, semliki-forest virus, friend murine leukaemia virus, herpes simplex virus, Newcastle disease virus [29, 33-35].

B. Selection Of Antigen For Virosomes

Antigen is selected as per our requirements. Antigens such a parasite, carcinogenic cell, bacterium or whole cell is used as antigens. Cell components such as DNA, RNA or plasmid can also be used as antigen. These antigens are coupled to lipid anchor so antigen will be ready to load on virosome (Figure 6).

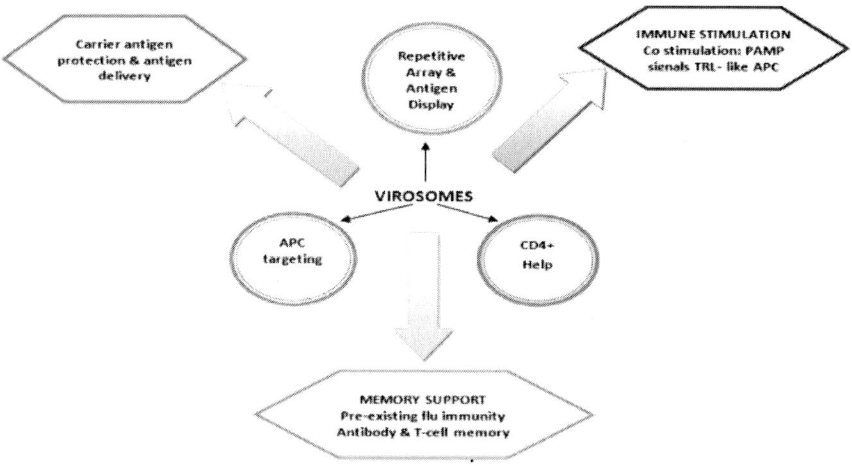

Figure 6: Showing activation of antibody through virosomes.

C. Reconstitution Of Virosome

Virosome solubilized with detergent of octaglucoside, triton X-100, nonidert p-40. Because of solubilization with detergent internal viral protein and genetic material will Sediment then detergent is removed by different method such as dialysis and hydrophobic resins from supernatant. Then using ultracentrifugation process viral matrix protein and nucleiocapsid is removed.

Viral phospholipids (82%) and viral protein is recovered in supernatant. Protein obtained in supernatant represents viral envelope protein only. Now antigen which is already coupled to lipid anchor is mixed with polymer or surfactant solution and this solution is processed with virosome carrier so that antigen bound virosome is obtained (Figure 7).

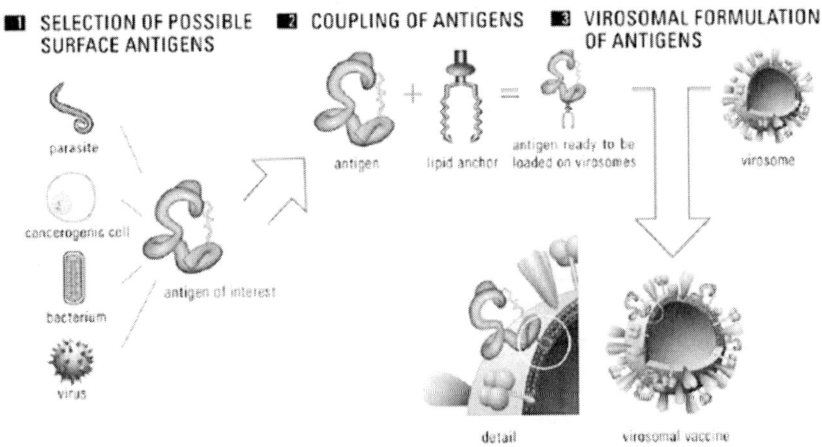

Figure 7: General method for preparation of virosomes.

Characterization Of Virosomes

A. Protein Detection

Preparation of virosome generally result in a relatively uniform protein-to-lipid ratio, sodium dodecyl sulfate polyacrylamide gel electrophoresis (SDS-PAGE) can confirm the presence of hemagglutinin (HA) protein in the virosomes [33].

B. Structure And Size

Negative-stain electron microscopy can generally be used to determine the ultra structure and different size of virosomes. The staining solutions should be neutral pH, to avoid acid-induced conformational changes of hemagglutinin (HA) [36].

C. Fusion Activity

Generally virosomes exhibit pH-dependent membrane fusion activity similar to native influenza virus. Virosomal fusion along with biological or artificial target membrane is visualized with a fluorescent resonance energy transfer assay (RET). Alternatively fusion can be assessed in vitro with an excimer assay using pyrene-labeled lipids and decrease of surface density of the pyrene-phosphatidylcholine-label on fusion with an unlabeled membrane corresponds to a reduction in excimer fluorescence [35].

Route Of Administration Of Virosomes

The virosomes are administered in a variety of parenteral routes including intravenous (IV), intramuscular (IM), subcutaneous (SC), intra-arterial and inhalable delivery. In addition, virosomes can be administered topically, orally or transdermally. The virosomes also can be incorporated into implantable devices for long-term release [37].

Virosome For Drug Targeting System

The major problem of combining chemotherapy and immunotherapy is the severe side effects that limit the use of doxorubicin as a cytotoxic drug. We can use virosomes (reconstituted fusion-active viral envelopes) as a new drug delivery system and have shown that virosomes are capable of binding and penetrating into tumor cells and delivering cytotoxic bioactive drugs. We have additionally demonstrated that conjugating Fab' fragments of an anti-rNeu monoclonal antibody (mAb) to irosomes selectively and efficiently inhibits tumor progression of established rNeu over expressing breast tumours. Fab'-Doxo-Virosomes combine the antiproliferative properties of the mAb and the cytotoxic effect of doxorubicin in vivo. Fab'-Doxo-Virosomes significantly inhibit tumor formation at a tumor load representing metastatic spread. The results indicate that virosomes conjugated with an antibody against a tumor antigen are a promising new selective drug delivery system for the treatment of tumors expressing a specific tumor antigen [38].

Novel Drug-Delivery Approaches

Virosomes are particularly useful for delivering nucleic acids or genes. These compounds are delivered into the host cell cytoplasm on fusion of the virosome with the endosome or cell plasma membrane. The nucleic acids or genes encoding a naturally occurring protein can be introduced into host cells and can be expressed, provided that the expression cassette contains the proper cis-acting regulatory elements. Drugs or nucleic acids can be incorporated into the virosome at the time of virosome targeting preparation. The bioactive compound is typically added to the lipid–HA-containing solution following removal of the nucleiocapsid. Alternatively, the bioactive compound is initially incorporated into a liposome, which is then fused with a virosome containing two haemagglutinin with different pH thresholds to form a virosome and liposome hybrid. Proteins also can be delivered to cells via virosome. For example, the gelonin subunit 'A' of diphtheria toxin and ovalbumin has been successfully delivered by virosome to target cells [31] (Figure 8).

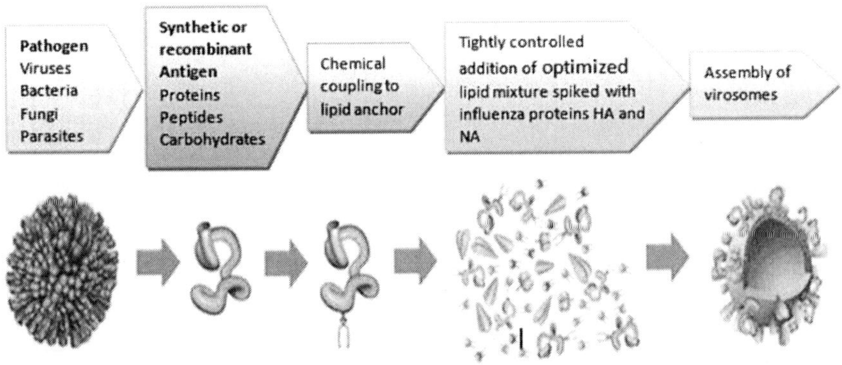

Figure 8: Showing assembly of virosome in a controlled manner.

Merits Of Virosomal Drug Delivery

1. Virosomal technology is approved by the FDA for use in humans and it has a high Safety profile.
2. Virosomes are nontoxic, biodegradable and biocompatible.
3. No disease-transmission risk
4. No auto immunogenity or anaphylaxis.
5. Broadly applicable with almost all important bioactive drugs enables drug delivery into the cytoplasm of target cell.
6. Promotes fusion activity in the endolysosomal pathway.
7. Protects drugs against degradation.

8. Target-specific delivery of antigens and amplification of the immune response.
9. Extended uptake, distribution and elimination of drug in body.
10. Promote fusion activity in endosomal pathway.
11. Virosome allow patient specific modular vaccine regimen.
12. Up scaling according to standard procedure.
13. The fully functional fusion-activity of virosomes enables receptor mediated uptake and natural intracellular of the antigen, which leads to the stimulation of immune system: humoral and cellular immune responses.
14. The antigen is partially protected from extra cellular degradation and the resulting depot effect greatly facilitates immune potentiation[31].

Applications Of Virosomes

Virosomes In Gene Delivery System

Haemagglutinin membrane fusion protein of influenza virus is known to mediate a low-pH- dependent fusion reaction between the viral envelope and the limiting membrane of the endosomal cell compartment following cellular uptake of the virus particles by receptor- mediated ndocytosis here, they exploited this activity of haemagglutinin to achieve efficient gene delivery to cultured cells [39].

Virosomes In RNA/DNA Delivery System

Small interfering RNA (siRNA) encapsulated in virosomes are able to down regulate the synthesis of newly induced and constitutively expressed proteins and overcoming the lack of suitable delivery methods for these molecules. Administration route is Intraperitoneal injection of siRNA loaded virosomes resulted in delivery of the nucleotides to cells in the peritoneal cavity [40].

Virosomes Activation Of Murine Lymphocyte

The incorporation of Salmonella Minnesota rough-LPS in liposome's reduced the potency of LPS to stimulate splenocyte proliferation and cell surface kappa-light chain expression on 70 Z/3 pre-B cells by over 100-fold. The Salmonella Minnesota rough-LPS inserted into virosomes was at least 10-fold more potent than free LPS, when both prebound virosomes were allowed to be taken up by the cells at neutral pH and when the virosomes were fused into the plasma membrane by low pH treatment. Virosomal LPS remained 2- to 10-fold more potent than free LPS in stimulating B lymphocytes and at least 100-fold more active than liposomal LPS or fusion inactivated virosomes. After low pH-induced fusion with the plasma membrane, the majority (80%) of the prebound virosomes had fused with the cells, compared with about 8% after neutral uptake [41].

Virosomes For Cancer Treatment

Virosomes have been also used in the oncology area to carry peptides corresponding to Tumour Associated Antigens (TAA), as in the case of peptides derived from the parathyroid hormone- related protein (PTH-rP) or from recombinant proteins such as Her-2/neu. Fab'-Doxo- virosomes combined the anti proliferate properties of the monoclonal antibody and the cytotoxic effect of doxorubicin in vivo. Fab'-Doxo-virosomes significantly inhibited tumour formation at a tumour load of metastasis spread, indicating that this can also be considered to be a promising new selective drug delivery system for the treatment of tumours expressing a specific tumour antigen. The immunogenic effect of the HER-2/neu protein was significantly increased when the protein was linked to virosomes; they are encapsulated as a soluble protein or bound to a virosomal membrane. Virosomes elicited humoral and cell-mediated responses against TAA, as well as inducing tumour rejection [42].

Virosomes For Malaria Therapy

Malaria vaccine, containing virosome-formulated anti-malaria peptides, shows a good tolerability and a highly specific immune response in humans. Scientists have identified and optimized synthetic peptide structures that mimic the surface loops of two candidate malaria vaccine antigens, the NPNA repeat region of the circumsporozoite protein (CSP), loop I of domain III of merozoite apical membrane antigen-1(AMA-1). Lead structures of additional antigens have been identified and additional optimised mimotopes are being developed. It is assumed that there is a need to add further mimotopes to produce an effective multistage, multicomponent malaria vaccine formulation [43-51].

Immune Stimulation

In addition to the influenza-specific antigens, virosomes provide pathogens-associated molecular patterns (PAMP) that deliver co-stimulatory signals to APC, which leads to a TLR-like activation [52, 53].

Possible Toxicity Of Virosomes

Virosome mediated delivery has low toxicity and high immunogenicity with various prospective applications for the treatment and prevention of cancer, neurodegenerative disorders and infectious diseases. The toxicity of cationic formulations might be ascribed to the cationic lipids themselves, and several studies have investigated the correlation between the chemical structure of lipids and their toxicity profile [54].

Safety Of Virosomes

So-called virosomes has been developed by incorporating the HA from an influenza virus A strain into liposomes composed of phosphatidylcholine. The influenza virus surface gly coprotein HA guides the virosomes specifically to antigen-presenting cells and leads to fusion with their endosomal membrane. Process provides optimal processing and presentation of the antigens to immunocompetent cells and T lymphocytes are activated to produce cytokines. The B lymphocytes to form large amounts of specific antibodies. Stimulation of B lymphocytes also occurs through direct contact with the antigen-virosome complex. When tested for safety and immunogenicity in elderly nursing home residents in comparison to whole-virion and subunit vaccines and the virosome-formulated influenza vaccine was found to be superior with regard to reactogenicity and immunogenicity. This trivalent virosome influenza vaccine (Inflexal Berna V) is currently licensed in several European countries (e.g., Switzerland since 1997 and Italy since 1998). We investigated the safety and comparative immunogenicity of this new virosome influenza vaccine in comparison with a standard subunit influenza vaccine for a pediatric group at risk, i.e., children and adolescents with CF[55].

Targeting Of Virosomes Influenza Vaccine

Influenza is a potentially serious disease in very young children due to no background immunity in the elderly due to innate decreased resistance to infections and a poorly functioning immune system, and in individuals with an underlying disease which may render them unable to handle infections.

Patients with chronic pulmonary dysfunction such as cystic fibrosis (CF) are at a particularly high risk for acquiring a severe influenza infection. An Influenza disrupts the normal defense system of the respiratory tract and may lead to secondary bacterial pneumonia. An Influenza vaccination has been shown to be beneficial to childrens, healthy working adults and elderly subjects with or without risk factors. Therefore, many public health authorities recommend routine annual immunization of high-risk individuals. In many countries, including Switzerland, targeted vaccinations are reimbursed by health insurance or by public funds. Despite these recommendations and incentives, at most half of Swiss citizens ≥ 65 years old are immunized annually against influenza. Recent surveys on influenza vaccination coverage showed these figures to be higher in France (≥ 70%), in The Netherlands (58 to 64%), and in the United States (55 to 75%), similar in Italy (26 to 49%), and lower in Austria (14%). For Switzerland, there are no figures on the influenza vaccination coverage of childrens an age group which is especially with regard to at-risk subjects, not adequately vaccinated worldwide.

Immunization of infants and young children requires two doses of vaccine spaced 1 or 2 months apart. However, current vaccines still do not result in a high, long-lasting protective immune response in this group, and vaccines with improved immunogenicity are clearly needed. However, reformulation of either whole-virus vaccines or subunit vaccines with new adjuvants or antigen delivery systems has been shown to greatly potentiate the immune response in animals [55].

Trafficking Of Virosomes

Trafficking of the virosomes to the cell surface has not been well characterized, but is presumed to occur via normal vesical maturation and exocytic process. The outcome is the nonlytic release of the vast majority of mature virions into the extracellular space. MHV and several other coronaviruses that can directly fuse with cells and there is a characteristic and rapidly detectable cytopathic effect of cell-cell fusion into multinucleated syncytia. The production of infectious virus continues even after the majority of cells are fused. Syncytia were recently reported as readout of SCoV receptor expression and cell infection. It is unknown whether SCoV is a respiratory virus or a pneumoenteric virus. This knowledge gap will be stymine efforts to develop a vaccine or drug against SCoV. Molecular biological studies have also identified several potential targets for antiviral drug discovery including viral binding and uncoating, replication, protein expression, processing and assembly, release cellular functions on which the virus depends on such as cholesterol synthesis membrane trafficking and autophagy [56].

Future Prospects Of Virosomes

Virosomes represent an innovative drug-delivery system for various biologically active molecules, especially nucleic acids or genes and for numerous indications. The outer surface of virosomes can be suitably modified to facilitate targeted drug delivery system. The comprehensive pharmacokinetic profile, bioavailability, clinical effects and stability should be studied thoroughly to ascertain their long-term reliability as a safe, effective, potent and affordable means for drug delivery and targeting.

CONCLUSION

Virosome is an emerging system of drug delivery and drug targeting on biological system. Improvisations of this tool will bring a new prospective and also open a new era in the modern pharmaceutical field and also human life too. Virosomes can be used to deliver an antigen in the administration by various routes like intranasal, intradermal, and intramuscular, depending on the aim of immunization without any side effects. An attractive feature of virosomes is the possibility to target them to selected cells using Fab fragments of monoclonal antibodies specific for the binding. Influenza virosomes can be a great tool for delivering antigens and molecules of different nature, such as proteins, peptides, plasmids, oligonucleoides and even drugs, to cells and due to their versatility and it is possible to exploit them in different scientific sectors. Virosomes could also be exploited as carriers for targeted drugs delivery and for immunomodulating molecules particularly in cancer therapy/treatment. All these features allow us to cons ider influenza virosomes as a promising model for antigen and/or unrelated molecules delivery and which could be helpful for the development of new vaccines or immunotherapy protocols that combine safety with immunogenicity and their applicability in different field of medical research.

ABBREVIATIONS

NA: Neuraminidase

HA: Haemagglutinin

IRIV: Immunopotentiatin reconstituted influenza virosome

PL: Phospholipids

PC: Phosphatidylcholine

APCs: Antigen presenting cells

CTLs: Cytotoxic T lymphocytes

PAMP: Pathogens-associated molecular patterns

TAA: Tumour Associated Antigens

CSP: circumsporozoite protein.

REFERENCES

1. Marc, P.G., Thomas, Cherian,. Yuri, Pervikar., et al. A review of vaccine research and development: human acute respiratory infections. (2005) Vaccine 23(50): 5708-5724.

2. Kay, M.A., Glorioso, J.C., Naldini, L. Viral vectors for gene therapy: the art of turning infectious agents into vehicles of therapeutics. (2001) Nat Med 7(1): 33-40.

3. Thomas, C.E., Ehrhardt, A., Kay, M.A. Progress and problems with the use of viral vectors for gene therapy. (2003) Nat Rev Genet 4(5): 346-358.

4. Hacein, B.S., Von, Kalle, C., Schmidt, M., et al. LMO2-associated clonal T cell proliferation in two patients after gene therapy for SCID-X1. (2003) Science 302(5644): 415-419.

5. Morral, N., O'Neal, W.K., Rice, K., et al. Lethal toxicity, severe endothelial injury, and a threshold effect with high doses of an adenoviral vector in baboons. (2003) Hum Gene Ther 13(1): 143-154.

6. Kafri, T., Morgan, D., Krahl, T., et al. Cellular immune response to adenoviral vector infected cells does not require de novo viral gene expression: implications for gene therapy. Proc. (1998) Natl Acad Sci USA. 95(19): 11377-11382.

7. Schimidt, W.G.D., Schimidt, W.I.G. Non-viral and hybrid vectors in human gene therapy: an update. (2003) Trends Mol Med 9(2): 67-72.

8. Kumar, V.V., Singh, R.S., Chaudhuri, A. Cationic transfection lipids in gene therapy: successes, set-backs, challenges and promises. (2003) Curr Med Chem 10(14): 1297–1306.

9. Crispin, R.D. Lipoplex-mediated delivery of nucleic acids: factors affecting in vivo transfection. (2004) J Mol Med 82(9): 579–591.

10. Lima, M.C., Neves, S., Filipe, A., et al. Cationic liposomes for gene delivery: from biophysics to biological applications. (2003) Curr Med Chem 10(14): 1221-1231.

11. Miller, A.D. The problem with cationic liposome/micelle-based non-viral vector systems for gene therapy. (2003) Curr Med Chem 10(14): 1195-1211.

12. Almeida, J.D., Edwards, D.C., Brand, C.M., et al. Formation of virosomes from influenza subunits and liposomes. (1975) Lancet 2(7941): 899-901.

13. Bagai, S., Anu, P., Robert, B., et al. Hemagglutinin-neuraminidase enhances F protein-mediated membrane fusion of reconstituted Sendai virus envelopes with cells. (1993) J Virol 67(6): 3312–3318.

14. Pöltl-Frank, F., Zurbriggen, R., Helg, A., et al. Use of reconstituted influenza virus virosomes as an immunopotentiating delivery system for a peptide-based vaccine. (1999) Clin Exp Immunol 117(3): 496-503.

15. Hunziker, I.P., Zurbriggen, R., Glueck, R., et al. Perspectives towards a peptide-based vaccine against hepatitis C virus. (2001) Mol Immunol 38(6): 475-84.

16. Mengiardi, B., Berger, R., Just, M., et al. Virosomes as carriers for combined vaccines. (1995) Vaccine 13(14): 1306-1315.

17. Mischler, R., Metcalfe, I.C. Inflexal V a trivalent virosome subunit influenza vaccine: production. (2002) Vaccine 20(5): 17-23.

18. Rafael, M., Luyong, J., Kerstin, M., et al. Exploiting conformationally constrained peptidomimetics and an efficient human-compatible delivery system in synthetic vaccine design. (2001) Chembiochem 2(11): 838-843.

19. Rock, K.L., York, L.A., Saric, T., et al. Protein degradation and the generation of MHC class-I presented peptides. (2002) Adv Immunol 80: 1-59.

20. Durrer, P., Glück, U., Spyr, C., et al. Mucosal antibody response induced with a nasal virosome-based influenza Vaccine. (2003) Vaccine 21(27-30): 4324-4334.

21. Both, G.W., Sleigh, M.J., Cox, N.J., et al. Antigenic drift in influenza virus H3 hemagglutinin from 1968 to 1980: multiple evolutionary

pathways and Sequential amino acid changes at key antigenic sites. (1983) J Virol 48(1): 52–60.

22. Carrat, F., Flahault, A. Influenza vaccine: the challenge of antigenic drift. (2007) Vaccine 25(39-40): 6852–6862.

23. WHO. Fact sheet Number 211(2003) Influenza.

24. Metsikkö, K., van, M. G., Simons, K. Reconstitution of the fusogenic activity of vesicular stomatitis virus. (1986) EMBO J. 5(13): 3429–3435.

25. Petri, W.A., Wagner, R.R. Reconstitution into liposomes of the glycoprotein of vesicular stomatitis virus by detergent dialysis. (1979) J Biol Chem 254(11): 4313-4316.

26. Glück, R., Mischler, R., Finkel, B., et al. Immunogenicity of new virosome influenza vaccine in elderly people. (1994) Lancet 344(8916): 160–163.

27. Prem, N.G., Singh, P., Mishra, V. et al. Topical immunization: Mechanistic insight and novel delivery systems. (2004) Indian Journal of Biotechnology 3: 9-21.

28. Rajat, S., Mohd, Yasir. Virosomes: A Novel Carrier for Drug Delivery. (2010) International Journal of PharmTech Research, 2(4): 2327-2339.

29. Huckriede, A., Bungener, L., ter Veer, W., et al. Influenza virosomes: combining optimal presentation of hemagglutinin with immunopotentiating activity. (2003) Immunopotentiators in Modern Vaccines. 21(9-10): 925–931.

30. Huckriede, A., Bungener, L., Stegmann, T., et al. The virosome concept for influenza vaccines. (2005) Vaccine 23(1): S26–38.

31. Kaneda, Y. Virosomes: evolution of the liposome as a targeted drug delivery system. (2000) Adv Drug Deliv Rev 43(2-3): 197–205.

32. Stegmann, T., Morselt, H.W., Booy, F.P., et al. Functional reconstitution of influenza virus envelopes. (1987) EMBO J 6(9): 2651-2659.

33. Bron, R., Ortiz, A., Dijkstra, J., et al. Preparation, properties, and applications of reconstituted influenza envelopes (virosomes). (1993) Methods in Enzimol 220: 313- 331.

34. Pieter, S., Romke, B., Wilschut, J. Delivery of foreign substances to cells mediated by fusion-active reconstituted influenza virus envelopes (virosomes). (1993) J Liposome Res 3(3): 767–792.

35. Romke, B., Antonio, Ortiz., Wilschut, J. Cellular cytoplasmic delivery of a polypeptide toxin by reconstituted influenza-virus envelopes (virosomes). (1994) Biochem 33(31): 9110–9117.

36. Asghar, A., Hoorieh, S., Masoumeh, T. K., et al. Reconstruction of H3N2 influenza virus based virosome in-vitro. (2013) Iran J Microbiol 5(2): 166-171.

37. Felnerova, D., Viret, J.F., Glück, R., et al. Liposomes and virosomes as delivery systems for antigens, nucleic acids and drugs. (2004) Curr Opin Biotechnol 15(6): 518–529.

38. Maria, G.C. Applications of influenza virosomes as a delivery system. (2006) Human Vaccines 2(1): 1–7.

39. Schoen, P., Chonn, A., Cullis, P.R., et al. Gene transfer mediated by fusion protein hemagglutinin reconstituted in cationic lipid vesicles. (1999) Gene Ther. 6(5): 823–832.

40. Jonge, J., Holtrop, M., Wilschut, J., et al. Reconstituted influenza virus envelopes as an efficient carrier system for cellular delivery of small-interfering RNAs. (2005) Gene Ther 13(5): 400-411.

41. Dijkstra, J., Bron, R., Wilschut, J., et al. Activation of murine lymphocytes by lipopolysaccharide incorporated in fusogenic, reconstituted influenza virus envelopes (virosomes). (1996) J Immunol 157(3): 1028- 1036.

42. Scardino, A., Correale, P., Firat, H., et al. In vivo study of the GC/90IRIV vaccine for immune response and autoimmunity into a novel humanised transgenic mouse. (2003) Br J Cancer 89(1): 199-205.

43. Waelti, E., Wegmann, N., Schwaninger, R., et al. Targeting HER/neu with antirat Neu virosomes for cancer therapy. (2002) Cancer Res 62(2): 437-444.

44. Markus, S. M., Annabelle, R., Francesca, B., et al. Induction of parasite growth inhibitory antibodies by a virosomal formulation of a peptidomimetic of loop I from domain III of Plasmodium falciparum apical membrane antigen1. (2003) Infec Immun 71(8): 4749-4758.

45. Maria, G.C., Rinaldo, Z., Marcello, V., et al. Intranasal immunization with mumps virus DNA vaccine delivered by influenza virosomes elicits mucosal and systemic immunity. (2000) Virology 277(1): 111-118.

46. Cusi, M.G., Del Vecchio, M.T, Terrosi, C., et al. Immune-Reconstituted Influenza Virosome containing CD40L gene enhances the

immunological and protective activity of a carcinoembryonic antigen anti-cancer vaccine. (2005) J Immunol 174(11): 7210-7216.

47. Waelti, E.R, Glück, R. Delivery to cancer cells of antisense L-myc oligonucleotides incorporated in fusogenic, cationic-lipid-reconstituted influenza-virus envelopes (cationic virosomes). (1998) Int J Cancer 77(5): 728-733.

48. Cusi, M.G., Zurbriggen, R., Correale, P., et al. Influenza virosomes are an efficient delivery system for respiratory syncytial virus-F antigen inducing humoral and cell-mediated immunity. (2002) Vaccine 20(29-30): 3436-3442.

49. Enrico, M., Pieter, S., Jan, W., et al. Targeting influenza virosomes to ovarian carcinoma cells. (2001) FEBS Letters. 509(1): 71-76.

50. Hunziker, I.P., Zurbriggen, R., Glueck, R., et al. Perspectives: towards a peptide- based vaccine against hepatitis C virus. (2001) Mol Immunol 38(6): 475-484.

51. Zurbriggen, R., Amacker, M., Kammer, A.R., et al. Virosome-based active immunization targets soluble amyloid species rather than plaques in a transgenic mouse model of Alzheimer's disease. (2005) J Mol Neurosci 27(2): 157-166.

52. Moser, C., Amacker, M., Kammer, A.R., et al. Influenza virosomes as a combined vaccine carrier and adjuvant system for prophylactic and therapeutic immunizations. (2007) Expert Rev Vaccines 6(5): 711-721.

53. Priyanka, R., Gaurav, S. A. Virosomes: Novel vaccination technology. (2012) Int J Pharma Sci Research 3(10): 3591-3597.

54. Erdmann, V.A., Barciszewski, J. DNA and RNA Nanobiotechnologies in medicine: Diagnosis and treatment of diseases. (2013) Springer Publisher 87-356 .

55. Schaad, U. B., Buhlmann, U., Burger, R., et al. Comparison of immunogenicity and safety of a virosome influenza vaccine with those of a subunit influenza vaccine in pediatric patients with cystic fibrosis. (2000) Antimicrob Agents Chemother 44(5): 1163-1167.

56. Knobler, S., Mahmoud, A., Lemon, S., et al. Learning from SARS: Preparing for the Next Disease Outbreak. Workshop Summary. (2004) Institute of medicine of The National Academies, The national Academies Press, Washington, D.C. 1-376.

Chapter 7

Polymer Nanoparticles for Smart Drug Delivery

Devasier Bennet[1] **and Sanghyo Kim**[1, 2]

[1] *Department of Bionanotechnology, Gachon University, Bokjeong-Dong, Sujeong-Gu, Seongnam-Si, Republic of Korea*

[2] *Graduate Gachon Medical Research Institute, Gil Medical Center, Inchon, Republic of Korea*

1. INTRODUCTION

In the recent decades, polymers are widely used as biomaterials due to their favorable properties such as good biocompatibility, easy design and preparation, a variety of structures and interesting bio-mimetic character. Especially in the field of smart drug delivery, polymer played a significant role because it can deliver therapeutic agents directly into the intended site of action, with superior efficacy. The ideal requirements for designing nano-particulate delivery system are to effectively be controlled particle size, surface character; enhance permeation, flexibility, solubility and release of therapeutically active agents in order to attain the target and specific activity at a predetermined rate and time. The smart drug delivery systems have been successfully made by the advances in polymer science in the bio-nanotechnology field. Recently, these advances have been found in various medical applications for nano-scale structures in smart drug delivery. The smart drug delivery systems should possess some important feature such as pre-scheduled rate, self controlled, targeted, pre-determined time and monitor the delivery. The smart drug delivery system enhances the polymer nanoparticle better stage to their therapy regimen. They are drug carriers of natural, semi-synthetic, and synthetic polymeric nature at the nano-scale to micro-scale range. The polymeric particles are collectively named as spheres and capsules. The most of the polymeric nanoparticles with surfactants offer stability of various forms of active drugs and have useful to smart release properties. There are numerous biological applications have been reported for the nano-scale to micro-scale sized particles, such as site-targeted, controlled, and enhanced bioavailability of hydrophobic drugs [1-4]. Due to the nanoparticles size the drugs have been targeting into various applications, such as, various cancers targeting has been shown to be promising [5]. Moreover, polymeric particles proved their effectiveness in stabilizing and protecting the drug molecules such as proteins, peptides, or DNA molecules from various environmental hazards degradation [2-4, 6, 7]. So these polymers are affording the potential for various protein and gene delivery. Numerous methods had been available to fabricate nanoparticles; it depends on the physical and chemical properties of polymer and active ingredients. Most of the formulation techniques involve different mechanisms such as using organic solvents, temperature, ultra-sonication and mechanical agitation which can degrade the pharmaceutical active ingredients. So the nano-particulate system can be developed to consider the formulation methodology should not damage the active pharmaceutical ingredients. There are numerous biodegradable and biocompatible polymers with different physicochemical characters are offered to prepare smart nanoparticles, those polymeric nano-carriers can be natural or semi-synthetic or synthetic. Those nanoparticles can enhance the systemic circulation half-life and minimize unwanted internalization and prevents the denaturation of the therapeutically active moiety and could use to deliver the target agents. Several polymer systems are approved by the U.S. Food and Drug Administration (FDA) for human use. It is the belief that when inventions in fabrication can catch up with those in materials, design and development of drug delivery system can enter a new generation of enhancing clinical healthcare.

The most recent advances in the uses of carriers for sustained and targeted delivery, micro and nano fabricated self-regulated devices [8], bio-recognizable systems; micro-needles for transdermal drug delivery have shown the flexibility and enhanced permeability of these polymeric materials. Ultimately the goal in smart drug delivery is the emergence of a micro and nano-fabricated therapeutic drug release device with the capacity to enough hold and release of various active agents on demand. In modern system the micro-electro-mechanical systems give a distinctive possibility to produce micro-fabricated biomedical devices for different intentions, from implantable systems to lab-on-a-chip systems. The constant and prolonged drug release micro-fabricated systems have the several benefits, such as many active ingredients could be stored in an nano form within the system and sustainably released, the drug release is initiated by the dissolution and disintegration of outer membrane barrier by an mechanical/electric stimuli, the most potential drugs could be released more specifically with this technique, the complex drug release system such as simultaneous stable and periodically could be attained for local therapy by the micro-fabricated system; it can be achieved in high or low dose of drugs at the targeted site and increase the stability of drugs by the membrane barrier for preventing water diffusion into the reservoirs [9]. Owing to the advanced scientific sophistication of the controlled drug release system that has been achieved till now, or that are in dynamic progress, this delivery model can be categorized into various classes. The controlled drug delivery systems can be categorize four main mode of drug delivery, such as (1) rate-programmed drug delivery, where drug diffusion from the system has follow a specific release rate profile, (ii) activation-modulated drug delivery, where the drug release is induced by various factors such as physical, chemical electrical or biochemical modules, (iii) feedback-regulated drug delivery, where the rate of release is determined by biochemical substance (triggering agent) concentrations, it is dependent on the concentration exhibit in the target and (iv) site-targeting drug delivery systems, this is a complex process that consists of multiple steps of diffusion rate and partitioning for the rate of drug release is regulated by the specific targeting moiety, solubilizer and drug moiety. This chapter will brief discussion on recent innovative nano-fabrication methods for novel drug delivery system. Also, highlights some of these new technologies and consider their possibility ongoing clinical transformation of nanoparticles, which the particles are well-controlled formulated. This chapter will be followed by a more detailed novel drug delivery system development from a polymeric material viewpoint and their various bio-applications will be covered without attempting to all the work that has been done in this field.

Over a decade, investigators have appreciated the enrichment of potential uses of bio-nanotechnology in offering huge advancements in novel drug delivery and targeting. The novel drug delivery platform that provides diminishes toxicity and enhances therapeutic efficacy gives most possible benefits to clinical levels. In approaches to drug delivery systems the route of administration is one of the crucial roles of drug targeting. These nanoparticles can be used for various routes, including oral, nasal, transdermal, parenterals, pulmonary, ocular, etc. Nonetheless, the oral route is most convenient, preferred, and in several cases, also its cost-effective, but it does not cross easily some biological barrier; also easily degraded by various body fluids, then rapid hepatic clearance and other organs. So the drug delivery systems focus on overcoming the various membrane barriers, such as the blood brain barrier, tight junction barrier, to achieve the effective drug target and enhance the efficacy. To find an alternative and satisfiable route of administration for the effective drug delivery system should overcome the digestive tract problems, where the degradation could take place via acid-hydrolysis, enzymatic degradation and bacterial fermentation in the alimentary canal. This chapter will cover the more detailed novel route of administration and development from a polymeric material viewpoint and their brief discussion will be covered without attempting to all the work that has been done in this field.

2. GENERAL METHODS FOR POLYMERIC NANOPARTICLES PREPARATION

Recently, various kinds of polymers are used to prepare the polymeric nanoparticles, among this all polymer biodegradable polymers and their co-polymers such as di-block, tri-block, multi-block or radial block copolymer structures have been generally used to prepare polymeric nanoparticles and to encapsulate the active ingredients. These multi-functionalized polymeric nano-carriers include micelles, capsules, platelets, fibers, spheroids colloids, dendrimers, core-shells, nanoparticle incorporated polymer matrixes, etc. The first polymeric nanoparticles were developed between the year of 1960 to 1970 for the therapeutic application, and this were Micelles[10-12].The micelles are formed by polymerisation methods, commonly the formation of polymer nano-carriers during the polymerization of monomers [13-16]. Then the various advanced polymerization techniques have been developed for the preparation polymeric based nanoparticles, and the nanoparticles were stabilised using various surfactants [1, 9]. The stabilised drug loaded nanoparticles consist of drug and non-toxic biocompatible polymer with stabilizing agents, the biocompatible polymer is either biodegradable or non-biodegradable. Numerous techniques are available for the preparation of the polymeric nanoparticles and mainly top-down and bottom up processes. The polymer nanoparticle drug carriers can be further categorized into nano/micro-capsules and nano/micro-spheres depends on the size and structure [1, 9, 17-19]. The fine particles are 100 - 2,500 nm and ultrafine particles are 1 to100 nm in size, and are collectively known as nanoparticles. 50 to 300 nm sized nanoparticle have been prepared by emulsion polymerization method [20]. Drawbacks in polymerization techniques are evolving noxious factors such as toxic, reactive residues, un-reacted monomers, the risk of a chemical reaction and the formation of unwanted oligomers [1], and these drawbacks are overcome by using preformed polymers for the polymerization process [1]. Generally the drug loaded nanoparticles were prepared by dissolving the drug and polymer into the water-immiscible organic solvents and producing a nano-emulsion, as an example by probe-sonication method. The organic solvent is removed by using elevated temperature or reduced pressure [21-23], as an example of rotary evaporation method, and the nanoparticle is washed and collected by certification. Followed by various changes and improvements of the emulsification techniques have been reported [24-29]. For example, the sonication process is a crucial step in the preparation of the sensitive drug loaded nanoemulsion, and the sonication process can increase the temperature, that leads to inactivate the active ingredients. In order to avoid the problems researchers utilized an on/off cycle to maintain a low temperature. Other examples of general methods to prepare the drug polymer nanoparticle are described in the Figure 1. The biodegradable polymeric nanoparticles are commonly prepared by five different techniques such as emulsification-solvent evaporation, solvent displacement, salting-out, emulsification-solvent diffusion and double emulsion solvent evaporation. The synthesizing methods include salting-out method [1, 30, 31]; it is based on the separation of a water miscible solvent from aqueous solution through the salting out effect, solvent displacement method [1, 32-34], phase separation method [35], evaporation precipitation [36, 37], antisolvent precipitation and electrospray methods [38].

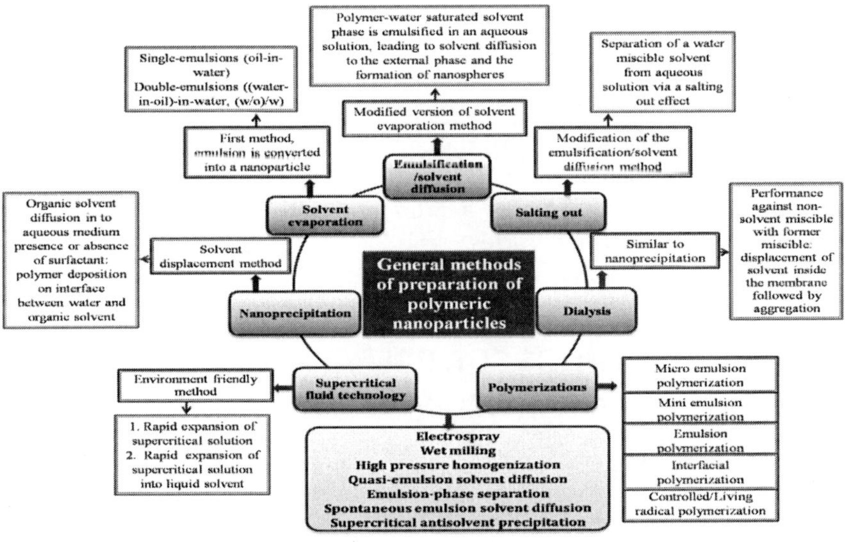

Figure 1. General methods of preparation of polymeric nanoparticles and their principle involved in the mechanisms

Also, many approaches have been developed for the drug particle size reduction (increase in the surface) to the nanometer size range. For size-reduction, high pressure homogenization or wet bead milling is frequently used technique to produce reduced size nanoparticle [39-43]. Among these the high-pressure homogenization has been shown to be effective methods to produce size reduction particle. Moreover, its need sophisticated equipment to resist increasing pressures and temperature. Then, in order to obtain dried polymeric nanoparticle formulations researchers used various drying techniques such as atmospheric freeze drying, spray freeze drying, vacuum freeze drying, and lyophilisation. The uniformity of spray-dried nanoparticle is better than a freeze-dried nanoparticle. Moreover the lyophilisation and spray-drying are used to prepare the nanoparticle [44, 45], these nanoparticles easily tends to aggregates. Also the polymeric nanoparticles have also been synthesized by supercritical fluid techniques [46-52]. This method can get a dry product without any solution, also no need additional drying stages, but the supercritical fluid can swell some of the polymers and act as a softener, extender, and lubricant, which lead to aggregation. Moreover, this method is not easy to get the mono-dispersed multi-component particles because of different kinetics [52]. Nanoparticles prepared by spray-drying technique are one-step based on the conversion of a droplet to a dry particle by evaporation [53-55]. These one-step techniques have been revealed that the nanoparticle could be prepared without any problems [56-58], and the drug content in the particles is almost high [59], but produce an amorphous residual structure. In all above technique induce some unwanted noxious factors, as well as the organic solvents used in the preparations are increasing the risk of pharmaceutical application, also the increased processing time leads to microbial contamination [60,61, 62]. Understanding the all risk factors, recently the modern instrument provides a promising and viable platform for the preparation polymeric nanoparticles.

3. MODERN METHODS FOR PREPARATION OF POLYMERIC NANOPARTICLES

Recently, the polymeric nanoparticles have emerged as a most promising and viable technology platform for recognizing the targeted, environment-responsive and, multi-functional with navigated controlled drug delivery system. Polymer in smart drug delivery is a rapid-emerging new technological discipline in which various therapeutic applications of nano products are expected to overcome the patient complaints in healthcare. Smart delivery will give new solutions for therapeutic interventions. There is great interest from the beginning in smart medicine of advanced and well-characterized bionanotechnological products that will be especially effective in fighting diseases like cardiovascular diseases [63], diabetes [64], cancer [65, 66], aging [67, 68], some chronic metabolic syndrome and various degenerative diseases and disorders [69, 70]. For example, the innovative smart polymers with nano-particulate drug-delivery systems can obviously advances in therapeutics by guiding the drugs to target cells and reducing the adverse-effect/side-effect on well being. At present, some of the smart polymer with multi-functioned nanoparticle system approaches in clinical trials, and it shows promising outcome. Certainly the morbidity and mortality rate of disease affected patients could improve their lifestyle by the early course of smart therapeutic intervention. This smart intervention can be attained by developing high sensitivity and reliable smart drug delivery.

The rapid advancement in the above direction has been made with the initiation and development of more advanced alternative nanofabrication techniques to produce structures in various nano-scales level of controlled manners. Drug loaded polymeric nano-systems can provide controlled release of both hydrophilic and hydrophobic drugs over a long period of time while minimizing unwanted side effects in the body. This involves the synthesis of various novel biocompatible polymers with well-defined nanometers to a few micro-meters structures using several modern techniques such as microelectromechanical systems [71] microfluidic systems [72-76], electrodropping system [77], microneedle based system [78-81], advanced high pressure homogenization, interfacial emulsion polymerization and combined systems. Figure 2 described the few modern techniques for polymeric nanoparticles preparation with various concepts. The physiochemical characters of polymeric nanoparticles have to be optimized based on the specific application. Various methods can be used to produce various nano-particulate systems with various polymers. The multifunctional polymeric nanoparticles developments such as environment-responsive micelles, colloids, nano hydrogel, core-shell nanoparticles, nano-spheres and core-shell nano-spheres with layer-by-layer assembly for single/dual or multi drug release have been achieved so far. In order to get the desired properties, the mechanism of formulation method plays a vital role. Thus, it is extremely beneficial to have synthesis mechanism at hand to approach multi-functional polymeric nanoparticles with exact physiochemical properties for a specific application.

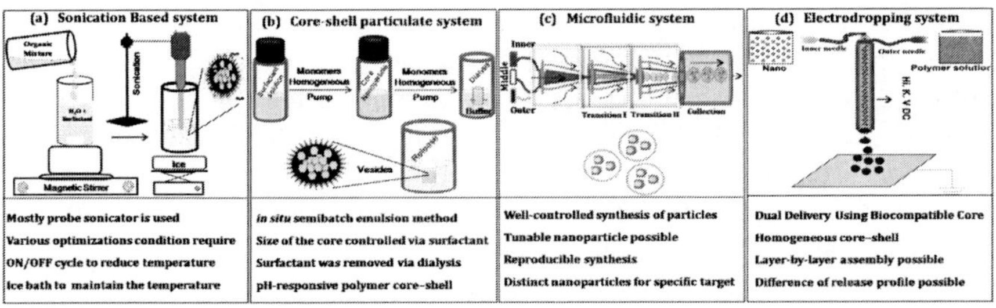

Figure 2. Schematic diagrams represent the advanced techniques of preparation of polymeric nanoparticles

The smart delivery systems of target bio-molecules have been concentrated of recent researches for various interventions. Particularly, various proteins, peptide, growth factors and cytokine therapy for various diseases play a vital role in regulating cellular responses, and thus the design of multi-functional polymeric particles delivery vehicles are closely associated with the regulation of multiple cellular events, likewise a wide variety of target bio-molecules have been investigated in numerous literature reports [82, 83]. Also numerous of delivery vehicles have been studied and reported recently, this chapter will cover same viewpoint and their brief discussion will be covered without attempting to all the work that has been done in this field. Various concepts are utilized in the design of delivery vehicles that are capable of ferrying multiple active ingredients in a self-controlled manner, with different release profile kinetics. The distinctive self-assembly of multifaceted nanostructures from an easy colloidal system has been of interest to design a material with distinctive characters for the use of drug delivery vehicles. The inter-and intra-molecular linkage via van der Waals interaction leads to dense-packed self-assembly periodic nanostructures. These structures could be colloidal particle or clusters, based on the assembly [84, 85]. The natural or semi-synthetic polymer-based self-assembled nanostructures have inherent capacity of the nano-carrier for delivering many kinds of active ingredients, because of good biocompatibility and degradation/resorption properties [86]. In the sonication methods (Figure 2a), the self-assembled nanoparticle was achieved by probe sonication, the process has been done by cavitation, nucleation and reversible locking concept, the formed nanostructure have more flexibility in the nature [87]. In this self-assembled and core-shell particulate delivery systems, including water-soluble polymeric drug compounds conjugates [88], block polymeric micelles [89-93], long-circulating polymeric micelles [94, 95], nano encapsulations [96, 97], and core-shell nano-spheres [98, 99] have been synthesized by in situ two-step semi-batch emulsion polymerization technique (Figure 2b), as vehicle to target suitable dose of drugs in an accurate and controlled manner. Also the core-shell nano-spheres have been achieved for pH-responsive controlled release, and delivery of hydrophobic anticancer agents for acidic tumor tissues [100]. Recently Choi DH, et al have optimized electrodropping system to produce a homogeneous biocompatible core shell capsules for angiogenesis in dual delivery system [77], and they particularly focused on regenerative medicine. This electro-dropping system can overcome from the particle aggregation and drug encapsulation efficiency (Figure 2d). Coming to the micro-fluidics, the recent science and advanced technology of manipulating micro/nano-scale volumes in micro-fluidic channels have significant impact on the various applications. Advances and inventions in micro-fluidics are awaited to enhance the preparation of polymer nanoparticles and shifting to clinical evaluation [101] most of the micro-fluidic systems for synthesis, polymer nanoparticles are still under development and they have the widest possible to develop because they are highly reproducible, easily modifiable and can be incorporated with other techniques [102]. Recently, various micro-fluidic systems provide rapid mixing without any stimulator, such as stirring or electric force; have been originated [103]. Among these various systems the flow-focusing [104], droplet mixers [105] are widely utilized and it enables micro-mixing within the micro channel [106]. The flow focusing squeezes the solvent stream between two anti-solvent streams, resulting in a rapid solvent exchange via diffusion take place (Figure 2c). The effectuation of these rapid mixing methods for the development of nanoparticles in continuous flow; the micro-fluidic system has been achieved the continuous flow, narrow sized, mono dispersed with high drug entrapment and better batch-to-batch uniformity in compared with conventional methods [107].

4. CONTROLLED DRUG DELIVERY SYSTEMS

4.1. Rate-Programmed Drug Delivery Systems

The recent advances in smart drug delivery systems with rate-programmed drug delivery systems have been achieved by functionalization of rate-controlling surface. The transdermal drug delivery have been achieved a new rate pre-programmed drug delivery system, transdermal patch which delivers a particular concentration of drugs to the blood circulation via the skin, it provides the therapeutic advantage to clinical levels. The rate-programmed drug delivery systems, the release of drug molecules from the rate controlling membrane system has been pre-programmed at particular rate kinetics. The rate controlling membranes made from natural and semi-synthetic polymeric material and proves their ability to use as a rate controlling membranes in any dosage form even nano to micro-scale level particle embedded matrixes or implantable or transdermal patches. It must be simple, cost-effective, and flexible enough not to split or crack on bending or stretching. Recently, some of novel rate-controlling composite membranes have been developed as rate controlling barriers for transdermal application, with flexible and smooth surface nanoparticles embedded scaffold which could reduce the risk of wounding or being rubbed off during dressing, and thereby improves upon traditional dressings and its can provides better patient compliance [108, 109]. This is achieved by optimized system design, which determines the diffusivity of active agents across the membrane. This rate-programmed drug delivery system can be categorized by various controlling dependencies, such as (1): membrane permeation-controlled, (2): diffusion-controlled, (3): membrane/matrix hybrid-type and (4): reservoir partition-controlled systems. The recent advance in the smart rate-programmed drug delivery systems the polymer and their scaffolds play vital roles, such as greater drug-loaded nano/micro-particle encapsulation ability, overcome pre-systemic metabolism, enhanced bioavailability and environmental responsive properties for various applications. For selecting the polymers, need to consider some important key factors for pharmaceutical application such as reduced tensile strength [110], water vapor permeability rate, biocompatibility, non-toxic [111], anti-infective, controlled release [112,113], flexibility, emollient, adhesion, spreadability and retention properties of the drug-loaded nano/micro-particle encapsulation scaffold or film preparation [114-116]. So it can prevent the immunogenesis, secondary damage to cells, disease recurrence and finally enhance patient compliance [117]. In this type of rate-programmed controlled drug delivery systems, a drug-loaded nano formulation or rate-controlled nano formulation can be either totally or partially loaded in the reservoir space whose surface is covered by the rate pre-programmed polymeric membrane. The pre-programmed polymeric membrane can be optimized and achieved by multi-functionalization with block copolymers. The scaffold or membrane can be produced by the homogeneous or heterogeneous non-porous polymeric compounds or a micro/nano-porous or semi-permeable material. The drug release profile should be at a constant pre-fixed rate. The release profile is controlled by a pre-programmed rate-controlling membrane; it's based on the molecules, diffusivity, partition co-efficient, and dimension of the outer membrane. Also the rate of release is determined by the cross-linking ratio of the polymer network. The rate controlled release profile exists in many kind therapeutic formulations such as intrauterine devices [118], ocular insert [119, 120], some transdermal therapeutic system [109], polymer matrix, sub-dermal [121] and subcutaneous implantation [122-125].

4.2. Activation-Modulated Drug Delivery

4.2.1. Environmental activation/stimuli responsive smart delivery system

The smart drug delivery with activation-modulated system has been achieved by external or environmental stimuli, these environmental responsive smart delivery systems achieved a lot more with double and multiple-responsive delivery system. The various activation/stimuli responsive drug delivery vehicles have been synthesized and tested, in various particle sizes, ranges from nanometers to a few micro-meters sized carriers for different routes of administration. The transdermal electro-activated or electro-modulated drug delivery has been established as an efficient model. In this group of activation-modulated controlled drug delivery system, the release of active agents from the systems is activated by some physical, chemical, electrical, environmental condition or biochemical processes and/or facilitated by an energy supplied externally. The release profile has been controlled by the input energy. Based

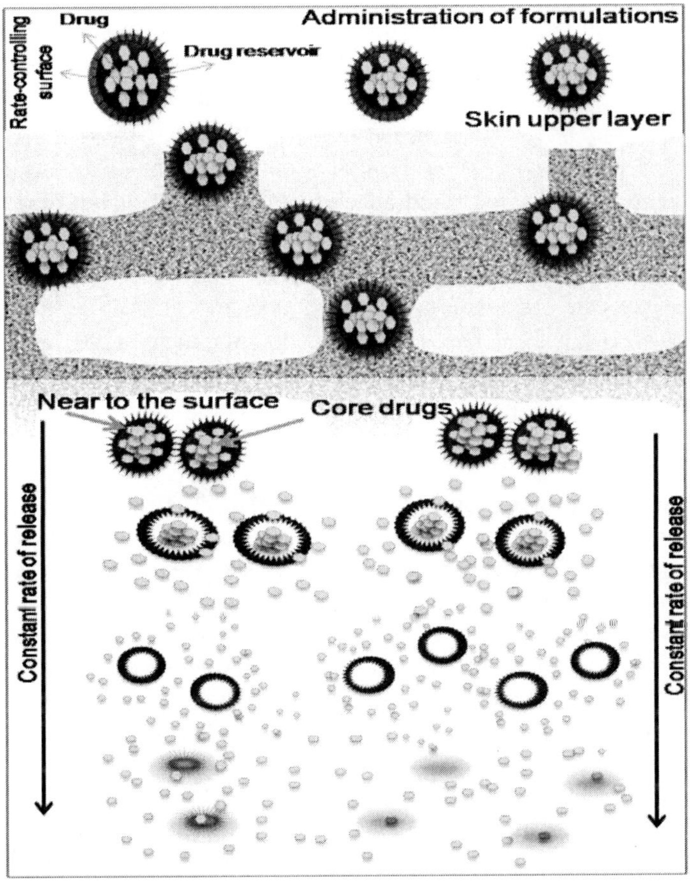

Figure 3. Schematic diagrams represent the rate controlled drug delivery systems of topical applications

on the activation/stimulation process applied or energy type used, this activation-modulated controlled drug delivery system can be categorized into the various classes which are given in the Table 1. These stimuli-responsive materials show changes in the physicochemical character during the environmental condition changes. These changing properties can be fully utilized in smart delivery system, which certainly similar to the biological response behavior. Different types of body organs, different tissues and various types of cellular compartments might have great differences in every stimulus with great response. So that all the important cases considered in this chapter, deal with various environmental responsive smart delivery systems. Any specific behavioral changes in the system lead to a phase transition, these transitions will be key factors for the stimuli-responsive drug delivery system and some selected examples of applications are described in the Figure 4. The preclinical and clinical studies have demonstrated that drug-loaded polymeric nanoparticles has been well tolerated, extended systemic circulation, higher accumulation in the tumor sites through enhanced permeability and retention effect, minimized side effects and adverse effect, and/or higher bioavailability [153-155]. And most of the drug delivery systems are based on biodegradable polymer [156, 157]. Most of the environment-sensitive polymeric nano-particulate systems are leading to degradation and or disintegration by the internal or external local environmental stimulus such as pH, glucose, low oxygen content, ions, redox potential, and lysosomal enzymes; and then temperature, magnetic field, electric, ultrasound, and light respectively (Table 1).

These activations grew to achieve smart, targeted drug release in a particular time (spatial and temporal control release) [158-160]. At this place we describe a few examples. Particularly, the acidic pH levels in the body vary according to the different body environments (site and the organ) such as tumor cells and tissues (pH 6.5-7.2), endosomes (pH 5.0-6.5), lysosomes (pH 4.5-5.0) and entire GI tract with different pH value as comparatively varied with normal physiological (pH of 7.4) conditions in blood and tissues. So, the pH-responsive nano system have been considered and formulated to release the active agents in pH sensitive targets such as cancer site or endo/lysosomal regions [161,162]. The cytosol and cell nuclei have surrounded with elevated redox potential (in reducing glutathione) it higher than normal body fluids and it have been developed for intracellular release of various active bio-molecules [163-165]. Additionally, the cancerous tissues are extremely low in oxygen content (hypoxia) with higher glutathione levels compared to normal tissues [166]. This has been targeted with hypoxia-responsive polymeric nanoparticles. These internal stimuli-responsive nanoparticles have their own benefit of self-regulated drug delivery and effective target in clinical therapeutics. Also the external activated nanoparticles provide their own advantages such as high reproducible nature, also remote controlled delivery possible, then the release profile can be pulsatile delivered (means that switched on and off) possible [167]. On the other hand, the various light-responsive polymeric nanoparticles system has been developed for activating antitumor drug release [168]. Also numerous of temperature-sensitive multi-functionalized polymeric and copolymers nanoparticles have been formulated based on thermally-responsive release [169, 170]. Magnetically guided nano-carriers have been developed for the remote controlled cancer therapy and diagnosis [171, 172]; also the core-shell nanoparticles have demonstrated for improved tumor accumulation and antitumor therapeutic efficacy in various models.

Table 1. Overview of various stimuli responsive nano-carriers for smart drug delivery systems with mode of drug release applications

Based on	Stimulus	Mode	Ref.
Physical stimuli	Osmotic pressure	Controlled through the permeability of water Controlled through a gradient of osmotic pressure	[126]
	Hydrodynamic pressure	Generate hydrodynamic pressure gradient Forces the drug to release through the orifice	[127]
	Vapor pressure	Pumping system contains vaporizable fluid Creates vapor pressure, vaporizes at body temperature	[128] [129]
	A mechanical force	Equipped with a mechanically activated pump First-pass elimination and pressure-sensitive delivery	[130]
	Magnetics	Electromagnetism-triggering vibration mechanism Magnetically activated, vibrate by an electromagnetic field	[131]
	Sonophoresis	Utilizes ultrasonic energy to activate the delivery	[132]
	Iontophoresis	Electrical current to activate and diffuse the charged drug	[133]
	Hydration	Utilized swellable polymer matrix Activated by hydration-induced swelling delivery	[128] [126]
	Electricity	Electric-sensitive capsule Electrically erodible matrix for delivery	[134] [135]
Chemical stimuli	pH	Deliver the drug in the intestinal tract not in the stomach Deliver the drug in the ulcer stomach by floating delivery	[136] [137]
	Salt concentration	Prepared by ionizable drug with ion-exchange resin Controlling the delivery of an ionic or an ionisable drug	[128] [138]
	Hydrolysis	Hydrolysis-induced degradation of polymer chains Hydrolysis activate the release of drug molecules	[139]
Biochemical stimuli	Enzyme	Polymer chains fabricated with biopolymers Deliver the drug by enzymatic hydrolysis of polymers	[140] [141]
	Biochemical	Enzymatic-activated, biodegradation Feedback-regulated delivery concept has been applied	[142] [143]
Environmental stimuli	Temperature	Depends on the transition temperature Shifting the hydrophilic/hydrophobic balance	[144] [145]
	Light	Polymers undergo isothermal phase transitions by photon Reversible phase separations through photo-irradiation	[146] [147]
	Hypoxia	Hydrophobically modified imidazole derivative was conjugated to the carboxymethyl dextran, it can release the hydrophobic agents under hypoxic conditions	[148]
Dual-stimuli	Two different responses	Based on the polymer architecture Micelles are reported pH and thermo-responsive	[149] [150]
Multi-stimuli	More than two responses	Functionalization of pyrene-quaternized segments form a light-responsive shell and the unquaternized segments form a temperature/pH-responsive core	[151] [152]

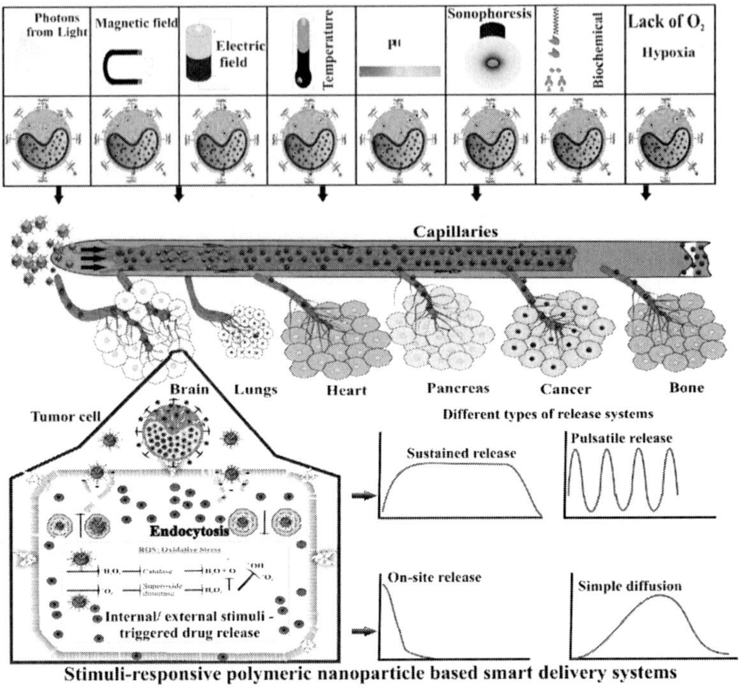

Figure 4. Schematic diagrams represent the activation-modulated drug delivery systems, which the polymeric nanoparticle activated by various stimuli such as physical, chemical, biochemical, environment, and/or a combination of two or more.

4.2.2. Dual and multi-stimuli responsive smart delivery system

In this chapter, provide the recent proposes and formulations of dual and multiple-stimuli responsive multi-functionalized polymeric nanoparticles and their promising targets in smart drug delivery in specific to the cancer therapy. With the booster development of the smart drug release and increase therapeutic efficiency of intelligent drug loaded nano-particulate system, polymeric nanoparticles that respond to dual and multi-stimuli, which have been aggressively reported. The double-response and multiple-responsive nano-particulate systems were described in the Table 2. It must be mentioned that the stimuli and responses happened at the same time at the same site or different mode. These dual and multi-stimuli responsive polymeric nanoparticles can provide control over the drug release profile, which leads to greater anti-tumor efficiency in vitro and in vivo models, and on the other side the nanoparticle formulation and drug loading under moderate conditions. In this section we describe a few examples. Especially, redox-responsive drug release multi-functionalized nano-particulate system have been formulated based on temperature and reduction, dual responsive tri-block copolymers functionalized by increasing temperature above the lower critical solution temperature after that cross-linking [173, 174]. These multi-functionalized nano-particulate systems were targeted to cancer cells and triggered by reduction oxidation mechanism, which leads to dissociate to release the active agents by de-crosslinking followed by disruption and degradation of nano-particulate system. pH/redox dual-stimuli multi-functionalized disulfide cross-linked micelles have been developed for increased drug release and accumulation in the cancer target, due to endo/lysosomal pH and intracellular redox environment the drug release was taken place [175].

4.2.3. Considerations for stimuli responsive targeted molecular systems

These multi-functional polymeric nanoparticles are capable to face the current problems of nanoparticle drug formulations including formulation and drug encapsulation, prolong stability, cellular internalization, site-targetability, enhanced cellular uptake, and inside cell target and drug release. These dual and multiple-activation responsive characteristics have provided novel and enthusiastic power over drug release kinetics and greater efficiency. All the described studies in dual and multiple-stimuli responsive drug delivery systems are mostly trial and error models, because most them non-biodegradable carriers, low encapsulation, and nonviable to clinical therapeutics. To overcome all the unfavorable conditions, immediate efforts could be focussed to improvement of dual and multiple-stimuli responsive biocompatible, biodegradable, non-toxic, and non-immunogenic smart polymeric nanoparticles that could effectively entrap and sustain the drug release in the systemic circulation, enhanced accumulation in the cancer target, and efficient release kinetics in response to more efficient external or internal stimuli. Moreover the smart polymeric nanoparticle system does not produce any secondary damage and any harmful to the healthy cells. In the case of clinical studies on dual and multiple stimuli responsive system shall be performed to obtain a real mechanism of action in anti-cancer target. In addition, the multi-functionalized smart polymeric nanoparticles system construct with targeting ligands and shall be incorporated into dual/multiple stimuli responsive nanoparticles to be achieved multidrug resistant cancers by site targeting, site-specific, and rapid/sustained release, and we sure that dual and multiple stimuli responsive smart nano-particulate system going to be a good future in cancer therapy.

Table 2. Overview of dual and multi-stimuli responsive materials for nano-carriers of various smart drug delivery systems

Responses	Stimulus	Nanoparticles	Ref.
Dual-stimuli	pH & Thermo	P(NIPAAm-co-DMAAm-co-UA) nanoparticles	[176]
		P(NIPAAm-co-AA)-b-PCL nanoparticles	[177]
		PLA-g-P(NIPAAm-co-MAA) nanoparticles	[178]
		P(NIPAAm-co-DMAAm)-b-PCL/PLA micelles	[179]
		PNIPAAm and PAA hollow nanogels	[180]
	pH & redox	PEG-SS-PDEA polymersomes	[181]
		DS-g-PEG/cRGD nanoparticles	[182]
		Poly(b-amino ester)s-PEG micelles	[183]
		PMAA-based nanogels	[184]
		mPEG-PAsp(MEA)-PAsp(DIP) micelles	[185]
	pH & magnetic	Fe_3O_4 nanocarrier with peptide mimic polymers DOX-tethered Fe3O4 conjugates nanoparticles mPEG-b-PMAA-b-PGMA-Fe_3O_4 nanoparticles Fe_3O_4-capped MSNs MCM-TAA-Fe_3O_4-capped MSNs	[186] [187] [188] [189]
	T & redox	EO-PAA-PNIPAAm polymersomes	[190] [191]
	Double pH	PPC-Hyd-DOX-DA nanoparticles	[192]
		Poly-b-amino ester ketal nanoparticles	[193]
	pH & diols	PEG-b-dendritic cholic acid telodendrimers nano-carriers containing boronic acid	[194]
	T & magnetic	Pluronic with Fe_3O_4 nanoparticles	[195]
	T & enzyme	DNA-capped MSNs	[196]
Multi- stimuli	T/pH/redox	PNIPAAm-SS-P(THP-protected HEMA) micelles	[197]
	T/pH/magnetic	P(NIPAAm-co-MAA) coated magnetic MSNs	[198]
	pH/redox/ magnetic	Fe(II) loaded PMAA crosslinked by N,N-methylene-bisacrylamide and N,N-bis(acryloyl)- cystamine	[199]
	T/redox/guest molecule	Vesicles based on hosteguest complex formation between C4AS and MVC12	[200]
	T/pH/guest molecule	Cucurbit(8)uril micelles, methylviologene-functionalize PNIPAAm and naphthalene-terminated PDMAEMA	[201]
	Light/pH/T	Pyrene-functionalized poly (dimethylaminoethyl methacrylate)	

4.3. Feedback-regulated drug delivery

The recent advances in smart delivery systems with feedback-regulation of drug release. This self-regulated or feedback-controlled drug delivery comes under closed-loop systems. The self-regulated system drug release rate is controlled by feedback information, without any external stimulation, and utilized several approaches to control the release rate [202-205]. The feedback-regulated drug delivery concepts were schematically depicted in Figure 5. The feedback-regulated drug delivery concept has been applied to the development of various controlled delivery systems such as bio-erosion regulated, bio-responsive regulated and self-regulating drug delivery systems. Among this one of the concepts has been involved in the smart controlled delivery systems. For that various research efforts are also in progress to develop such nanoparticles that contain drugs capable of a feedback-modulated drug release. The drug release is activated by a triggering agent, such as a biochemical substance, in the body via some feedback mechanisms. The release rate has been determined by triggering agent concentration. When the triggering agent is above a certain level, the release is activated. This can induce and stop the drug release. It would be a high potential benefits if they were delivered by a system that recognized the particular warning signal caused by disease affected part, then they estimated the magnitude ratio of the signal, and then acted to release the exact quantity of active drugs in response. This kind of drug delivery system required to fulfil the physiological need by means of some feedback mechanism. The self-regulated drug delivery systems utilize several approaches for the rate-control release: pH-responsive polymers, temperature-responsive polymers, enzyme-substrate reactions, antibody interactions, enzyme-mediated, pH-dependent drug solubility nature, competitive binding mechanism and metal concentration-dependent hydrolysis. A hydrogel can swell in aqueous medium and retain their structure. The multi-functionalized polymer nanoparticle can be incorporated into hydrogel, such hydrogel used for the feedback-regulated drug delivery system. This hydrogels can protect the drug from dangerous environments such as enzymes and low pH in the stomach. This can control drug release through changing the network structure in response to particular stimuli, which can enable the sensor leads to reversible volume phase transitions upon small changes in the environment condition. For example, the polymers characterized by lower critical solution temperatures generally shrink, as the temperature is increased via lower critical solution temperature. Decreasing the temperature below lower critical solution temperature, the polymer can swell. Biomolecules can be encapsulated on or within the heat responsive polymers.

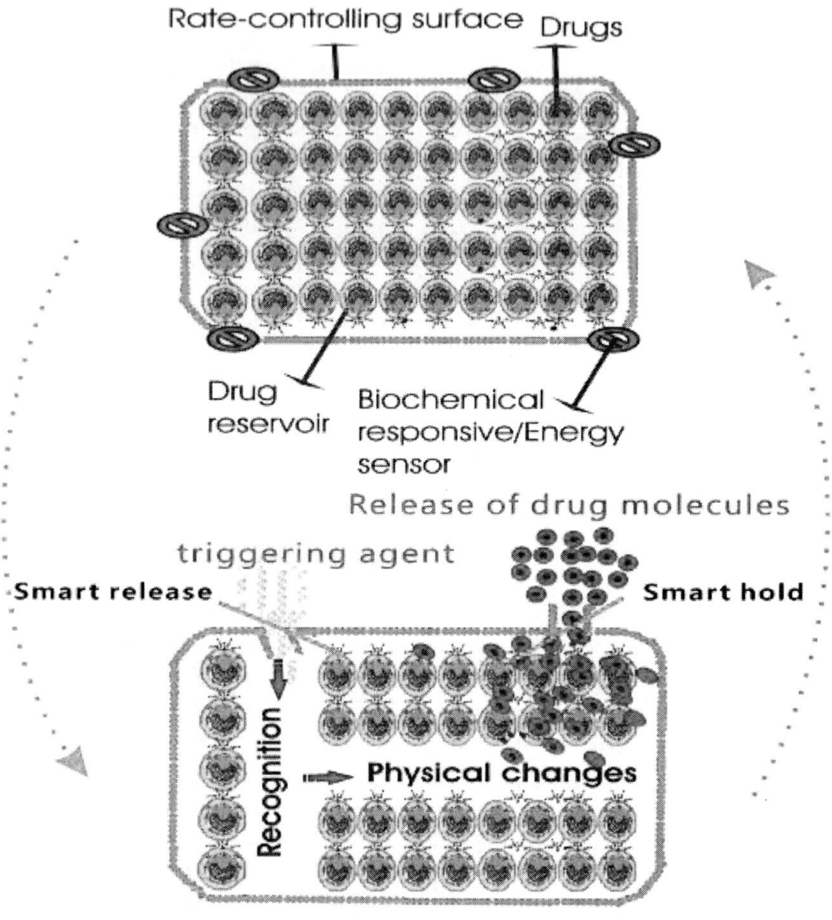

Figure 5. Schematic diagrams represent the feedback-regulated drug delivery systems

The sensor grafted in the delivery system can enable to mimic the recognition function of various bio-chemicals such as enzymes, cell mediated receptors and various proteins in human beings for maintaining the regulation and equilibrium. This approach is utilized for drug incorporated polymeric feedback controlled delivery systems, and this system approach is based on the observation that changes in control mechanisms, e.g.: pH or ionic strength or temperatures can affect large changes in drug solubility; this can be the main factor for control release rate. The external trigger molecule and polymer-bound enzyme can alter the pH inside the polymeric system. If the pH alteration happened inside the polymer system that can lead to changes in drug solubility, which is induces the diffusion or dissolution or disintegration, and rate of release has been changed accordingly. Many researchers have been developed a membrane to bypass the rumen but it allows the polymeric system to release the drug in the stomach via gastric retention mechanism [206]. Because of the polymer membrane it is impermeable to the rumen pH 7, but the swells and release at pH 4, which is the fourth stomach. Several studies have been performed on various polymers holding weakly acidic or basic functional groups in the polymeric backbone [207-112]. This polymeric system can swell or de-swell by changing the pH of the environments. By this way the drug will release from a matrix or device, which is developed by pH dependent polymers and this system can provides controlled release rates.

The bio-erosion controlled drug delivery system comprises of a drug-encapsulated bio-erodible scaffolds developed from biocompatible polymers (poly (vinyl methyl ether)), and were layered using immobilized urease. In a neutral pH the polymer erodes gradually, but in existing with urea, urea is metabolized by the system containing urea to form ammonia, it leads to increase the pH in the surrounding area, this increased pH degrade the polymer scaffolds then the drugs has been released [213], and some polymers require high pH to degrade.

The bio-responsive controlled drug delivery system, glucose-triggered insulin delivery has developed [214], the insulin is encapsulated within biocompatible polymer hydrogel scaffold comprising abundant NR2 functional groups present in the normal state. So in this state scaffolds are un-swollen and thus impermeable to insulin molecules. Enzymatically oxidized glucose is to form gluconic acid, this triggers the NR2 groups to form NR2 H+, it leads to swollen and insulin molecules deliver through the polymer membrane, and the amount of delivery has been controlled by glucose penetrating concentration.

The reversible and competitive binding mechanism also has been reported to insulin delivery. This mechanism role is to activate and to regulate the release of drug in the target; also it depends upon the glucose level present in the systemic circulation. Insulin-sugar-lectin complex has been prepared and entrapped into the semi-permeable polymeric membrane to achieve controlled release. The diffused blood glucose has competitively bound to particular binding sites, then activates the complex to release insulin derivatives, and the release acted based on the concentration of glucose presented in the systemic circulation. By this way the self-controlled drug delivery has been achieved. A further improvement on insulin delivery, they used glycosylated insulin-concanavalin A complex and entrapped inside polymeric membrane and the release has been achieved by self-regulated mechanism, depends on the glucose concentration permeate into the system [215]. Again in the development of self-regulating insulin delivery has achieved by enzymatically controlled implantable glucose-dependent insulin delivery systems [216]. Followed by various researches developed the different kinds of glucose-responsive insulin delivery [217-223]. Also the molecular imprinting technology developed system able to identify the specific compounds on the cell surface, and this can be appropriate for further developing and targeting the delivery system to specific tissues or cells. Recently, the pH-Sensitive polymer multi-functionalized with block co-polymeric nanoparticles have been developed for the triggered release of paclitaxel within a tumor microenvironment which the polymer acted as a feedback-regulated drug delivery carrier [224], and this carrier have a reversed swelling behavior. Most recently, the feedback controlled drug delivery system has been developed for cerebral cortical disorders with a feedback controlled mechanism. Drugs have been delivered via subdural/subarachnoid space, then diffuse into neocortical tissue and this diffusion can be controlled by electrophysiological feedback, the cerebral cortical area is exposed to the drug, and they were optimized for the drug concentration, delivery, frequency of delivery [225]. Moreover, the molecular imprinting technology has a huge possibility for producing acceptable dosage forms in the feedback-regulated drug delivery systems. The application of molecular imprinting enables the design of new systems and also in polymer based device fabrications. The advances in the preparation of molecular imprinting as spherical uniform particles [226] and scaffolds [227] can increase the field application potentiality of several polymers in drug delivery system. Moreover, these imprinted delivery systems have not yet touched in clinical therapeutics.

4.4. Site-targeting drug delivery systems

The recent advances in the smart delivery systems with site-targeting drug release. A site targeted drug delivery systems are complex of multiple steps of diffusion and partitioning. Nowadays the site targeted drug delivery systems involve deep investigation as they are very eager to overcome the modern medical application [228]. A well-designed multi-functionalized polymeric carrier for site-targeted drug delivery in the interventions of various diseases such as colon disease, kidney/renal disease, nasal disease and genitourinary disease has been reported recently [229-234]. A variety of both natural and synthetic water-soluble polymers have been used for biomedical applications. These polymers have been used routinely in bio-pharmaceutics because of the effectiveness in controlled drug release. The traditional formulations are not significantly efficient at targeting molecules, thus the new and smart drug delivery systems are being studied to overcome the problem. The goal of the smart drug delivery systems is to allow a localized drug delivery, at the same time; it does not affect the healthy tissues and no unwanted effects. The drugs composed of micro-or nano-sized particulate system, which is able to spread through the systemic circulation, and transport through various body organs and body areas such as arteries, veins, and capillaries and even cross membrane barriers. The nanoparticle transport and targeting tissue are the complex process, so the transportation and communication have been viewed by the molecular communication paradigm. This transport of drug-loaded particles in the human body has been viewed, where the nanoparticle has transported this information is conveyed by signaling molecule. This communication system provides a clear reading of particle diffusion, distribution, disintegration over time throughout the biological system, which provides the importance to the invention of a smart particulate delivery system. Initially, the kinetic Monte Carlo method [235, 236], have been used computer simulation to solve the communication system. Lately, researchers developed an analytical approach based on the abstraction of targeted particulate delivery systems as a communication mechanism. This information is passed between sender and receiver by intracellular and intercellular signalling [237]. Different kinds of molecular communication have been analyzed so far, which involve passive or active transport of molecules [238,239]). The smart site targeted delivery system takes an advantage of the systemic circulation for the distribution of active drug particle from where it's ingested to the systemic circulation to a targeted site. Basically, the delivery systems have been made with purpose and intention to control the rate of release from the systems, but the transport of nanoparticle to the target site still needs more control. Preferably, the route of administration and nanoparticle transport should also be strong enough controlled.

In this section also provides a few examples of site-targeted drug delivery systems, The ideal example is that the kidney site-targeted drug delivery systems, it acted as a smart delivery to enhance drug efficacy and safety in the therapeutics of kidney diseases. By this smart drug delivery treatment provides that reduces inflammation and reduce the formation of excess fibrous to proximal tubular cells, it can protect systemic infection and renal tubular inflammations. So targeting the renal proximal tubular cells is the novel and efficient routes to cure kidney disease [240-244]. Kidney-targeted drug delivery system can overcome from the various obstacles such as kidney transplantation, ureteral obstruction, diabetes, and other some important kidney disease. Figure 6 shows the kidney drug delivery of nano-particulate systems. Among all drug carriers the macromolecular carriers are extremely powerful targeting the kidney, because of the selective accumulation in the kidneys. Macromolecular carriers with prodrugs play crucial roles in targeting drugs to particular target cells in the kidney. The molecular weight and electric charge of polymers is one of the crucial role for effective renal clearance [245, 246], thus the active polymeric system can uptake and exists in the renal cells [247]. Especially the multi-functionalized polymeric nanoparticles showed higher uptake in glomerular mesangial cells [248, 249]. For nasal site-targeting specificity, the multi-functional particulate system design is the main role for site-targeting. So, design and preparation method has to be controlled

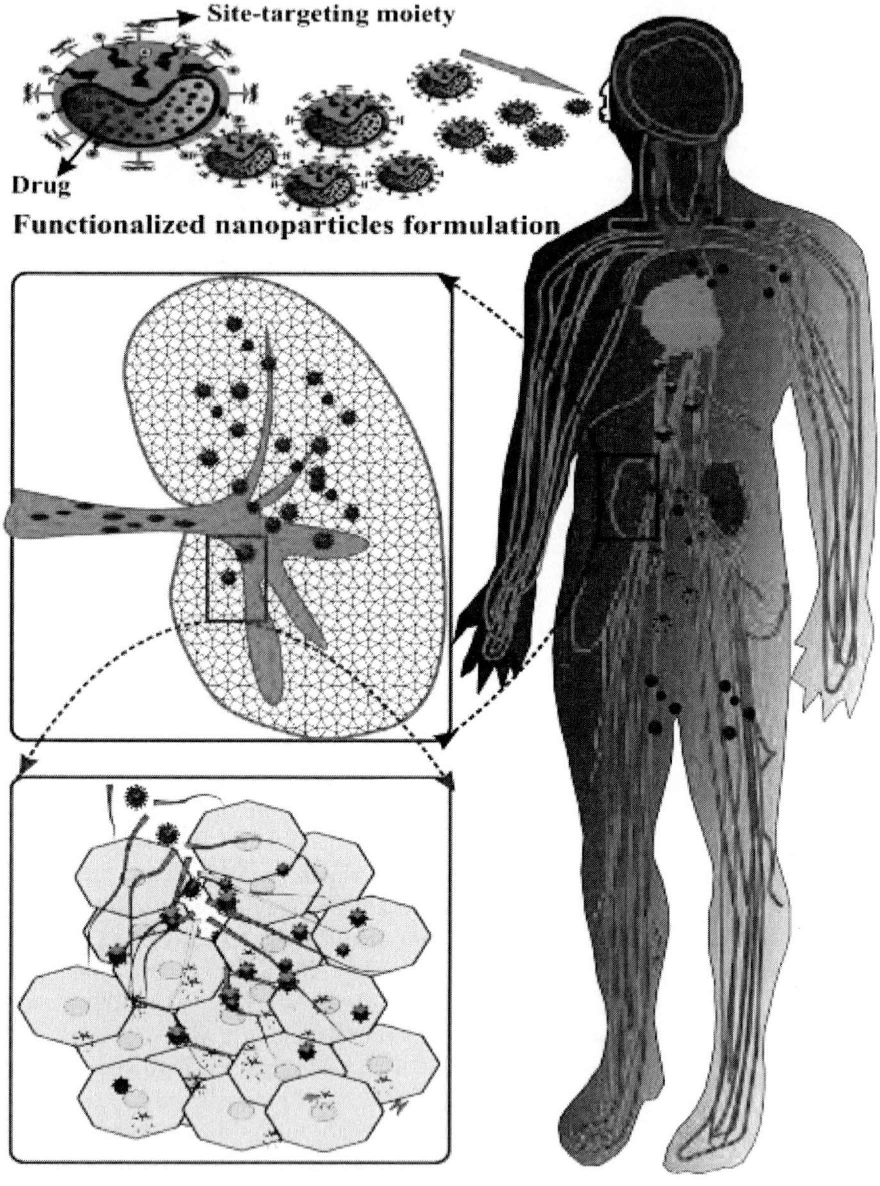

Figure 6. Schematic diagrams represent the site-targeting specificity particulate drug delivery systems

according to the needs, the materials should be with quality of properties such as biocompatible, biodegradable, modifiable, mucoadhesive, antimicrobial, tumor or particular cell recognition, and maintain the drug release. In the example, N,N,N-Trimethyl chitosan nanoparticles achieved controlled intra nasal delivery to treat various diseases including hepatitis B and allergic rhinitis [250]. Also the amine functionalized chitosan has been shown their eminent characters such as biocompatible, enhanced solubility, strength, porosity, absorption efficacy, chemical tolerance, non-immunogenic and non-antigenic properties, and it has been used for various nasal delivery.

4.5. Targeting strategies for kidney diseases

Macromolecule is a very large molecule, which can accumulate in the kidneys. Generally, the molecular weight of the macromolecular vehicle is bigger than that of the prodrugs, so this kind of system can achieve the goal. Pro-drugs have the ability to select the target in the kidney because it can release the active drug by the action of renal enzymes. The various strategies of kidney-targeted drug delivery systems has to be considered such as biodynamical strategy of renal artery perfusion, macromolecular carriers which includes enzymes, immune proteins and peptide hormones, pro-drugs which includes folate, sugars, and amino acids, and other strategies including various nano-particulate systems. The molecular weight and charge [245, 246] of polymers is the main factor, it can influence their distribution in various organs including kidney. In general, increasing the molecular weight of polymers leads to decreases urinary clearance. Some of the polymers have been eliminated rapidly from the systemic circulation but it does not excrete from the kidney, and its accumulated in the renal systems. So it clearly proposed that the selection of effective and active multi-functionalized polymeric nanoparticles can uptake by the particular kidney cell types. So the selection of polymers is one of the prime strategies for consideration to achieve the efficient kidney targeting. These new possibilities to develop kidney targeting conjugates and other nano-particulate drug delivery systems. Including various polymers based nanoparticles give excellence strategies to achieve the goal of targeting drugs to the various renal diseases.

4.6. Common strategies for smart polymeric particulate targeted delivery

The ideal proposed model for site-targeting delivery is fabricated from a biocompatible, non-immunogenic and biodegradable polymer and acts as the central of support to three main characteristics of attachments such as site-specific targeting moiety, solubilizer and drug moiety, which should have drug delivery capacity, capable of transport and active molecule should bonded to the polymer via spacer, and the linkage is cleaved by particular enzyme(s) at the final targeted site respectively. In order to develop a new polymeric vehicle for a particular drug, the polymer distribution in the systemic circulation has to be analyzed since it's right away affects on activity of drugs. For controlling the systemic distribution of drugs, we need to consider minimum two strategies which are active or passive targeting. Previously, the drug is delivered to target site using some specific antibodies, which are specific to target cell-surface [251-254]. This method gives efficient targeting to tumor site; however, the antibodies can produce immunogenic activity. But, the passive targeting with bio-polymers vehicles cannot produce immunogenicity or toxicity, this might enhance the active molecule efficacy, such as increased half-life by increased size of the nano-particulate complex, increased permeability at the targeted area and polymer vehicle interacts to the body organs. Those elements must be increase the absorption of the drug molecule; which minimize the dosage and low unwanted effects [255, 256]. Moreover, in the advanced fabrication of molecular imprinting technology can provide efficient smart polymeric systems with the ability to recognize specific bio active molecules. This advanced fabrication technology has tremendous possibility to meet the requirements for satisfactory dosage forms developments. Depends upon the particular application the fabricated systems can decide the delivery, efficiency, safety of the drugs, and when it should be reached. Described all above application strategies have a significant interest in targeting drugs into specific regions [257, 258].

5. BIOENGINEERED MATERIALS: IDEAL AND RECENT ADVANCES FOR DRUG DELIVERY SYSTEMS

5.1. Nano-engines of drug delivery systems

Engineered materials have been utilized for developing smart drug delivery systems. Design and multi-functionalities fabricate of efficient smart drug delivery systems are vitally necessary for medicine and healthcare development. In the material science field provides biodegradable, biocompatible, environment-responsive, and highly effective novel polymeric system for targeted delivery. Nanotechnology provides bottom-up and top-down nanofabrication with size controlled and multi-functionality of particulate for targeted delivery. New materials invention and advanced technology have been synergistically achieved in drug delivery so far. The essential goals of medical pharmacology provide the right medicine, right dosage, and right route at the right time to the right patient, so more research need to optimize the therapeutic efficacy of the drug. This is the essential principles is behind the smart drug delivery. A smart, controlled delivery system needs synergistic consideration of several factors; these have been summarized in Figure. 7. It is difficult to get all consideration factors in a smart controlled delivery system due to other influencing factors. Also high quality, reliability, efficiency and reproducibility are the most significant issue while designing such a smart system. Also the smart systems have to induce the drug release and stop the release by their own manner. It would be highly benefited, if the system recognizes the disease affected part, estimated the disease affected ratio, and then acted to release the exact quantity of active drugs. This kind of drug delivery system can fulfil the medicine and healthcare requirements.

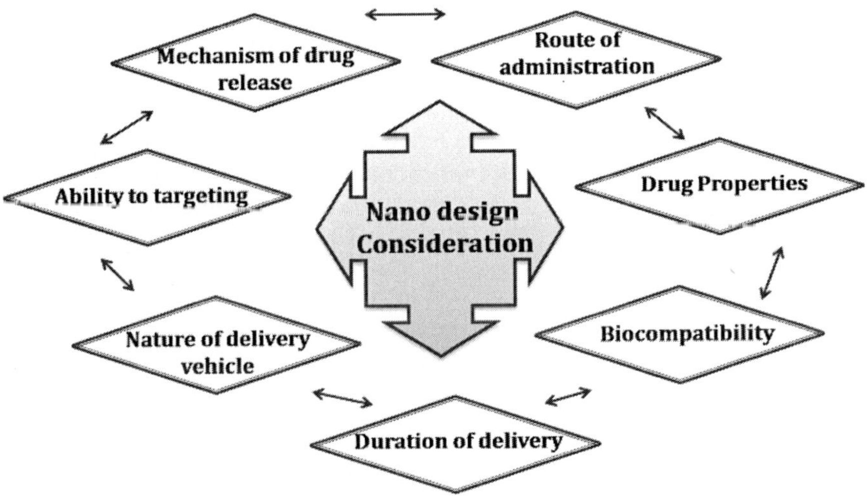

Figure 7. Requirements of several factors for simultaneous consideration to design a polymeric nanoparticle for the smart drug delivery system

6. POLYMERIC NANOPARTICLES FUNCTIONALIZATION AND CONSIDERATIONS FOR SMART APPLICATION

In this section provides the recent research on the preparation and functionalization of various polymeric hybrid nano-materials including nanoparticles and microparticles by various techniques. Several techniques have been developed for the functionalization of polymeric nanoparticles with different therapeutic applications. The polymeric nanoparticles have been studied for their enriched properties in biological systems, with the nature of the materials and whether it has the specific properties for chemical modification and functionalization of the nanoparticle developed from various materials including bio-macromolecules. There are several researchers have been studied for functionalization and surface modification of nanoparticles and it would not cover all this in this section; so, this section covers some examples of nanoparticles functionalization and some important criteria to consider the fabrication process. In addition, the richness of surface chemistry and potential biomedical applications are described. The polymeric nanoparticles surface functionalization are mainly two types, one is functionalization with biological (macro)molecules such as peptides, carbohydrates, lipids, fatty acids, proteins, and nucleic acids (genes, oligomers, aptamers, and ribozymes/DNAzymes); another one is functionalization with specific ligands such as mono-or oligosaccharides (carbohydrates), folate receptor, antibodies and biotin are commonly used. This surface functionalization have been made by various modifications on preformed nanoparticles through adsorption, functional surfactants, emulsification, polymerization, covalently bounded functional molecules and various forms of bio-conjugation. There are few considerations for functionalization of polymeric nanoparticles properties such as: 1) the bio-molecule ratio should controlled by calculating the number of conjugate sites presents in the nanoparticles with different applications, 2) due to the environment and electrostatic interactions the alignment of functionalization has been varying, so the non specific attachment should be avoided in the performed nanoparticles, 3) depends on the applications requirements the nanoparticles bio-molecule distance should be maintained, 4) control the conjugation moiety attachment/linking affinity to the performed nanoparticles, 5) should maintain the optimal efficiency of physiochemical characters and 6) it should be high reproducible for all batches. The above all criteria can fulfil the requirement of design and functionalization of nanoparticles for a controllable release profile that satisfies the desired application. And better protection against environmental factors and maximum optimal control is achieved if drug loading is carried out by encapsulation instead of adsorption on to the particle surface. With the combinations of these above criteria in the fabrication of nanoparticles are potential to increase the clinical therapeutics by reducing unwanted effects.

With the field of bio-nanotechnology, enormous new research on the synthesis of polymeric nanoparticle based top-down or bottom-up approaches have been recently developed. Recent developed polymeric systems engrafted nanoparticles provide the optimal characteristic of the functionalized nanoparticles for various therapeutic approaches in harsh environments such as in the acidic and alkali environment [259]. Also polymer nanoparticles are broadly used in several therapeutic applications, mostly cancer targeting and therapeutics. And we provide some examples of various nanoparticles with different functionalization and different therapeutic uses based on the target, shown in Table 3. Therefore, the multi-functionalized nanoparticle over comes from the drawbacks of conventional therapy. In the latest study provided that more than 26 nanoparticle based therapeutic system have been approved for clinical treatment and several nanoparticles are under consideration [281]. In order to achieve the efficient nano-particulate system based therapeutics the nanoparticle synthesis and functionalization methods have to consider very carefully. Although several surface modified methods for various bio-applications have been reported previously, in this section highlight particular examples where this type of functionalization has been used.

Table 3. Examples of various nanoparticles with different functionalization and therapeutic uses based on the target

Nanoparticles	Functionalization	Drug	Use	Refs.
Human serum albumin	Amino/acid group	Doxorubicin	Antineoplastic	[260]
Trimyristin	Sterically stabilized	Paclitaxel	Ovarian, lung, breast cancer	[261]
PLLA-b-PEG	Folate targeted	Doxorubicin	Solid tumors	[262]
PEG-PE	Lipid conjugated	Paclitaxel	Various cancers	[263]
PEG	Lipid conjugated	Tamoxifen	Lung carcinoma	[264]
Polymer-lipid hybrid	Lipid conjugated	Doxorubicin	Solid cancer	[265]
PCL-b-trimethylene carbonate-PEG	Serum protein	Ellipticin	Anticancer	[266]
PAMAM dendrimers	Folic acid	ethotrexate	Epithelial cancer	[267]
PEG	Albumin bound	Doxorubicin	Various cancers	[268]
Micelles	Biotin-antibody-conjugated	Daunomycin	Brain tumor	[269]
PLGA	Alendronate	Estrogen	Bone-osteoporosis	[270]
Poly(DEAP-Lys)-b-PEG -b-PLLA	Poly(lysine)	Doxorubicin	pH sensitive tumor	[271]
PLGA-b-PEG-COOH	PSMA	Anti cancer	Prostate- cancer	[272]
PEG or PE particles	Transferrin	Oligonucleotide	Brain- gene	[273]
PLLA-PEG	Biotin	Anti cancer	Cancer therapy	[274]
Polystyrol	Sc-TNF	Anti cancer	Cancer therapy	[275]
PLA	Aptamer	Anti cancer	Prostate cancer	[276]
PE	RGD peptides	siRNA	Vasculature cancer	[277]
mPEG/PLGA	Peptidomimetics	Anti cancer	Brain cells cancer	[278]
PLA	Galactose	Retinoic acid	Hepatocytes	[279]
PLGA	MP lipid A	Anti cancer	Dentritic cells	[280]

Functionalization is defined as the improving performance of nanoparticle by a chemical functional group on their surface. Some basic components of functionalized nanoparticle are enabling to increasing the multifunctional applications in the field of biomedicine; the basic components are diagnostic agent, targeting ligand, spacer group, therapeutic agents, and polymer nano-carrier with proper functionalization. Here we introducing two strategies for surface functionalization, first one is direct functionalization, where the functional ligand is a bi-functional compound. In this method, one of the reactive groups is used to bind to the nanoparticle surface and the second group contains the required active functionality. Another one is post-functionalization, here the strategy is not changeable and the nature of the functionalizing group cannot be compatible with good control over the size and dispersion of the nanoparticles in the solvent used for the fabrication. Commonly, the nano-carriers have been functionalized with various chemical functional groups such as thiols, disulfides, amines, nitriles, carboxylic acids, phosphines and bio-macromolecules [282-287], based on their application. The functionalization of nanoparticle is to modify their outer surface with other specific chemical agents based on the desired application. After functionalization the particle physiochemical character has been changed. Also, it is a very important step for control because it can change their size and self-organization during the formation and should not promote aggregation. The prepared polymeric nanoparticles have emerged promising technology platform for recognizing the target with navigated controlled drug delivery system. Figure 8 shows the various functionalizations of the nano-engines for the development of smart drug delivery systems (Left side) and pre-regulated nanoparticle recognizes the tumor cells not the healthy (right side). This therapeutic drug concentration reaches the tumor site not in the normal cells or tissues. Polymer base smart drug delivery can overcome the patient complaints in healthcare.

In polymeric based nano-composites fabrication, the nanoparticles is used as backbone to enhance the physiochemical characters [288-290] such as flexibility, smoothness, enough strength and stiffness, which are much essential in the field of tissue engineering and bio-medical applications. The mechanical strength of polymer based nanocomposites is low due to the poor linkage between nanoparticles and the polymer, which leads to artificial defects in the composites [291-293]. It could be engineered with the appropriate interface to enhance the flexibility, smoothness, strength, stiffness and compatibility of the composite character [294]. The advanced functionalization of the nanocomposite have been prepared with suitable surface active agents, including anionic and non-ionic surfactants, it can lead to strong linkage between the nanoparticle and the polymer. The multi-functionalized nanocomposite enhances the physicochemical properties and no untoward effect on the biological system had been reported [295]. For the hydrophobic drug the phage display technique has been used for the functionalization [296], and the bioavailability have enhanced by post-polymerization. Additionally, the post-polymerization with copolymer produces efficient targeting in the extracellular compartment of the biological system [297-300]. With the nanoparticles the polymers like PEG establishes for prolonged systemic circulation [301, 302]. For the stimuli responsive targeted drug delivery has been achieved by the functionalization of suitable materials (light or magnetic or thermal or ionic responsive material). Particularly, the magnetic induction systems have been used with functionalized magnetic nanoparticles for cell or tissue specific targeted delivery. For targeting brain delivery system the nanoparticles has been functionalized for specific or nonspecific binding mechanisms [303]. The fabrication and functionalization science has merged with software oriented technology for the development of controlled and targeted nanoparticle loaded micro-device system [304]. The recent trends in novel polymer and block co-polymer synthesis methods like radical polymerization and click chemistry has been provide well-desired multi functionality polymeric structures [305-312]. This is the potential method to fabricate the desired molecular weight polymer with well-defined characteristic features. This unique method of polymer synthesis gives the successful nano formulation for potential bio-application. The functionalized nanoparticles have been synthesized with potential biochemical moieties. Then these multi-functionalized nanoparticles have been examined for desired physicochemical property and biocompatibility.

7. RECENT DEVELOPMENTS, SIGNIFICANT ROUTE OF ADMINISTRATION AND TARGETING STRATEGIES

The route of administration of therapeutics is crucially important to cure the disease. Despite the invention of potential therapeutic moieties, the inefficient drug targeting by pills or injection on the appropriate site of the body limits therapeutics values to a larger extend. There are multiple barriers involve in the anatomical and physiological system to lack the drug efficiency, including enzymatic degradation in the stomach, absorption across the intestinal epithelium, hepatic clearance, and accumulation in non-targeted tissues. These barriers also involve a range of complexities from the tissue to the organelle level along with the time that mismatch the drug potency in vivo. Collectively, these conditions challenge the active utilization of potent therapeutic molecules for disease treatment or prevention. Extensive research has been carried out in the field of drug delivery to overcome these challenges and thus to contribute a significant role in the overall drug-development process.

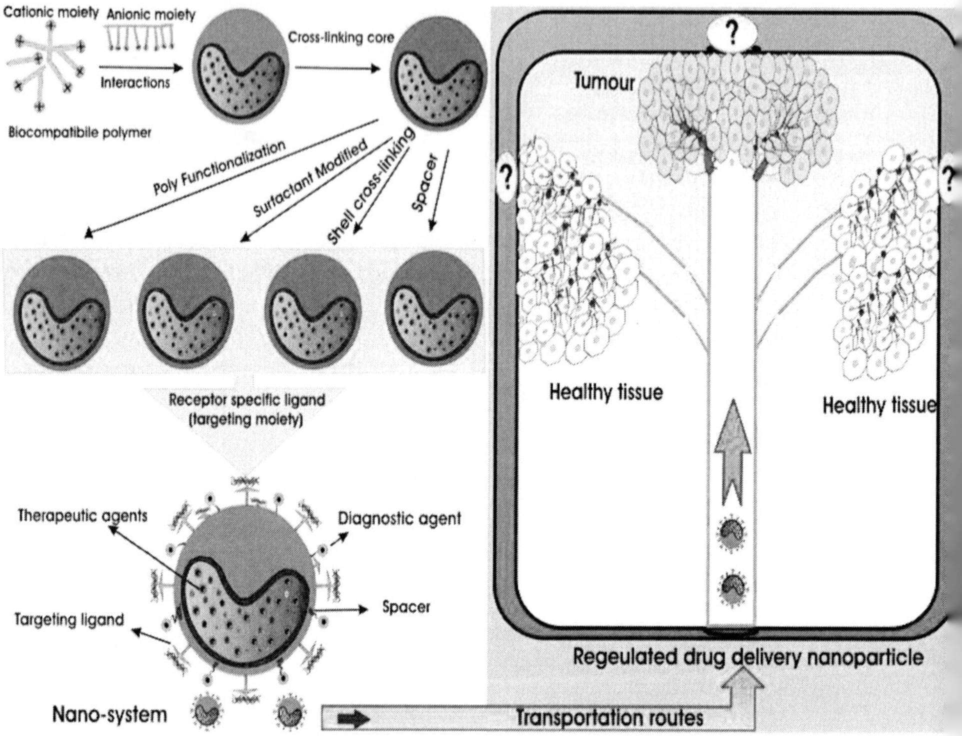

Figure 8. Schematic diagrams represent the various functionalizations of the nano-engines for smart drug delivery systems, which the pre-regulated nanoparticle recognizes the tumor cells not the healthy.

After the evolution of nanotechnology and vast increment in knowledge about the human body, advances have been achieved in the drug delivery field as targeted delivery and sustained/controlled delivery system. By tuning the kinetic properties of therapeutics, the potentiality could be secured until it reaching the targeted organ and this factor is considered to be the most important in the field of pharmacology. Progresses in the nanomaterials development have been fruitful to fulfil the goals of drug delivery. Pharmacologically, the drug delivery is better explained based on the routes of drug administrations. Development of alternative drug delivery methods is crucially important to overcome the challenges experienced throughout the history of medicine. Scientists have been working on the creation of the smart drug delivery system and such approaches could provide an easy route of administration, ensuring patient compliance, decreasing toxicity, improving bioavailability and achieving precise therapeutic targeting. Creation of smart drug carrier as delivery systems and the discovery of new pharmacological compounds will potentially advance disease diagnosis and treatment beyond expectation. A variety of novel drug delivery systems have been developed using various nanomaterials during the last decade and several of them are already marketed. Nanotechnology manipulates the multiple properties including the size and other physical characteristics and thus achieves both controlled and targeted delivery of drugs. The bio-adaptability and multi-functional properties of smart delivery system minimize the undesirable properties of drugs in various routes of administration, including oral, rectal, nasal, ocular, topical route such as transdermal, and dermal, parenteral route such as intravenous/intravascular, intramuscular, subcutaneous, intradermal/intracutaneous, intraperitoneal and intrathecal. Figure 9 depicts the tremendous applications of new nanomaterials for the development of various routes of administration and targeting for therapeutics such as transdermal vaccine delivery, intranasal vaccine delivery and lung targeted delivery. Nasal mucosa offers numerous benefits as a target tissue for drug delivery, particularly for brain targeting because drug penetration through the BBB is favored by lipophilicity.

In particular, the non-invasive intranasal delivery offers large interests in the targeted route of administration. Nasal delivery helps drugs to bypass the blood-brain barrier and hence acts as an excellent platform for brain targeting. The intranasal drug delivery several approaches should be considered, attending, specifically, to the nature of pathological condition (acute or chronic) and intended effects of drug treatment (local, systemic or at CNS). Local delivery, nasal vaccines, systemic delivery and CNS delivery through nasal route is the prime route for drug administration to treat the various diseases. So the nasal vaccination is a promising alternative to the classic parenteral route because the nasal mucosa possesses abundant nasal associated lymphoid tissue (NALT), dentritic cells, large surface area, and low proteolytic enzymes that serve as a primary defense system against pathogens. It can exhibit high drug concentration, permeation, no first-pass effect and compliance administration without enzymatic destruction. Moreover, antigens encapsulated nanoparticles ensure enhanced uptake and controlled release of antigens from the nasal vasculature membrane with strong immunogenicity and improved systemic therapeutic responses. Also, the bio-nanotechnology applied to the parenteral administrations techniques such as microneedles, jet-injections, ultrasound, iontophoresis, and electrophoresis. Theses systems extend painless, patient-friendly alternatives to injections for the delivery of molecule [313-317]. Drug administration using microneedles for the transdermal delivery routes have been reported elsewhere [318-320].

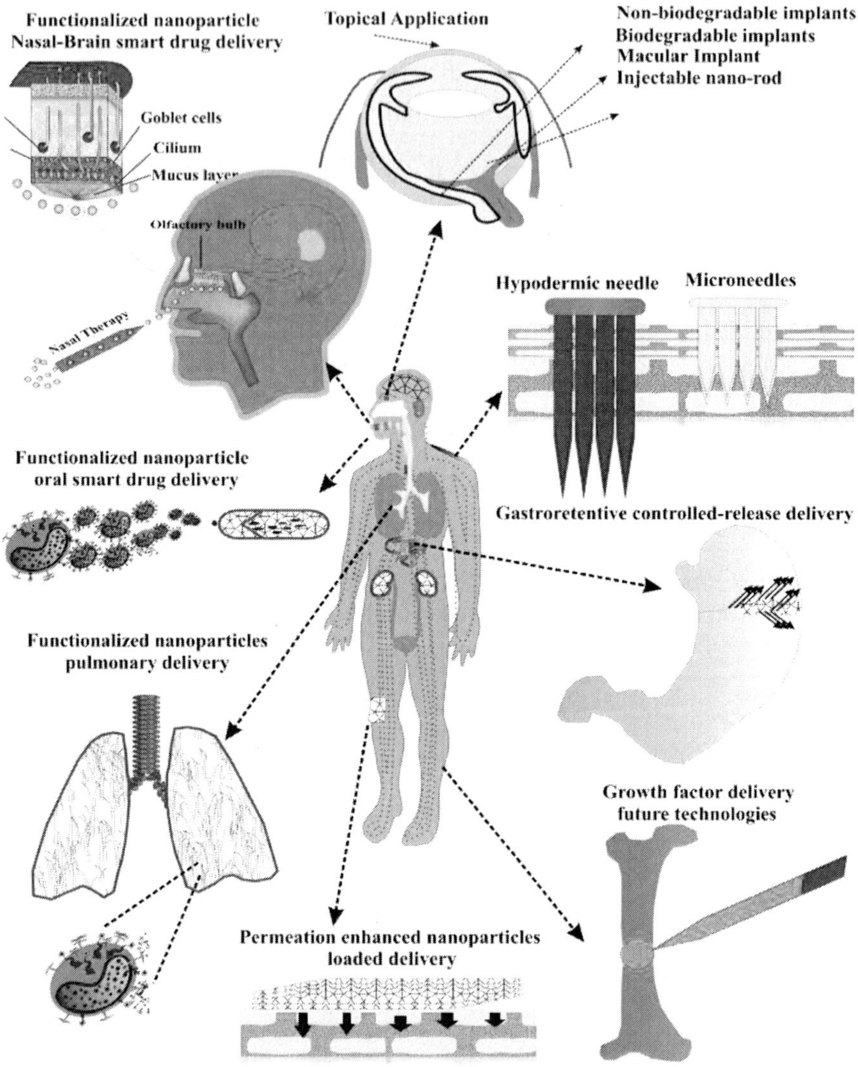

Figure 9. Schematic diagrams represent the recent developments of various significance routes of administration and targeting strategies

Microneedles are arrays of micrometer-sized shallow needles that penetrate only into the superficial layers of skin, thereby eliminating the pain associated with standard hypodermic needles [321]. Microneedles have been made from a variety of materials and in particular the polymers have been shown to be effective. They have also been produced in solid and as well as in hollow forms.

Solid microneedles are used to render skin permeable, whereas hollow microneedles actively deliver drugs into the skin at a controlled rate. In contrast, jet injectors deliver a high-velocity liquid jet stream into the skin, delivering drugs into various skin layers, depending on the jet parameters [322]. Jet injectors have a long history, particularly in the delivery of vaccines, insulin, and growth hormone. Ultrasound enhances skin permeability by cavitation, which temporarily disrupts skin structure [323]. Iontophoresis and electroporation use electric fields to alter the skin structure and/or provide additional driving force for drug penetration through the skin [324]. These new routes of administration of therapeutics with improved responses have been achieved by high drug concentration in target, permeation, no first-pass effect, high bioavailability and compliance administration without enzymatic destruction [325, 326].

8. CONCLUSION

The uses of bio-nanotechnology in therapeutics a number of unexpected inventions have been done recently on polymer based nanometers, which have great attention in the field of smart drug delivery applications. The biomaterials including protein based polymers, polysaccharide based polymers, natural or synthetic or semi-synthetic polymers, various biomaterials and combination of polymer have utilized to prepare various kinds of nano-formulations towards the smart drug delivery applications. Several polymeric nanoparticle-based therapeutic systems have been established for the treatment of various diseases. Several nanoparticle based drug delivery systems have been approved in clinical trials, some of them in under pre-clinical trial levels, this nanoparticle based system can provide the increased half-life, high biocompatibility, and minimum immunogenicity, site targeting and overcome the membrane barriers. Also the last era, major and new identifications have been drastically established in the smart material that alter its own structure and function in response to the environment. This performance has been used for the fabrication smart drug delivery systems, Smart polymer matrices release drugs by environment responses this system have been successfully achieved. In parallel the new method of bottom-up and top-down nanofabrication technologies provided precisely controlled size and shaped nano-particulate delivery system. Simultaneously, various advanced significant routes of targeting have developed and successfully achieved to the site of action. At present, the field of microfluidics for synthesis, micro-needle for transdermal and site targeted delivery is still in its infancy. So the pharmaceutical industry has to bring these products into industry-led investigation and the improvement in this would possibly to quicken their progress.

9. FUTURE PERSPECTIVES

Although there are considerable amount researches have been done in the field of drug delivery so far. In the polymeric nanoparticle based drug therapy has to be enhanced by incorporating by the combination therapies, Smart delivery has been achieved successfully in the case of cancer, but need to be concentrating more on other pathologies, also numerous challenges remain. From the material viewpoint, most of the smart delivery systems mechanism do well in vitro studies but flops the in vivo studies. So the research has to be re-considering to come up with simple, straightforward, efficient and reasonably accurate preparations with broadly applicable strategies, the pharmacologically active agent targeting to pathological sites, for the development of smart drug delivery systems. In technology vice the research has to focus into the fusion technologies. Although several specific specialized technologies have been shown to in polymer synthesis, functionalization, analysis, in vitro and in vivo study in the field of polymer science, the combinations of two or more techniques are often more effective than single technologies like a combination of controlled radical polymerization with click chemistry. The fusion technologies can fulfil the various existing drawbacks of some individual technologies, and this has the high potentiality, synergistic enhancement in safest nanoparticle based drug delivery. Consider merging and adopting two or more right technologies for getting a high-throughput technology by selecting the right combinations is a fruitful area for research that is still largely unexplored. This new understanding must be incorporated into the future of newer polymeric based nanoparticle synthesis development and evaluation of smart drug delivery. Also the next generation of polymeric nanoparticle based delivery systems with drugs like growth factors, hormones, antibodies, genes, peptides, etc.; should also enhance the efficiency and minimize the unwanted effects.

10. ACKNOWLEDGEMENTS

This work was supported by the R&D Program for Society of the National Research Foundation(NRF) funded by the Ministry of Science, ICT & Future Planning (2013M3C8A3078806 and 2013M3C1A8A01072922).

REFERENCES

1. Allemann E, Gurny R, Doelker E. Drug-Loaded Nanoparticles: Preparation Methods and Drug Targeting Issues. European Journal of Pharmaceutics and Biopharmaceutics 1993;39(5) 173-191.

2. Kawashima Y. Nanoparticulate Systems for Improved Drug Delivery. Advanced Drug Delivery Reviews 2001;47(1) 1-2.

3. Soppimath KS, Aminabhavi TM, Kulkarni AR, Rudzinski WE. Biodegradable Polymeric Nanoparticles as Drug Delivery Devices. Journal of Controlled Release 2001;70(1-2) 1-20.

4. Panyam J, Labhasetwar V. Biodegradable Nanoparticle from Drug and Gene Delivery to Cells and Tissue. Advanced Drug Delivery Reviews 2003;55(3) 329-347.

5. Brigger I, Dubernet C, Couvreur P. Nanoparticles in Cancer Therapy and Diagnosis. Advanced Drug Delivery Reviews 2002;54(5) 631-651.

6. Cui Z, Mumper RJ. Plasmid DNA-Entrapped Nanoparticles Engineered from Microemulsion Precursors: In Vitro and In Vivo Evaluation. Bioconjugate Chemistry 2002;13(6) 1319-1327.

7. Cohen H, Levy RJ, Gao J, Fishbein I, Kousaev V, Sosnowski S, Slomkowski S, Golomb G. Sustained Delivery and Expression of DNA Encapsulated in Polymeric Nanoparticles. Gene Therapy 2000;(22) 71896-1905.

8. Cao X, Lai S, Lee LJ. Design of a Self-Regulated Drug Delivery Device. Biomedical Micro devices 2001;3(2)109-118.

9. Kasagana VN, Karumuri SS, Thirumal. M. Recent Advances in Smart Drug Delivery Systems. International Journal of Pharmacy and Biotechnology 2011;1(3) 201-207.

10. Kreuter, J. Nanoparticles and Nanocapsules-New Dosage Forms in the Nanometer Range. Pharmaceutica Acta Helvetiae 1978;53(2) 33-39.

11. Kreuter J. Nanoparticles. In: Swarbrick J, Boylan JC. (ed.) Encyclopedia of Pharmaceutical Technology. Marcel Dekker Inc: New York, NY, 1994. p165-190.

12. Birrenbach G, Speiser PP. Polymerized Micelles and their use as Adjuvants in Immunology. Journal of Pharmaceutical Sciences 1976;65(12) 1763-1766.

13. Fresta M, Cavallaro G, Giammona G, Wehrli E, Puglisi G. Preparation and Characterization of Polyethyl-2-Cyanoacrylate Nanocapsules containing Antiepileptic Drugs. Biomaterials 1996;17(8) 751-758.

14. Vauthier-Holtzscherer C, Benabbou S, Spenlehauer G, Veillard M, Couvreur P. Methodology for the Preparation of Ultra-Dispersed Polymer Systems. STP Pharma Sciences 1991;1 109-116.

15. Al Khouri Fallouh N, Roblot-Treupel L, Fessi H, Devissaguet JP, Puisieux F. Development of a New Process for the Manufacture of Polyisobutylcyanoacrylate Nanocapsules. International Journal of Pharmaceutics 1986;28(2-3) 125-132.

16. Rollot JM, Couvreur P, Roblot-Treubel L, Puisieux F. Physicochemical and Morphological Characterization of Polyisobutyl Cyanoacrylate Nanocapsules. Journal of Pharmaceutical Sciences 1986;75(4) 361-364.

17. Legrand P, Barratt G, Mosqueira V, Fessi H, Devissaguet JP. Polymeric Nanocapsules as Drug Delivery Systems. A review. STP Pharma Sciences 1999;9(5) 411-418.

18. Barratt GM. Therapeutic Applications of Colloidal Drug Carriers. Pharmaceutical Science and Technology Today 2000;3(5) 163-171.

19. Fresta M, Cavallaro G, Giammona G, Wehrli E, Puglisi G. Preparation and Characterization of Polyethyl-2-Cyanoacrylate Nanocapsules containing Antiepileptic Drugs. Biomaterials 1996;17(8) 751-758.

20. Schroeder U, Sommerfeld P, Ulrich S, Sabel BA. Nanoparticle Technology for Delivery of Drugs across the Blood-Brain Barrier. Journal of Pharmaceutical Sciences 1998;87(11) 1305-1307

21. Hans ML. Lowman AM. Biodegradable Nanoparticles for Drug Delivery and Targeting. Current Opinion in Solid State and Materials Science 2002;6(4) 319-327.

22. Arshady R. Preparation of Biodegradable Microspheres and Microcapsules: 2. Polylactides and Related Polyesters. Journal of Controlled Release 1991;17(1) 1-22.

23. Bodmeier R, Chen H, Tyle P, Jarosz P. Spontaneous Formation of Drug-containing Acrylic Nanoparticles. Journal of Microencapsulation 1991;8(2) 161-170.

24. Niwa T, Takeuchi H, Hino T, Kunou N, Kawashima Y. Preparations of Biodegradable Nanospheres of Water-Soluble and Insoluble Drugs with D,L-Lactide/Glycolide Copolymer by a Novel Spontaneous

Emulsification Solvent Diffusion Method, and the Drug Release Behaviour. Journal of Controlled Release 1993;25(1-2) 89-98.

25. Leroux J-C, Allemann E, Doelker E, Gurny R. New Approach for the Preparation of Nanoparticles by an Emulsification-Diffusion Method. European Journal of Pharmaceutics and Biopharmaceutics 1995;41(3) 14-18.

26. Quintanar-Guerrero D, Fessi H, Allemann E, Doelker E. Influence of Stabilizing Agents and Preparative Variables on the Formation of Poly(D,L-Lactic Acid) Nanoparticles by an Emulsification-Diffusion Technique. International Journal of Pharmaceutics 1996;143(2) 133-141.

27. Kawashima Y, Niwa T, Handa T, Takeuchi H, Iwamoto T, Itoh K. Preparation Of Controlled-Release Microspheres of Ibuprofen with Acrylic Polymers by a Novel Quasi-Emulsion Solvent Diffusion Method. Journal of Pharmaceutical Sciences 1989;78(7) 68-72.

28. Kawashima Y, Iwamoto T, Niwa T, Takeuchi H, Hino T. Size Control of Ibuprofen Microspheres with an Acrylic Polymer by Changing the pH In an Aqueous Dispersion Medium and its Mechanism. Chemical and Pharmaceutical Bulletin 1993;41(1) 191-195.

29. Quintanar-Guerrero D, Allemann E, Doelker E, Fessi H. Preparation and Characterization of Nanocapsules from Preformed Polymers by a New Process based on Emulsification-Diffusion Technique. Pharmaceutical Research 1998;15(7) 1056-1062.

30. Allemann E, Doelker E, Gurny R. Drug Loaded Poly(lactic acid) Nanoparticles Produced by a Reversible Salting-out Process: Purification of an Injectable Dosage Form. European Journal of Pharmaceutics and Biopharmaceutics 1993;39 13-18.

31. Allemann E, Gurny R, Doelker E. Preparation of Aqueous Polymeric Nanodispersions by a Reversible Salting-Out Process: Influence of Process Parameters on Particle Size. International Journal of Pharmaceutics 1992;87(1-3) 247-253.

32. Rodrigues Jr JM, Fessi H, Bories C, Puisieux F, Devissaguet JP. Primaquine-Loaded Poly(Lactide) Nanoparticles: Physicochemical Study and Acute Tolerance in Mice. International Journal of Pharmaceutics 1995;126(1-2) 253-60.

33. Fessi H, Puisieux F, Devissaguet JP, Ammoury N, Benita S. Nanocapsule Formation by Interfacial Polymer Deposition Following Solvent

Displacement. International Journal of Pharmaceutics 1989;55(1) R1-R4

34. Peltonen L, Koistinen P, Karjalainen M, Hakkinen A, Hirvonen J. The Effect of Cosolvents on the Formulation of Nanoparticles from Low-Molecular-Weight Poly(L)Lactide. AAPS PharmSciTech 2002;3(4) E32.

35. Niwa T, Takeuchi H, Hino T, Nohara M, Kawashima Y. Biodegradable Submicron Carriers for Peptide Drugs: Preparation of Dl-Lactide/Glycolide Copolymer (PLGA) Nanospheres with Nafarelin Acetate by a Novel Emulsion-Phase Separation Method in an Oil System. International Journal of Pharmaceutics 1995;121(1) 45-54.

36. Chen X, Young TJ, Sarkari M, Williams RO 3rd, Johnston KP. Preparation of Cyclosporine a Nanoparticle by Evaporative Precipitation into Aqueous Solution. International Journal of Pharmaceutics 2002;242(1-2) 3-14.

37. Sarkari M, Brown J, Chen X, Swinnea S, Williams RO 3rd, Johnston KP. Enhanced Drug Dissolution using Evaporative Precipitation into Aqueous Solution. International Journal of Pharmaceutics 2002;243(1-2) 17-31.

38. Gomez A, Bingham D, de Juan L, Tang K. Production of Protein Nanoparticles by Electrospray Drying. Journal of Aerosol Science 1998;29(5-6) 561-574.

39. Liversidge GG, Cundy KC. Particle Size Reduction for Improvement of Oral Bioavailability of Hydrophobic Drugs: I. Absolute Oral Bioavailability of Nanocrystalline Danazol in Beagle Dogs. International Journal of Pharmaceutics 1995;125(1) 91-97.

40. Jacobs C, Kayser O, Muller RH. Nanosuspensions as a New Approach for the Formulation for the Poorly Soluble Drug Tarazepide. International Journal of Pharmaceutics 2000;196(2) 161-164.

41. Merisko-Liversidge E, Sarpotdar P, Bruno J, Hajj S, Wei L, Peltier N, Rake J, Shaw JM, Pugh S, Polin L, Jones J, Corbett T, Cooper E, Liversidge GG. Formulation and Antitumor Activity Evaluation of Nanocrystalline Suspensions of Poorly Soluble Anticancer Drugs. Pharmaceutical Research 1996;13(2) 272-278.

42. Jacobs C, Kayser O, Muller RH. Production and Characterisation of Mucoadhesive Nanosuspensions for the Formulation of Bupravaquone. International Journal of Pharmaceutics 2001;214(1-2) 3-7.

43. Merisko-Liversidge E, Liversidge GG, Cooper ER. Nanosizing: A Formulation Approach for Poorly-Water-Soluble Compounds. European Journal of Pharmaceutical Sciences 2003;18(2) 113-120.

44. Muller CR, Schaffazick SR, Pohlmann AR, de Lucca Freitas L, Pesce da Silveira N, Dalla Costa T, Guterres SS. Spray-Dried Diclofenac-Loaded Poly(E-Caprolactone) Nanocapsules and Nanospheres. Preparation and Physicochemical Characterization. Pharmazie 2001;56(11) 864-867.

45. Vergote GJ, Vervaet C, Van Driessche I, Hoste S, De Smedt S, Demeester J, Jain RA, Ruddy S, Remon JP. An Oral Controlled Release Matrix Pellet Formulation Containing Nanocrystalline Ketoprofen. International Journal of Pharmaceutics 2001;219(1-2) 81-87.

46. Bodmeier R, Wang H, Dixon DJ, Mawson S, Johnston KP. Polymeric Microspheres Prepared by Spraying into Compressed Carbon Dioxide. Pharmaceutical Research 1995;12(8) 1211-1217.

47. Reverchon E. Supercritical Antisolvent Precipitation of Micro-and Nano-Particles. Journal of Supercritical Fluids 1999;15(1) 1-21.

48. Reverchon E. Della Porta G. Production of Antibiotic Micro-and Nano Particles by Supercritical Antisolvent Precipitation. Powder Technology 1999;106 23-29.

49. Reverchon E, Marco De I, Della Porta G. Rifampicin Micoparticles Production by Supercritical Antisolvent Precipitation. International Journal of Pharmaceutics 2002;243(1-2) 83-91.

50. Rogers TL, Johnston KP, Williams RO 3rd. Solution-based Particle Formation of Pharmaceutical Powders by Supercritical or Compressed Fluid Co2 and Cryogenic Spray-Freezing Technologies. Drug Development and Industrial Pharmacy 2001;27(10) 1003-1015.

51. Tom JW, Debenedetti PG. Particle Formation with Supercritical Fluids-A Review. Journal of Aerosol Science 1991;22(5) 555-584.

52. Tu LS, Dehghani F, Forster NR. Micronisation and Microencapsulation of Pharmaceuticals using a Carbon Dioxide Antisolvent. Powder Technology 2002;126(2) 134-149

53. Broadhead J, Rouan SKE, Rhodes CT. The Spray Drying of Pharmaceuticals. Drug Development and Industrial Pharmacy 1992;18(11-12) 1169-1206.

54. Giunchedi P, Conte U. Spray-Drying as a Preparation Method of Microparticulate Drug Delivery System: An Overview. STP Pharma Sciences 1995;5 276-290.

55. Nielsen F. Spray Drying Pharmaceuticals. Manufacturing Chemist 1982;57 38-41.

56. Esposito E, Cervellati F, Menegatti E, Nastruzzi C, Cortesi R. Spray Dried Eudragit Microparticles as Encapsulation Devices for Vitamin C. International Journal of Pharmaceutics 2002;242(1-2) 329-334.

57. Bodmeier, R. and Chen, H. Preparation of Biodegradable Poly(+)Lactide Microparticles using a Spray-Drying Technique. Journal of Pharmacy and Pharmacology 1988;40(11) 754-757.

58. Wang FJ, Wang CH. Sustained Release of Etanidazole from Spray Dried Microspheres Prepared by Non-Halogenated Solvents. Journal of Controlled Release 2002;81(3) 263-280.

59. Pignatello R, Vandelli MA, Giunchedi P, Puglisi G. Properties of Tolmetin-Loaded Eudragit RL100 and Eudragit RS100 Microparticles Prepared by Different Techniques. STP Pharma Sciences 1997;7 148-157.

60. Magenheim B, Benita S. Nanoparticle Characterization: A Comprehensive Physicochemical Approach. STP Pharma Sciences 1991;1 221-241.

61. Muller RH, Jacobs C, Kayser O. Nanosuspensions as Particulate Drug Formulations in Therapy Rationale for Development and what can we expect for the Future. Advanced Drug Delivery Reviews 2001;47(1) 3-19.

62. Palakodaty S, York P. Phase Behavioural Effects on Particle Formation Processes using Supercritical Fluids. Pharmaceutical Research 1999;16(7) 976-985.

63. Kong DF, Goldschmidt-Clermont PJ. Tiny Solutions for Giant Cardiac Problems. Trends in Cardiovascular Medicine 2005;15(6)207-11.

64. Khafagy el S, Morishita M, Onuki Y, Takayama K. Current Challenges in Non-Invasive Insulin Delivery Systems: A Comparative Review. Advanced Drug Delivery Reviews 2007;59(15) 1521-46.

65. Ferrari M. Cancer Nanotechnology: Opportunities and Challenges. Nature Reviews. Cancer 2005;5(3) 161-71.

66. Duncan R. Polymer Conjugates as Anticancer Nanomedicines. Nature Reviews. Cancer 2006; 6(9) 688-701.

67. Nasir A. Nanodermatology: A Bright Glimpse just Beyond the Horizon-Part I. Skin Therapy Letter 2010;15(8) 1-4.

68. Gupta S, Bansal R, Gupta S, Jindal N, Jindal A. Nanocarriers and Nanoparticles for Skin Care and Dermatological Treatments. Indian Dermatology Online Journal 2013;4(4) 267-272.

69. Silva GA. Neuroscience Nanotechnology: Progress, Opportunities and Challenges. Nature Reviews. Neuroscience 2006;7(1) 65-74.

70. Pardridge WM, Blood-Brain Barrier Delivery. Drug Discovery Today 2007;12(1-2) 54-61.

71. Nuxoll E. BioMEMS in Drug Delivery. Advanced Drug Delivery Reviews 2013;65(11-12) 1611-25.

72. Wang Y, Byrne JD., Napier ME, DeSimone JM. Engineering Nanomedicines using Stimuli-Responsive Biomaterials. Advanced Drug Delivery Reviews 2012;64(11) 1021-1030.

73. Shim TS, Kim S, Yang S, Elaborate Design Strategies Toward Novel Microcarriers for Controlled Encapsulation and Release. Particle and Particle Systems Characterization 2013;30(1) 9-45.

74. Christopher GF, Anna SL. Microfluidic Methods for Generating Continuous Droplet Streams. Journal of Physics D: Applied Physics 2007;40(19) R319-R336.

75. Dendukuri D, Doyle PS. The Synthesis and Assembly of Polymeric Microparticles using Microfluidics. Advanced Materials 2009;21(41) 4071-4086.

76. Valencia PM, Farokhzad OC, Karnik R, Langer R. Microfluidic Technologies for Accelerating the Clinical Translation of Nanoparticles. Nature Nanotechnology 2012;7(10) 623-9.

77. Choi DH, Subbiah R, Kim IH, Han DK, Park K. Dual Growth Factor Delivery using Biocompatible Core-Shell Microcapsules for Angiogenesis. Small 2013;9(20) 3468-76.

78. Luttge R, Berenschot E, De Boer M, Altpeter D, Vrouwe E, Van den Berg A, Elwenspoek M. Integrated Lithographic Molding for Microneedle-Based Devices. Journal of Microelectromechanical Systems 2007;6(4) 872-884.

79. Park J, Allen M, Prausnitz M, Biodegradable Polymer Microneedles: Fabrication, Mechanics and Transdermal Drug Delivery, Journal of Controlled Release 2005;104(1) 51-66.

80. Wendorf JR, Ghartey-Tagoe EB, Williams SC, Enioutina E, Singh P, Cleary GW, Transdermal Delivery of Macromolecules using Solid-State Biodegradable Microstructures. Pharmaceutical Research 2011;28(1) 22-30.

81. Raphael AP, Prow TW, Crichton ML, Chen X, Fernando GJP, Kendall MAF, Targeted Needle-Free Vaccinations in Skin Using Multilayered, Densely-Packed Dissolving Microprojection Arrays. Small 2010;6(16) 1785-1793.

82. Kronenberg HM. Developmental Regulation of the Growth Plate. Nature 2003;423(6937) 332-336.

83. Karsenty G. The Complexities of Skeletal Biology. Nature 2003;423(6937) 316-318.

84. Zhuang J, Wu H, Yang Y, Cao YC. Controlling Colloidal Superparticle Growth through Solvophobic Interactions. Angewandte Chemie 2008;47(12) 2208-2212.

85. Manoharan VN, Elsesser MT, Pine DJ. Dense Packing and Symmetry in Small Clusters of Microspheres. Science 2003;301(5632) 483-487.

86. Brannon-Peppas L. Recent Advances on the use of Biodegradable Microparticles Andnanoparticles in Controlled Drug Delivery. International Journal of Pharmaceutics 1995;116(1) 1-9.

87. Marimuthu M, Bennet D, Kim S. Self-assembled Nanoparticles OF PLGA-Conjugated Glucosamine as a Sustained Transdermal Drug Delivery Vehicle. Polymer Journal 2013;45 202-209

88. Kopecek J, Kopeckova P, Minko T, Lu ZR, Peterson CM. Water Soluble Polymers in Tumor Targeted Delivery. Journal of Controlled Release 2001;74(1-3) 147-158.

89. Nakanishi T, Fukushima S, Okamoto K, Suzuki M, Matsumura Y, Yokoyama M, Okano T, Sakurai Y, Kataoka K. Development of the Polymer Micelle Carrier System for Doxorubicin. Journal of Controlled Release 2001;74(1-3) 295-302,

90. Tian Y, Bromberg L, Lin SN, Alan Hatton T, Tam KC. Complexation and Release of Doxorubicin from its Complexes with Pluronic P85-b-

Poly(Acrylic Acid) Block Copolymers. Journal of Controlled Release 2007;121(3) 137-145.

91. Cao T, Munk P, Ramireddy C, Tuzar Z, Webber SE. Fluorescence Studies of Amphiphilic Poly(Methacrylic Acid)-Block-Polystyrene-Block-Poly(Methacrylic Acid) Micelles. Macromolecules 1991;24(23) 6300-6305.

92. Zhang L, Yu K, Eisenberg A. Ion-Induced Morphological Changes in "Crew-Cut" Aggregates of Amphiphilic Block Copolymers. Science 1996;272(5269) 1777-1779.

93. Discher DE, Eisenberg A. Polymer Vesicles. Science 2002;2979(5583) 967-973.

94. Lee CM, Tanaka T, Murai T, Kondo M, Kimura J, Su W, Kitagawa T, Ito T, Matsuda H, Miyasaka M. Novel Chondroitin Sulfate-Binding Cationic Liposomes Loaded with Cisplatin Efficiently Suppress the Local Growth and Liver Metastasis of Tumor Cells In Vivo. Cancer Research 2002;62(15) 4282-4288.

95. Gabizon AA. Selective Tumor Localization and Improved Therapeutic Index of Anthracyclines Encapsulated in Long-Circulating Liposomes. Cancer Research 1992;52(4) 891-896.

96. Cleland JL, Lim A, Barron L, Duenas ET, Powell MF. Development of a Single-Shot Subunit Vaccine for HIV-1: Part 4. Optimizing Microencapsulation and Pulsatile Release of MN rgp120 from Biodegradable Microspheres. Journal of Controlled Release 1997;47(2) 135-150.

97. Rilling P, Walter T, Pommershein R, Vogt W. Encapsulation of Cytochrome C by Multilayer Microcapsules. A Model for Improved Enzyme Immobilization. Journal of Membrane Science 1997;129(2) 283-287.

98. Fonseca T, Relogio P, Martinho JMG, Farinha JPS. Preparation and Surface Characterization of Polymer Nanoparticles Designed for Incorporation into Hybrid Materials. Langmuir 2007;23(10) 5727-5734.

99. Sajjadi S. Population Balance Modeling of Particle Size Distribution in Monomer-Starved Semibatch Emulsion Polymerization. AIChE Journal 2009;55(12) 3191-3205.

100. Hui Wang, Garry L, Rempel. pH-Responsive Polymer Core-Shell Nanospheres for Drug Delivery. Journal of Polymer Science, Part A: Polymer Chemistry 2013;51(20) 4440-4450

101. Valencia PM, Farokhzad OC, Karnik R, Langer R. Microfluidic Technologies for Accelerating the Clinical Translation of Nanoparticles. Nature Nanotechnology 2012;7(10) 623-9.

102. DeMello AJ. Control and Detection of Chemical Reactions in Microfluidic Systems. Nature 2006;442(7101) 394-402.

103. Capretto L, Cheng W, Hill M, Zhang X. Micromixing within Microfluidic Devices. Topics in Current Chemistry 2011;304 27-68.

104. Rhee M, Valencia PM, Rodriguez MI, Langer R, Farokhzad OC, Karnik R. Synthesis of Size-Tunable Polymeric Nanoparticles Enabled by 3D Hydrodynamic Flow Focusing in Single-Layer Microchannels. Advanced Materials 2011;23(12) H79–H83.

105. Liu K, Wang H, Chen KJ, Guo F, Lin WY, Chen YC, Phung DL, Tseng HR, Shen CK. A Digital Microfluidic Droplet Generator Produces Self-Assembled Supramolecular Nanoparticles for Targeted Cell Imaging. Nanotechnology 2010;21(44) 445603.

106. Valencia PM, Basto PA, Zhang L, Rhee M, Langer R, Farokhzad OC, Karnik R. Single-Step Assembly of Homogenous Lipid-Polymeric and Lipid-Quantum Dot Nanoparticles Enabled by Microfluidic Rapid Mixing. ACS Nano 2010;4(3) 1671-1679.

107. Jahn A, Reiner JE, Vreeland WN, DeVoe DL, Locascio LE, Gaitan M. Preparation of Nanoparticles by Continuous-Flow Microfluidics. Journal of Nanoparticle Research 2008;10(6) 925-934.

108. Bennet D, Kim S. A Transdermal Delivery System to Enhance Quercetin Nanoparticle Permeability, Journal of Biomaterials Science. Polymer Edition 2013;24(2) 185-209.

109. Bennet D, Marimuthu M, Kim S, An J. Dual Drug-Loaded Nanoparticles on Self-Integrated Scaffold for Controlled Delivery. International Journal of Nanomedicine 2012;2012(7) 3399-419.

110. Srinivasa PC, Ramesh MN, Tharanathan RN. Effect of Plasticizers and Fatty Acids on Mechanical and Permeability Characteristics of Chitosan Films. Food Hydrocolloids 2007;21(7) 1113-22.

111. Zhang ML, Gong XH, Zhao YD, Zhang NM. Properties and Biocompatibility of Chitosan Films Modified by Blending with PEG. Biomaterials 2002;23(13) 2641-8

112. Badet C, Furiga A, Thebaud N. Effect of Xylitol on an In Vitro Model of Oral Biofilm. Oral Health & Preventive Dentistry 2008;6(4) 337-41.

113. Chandy T, Mooradian DL, Rao GH. Chitosan/Polyethylene Glycol-Alginate Microcapsules for Oral Delivery of Hirudin. Journal of Applied Polymer Science 1998;70(11) 2143-2153.

114. Rajangam T, Paik HJ, An SSA. Development of Fibrinogen Microspheres as a Biodegradable Carrier for Tissue Engineering. BioChip Journal 2011;5(2) 175-183.

115. Bromberg LE, Ron ES. Temperature-Responsive Gels and Thermogelling Polymer Matrices for Protein and Peptide Delivery. Advanced Drug Delivery Reviews 1998;31(3)197-221.

116. Jain GK, Sharma AK, Agrawal SS. Transdermal Controlled Administration of Verapamil-Enhancement of Skin Permeability. International Journal of Pharmaceutics 1996;130(2) 169-177.

117. Ding H, Triggle CR. Endothelial Cell Dysfunction and the Vascular Complications Associated with Type 2 Diabetes: Assessing the Health of the Endothelium. Vascular Health and Risk Management 2005;1(1) 55-71.

118. Chien YW. Novel Drug Delivery Systems: 2nd ed, Revised and Expanded; Marcel Dekker, Inc.: New York, 1992.

119. Chien YW. Rate-Control Drug Delivery Systems: Controlled Release vs. Sustained Release. Medical Progress Through Technology 1989;15(1-2) 21-46.

120. Robinson JR. Sustained and Controlled Release Drug Delivery Systems; Marcel Dekker, Inc.: New York, 1978.

121. Hsieh DST. Subcutaneous Controlled Delivery of Estradiol by Compudose Implants: In Vitro and In Vivo Evaluations. Drug Development and Industrial Pharmacy 1987;13(15) 2651-2666.

122. Segal SJ. The Development of NORPLANT Implants. Studies in Family Planning 1983;14(6-7) 159-163.

123. Diaz S, Pavez M, Miranda P, Robertson DN, Sivin I, Croxatto HB. A five-Year Clinical Trial of Levonorgestrel Silastic Implants (Norplant 2). Contraception 1982;25(5) 447-456.

124. Weiner E, Victor A, Johansson ED. Plasma Levels of D-Norgestrel after Oral Administration. Contraception 1976;14(5) 563-570.

125. Croxatto HB, Diaz S, Miranda P, Elamsson K, Johansson ED. Plasma Levels of Levonorgestrel in Women during Longterm use of Norplant. Contraception 1981;23(2) 197-209.

126. Chien YW. Microsealed Drug Delivery Systems: Theoretical Aspects and Biomedical Assessments. In Recent Advances in Drug Delivery Systems; Anderson, JM, Kim, SW. Ed. Plenum Press: New York; 1984. p367-387.

127. Sunil K, Anil K, Vaibhav G, Kuldeep M, Pankaj R. Oral Extended Release Drug Delivery System A Promising Approach. Asian Pharma Press. Asian Journal of Research in Pharmaceutical Sciences 2012;2(3) 101-106.

128. Chien YW. Novel Drug Delivery Systems: Fundamental, Developmental Concepts and Biomedical Assessments; Marcel Dekker, Inc.: New York, 1982.

129. Haznar-Garbacz D, Garbacz G, Eisenacher F, Klein S, Weitschies W. A Novel Liquefied Gas based Oral Controlled Release Drug Delivery System for Liquid Drug Formulations. European journal of Pharmaceutics and Biopharmaceutics 2012;81(2) 334-8.

130. Rajesh A, Jaimin P, Sangeeta A. A Novel Approach: Pulsatile Drug Delivery System. International Research Journal of Pharm 2012;3(9) 43-49

131. Hsieh, DST, Langer R. Zero-order Drug Delivery Systems with Magnetic Control. In Controlled Release Delivery Systems; Roseman TJ, Mansdorf SZ. Ed. Marcel Dekker, Inc.: New York, 1983.

132. Tyle P, Agrawala P. Drug Delivery by Phonophoresis. Pharmaceutical Research 1989;6(5) 355-361.

133. Dhote V, Bhatnagar P, Mishra PK, Mahajan SC, Mishra DK. Iontophoresis: A Potential Emergence of a Transdermal Drug Delivery System. Scientia pharmaceutica 2012;80(1) 1-28.

134. Okahata Y, Hachiya S, Ariga K, Seki T. The Electrical Breakdown and Permeability Control of a Bilayer-Corked Capsule Membrane in an External Electric Field. Journal of the American Chemical Society 1986;108(11) 2863-2869.

135. Kwon IC, Bae YH, Kim SW. Electrically Erodible Polymer Gel for Controlled Release of Drugs. Nature 1991;354(6350) 291-293.

136. Foss AC, Goto T, Morishita M, Peppas NA. Development of Acrylic-based Copolymers for Oral Insulin Delivery. European Journal of Pharmaceutics and Biopharmaceutics 2004;57(2) 163-169.

137. Ramachandran S, Shaheedha SM, Thirumurugan G, Dhanaraju MD. Floating Controlled Drug Delivery System of Famotidine Loaded Hollow Microspheres (Microballoons) in the Stomach. Current Drug Delivery 2010;7(1) 93-7.

138. Chu LY, Yamaguchi T, Nakao S. A Molecular-Recognition Microcapsule for Environmental Stimuli-Responsive Controlled Release. Advanced Materials 2002;14(5) 386-389.

139. Heller J. Biodegradable Polymers in Controlled Drug Delivery. Critical Reviews in Therapeutic Drug Carrier Systems 1984;1(1) 39-90.

140. Morimoto Y, Fujimoto S. Albumin Microspheres as Drug Carriers. Critical Reviews in Therapeutic Drug Carrier Systems 1985;2(1) 19-63.

141. Veronese FM, Schiavon O, Pasut G, Mendichi R, Andersson L, Tsirk A, Ford J, Wu G, Kneller S, Davies J, Duncan R. PEG-Doxorubicin Conjugates: Influence of Polymer Structure on Drug Release, In Vitro Cytotoxicity, Biodistribution, and Antitumor Activity. Bioconjugate Chemistry 2005;16(4) 775-784.

142. You L-C, Lu F-Z, Li Z-C, Zhang W, Li F-M, Glucose-Sensitive Aggregates Formed by Poly(Ethylene Oxide)-Block-Poly(2-Glucosyloxyethyl Acrylate) with Concanavalin A in Dilute Aqueous Medium. Macromolecules 2003;36(1) 1-4.

143. Prausnitz MR, Langer R. Transdermal Drug Delivery. Nature biotechnology 2008;26(11) 1261-8.

144. Kaneko Y, Nakamura S, Sakai K, Kikuchi A, Aoyagi T, Sakurai Y, Okano T. Synthesis and Swelling-Deswelling Kinetics of Poly(n-Isopropylacrylamide) Hydrogels Grafted with LCST Modulated Polymers. Journal of Biomaterials Science. Polymer Edition 1999;10(11) 1079-1091.

145. Nakayama M, Okano T, Miyazaki T, Kohori F, Sakai K, Yokoyama M. Molecular Design of Biodegradable Polymeric Micelles for Temperature-Responsive Drug Release, Journal of Controlled Release 2006;115(1) 46-56.

146. Irie M. Stimuli-Responsive Poly(N-Isopropylacrylamide). Photo and Chemical-Induced Phase Transitions. Advances in Polymer Science 1993;110 49-65.

147. Suzuki A, Tanaka T. Phase Transition in Polymer Gels Induced by Visible Light. Nature 1990;346 345-347.

148. Thambi T, Deepagan VG, Yoon HY, Han HS, Kim SH, Son S, Jo DG, Ahn CH, Suh YD, Kim K, Kwon IC, Lee DS, Park JH. Hypoxia-Responsive Polymeric Nanoparticles for Tumor-Targeted Drug Delivery. Biomaterials 2014;35(5) 1735-43.

149. Schmaljohann D. Thermo-and pH-Responsive Polymers in Drug Delivery. Advanced Drug Delivery Reviews 2006;58(15)1655-70.

150. Wei H, Zhang XZ, Cheng H, Chen WQ, Cheng SX, Zhuo RX. Self-Assembled Thermo-and pH Responsive Micelles of Poly(10-Undecenoic Acid-B-N-Isopropylacrylamide) for Drug Delivery. Journal of Controlled Release 2006;116(3) 266-74.

151. Medeiros SF, Santos AM, Fessi H, Elaissari A. Stimuli-Responsive Magnetic Particles for Biomedical Applications. International Journal of Pharmaceutics 2011;403(1-2) 139-61.

152. Cheng R, Meng F, Deng C, Klok HA, Zhong Z. Dual and Multi-Stimuli Responsive Polymeric Nanoparticles for Programmed Site-Specific Drug Delivery. Biomaterials 2013;34(14) 3647-57.

153. Torchilin V. Tumor Delivery of Macromolecular Drugs based on the EPR Effect. Advanced Drug Delivery Reviews 2011;63(3) 131-5.

154. Hrkach J, Von Hoff D, Mukkaram Ali M, Andrianova E, Auer J, Campbell T, De Witt D, Figa M, Figueiredo M, Horhota A, Low S, McDonnell K, Peeke E, Retnarajan B, Sabnis A, Schnipper E, Song JJ, Song YH, Summa J, Tompsett D, Troiano G, Van Geen Hoven T, Wright J, LoRusso P, Kantoff PW, Bander NH, Sweeney C, Farokhzad OC, Langer R, Zale S. Preclinical Development and Clinical Translation of a PSMA-Targeted Docetaxel Nanoparticle with a Differentiated Pharmacological Profile. Science Translational Medicine 2012;4(128) 128ra139.

155. Gong J, Chen MW, Zheng Y, Wang SP, Wang YT. Polymeric Micelles Drug Delivery System in Oncology. Journal of Controlled Release 2012;159(3) 312-23.

156. Deng C, Jiang YJ, Cheng R, Meng FH, Zhong ZY. Biodegradable Polymeric Micelles for Targeted and Controlled Anticancer Drug Delivery: Promises, Progress and Prospects. Nano Today 2012;7(5) 467-80.

157. Meng FH, Cheng R, Deng C, Zhong ZY. Intracellular Drug Release Nanosystems. Materials Today 2012;15(10) 436-42.

158. Ganta S, Devalapally H, Shahiwala A, Amiji M. A Review of Stimuli-Responsive Nanocarriers for Drug and Gene Delivery. Journal of Controlled Release 2008;126(3) 187-204.

159. Meng FH, Zhong ZY, Feijen J. Stimuli-Responsive Polymersomes for Programmed Drug Delivery. Biomacromolecules 2009;10(2) 197-209.

160. Rapoport N. Physical Stimuli-Responsive Polymeric Micelles for Anti-Cancer Drug Delivery. Progress in Polymer Science 2007;32(8-9) 962-90.

161. Chen W, Meng FH, Li F, Ji SJ, Zhong ZY. pH-Responsive Biodegradable Micelles based on Acid-Labile Polycarbonate Hydrophobe: Synthesis and Triggered Drug Release. Biomacromolecules 2009;10(7) 1727-35.

162. Du JZ, Tang YQ, Lewis AL, Armes SP. pH-Sensitive Vesicles based on a Biocompatible Zwitterionic Diblock Copolymer. Journal of the American Chemical Society 2005;127(51) 17982-3.

163. Saito G, Swanson JA, Lee KD. Drug Delivery Strategy Utilizing Conjugation via Reversible Disulfide Linkages: Role and Site of Cellular Reducing Activities. Advanced Drug Delivery Reviews 2003;55(2) 199-215.

164. Meng FH, Hennink WE, Zhong ZY. Reduction-Sensitive Polymers and Bio-Conjugates for Biomedical Applications. Biomaterials 2009;30(12) 2180-98.

165. Cheng R, Feng F, Meng FH, Deng C, Feijen J, Zhong ZY. Glutathione-Responsive Nano-Vehicles as a Promising Platform for Targeted Intracellular Drug and Gene Delivery. Journal of Controlled Release 2011;152(1) 2-12.

166. Kuppusamy P, Li H, Ilangovan G, Cardounel AJ, Zweier JL, Yamada K, Krishna MC, Mitchell JB. Noninvasive Imaging of Tumor Redox Status and its Modification by Tissue Glutathione Levels. Cancer Research 2002;62(1) 307-12.

167. Chan A, Orme RP, Fricker RA, Roach P. Remote and Local Control of Stimuli Responsive Materials for Therapeutic Applications. Advanced Drug Delivery Reviews 2013;65(4) 497-514.

168. Alvarez-Lorenzo C, Bromberg L, Concheiro A. Light-Sensitive Intelligent Drug Delivery Systems. Photochemistry and Photobiology 2009;85(4) 848-60.

169. Chilkoti A, Dreher MR, Meyer DE, Raucher D. Targeted Drug Delivery by Thermally Responsive Polymers. Advanced Drug Delivery Reviews 2002;54(5) 613-30.

170. Wei H, Cheng SX, Zhang XZ, Zhuo RX. Thermo-Sensitive Polymeric Micelles based on Poly(N-Isopropylacrylamide) as Drug Carriers. Progress in Polymer Science 2009;34(9) 893-910.

171. Arruebo M, Fernandez-Pacheco R, Ibarra MR, Santamaria J. Magnetic Nano-Particles for Drug Delivery. Nano Today 2007;2(3) 22-32.

172. Sun C, Lee JSH, Zhang M. Magnetic Nanoparticles in MR Imaging and Drug Delivery. Advanced Drug Delivery Reviews 2008;60(11) 1252-65.

173. Xu HF, Meng FH, Zhong ZY. Reversibly Crosslinked Temperature-Responsive Nano-Sized Polymersomes: Synthesis and Triggered Drug Release. Journal of Materials Chemistry 2009;19(24) 4183-90.

174. Cheng R, Meng FH, Ma SB, Xu HF, Liu HY, Jing XB, Zhong Z. Reduction and Temperature Dual-Responsive Crosslinked Polymersomes for Targeted Intracellular Protein Delivery. Journal of Materials Chemistry 2011;21(47) 19013-20.

175. Dai J, Lin SD, Cheng D, Zou SY, Shuai XT. Interlayer-Crosslinked Micelle with Partially Hydrated Core Showing Reduction and pH Dual Sensitivity for Pin-Pointed Intracellular Drug Release. Angewandte Chemie 2011;50(40):9404-8.

176. Soppimath KS, Tan DCW, Yang YY. pH-Triggered Thermally Responsive Polymer Core-Shell Nanoparticles for Drug Delivery. Advanced Materials 2005;17(3) 318-23.

177. Zhang LY, Guo R, Yang M, Jiang XQ, Liu BR. Thermo and pH Dual-Responsive Nanoparticles for Anti-Cancer Drug Delivery. Advanced Materials 2007;19(19) 2988-92

178. Lo CL, Lin KM, Hsiue GH. Preparation and Characterization of Intelligent Core-Shell Nanoparticles based on Poly(D, L-lactide)-g-Poly(N-Isopropyl-Acryl-Amide-Co-Methacrylic Acid). Journal of Controlled Release 2005;104(3) 477-88.

179. Li W, Li JF, Gao J, Li BH, Xia Y, Meng YC, Yu Y, Chen H, Dai J, Wang H, Guo Y. The Fine-Tuning of Thermosensitive and Degradable Polymer Micelles for Enhancing Intracellular Uptake and Drug Release in tumors. Biomaterials 2011;32(15) 3832-44.

180. Xing ZM, Wang CL, Yan J, Zhang L, Li L, Zha LS. Dual stimuli responsive hollow nanogels with IPN structure for temperature controlling drug loading and pH triggering drug release. Soft Matter 2011;7(18) 7992-7.

181. Zhang JC, Wu LL, Meng FH, Wang ZJ, Deng C, Liu H, Zhong Z. pH and Reduction Dual-Bioresponsive Polymersomes for Efficient Intracellular Protein Delivery. Langmuir 2011;28(4) 2056-65.

182. Bahadur KCR, Thapa B, Xu P. pH and Redox Dual Responsive Nanoparticle for Nuclear Targeted Drug Delivery. Molecular Pharmaceutics 2012;9(9) 2719-29.

183. Chen J, Qiu XZ, Ouyang J, Kong JM, Zhong W, Xing MMQ. pH and Reduction Dual-Sensitive Copolymeric Micelles for Intracellular Doxorubicin Delivery. Biomacromolecules 2011;12(10) 3601-11.

184. Pan YJ, Chen YY, Wang DR, Wei C, Guo J, Lu DR, Chu CC, Wang CC. Redox/pH Dual Stimuli-Responsive Biodegradable Nanohydrogels with Varying Responses to Dithiothreitol and Glutathione for Controlled Drug Release. Biomaterials 2012; 33(27) 6570-9.

185. Shao Y, Huang W, Shi C, Atkinson ST, Luo J. Reversibly Crosslinked Nanocarriers for On-Demand Drug Delivery in Cancer Treatment. Therapeutic delivery 2012;3(12) 1409-27.

186. Barick KC, Singh S, Jadhav NV, Bahadur D, Pandey BN, Hassan PA. pH-Responsive Peptide Mimic Shell Cross-Linked Magnetic Nanocarriers for Combination Therapy. Advanced Functional Materials 2012;22(23) 4975-4.

187. Zhao ZH, Huang DT, Yin ZY, Chi XQ, Wang XM, Gao JH. Magnetite Nanoparticles as Smart Carriers to manipulate the Cytotoxicity of Anticancer Drugs: Agnetic Control and pH-Responsive Release. Journal of Materials Chemistry 2012;22(31) 15717-5.

188. Gan Q, Lu XY, Yuan Y, Qian JC, Zhou HJ, Lu X, Shi J, Liu C. A Magnetic, Reversible pH-Responsive Nanogated Ensemble based on Fe3O4 Nanoparticles-Capped Mesoporous Silica. Biomaterials 2011;32(7) 1932-2.

189. Gan Q, Lu XY, Dong WJ, Yuan Y, Qian JC, Li YS, Shi J, Liu C. Endosomal pH-Activatable Agnetic Nanoparticle-Capped Mesoporous Silica for Intracellular Controlled Release. Journal of Materials Chemistry 2012;22(31) 15960-8.

190. Xu HF, Meng FH, Zhong ZY. Reversibly Crosslinked Temperature-Responsive Nano-Sized Polymersomes: Synthesis and Triggered Drug Release. Journal of Materials Chemistry 2009;19(24) 4183-90.

191. Cheng R, Meng FH, Ma SB, Xu HF, Liu HY, Jing XB, Zhong Z. Reduction and Temperature Dual-Responsive Crosslinked Polymersomes for Targeted Intracellular Protein Delivery. Journal of Materials Chemistry 2011;21(47) 19013-20.

192. Du JZ, Du XJ, Mao CQ, Wang J. Tailor-Made Dual pH-Sensitive Polymer-Doxorubicin Nanoparticles for Efficient Anticancer Drug Delivery. Journal of the American Chemical Society 2011;133(44) 17560-3.

193. Sankaranarayanan J, Mahmoud EA, Kim G, Morachis JM, Almutairi A. Multi-Response Strategies to Modulate Burst Degradation and Release from Nanoparticles. ACS Nano 2010;4(10) 5930-6.

194. Li YP, Xiao WW, Xiao K, Berti L, Luo J, Tseng HP, Fung G, Lam KS. Well-Defined, Reversible Boronate Crosslinked Nanocarriers for Targeted Drug Delivery in Response to Acidic pH Values AND Cis-Diols. Angewandte Chemie 2012;124(12) 2918-23.

195. Liu TY, Hu SH, Liu KH, Shaiu RS, Liu DM, Chen SY. Instantaneous Drug Delivery of Magnetic/Thermally Sensitive Nanospheres by a High-Frequency Magnetic Field. Langmuir 2008;24(23) 13306-11.

196. Chen C, Geng J, Pu F, Yang XJ, Ren JS, Qu XG. Polyvalent Nucleic Acid/Meso-Porous Silica Nanoparticle Conjugates: Dual Stimuli-Responsive Vehicles for Intracellular Drug Delivery. Angewandte Chemie 2011;123(4) 912-6.

197. Klaikherd A, Nagamani C, Thayumanavan S. Multi-Stimuli Sensitive Amphiphilic Block Copolymer Assemblies. Journal of American Chemical Society 2009;131(13) 4830-8.

198. Chang BS, Sha XY, Guo J, Jiao YF, Wang CC, Yang WL. Thermo and pH Dual Responsive, Polymer Shell Coated, Magnetic Mesoporous Silica Nanoparticles for Controlled Drug Release. Journal of Materials Chemistry 2011;21(25) 9239-47.

199. Bilalis P, Chatzipavlidis A, Tziveleka LA, Boukos N, Kordas G. Nanodesigned Magnetic Polymer Containers for Dual Stimuli Actuated Drug Controlled Release and Magnetic Hyperthermia Mediation. Journal of Materials Chemistry 2012;22(27) 13451-4.

200. Wang K, Guo DS, Wang X, Liu Y. Multistimuli Responsive Supramolecular Vesicles based on the Recognition of P-

Sulfonatocalixarene and its Controllable Release of Doxorubicin. ACS Nano 2011;5(4) 2880-94.

201. Loh XJ, Jesus del B, Toh PPC, Lee TC, Jiao DZ, Rauwald U, Appel EA, Scherman OA. Triply Triggered Doxorubicin Release from Supramolecular Nanocontainers. Biomacromolecules 2012;13(1) 84-91.

202. Heller J, Self-regulated drug delivery systems. Medical Device and Diagnostic Industry 1985;7 32-37.

203. Zhao L, Xiao C, Ding J, He P, Tang Z, Pang X, Zhuang X, Chen X. Facile One-Pot Synthesis of Glucose-Sensitive Nanogel via Thiol-ene Click Chemistry for Self-Regulated Drug Delivery. Acta Biomaterialia 2013;9(5) 6535-43.

204. Heller J. Chemically Self-Regulated Drug Delivery Systems. Journal of Controlled Release 1988;8(2) 111-125.

205. Zhou G, Lu Y, Zhang H, Chen Y, Yu Y, Gao J, Sun D, Zhang G, Zou H, Zhong Y. A novel pulsed drug-delivery system: polyelectrolyte layer-by-layer coating of chitosan-alginate microgels. International Journal of Nanomedicine 2013;8 877-87.

206. Singh BN, Kim KH. Floating Drug Delivery Systems: An Approach to Oral Controlled Drug Delivery via Gastric Retention. Journal of Controlled Release 2000;63(3) 235-59.

207. Alhaique F, Marchetti M, Riccieri F, Santucci E. A Polymeric Film Responding in Diffusion Properties to Environmental PH Stimuli: A Model for a Self-Regulating Drug Delivery System. The Journal of pharmacy and pharmacology 1981;33(7) 413-6.

208. Alhaique F, Riccieri FM, Santucci E, Crescezi V, Gamini A. A Possible pH-Controlled Drug Delivery System based on a Derivative of the Polysaccharide Scleroglucan, Journal of Pharmacy and Pharmacology 1984;37(5) 310-313.

209. Bala K, Vasudevan P. pH-Sensitive Microcapsules for Drug Release, Journal of Pharmaceutical Sciences 1982;71(8) 960-962.

210. Okahata Y, Ozaki K, Seki T. pH-Sensitive Permeability Control of Polymer Grafted Nylon Capsule Membranes. Journal of the Chemical Society, Chemical Communications 1984;(8) 518-521.

211. Okahata Y, Seki T, pH-Sensitive Capsule Membranes. Reversible Permeability Control from the Dissociative Bilayer-Coated Capsule

Membrane by an Ambient pH Change. Journal of American Chemical Society 1984;106(26) 8065–8070.

212. Siegel RA, Firestone BA. pH-Dependent Equilibrium Swelling Properties of Hydrophobic Polyelectrolyte Copolymer Gels. Macromolecules 1988;21(11) 3254-3259.

213. Heller J, Trescony PV. Controlled Drug Release by Polymer Dissolution. II: Enzyme-Mediated Delivery Device. Journal of Pharmaceutical Sciences 1979;68(7) 919-921.

214. Trehan A, Ali A. Recent Approaches in Insulin Delivery. Drug Development and Industrial Pharmacy 1998;24(7) 589-97.

215. Jeong SY, Kim SW, Eenink MJD, Feijen J. Self-Regulating Insulin Delivery Systems. I. Synthesis and Characterization of Glycosylated Insulin. Journal of Controlled Release 1984;1(1) 57-66.

216. Fischel-Ghodsian F, Brown L, Mathiowitz E, Brandenburg D, Langer R. Enzymatically Controlled Drug Delivery. Proceedings of the National Academy of Sciences of the United States of America 1988;85(7) 2403-2406.

217. Hassan CM, Doyle III FJ, Peppas NA.Dynamic Behavior of Glucose-Responsive Poly(methacrylic acid-g-ethylene glycol) Hydrogels. Macromolecules 1997;30 6166-6173.

218. Kost J, Horbett TA, Ratner BD, Singh M. Glucose Sensitive Membranes Containing Glucose Oxidase: Activity, Swelling and Permeability Studies. Journal of Biomedical Materials Research 1985;19(9) 1117-1133.

219. Albin G, Horbett TA,. Ratner BD. Glucose Sensitive Membranes for Controlled Delivery of Insulin: Insulin Transport Studies. Journal of Controlled Release 1985;2 153-164.

220. Jin X, Zhang X, Wu Z, Teng D, Zhang X, Wang Y, Wang Z, Li C. Amphiphilic Random Glycopolymer Based on Phenylboronic Acid: Synthesis, Characterization, and Potential as Glucose-Sensitive Matrix. Biomacromolecules 2009;10(6) 1337-45.

221. Ishihara K, Kobayashi M, Shonohara I. Insulin Permeation through Amphiphilic Polymer Membranes having 2-Hydroxyethyl Methacrylate Moiety. Polymer Journal 1984;16 647-651.

222. Ishihara K, Matsui K. Glucose Responsive Insulin Release from Polymer Capsule. Journal of Polymer Science Part C: Polymer Letters 1986;24(8) 413-417.

223. Ishihara K. Glucose-Responsive Polymers for Controlled Insulin Release. Proceedings International Symposium Controlled Release Bioact. Mater. 1988;15 168-169.

224. You JO, Auguste DT. Feedback-Regulated Paclitaxel Delivery based on Poly(N,N-Dimethylaminoethyl Methacrylate-Co-2-Hydroxyethyl Methacrylate) Nanoparticles. Biomaterials 2008;29(12) 1950-7.

225. Ludvig N, Medveczky G, Rizzolo R, Tang HM, Baptiste SL, Doyle WK, Devinsky O, Carlson C, French JA, Kral JG, Charchaflieh J, Kuzniecky RI. An Implantable Triple-Function Device for Local Drug Delivery, Cerebrospinal Fluid Removal and EEG Recording in the Cranial Subdural/Subarachnoid Space of Primates. Journal of Neuroscience Methods 2012;203(2) 275-83.

226. Hiratani H, Alvarez-Lorenzo C. The Nature of Backbone Monomers Determines the Performance of Imprinted Soft Contact Lenses as Timolol Drug Delivery Systems. Biomaterials 2004;25(6) 1105-13.

227. Duffy DJ, Das K, Hsu SL, Penelle J, Rotello VM, Stidham HD. Binding Efficiency and Transport Properties of Molecularly Imprinted Polymer Thin Films. Journal of the American Chemical Society 2002;124(28) 8290-6.

228. Kumar N. Handbook of Particulate Drug Delivery (Nanotechnology book Series). Valencia, CA, USA: American Scientific Publishers, 2008, vol. 1.

229. Yamamoto Y, Tsutsumi Y, Yoshioka Y, Nishibata T, Kobayashi K, Okamoto T, Mukai Y, Shimizu T, Nakagawa S, Nagata S, Mayumi T. Site-Specific PEGylation of a Lysine-Deficient TNF-Alpha with Full Bioactivity. Nature Biotechnology 2003;21(5) 546-552.

230. Farokhzad OC, Dimitrakov JD, Karp JM, Khademhosseini A, Freeman MR, Langer R. Drug Delivery Systems in Urology--Getting "Smarter". Urology 2006;68(3) 463-9.

231. Patel MP, Patel RR, Patel JK. Chitosan Mediated Targeted Drug Delivery System: A Review. Journal of Pharmaceutical Sciences 2010;13(4) 536-57.

232. Kishida A. A Site-Specific Polymeric Drug Carrier for Renal Disease Treatment. Trends in Pharmacological Sciences 2003;24(12) 611-3.

233. Liu L, Fishman ML, Kost J, Hicks KB. Pectin-Based Systems for Colon-Specific Drug Delivery via Oral Route. Biomaterials. 2003;24(19) 3333-43.

234. Shirota K, Kato Y, Suzuki K, Sugiyama Y. Characterization of Novel Kidney-Specific Delivery System using an Alkylglucoside Vector. Journal of Pharmacology and Experimental Therapeutics 2001;299(2) 459-67.

235. Heaton LL, Lopez E, Maini PK, Fricker MD, Jones NS. Advection, Diffusion, and Delivery over a Network. Physical Review. E, Statistical, Nonlinear, and Soft Matter Physics 2012;86(2 pt 1) 021905-10.

236. Watkins PK, Walker AB, Verschoor GL. Dynamical Monte Carlomodeling of Organic Solar Cells: The Dependence of Internal Quantum Efficiency on Morphology. Nano Letters 2005;5(9) 1814-1818.

237. Basu S, Gerchman Y, Collins CH, Arnold FH, Weiss R. A Synthetic Multicellular System for Programmed Pattern Formation. Nature 2005;434(7037) 1130-4.

238. Pierobon M, Akyildiz I. Capacity of a Diffusion-based Molecular Communication System with Channel Memory and Molecular Noise. IEEE Transactions on Information Theory 2013;59(2) 942-954.

239. Moore M, Enomoto A, Nakano T, Egashira R, Suda T, Kayasuga A, Kojima H, Sakakibara H, Oiwa K. A Design of a Molecular Communication System for Nanomachines using Molecular Motors. Pervasive Computing and Communications Workshops, 2006. PerCom Workshops 2006. Fourth Annual IEEE International Conference 2006; 6 p559.

240. Haas M, Mooletmar F, Meijer DK, de Zeeuw D. Specific Drug Delivery to the Kidney. Cardiovascular Drugs and Therapy 2002;16(6) 489-96.

241. Kitamura M, Fine LG. The Concept of Glomerular Self-Defense. Kidney International 1999;55(5) 1639-71.

242. Christensen EI, Bim H, Verroust P, Moestrup SK. Membrane Receptors For Endocytosis in the Renal Proximal Tubule. International Review Of Cytology 1998;180 237-84.

243. Leung S, Bendayan R. Role of P-Glycoprotein in the Renal Transport of Dideoxynucleoside Analog Drugs. Canadian Journal of Physiology and Pharmacology 1999;77(8) 625-30.

244. van Ginneken CA, Russel FG. Saturable Pharmacokineticsin the Renal Excretion of Drugs. Clinical Pharmacokinetics 1989;16(1) 38-54.

245. Brenner BM, Hostetter TH, Humes HD. Glomerular Permselectivity: Barrier Function based on Discrimination of Molecular Size and Charge. The American Journal of Physiology 1978;234(6) F455-F460.

246. Takakura Y, Fujita T, Hashida M, Sezaki H. Disposition Characteristics of Macromolecules in Tumor-Bearing Mice. Pharmaceutical Research 1990;7(4) 339-346.

247. Kamada H, Tsutsumi Y, Sato-Kamada K, Yamamoto Y, Yoshioka Y, Okamoto T, Nakagawa S, Nagata S, Mayumi T. Synthesis of a Poly(Vinylpyrrolidone-Co-Dimethyl Maleic Anhydride) Co-Polymer and its Application for Renal Drug Targeting. Nature Biotechnology 2003;21(4) 399-404.

248. Manil L, Davin JC, Duchenne C, Kubiak C, Foidart J, Couvreur P, Mahieu P. Uptake of Nanoparticles by Rat Glomerular Mesangial Cells In Vivo and In Vitro. Pharmaceutical Research 1994;11(8) 1160-5.

249. Choi CH, Zuckerman JE, Webster P, Davis ME. Targeting Kidney Mesangium by Nanoparticles of Defined Size. Proceedings of the National Academy of Sciences of the United States of America 2011;108(16) 6656-61.

250. Subbiah R, Ramalingam P, Ramasundaram S, Kim DY, Park K, Ramasamy MK, Choi KJ. N,N,N-Trimethyl Chitosan Nanoparticles for Controlled Intranasal Delivery of HBV Surface Antigen. Carbohydrate Polymers 2012;89(4) 1289-1297.

251. Brich Z, Ravel S, Kissel T, Fritsch J, Schoffmann A. Preparation and Characterization of a Water Soluble Dextran Immunoconjugate of Doxorubicin and the Monoclonal Antibody. Journal of Controlled Release 1992;19(1-3) 245-258.

252. Igarashi R, Mizushima Y, Takenaga M, Matsumoto K, Morizawa Y, Yasuda A. A Stable PGE1 Prodrug for Targeting Therapy. Journal of Controlled Release 1992;20(1) 37-46.

253. Kopecek J. Targetable Polymeric Anticancer Drugs. Temporal Control of Drug Activity. Annals of the New York Academy of Sciences 1991;618 335-344.

254. Nishikawa M, Ohtsubo Y, Ohno J, Fujita T, Koyama Y, Yamashita F, Hashida M, Sezaki H. Pharmacokinetics of Receptor-Mediated Hepatic

Uptake of Glycosylated Albumin in Mice. International Journal of Pharmaceutics 1992;85(1-3) 75-85.

255. Yamaoka T, Tabata Y, Ikada Y. Fate of water-Soluble Polymers Administered via Different Routes. Journal of pharmaceutical sciences 1995;84(3) 349-354.

256. Yamaoka T, Tabata Y, Ikada Y. Distribution and Tissue Uptake of Poly (Ethylene Glycol) with Different Molecular Weights after Intravenous Administration to Mice. Journal of Pharmaceutical Sciences 1994;83(4) 601-606.

257. Wang G, Kuroda K, Enoki T, Grosberg A, Masamune S, Oya T, Takeoka Y, Tanaka T. Gel Catalysts That Switch On and Off. Proceedings of the National Academy of Sciences of the United States of America 2000;97(18) 9861-4.

258. Alvarez-Lorenzo C, Concheiro A. Molecularly Imprinted Polymers for Drug Delivery. Journal of chromatography. B, Analytical Technologies in the Biomedical and Life Sciences 2004;804(1) 231-45.

259. Guo Z, Pereira T, Choi O, Wang Y, Hahn HT. Surface Functionalized Alumina Nanoparticle Filled Polymeric Nanocomposites with Enhanced Mechanical Properties. Journal of Materials Chemistry 2006;16(1) 2800-2808.

260. Dreis S, Rothweiler F, Michaelis M, Cinatl J, Kreuter J, Langer K. Preparation, Characterization and Maintenance of Drug Efficacy of Doxorubicin-Loaded Human Serum Albumin (HSA) Nanoparticles. International Journal of Pharmaceutics 2007;341(1-2) 207-214.

261. Lee MK, Lim SJ, Kim CK. Preparation, Characterization and In Vitro Cytotoxicity of Paclitaxel-Loaded Sterically Stabilized Solid Lipid Nanoparticles. Biomaterials 2007;28(12) 2137-2146.

262. Lee ES, Na K, Bae YH. Polymeric Micelle for Tumor pH and Folate-Mediated Targeting. Journal of Controlled Release 2003;91(1-2) 103-113.

263. Wang J, Mongayt D, Torchilin VP. Polymeric Micelles for Delivery of Poorly Soluble Drugs: Preparation and Anticancer Activity In Vitro of Paclitaxel Incorporated into Mixed Micelles based on Poly(Ethylene Glycol)-Lipid Conjugate and Positively Charged Lipids. Journal of Drug Targeting 2005;13(1-2) 73-80.

264. Gao Z, Lukyanov A, Singhal A, Torchilin V. Diacyllipid-Polymer Micelles as Nanocarriers for Poorly Soluble Anticancer Drugs. Nano Letters 2002;2(9) 979-982.

265. Wong HL, Rauth AM, Bendayan R, Wu XY. In Vivo Evaluation of a New Polymer–Lipid Hybrid Nanoparticle (Pln) Formulation of Doxorubicin in a Murine Solid Tumor Model. European Journal of Pharmaceutics and Biopharmaceutics 2007;65(3) 300-308.

266. Liu J, Zeng F, Allen C. Influence of Serum Protein on Polycarbonate-based Copolymer Micelles as a Delivery System for a Hydrophobic Anti-Cancer Agent. Journal of Controlled Release 2005;103(2) 481-497.

267. Latallo JF, Candido KA, Cao Z, Nigavekar SS, Majoros IJ, Thomas TP, Balogh LP, Khan MK, Baker J. Nanoparticles Targeting of Anticancer Drug Improves Therapeutic Response in Animal Model of Human Epithelial Cancer. Cancer Research 2005;65(12) 5317-5324.

268. Wosikowski K, Biedermann E, Rattel B, Breiter N, Jank P, Loser R, Jansen G, Peters GJ. In Vitro and In Vivo Antitumor Activity of Methotrexate Conjugated to Human Serum Albumin in Human Cancer Cells. Clinical Cancer Research 2003;9(5) 1917-1926.

269. Schnyder A, Krahenbuhl S, Drewe J, Huwyler J. Targeting of Daunomycin using Biotinylated Immunoliposomes: Pharmacokinetics, Tissue Distribution and In Vitro Pharmacological Effects. Journal of Drug Targeting 2005;13(5) 325-335.

270. Choi SW, Kim JH. Design of Surface Modified Poly (D, L-Lactide-Co-Glycolide) Nanoparticles for Targeted Drug Delivery to Bone. Journal of Controlled Release 2007;122(1) 24-30.

271. Oh KT, Oh YT, Oh NM, Kim K, Lee DH, Lee ES. A Smart Flower-Like Polymeric Micelle for PH-Triggered Anticancer Drug Release. International Journal Of Pharmaceutics 2009;375(1-2) 163-169.

272. Cheng J, Teply BA, Sherifi I, Sung J, Luther G, Gu FX, Levy-Nissenbaum E, Radovic-Moreno AF, Langer R, Farokhzad OC. Formulation of Functionalized PLGA-PEG Nanoparticles for In Vivo Targeted Drug Delivery. Biomaterials 2007;28(5) 869-876.

273. Vinogradov SV, Batrakova EV, Kabanov AV. Nanogels for Oligonucleotide Delivery to the Brain. Bioconjugate Chemistry 2004;15(1) 50-60.

274. Patil YB, Toti US, Khadir A, Ma L, Panyam J. Single-Step Surface Functionalization of Polymeric Nanoparticles for Targeted Drug Delivery. Biomaterials 2009;30(5) 859-866.

275. Messerschmidt SKE, Musyanovych A, Altvater M, Scheurich P, Pfizenmaier K, Landfester K, Kontermann RE. Targeted Lipid-Coated Nanoparticles: Delivery of Tumor Necrosis Factor-Functionalized Particles to Tumor Cells. Journal of Controlled Release 2009;137(1) 69-77.

276. Farokhzad OC, Jon S, Khademhosseini A, Tran TT, LaVan A, Langer R. Nanoparticle-Aptamer Bioconjugates: A New Approach for Targeting Prostate Cancer Cells. Cancer Research 2004;64(21) 7668-7672.

277. Schiffelers RM, Ansari A, Xu J, Zhou Q, Tang Q, Storm G, Molema G, Lu PY, Scaria PV, Woodle MC. Cancer siRNA Therapy by Tumor Selective Delivery with Ligand-Targeted Sterically Stabilized Nanoparticle. Nucleic Acids Research 2004;32(19) e149-e150.

278. Olivier JC. Drug Transport to Brain with Targeted Nanoparticles. NeuroRx 2005;2(1) 108-119.

279. Cho CS, Cho KY, Park IK, Kim SH, Sasagawa T, Uchiyama M, Akaike T. Receptor-Mediated Delivery of All Trans-Retinoic Acid to Hepatocyte Using Poly(L-Lactic Acid) Nanoparticles Coated with Galactose-Carrying Polystyrene. Journal of Controlled Release 2001;77(1-2) 7-15.

280. Elamanchili P, Diwan M, Cao M, Samuel J. Characterization of Poly(D,L-Lactic-Co-Glycolic Acid) based Nanoparticulate System for Enhanced Delivery of Antigens to Dendritic Cells. Vaccine 2004;22(19) 2406-2412.

281. Zhang L, Gu FX, Chan JM, Wang AZ, Langer RS, Farokhzad OC. Nanoparticles in Medicine: Therapeutic Applications and Developments. Clinical Pharmacology and Therapeutics 2008;83(5) 761-769.

282. Roux S, Garcia B, Bridot JL, Salome M, Marquette C, Lemelle L, Gillet P, Blum L. Perriat P, Tillement O. Synthesis and Characterization of Dihydrolipoic Acid Capped Gold Nanoparticles and Functionalization by the Electroluminescent Luminal. Langmuir 2005;21(6) 2526-2536.

283. Zatats M, Katz E, Baron R, Willner I. Reconstitution of Apo Glucose Dehydrogenase on Pyrroloquinoline Quinine-Functionalized Au Nanoparticles Yields an Electrically Contacted Biocatalyst. Journal of the American Chemical Society 2005;127(35) 12400-12406.

284. Ulman A. Formation and Structure of Self-Assembled Monolayers. Chemical Reviews 1996;96(4) 1533-1554.

285. Fan H, Chen Z, Brinker CJ, Clawson J, Alam T. Synthesis of Organo-Silane Functionalized Nanocrystal Micelles and their Self-Assembly. Journal of the American Chemical Society 2005;127(40) 13746-13747.

286. Ramirez E, Jansat S, Philippot K, Lecante P, Gomez M, Masdeu-Bulto AM, Chaudret B. Influence of Organic Ligands on the Stabilization of Palladium Nanoparticles. Journal of Organometallic Chemistry 2004;689(24) 4601-4610.

287. Woehrle GH, Hutchison JE. Thiol-Functionalized Undecagold Clusters by Ligand Exchange: Synthesis, Mechanism, and Properties. Inorganic Chemistry 2005;44(18) 6149-6158.

288. Sandi G, Kizilel R, Carrado KA, Fernandez-saavedra R Castagnola N. Effect of the Silica Precursor on the Conductivity of Hectorite-Derived Polymer Nanocomposites. Electrochimica Acta 2005;50(19) 3891-3896.

289. Huang WY, Han CD. Dispersion Characteristics and Rheology of Organoclay Nanocomposites based on a Segmented Main-Chain Liquid-Crystalline Polymer Having Pendent Pyridyl Group. Macromolecules 2006;39(1) 257-267.

290. Mammeri F, Le Bourhis E, Rozes L, Sanchez CJ. Mechanical Properties of Hybrid Organic-Inorganic Materials. Journal of Materials Chemistry 2005;15(1) 3787-3811.

291. Sanchez C, Ribot F. Design of Hybrid Organic-Inorganic Materials Synthesized Via Sol-Gel Chemistry. New Journal of Chemistry 1994;18(1) 1007-1047.

292. Judeinstein P, Sanchez C. Hybrid Organic-Inorganic Materials: A Land of Multidisciplinarity. Journal of Materials Chemistry 1996;6(1) 511-525.

293. Zhang X, Simon LC. In Situ Polymerization of Hybrid Polyethylene-Alumina Nanocomposites. Macromolecular Materials and Engineering 2005;290(6) 573-583.

294. Gao SL, Mader E. Characterization of Interphase Nanoscale Property Variations in Glass Fibre Reinforced Polypropylene and Epoxy Resin Composites. Composites Part A: Applied Science and Manufacturing 2002;33(4) 559-576.

295. Shenhar R, Norsten TB, Rotello VM. Polymer-Mediated Nanoparticle Assembly: Structural Control and Applications. Advanced Materials 2005;17(6) 657-669.

296. Rothenfluh DA, Bermudez H, O'neil1 CP, Hubbell JA. Biofunctional Polymer Nanoparticles for Intra-Articular Targeting and Retention in Cartilage. Nature Materials 2008;7(3) 248-254.

297. Arap W, Kolonin MG, Trepel M, Lahdenranta J, Cardo-vila M, Giordano RJ, Mintz PJ, Ardelt PU, Yao VJ, Vidal CL, Flamm CL, Valtanen H, Weavind LM, Hicks ME, Pollock RE, Botz GH, Bucana CD, Koivunen E, Cahill D, Troncoso P, Baggerly KA, Pentz RD, Do KA, Logothetis CJ, Pasqualini R. Steps Toward Mapping the Human Vasculature by Phage Display. Nature medicine 2002;8(2) 121-127.

298. Kolonin MG, Sun J, Do KA, Vidal CI, Ji Y, Baggerly KA, Pasqualini R, Arap W. Synchronous Selection of Homing Peptides for Multiple Tissues by In Vivo Phage Display. FASEB Journal 2006;20(7) 979-981.

299. Smith GP, Petrenko VA. Phage Display. Chemical Reviews 1997;97(2) 391-410.

300. Rehor A, Hubbell JA, Tirelli N. Oxidation-Sensitive Polymeric Nanoparticles. Langmuir 2005;21(1) 411-417.

301. Harris JM, Martin NE, Modi M. Pegylation: A Novel Process for Modifying Pharmacokinetics. Clinical Pharmacokinetics 2001;40(7) 539-551.

302. Orringer DA, Koo YE, Chen T, Kopelman R, Sagher O, Philbert MA. Small Solutions for Big Problems: The Application of Nanoparticles to Brain Tumor Diagnosis and Therapy. Clinical Pharmacology & Therapeutics 2009;85(5) 531-534.

303. Prescott JH, Lipka S, Baldwin S, Sheppard NF, Maloney JM, Coppeta J, Yomtov B, Staples MA Santini JT. Chronic, Programmed Polypeptide Delivery from an Implanted, Multireservoir Microchip Device. Nature Biotechnology 2006;24(4) 437-438.

304. Lutz JF. Solution Self-Assembly of Tailor-Made Macromolecular Building Blocks Prepared by Controlled Radical Polymerization Techniques. Polymer International 2006;55 979-993.

305. Jagur-Grodzinski J. Preparation of Functionalized Polymers using Living and Controlled Polymerizations. Reactive & Functional Polymers 2001;49(1) 1-54.

306. Matyjaszewski K. Macromolecular Engineering: From Rational Design through Precise Macromolecular Synthesis and Processing to Targeted Macroscopic Material Properties. Progress in Polymer Science 2005;30(8-9) 858-875.

307. Taton D, Gnanou Y, Matmour R, Angot S, Hou SJ, Francis R, Lepoittevin B, Moinard D, Babin J. Controlled Polymerizations as Tools for the Design of Star-like and Dendrimer-like Polymers. Polymer International 2006;55(10) 1138-1145.

308. Brauncker WA, Matyjaszewski K. Controlled/Living Radical Polymerization: Features, Developments, and Perspectives. Progress in Polymer Science 2007;32(1) 93-146.

309. Zhang XW, Lian XM, Liu L, Zhang J, Zhao HY. Synthesis of Comb Copolymers with Pendant Chromophore Groups based on RAFT Polymerization and Click Chemistry and Formation of Electron Donor-Acceptor Supramolecules. Macromolecules 2008;41(21) 7863-7869.

310. Gondi SR, Vogt AP, Sumerlin BS. Versatile Pathway to Functional Telechelics via RAFT Polymerization and Click Chemistry. Macromolecules 2007;40(3) 474-481.

311. Gao H, Matyjaszewski K. Synthesis of Molecular Brushes by "Grafting Onto" Method: Combination of ATRP and Click Reactions. Journal of the American Chemical Society 2007;129(20) 6633-6639.

312. Liu H, Li CH, Liu HW, Liu SY. pH-Responsive Supramolecular Self-Assembly of Well-Defined Zwitterionic ABC Miktoarm Star Terpolymers. Langmuir 2009;25(8) 4724-4734.

313. Arora A, Hakim I, Baxter J, Rathnasingham R, Srinivasan R, Fletcher DA, Mitragotri S. Needle-Free Delivery of Macromolecules Across the Skin by Nano Liter Volume Pulsed Microjets. Proceedings of the National Academy of Sciences of the United States of America 2007;104(11) 4255-4260.

314. Bashir SL, Chew AL, Anigbogu A, Dreher F, Maibach HI. Physical and Physiological Effects of Stratum Corneum Tape Stripping. Skin Research Technology 2001;7(1) 40-48.

315. Doukas AG, Kollias N. Transdermal Drug Delivery with a Pressure Wave. Advanced Drug Delivery Reviews 2004;56(5) 559-579.

316. Habash RW, Bansal R, Krewski D, Alhafid HT. Thermal Therapy, Part 1: An Introduction to Thermal Therapy. Critical Reviews in Biomedical Engineering 2006;34(6) 459-489.

317. Karande P, Jain A, Mitragotri S. Discovery of Transdermal Penetration Enhancers by High-Throughput Screening. Nature Biotechnology 2004;22(2) 192-197.

318. Lee SH, Lee HH, Choi SS. Nanoparticle Popsicle: Transdermal Delivery of Nanoparticles using Polymeric Microneedle array. Korean Journal of Chemical Engineering 2011;28(9) 1913-1917.

319. Demir YK, Akan Z, Kerimoglu O. Characterization of Polymeric Microneedle Arrays for Transdermal Drug Delivery. 2013;8(10) e77289.

320. Tuan-Mahmood TM, McCrudden MT, Torrisi BM, McAlister E, Garland MJ, Singh TR, Donnelly RF. Microneedles for Intradermal and Transdermal Drug Delivery. European Journal of Pharmaceutical Sciences 2013;50(5) 623-37.

321. Prausnitz MR. Microneedles for Transdermal Drug Delivery. Advanced Drug Delivery Reviews 2004;56(5) 581-587.

322. Mitragotri S. Current Status and Future Prospects of Needle-Free Liquid Jet Injectors. Nature Reviews. Drug Discovery 2006;5(7) 543-548.

323. Paliwal S, Menon GK, Mitragotri S. Low-Frequency Sonophoresis: Ultrastructural basis for Stratum Corneum Permeability Assessed using Quantum Dots. Journal of Investigative Dermatology 2006;126(5) 1095-1101.

324. Guy RH, Kalia YN, Delgado-Charro MB, Merino V, Lopez A, Marro D. Iontophoresis: Electrorepulsion and Electroosmosis. Journal of Controlled Release 2000;64(1-3) 129-132.

325. Al-Qadi S, Grenha A, Remunan-Lopez C. Microspheres Loaded with Polysaccharide Nanoparticles for Pulmonary Delivery: Preparation, Structure and Surface Analysis. Carbohydrate Polymers 2011;86(1) 25-34.

326. Taranejoo S, Janmaleki M, Rafienia M, Kamali M, Mansouri M. Chitosan Microparticles Loaded with Exotoxin A Subunit Antigen for Intranasal Vaccination Against Pseudomonas Aeruginosa: An In Vitro Study. Carbohydrate Polymers 2011;83(4) 1854-1861.

Chpater 8

Liposomes as Potential Drug Carrier Systems for Drug Delivery

Melis Çağdaş[1], Ali Demir Sezer[2] and Seyda Bucak[3]

[1] *Department of Chemistry, Boğaziçi University, Bebek, Istanbul, Turkey*

[2] *Department of Pharmaceutical Biotechnology, Faculty of Pharmacy, Marmara University, Haydarpaşa, Istanbul, Turkey*

[3] *Department of Chemical Engineering, Yeditepe University, Kayışdağı, Istanbul, Turkey*

1. INTRODUCTION

Lipids are amphiphilic molecules, where one part of the molecule is water-loving (hydrophilic) and the other water-hating (hydrophobic). When lipids are placed in contact with water, the unfavorable interactions of the hydrophobic segments of the molecule with the solvent result in the self assembly of lipids, often in the form of liposomes. Liposomes consist of an aqueous core surrounded by a lipid bilayer, much like a membrane, separating the inner aqueous core from the bulk outside. They were first discovered by Bangham and his co-workers in 1961 [1] and described as swollen phospholipid systems [2]. In the following years, a variety of enclosed phospholipid bilayer structures were defined which were initially called bangosomes and then liposomes, which was derived by the combination of two Greek words, "lipos" meaning fat and "soma" meaning body.

Liposomes have been used to improve the therapeutic index of new or established drugs by modifying drug absorption, reducing metabolism, prolonging biological half-life or reducing toxicity. Drug distribution is then controlled primarily by properties of the carrier and no longer by physicochemical characteristics of the drug substance only.

Lipids forming liposomes may be natural or synthetic, and liposome constituents are not exclusive of lipids, new generation liposomes can also be formed from polymers (sometimes referred to as polymersomes). Whether composed of natural or synthetic lipids or polymers, liposomes are biocompatible and biodegradable which make them suitable for biomedical research. The unique feature of liposomes is their ability to compartmentalize and solubilize both hydrophilic and hydrophobic materials by nature. This unique feature, coupled with biocompatibility and biodegradability make liposomes very attractive as drug delivery vehicles.

Hydrophobic drugs place themselves inside the bilayer of the liposome and hydrophilic drugs are entrapped within the aqueous core or at the bilayer interface. Liposomal formulations enhance the therapeutic efficiency of drugs in preclinical models and in humans compared to conventional formulations due to the alteration of biodistribution. Liposome binding drugs, into or onto their membranes, are expected to be transported without rapid degradation and minimum side effects to the recipient because generally liposomes are composed of biodegradable, biologically inert and non-immunogenic lipids. Moreover, they produce no pyrogenic or antigenic reactions and possess limited toxicity [3-5]. Consequently, all these properties as well as the ease of surface modification to bear the targetable properties make liposomes more attractive candidates for use as drug-delivery vehicles than other drug carrying systems such as nanoparticles [6, 7] and microemulsions [8, 9]. In the 1970s [1,10-13], liposomes were introduced as drug delivery vehicles but the initial clinical results were not satisfactory due to their colloidal and biological instability and their inefficient encapsulation of drug molecules.

Subsequent research on their stability and drug interactions resulted in several commercial liposome products in the market in the 1980s and early 1990s [14]. A schematic representation of liposomal drug delivery is given in Figure 1.

Liposomes represent versatile and advanced nanodelivery systems for a wide range of biologically active compounds [16]. The final amount of the encapsulated drug is affected by a selection of an appropriate preparation method providing a preparation of liposomes of various size, lamellarity and physicochemical properties [17]. The entrapment of the drugs, both hydrophilic and hydrophobic, into the liposomes is used to bypass the frequent generic toxicity associated with the drug as often seen in cancer drugs [18]. Thus, it represents a very effective route that enhances the drug therapeutic effect. The modification of liposomes permits a passive or active targeting of the tumor site. This effect enables an efficient drug payload into the malignant cell of tumors, while the non-malignant cells become minimally impacted.

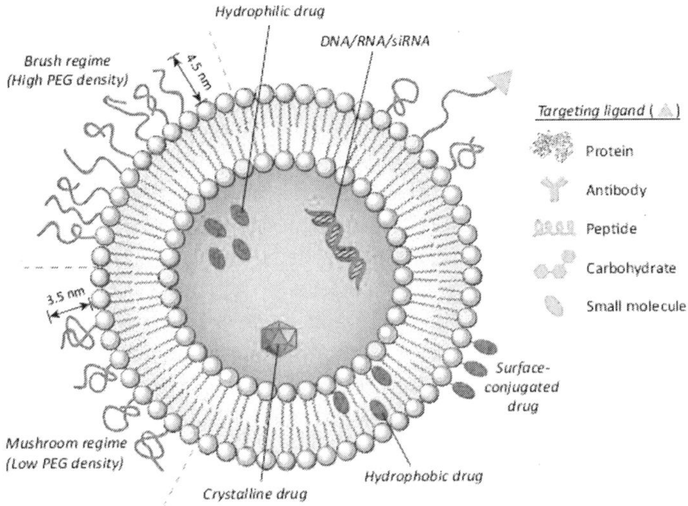

Figure 1. Structural and design considerations for liposomal drug delivery. Liposomes can be surface functionalized to endow stealth through PEGylation and to promote receptor-mediated endocytosis by using targeting ligands such as antibodies, peptides, proteins, carbohydrates, and various other small molecules. PEGylation extends liposomal circulation half-life in vivo by reducing clearance, immune recognition, and the non-specific absorption of serum proteins. Polyethylene glycol (PEG) density determines its structure at the liposome surface, with densities below 9% adopting a mushroom-like globular structure and those above 9% adopting a more rigid, extended, brush-like morphology. Chemotherapeutics or diagnostics can be encapsulated into the aqueous lumen, incorporated into the lipid bilayer, or conjugated to the liposome surface. Abbreviation: siRNA, small interfering RNA [15].

In some of the first demonstrations of the improved in vivo activity of liposome-encapsulated drugs in animal models, the anti-cancer drug cytosine arabinoside used which showed a significant increase in the survival times of the mice bearing leukemia [19, 20] which became a popular model for testing the effects of a wide range of liposome characteristics on therapeutic outcomes. Following experiments include liposomal amphotericin B [21] and liposomal doxorubicin [22] that finally led to the first clinical trials of liposomal drugs. Nowadays; the liposomal products (as a suspension, as an aerosol or in a semi-solid form such as a gel, cream, or powder) in the market still include mostly anticancer preparations as well as antifungal and antibacterial preparations and cosmetics. In addition, liposomes are recently used as therapeutic agents to treat a disease because increased gene transfer efficiencies have been obtained via liposomal gene vectors in gene therapy.

The benefits and limitations of liposome drug carriers critically depend and based on physicochemical and colloidal characteristics such as size, composition, loading efficiency and stability, as well as their biological interaction with the cell membranes. There are four major interactions between liposomes and cells [23]. The predominant interaction among them is either simple adsorption or subsequent endocytosis. Adsorption occurs when the attractive forces exceed the repulsive ones and obviously this type of interaction depends on the surface properties of liposomes. In the delivery through endocytosis, liposome and its contents indirectly place themselves in the cytoplasm. Fusion with cell membranes, delivery of the liposomal content directly into the cell through the merge of liposome lipids into the membrane, is much rarer. The last possible interaction is the lipid exchange which is a long-range interaction that involves the exchange of bilayer constituents, such as lipids, cholesterol, and membrane bound molecules with components of cell membranes. Upon entering into the body, the delivered liposomes via one of these interaction types trigger the response of the immune system and the encapsulated material may become inactive. Therefore; substantial researches have been carried out in the development of the biocompatible and nonrecognizable liposomal surfaces.

Various types of liposomes can be prepared by different preparation methods, depending on the required application. In this chapter, these methods are summarized to give a general understanding of the relationship between structure and functionality of liposomes. As one of the advantages of liposomal formulations is the encapsulation ability of both hydrophobic and hydrophilic drugs, incorporation methods are shortly visited. Physical properties of liposomes such as stability, storage and sterilization are discussed along with the characterization techniques for size, charge, etc. Clinical applications of liposomes are a vast area of research where cancer therapy is the area of highest impact. Different clinical applications of liposomes and most recent advances in cancer therapy are summarized. New generation involving constituents other than conventional ones such as phospholipids prove to be a growing field in nanotechnology. A brief list of different types of new generation liposomes are given with short descriptions at the end of this chapter.

2. LIPOSOME PREPARATION METHODS

The manufactured liposome features are directly related to the preparation method. Although liposome formation may be spontaneous, often some mechanical agitation is required. In order to have control over the size and structure of the liposomes that are formed, increase the efficiency of entrapment of the desired molecules, and prevent subsequent leakage from the liposomes, different preparation methods have been devised.

There are a few parameters that should be considered during the method selection: 1) the physicochemical characteristics of the material to be entrapped and those of the liposomal ingredients, 2) the nature of the medium in which the liposomes are dispersed, 3) the effective concentration of the encapsulated material and its potential toxicity, 4) additional processes involved during application (delivery of the liposomes), 5) optimum size, polydispersity and shelf-life of the liposomes for the intended application and 6) batch-to-batch reproducibility and possibility of large-scale production of safe and efficient liposomal products [24-26].

Liposome size is a crucial parameter in determining the circulation half-life of liposomes in drug delivery. The amount of encapsulated drug is also related with the size and the number of bilayers of the prepared liposome. According to the desired formulation, different liposome preparation methods can be employed. The main difference in these methods is their approach to overcome the low solubility of lipids in water. Accordingly, these methods can be classified as mechanical agitation, solvent evaporation, solvent injection, and detergent solubilization. In all the above mentioned methods, drug loading is passive.

2.1. Mechanical Agitation

In this method, lipids are directly solubilized in water upon application of high mechanical agitation, through the use of probe sonication. It is one of the simplest methods of liposome preparation, however, yields small liposomes that are highly unstable in terms of their size and suffers from the drawback that it is impossible to remove completely the risk of lipid degradation by contact with the hot probe, and contamination with titanium from the probe. Its advantage is the exclusion of use of organic solvents as described in the following methods. However, for drug delivery applications, liposomes prepared with mechanical agitation are not suitable due to their size instability and high leakage of encapsulated drugs [27].

2.2. Solvent Evaporation

In general this method consists of four major steps; first is the solubilization of the lipid (and a hydrophobic compound) in an organic solvent; second is solvent evaporation; third is hydration with a buffer (and the hydrophilic compound) and if need the fourth often involves obtaining unilamellar liposomes from the obtained multilamellar ones.

The aqueous volume enclosed within these lipid membranes is very small proportion of total volume used for preparation (5-10%). Consequently, large amount of water soluble drug is wasted during the preparation. On the other hand, lipid soluble drug can be encapsulated with 100% efficiency, providing that they are not present in quantities which overwhelm the structural components of the membrane [28]. The volume of entrapment can be significantly increased by the usage of negatively charged lipids in the membrane which tend to push the bilayers apart from each other. The same effect can also be achieved in the presence of neutral lipids by freezing and thawing repeatedly the obtained liposomes. 30% volume of entrapment can be achieved, which can further be increased at higher lipid concentrations [29]. The freeze-thaw protocol results in a dramatic change in liposome morphology followed by freeze-fracture electron micrographs. Before freeze-thawing, the samples exhibit the tightly packed “onions skin” arrangements of concentric bilayers normally associated with liposomal systems. After a few freeze-thaw steps, however, new structures are observed where the interlamellar spaces are much increased, and where closed lamellar systems can be intercalated between bilayers [30].

2.2.1. Solubilization Of The Lipid

The starting point of this liposome preparation method is to prepare an organic solution of membrane lipids in order to ensure complete and homogenous mixing of all the components as they are required in the final membrane preparation. Compounds to be incorporated which are lipid soluble will be added to the organic solution, while compounds to be entrapped in the aqueous compartment of liposomes will be dissolved in the aqueous environment. In this method, phospholipids are first dissolved in an organic solvent along with lipid soluble compounds (if any) to be incorporated in the liposome to ensure complete and homogenous mixing.

2.2.2. Solvent Evaporation

The next step is the evaporation of the organic solvent. The simplest is to allow the solvent to evaporate in a glass container. A better method is evaporating the solvent using a rotary evaporator connected to a vacuum pump to obtain a thin film of the lipid on the walls of a round bottom flask. In order to increase encapsulation, it is recommended to start with a large volume round bottom flask so that the lipids will be dried down onto a large surface area possible to form a very thin film. The evaporator is detached from vacuum pump and introduced to nitrogen. The container is then removed from the evaporator and fixed to a lyophilizer or exposed to high vacuum overnight to remove the residual solvent.

An alternative method of dispersing the lipids in a finely-divided form before the addition of aqueous media is to freeze-dry the dissolved lipids in an organic solvent [31]. The important concept in this method is the choice of the organic solvent which should have a freezing point above the temperature of the condenser of the freeze-drying and also be inert with regard to rubber seals of commercial lyophilizers. When these restrictions are concerned, the most suitable organic solvent happens to be tertiary buthanol.

2.2.3. Hydration

Evaporation (or freeze-drying) of the solvent is followed by hydration of lipids with the aqueous medium. Often for hydration, a suitable buffer at a temperature above the phase transition temperature of the phospholipid is employed. The solution is swirled manually or mechanically (either with a bath sonicator or vortex mixer) until all the lipids have been incorporated into the solution. The resulting product is a milky suspension of lipids which is allowed to stand for a while for the complete swelling to give MLVs [28]. Further treatment is required for the preparation of ULVs, which will be discussed later in the text.

It is possible to obtain LUVs instead of MLVs during hydration by introducing an aqueous sucrose solution down the side of the flask by inclining the flask to one side and slowly returning the flask to the upright orientation, allowing the fluid to run gently over the lipid layer on the bottom of the flask. The swelling is carried out as usual without any shaking or agitation. The suspension is then centrifuged and the layer of MLVs floating on the surface is removed, leaving LUVs in solution.

2.2.4. Obtaining Suvs From Mlvs

After preparation of MLVs by hydration of dried lipid, it is possible to continue processing the liposomes in order to modify their size and other characteristics. For many purposes, MLVs are too large of too heterogeneous population to work with. There are several methods devised to reduce their size. These include techniques such as micro-emulsification, extrusion, and ultrasonication. A second set of methods is designed to increase the entrapment volume of hydrated lipids, and/or reduce the lamellarity of the liposomes formed, and involves procedures such as freeze-drying, freeze-thawing or induction of vesiculation by ions or pH change.

Microemulsification of liposomes is performed with an equipment called micro fluidizer to prepare small vesicles from concentrated lipid suspension. This method can produce liposomes in 50-200 nm size range with the encapsulation efficiency of up to 75% [32].

Sonication [33] disrupts MLV suspensions by using sonic energy to produce SUVs with diameters in the range of 15-50 nm. There are two methods of sonication; bath sonication and probe sonication. The former method is used for large volumes of dilute lipids whereas the latter one is used for suspensions which require high energy, such as high concentration of lipid suspensions. The disadvantage of probe sonication is the contamination of preparation with metal from the tip of the probe which should be removed by centrifugation prior to use. Also, as a result of high energy, probe sonication suffers from overheating the lipid suspension causing degradation. For these reasons, bath sonicators are the most widely used instrumentation for SUV preparation.

An even gentler method of reducing the size of the liposomes is to pass through a membrane filter of defined pore size [34]. This can be at much more lower pressure and can give populations in which one can choose the upper size limit depending on the exact pore size of the filter used. This membrane extrusion technique can be used to process both LUVs and MLVs in which liposome contents are exchanged with the suspending medium during breaking and resealing of the phospholipid bilayers as they pass through the polycarbonate membrane. In order to achieve as high an entrapment as possible of water-soluble compounds, it is crucial to have these compounds present in the suspending medium during the extrusion. An almost completely unilamellar population can be produced after 5-10 repeated extrusions through two stacked membranes.

In freezing-thawing method, SUVs are rapidly frozen and thawed slowly. The short-lived sonication disperses aggregated materials to LUV. The creation of unilamellar vesicles is as a result of the fusion of SUV throughout the processes of freezing and thawing [35-37].

2.3. Solvent Injection

In this type of preparation methods, lipids are first dissolved in an organic solvent and then brought into contact with the aqueous phase containing the materials to be encapsulated within the liposome. The lipids align themselves into a monolayer at the interface between the organic and aqueous phase which is an important step to form the bilayer of the liposome [29]. There are three categories in solvent dispersion method including; (i) a miscible organic solvent with the aqueous phase, (ii) an immiscible organic solvent with the aqueous phase that is used in excess, and (iii) an immiscible organic solvent used in excess with the aqueous phase.

2.3.1. Ethanol Injection Method

In this method an ethanol solution of lipids is injected rapidly into an excess saline or other aqueous medium by a fine needle [38]. The injection force is usually sufficient to achieve complete mixing, so that ethanol is diluted in water, and lipids are dispersed evenly throughout the medium. This method yields a high proportion of SUVs. This method is extremely simple and it has a very low risk of degradation for sensitive lipids. Its major disadvantages are the limitation of solubility of lipids in ethanol and the volume of ethanol that can be introduced into the medium, which in turn limits the quantity of lipid dispersed, so that the resulting liposome solution is generally dilute. As a result, the percentage encapsulation for hydrophilic materials is very low. One last disadvantage for this method is the difficulty of the removal of ethanol from the lipid membranes.

2.3.2. Ether Injection Method

This method [39, 40] involves injecting the immiscible organic solution very slowly into an aqueous phase through a narrow needle at a temperature that the organic solvent is removed by vaporization during the process. In this method, large vesicles are formed which might be due to the slow vaporization of solvent giving rise to an ether: water gradient extending on both sides of the interfacial lipid monolayer, resulting in the eventual formation of a bilayer sheet which folds in on to itself to form a sealed vesicle [29]. Ether injection treats sensitive lipids very gently and runs very little risk of causing oxidative degradation. Since the solvent is removed at the same rate as it is introduced, there is no limit to the final concentration of lipid which can be achieved, since the process can be run continuously for a long period of time, giving rise to a high percentage of the aqueous medium encapsulated within the liposomes. The major drawbacks of this method are the long time taken to produce a batch of liposomes and the need of careful control for the introduction of lipid solution.

2.4. Surfactant (Detergent) Solubilization Method

In this method, the phospholipids are brought into contact with the aqueous phase via the intermediary of surfactants. Phospholipid molecules associate with surfactants and form mixed micelles. The basic feature of this method is the removal of the surfactant from pre-formed mixed micelles containing phospholipids, whereupon unilamellar liposomes form spontaneously. However, removal of surfactants is carried out using techniques such as, dialysis and column chromatography, inevitably remove other small water-soluble molecules, making this method not very efficient in terms of percentage encapsulation values attainable for water soluble compounds. On the other hand, surfactant solubilization method has the ability to vary the size of the liposomes by precise control of the conditions of surfactant removal and to obtain liposomes of very high size homogeneity [29].

The transfer from laboratory to industry was very important for liposomes, as it is for any biotechnological discipline. The first liposomal drug delivery experiments in humans were carried out by freshly prepared liposomes but in order to be a commercial product the liposome-drug formulation must have well-defined stability and a shelf life over a year. Of the several preparation methods described in the literature, only a few of them have the potential to be used in the large scale liposome manufacturing. The crucial problem is the presence of organic solvent residues, pyrogen control, stability, sterility, size and size distribution as well as batch to batch reproducibility.

In the parental administration the liposomes two important conditions involve being sterile and pyrogen free. In the case of animal experiments, the sufficient sterility can be obtained by the passage of the liposome preparations through the 400 nm pore size Millipore filters. In human experiments the sterilization depyrogenation techniques should be taken much more seriously starting from the raw materials, containers and working areas [41].

2.5. Loading Of Drugs In Liposome Formulations

2.5.1. Encapsulation Of Hydrophilic Drugs

Once lipids are hydrated in the presence of hydrophilic drugs, a portion of the drug gets entrapped inside the liposome and another portion remains in the bulk, outside the aqueous core of the liposome. As only the entrapped drug is of interest, drug in the bulk should be removed. This purification is generally done by gel filtration column chromatography (Sephadex G-50, Pharmacia LKB) and dialysis (hollow fiber dialysis cartridge) on the basis of size differences between the liposomes and the non-encapsulated material. In the cases where DNA or proteins are being encapsulated, or where there is concern that non-encapsulated material may form large aggregates, techniques such as centrifugation can be employed due to the differences in the buoyant densities of liposomes and non-encapsulated material [42, 43].

A hydrophilic drug may not be encapsulated with high efficiency because the drug molecules can diffuse in and out of the lipid membrane. Thus, the drug would be difficult to retain inside the liposomes. However, compounds with ionizable groups and those that are both water and lipid soluble can be encapsulated with high efficiency (up to 90%) by the liposomes after the formation of membranes [44] by active loading. In this technique, the pH of the interior part of the liposome is such that the unionized drug which enters the liposome by passive loading is ionized inside the liposome, and ionized drug molecules lose their ability to diffuse through the lipid membrane. Therefore, high concentration of the ionized drug is obtained inside the liposome. For example, doxorubicin and epirubicin can be entrapped in preformed SUV with high efficiency through active loading [45, 46].

The pH difference can be brought about by encapsulating a non-permeating buffer ion such as glutamate inside the liposomes at low pH and replacing the extra-liposomal buffer with one which is iso-osmolar at pH 7.0. Alternatively, charged lipids may be incorporated into the membrane at low pH, followed by adjustment of the suspending medium to neutrality. A similar approach may be adopted by using a potassium gradient, in which the membrane is made selectively permeable to potassium ions entrapped inside the liposome by incorporation of valinomycin into the lipid membrane [47, 48].

2.5.2. Encapsulation Of Hydrophobic Drugs

Hydrophobic drugs are solubilized in the phospholipid bilayer of the liposomes that mainly provide a hydrophobic environment. Once trapped, they remain in the liposome bilayer as they have very low affinity towards the inner or outer aqueous regions of the liposomes. During the preparation of liposomes, hydrophobic drugs are solubilized in the organic solvent along with the phospholipids and during the subsequent hydration phase, they remain entrapped in the hydrophobic bilayer region. For example, the liposomal photosensitizer verteporfin (Visudyne) contains a hydrophobic drug that is rapidly transferred to blood proteins in vivo. Activation of the drug by targeting laser light to blood flowing though the eye causes its site-specific activity in the treatment of wet macular degeneration [49]. Amphotericin B and paclitaxel are the other most commonly investigated hydrophobic drugs in liposome formulations.

3. STABILITY OF LIPOSOMES

Liposome stability can be explained by physical, chemical and biological means which are all interrelated. Generally, chemical (degradation of phospholipids structures) and physical (uniformity of size distribution and encapsulation efficiency) stability determine the shelf-life of liposomes. Once the liposomal formulations have been obtained, maintenance of the physical properties of these preparations can be difficult. Leakage of the encapsulated material due to the permeability of the membrane, change in the size distribution and stability problems due to the hydrolytic and oxidative degradation are the general problems upon storage. Methods are devised to overcome these instability problems, those designed to minimize the degradation processes and those which help liposomes to survive in the face of conditions which encourages these processes.

Two different types of chemical degradation can affect the performance of the phospholipids bilayers; hydrolysis of the ester bonds linking the fatty acids to the glycerol backbone and oxidation of the unsaturated acyl chains, if present. The level of oxidation can be kept to a minimum by taking some precautions like starting with freshly purified lipids and freshly distilled solvents, avoiding procedures involving high temperatures, carrying out the manufacturing process in the absence of oxygen, deoxygenating the aqueous solutions by passing nitrogen, storing all liposome suspensions in an inert atmosphere and including an anti-oxidant, e.g. α-tocopherol [50], a common non-toxic dietary lipid, as a component of the lipids membrane. An alternative solution to the oxidation problem is to reduce the level of oxidizable lipids in the membrane by using saturated lipids instead of the unsaturated ones. Also, the mono-unsaturated ones have much less tendency of oxidation than the polyunsaturated ones. Thus; sphingomyelins, usually having only one double bond, are expected to degrade more slowly than other mammalian origin lipids. Entirely synthetic and saturated phospholipids; DMPC, DPPC and DSPC, can also be considered as a solution for the oxidative degradation of liposomes.

Hydrolysis type of chemical degradation of the ester linkages in the phospholipid structure occurs most slowly at pH values close to neutral. In general, the rate of hydrolysis has a "V-shaped" dependence, with a minimum at pH 6.5 and an increased rate at both higher and lower pH. In the active loading of drugs, as it is mentioned before, low pH levels are required which triggers the hydrolysis. This hydrolysis kind of chemical degradation is also very effective on the aqueous solutions of liposome due to the presence of water. Temperature also triggers the hydrolysis of the lipids which creates the need for refrigeration. In order to keep hydrolysis to a minimum during active loading, attention must be paid for the removal of residual solvent from the dried lipids. To avoid hydrolysis, instead of ester linked lipids, the usage of ether linkage containing lipids (e.g. found in the membrane of halophilic bacteria) would be an absolute solution [51]. Another chemical degradation, oxidation of the lipids in the liposome structures can be prevented by the addition of small amounts of antioxidants during the manufacturing steps.

The problems related to the lipid oxidation and hydrolysis during the shelf-life of the liposomal product can be reduced by the storage of liposomal dispersion in the dry state by freeze-drying (lyophilization), without compromising their physical state or encapsulation capacity [52]. However, freeze-drying of liposome systems without appropriate stabilizers will lead to fusion of vesicles, i.e. physical instability. To promote vesicle stability during the freeze-drying process, cycloprotectants [53-55], including saccharides (e.g. sucrose, trehalose, and lactose) and their derivatives are employed [56]. Cycloprotectants, especially sucrose because of its high glass transition temperature, are believed to be effective to protect the liposome membranes against possible fracture and rapture that might cause a change in size distribution and a loss of the encapsulated material presumably by forming glasses under the typical freezing conditions used for lyophilization [57]. Lyophilization increases the shelf-life of the finished product by preserving in a relatively more stable dry state. Some liposome products on market or clinical trials are provided as lyophilized powder. For example, AmBisomeTM, a liposomal amphotericin, is the first liposome product to be marketed in several countries is supplied as a lyophilized powder to be reconstituted with sterile water injection. Additionally, paclitaxel-liposome formulations have been developed which show good stability [58, 59]. These formulations once lyophilized can be stored at room temperature for extended time. On the other hand, once the preparation is reconstituted, it is not stable for more than a day in terms of size.

The physical degradation, leakage and fusion of liposomes, can occur as a result of the lattice defects in the membrane introduced during the manufacture, particularly in SUVs that are prepared below the membrane phase transition temperature. Annealing process, incubating the liposomes at a higher temperature than the phase transition temperature, can wipe out these defects by equalizing the differences in packing density between opposite sides of the bilayers. Even in annealed vesicles, aggregation and fusion can occur over a long period of time. In neutral liposomes, aggregation takes place because of the van der Waals interactions and because of the increased surface area it tends to be more pronounced in large liposomes. The simplest solution to overcome this aggregation is to add a small amount of negatively charged phospholipid (e.g. 10% PA or PG) to the liposome composition [29]

SUVs have much more tendency to fusion when compared to large liposomes due to the presence of stress arising from the high curvature of the membrane. Since this can occur specifically at the transition temperature of the membrane, it would be better to store these liposomes at a temperature much lower than the transition temperature of the lipids. For example, SUVs should be stored above their transition temperature for no longer than 24 hours but LUVs can be stored for a longer period of time if the temperature of the solution is kept in a range of 4-8 0C for approximately 1 week before the leakage of the encapsulated material starts due to the hydrolytic degradation on the membrane structure [60]. Also, addition of cholesterol to the phospholipid mixture would be a solution to reduce or eliminate the transition. The presence of cholesterol prevents packing and aggregation by inducing orientation and more rigidity to the phospholipids. Other than cholesterol, peptide incorporation to the lipid membrane also enables the lipid membrane to be more rigid at physiological temperature [61-63].

Permeability of liposome membranes depends highly on the membrane lipid composition, as well as on the encapsulated material. Large polar or ionic molecules will be retained much more efficiently than low molecular weight lipophilic compounds. Generally, for both type of encapsulated material, a rigid, more saturated membrane with a higher ratio of cholesterol forms the most stable lipid membrane concerning the leakage of the encapsulated material.

Many attempts have been made to enhance the physical stability of liposomes. Among these, surface modification of liposomes is an attractive method to improve liposomal stability both in vitro and in vivo. Some improvements in chemical and physical stability of polymer coated liposomes prepared with polysaccharide derivatives, such as mannan or amylopectin, have been demonstrated [64]. Several other substances also have been used for preparation of polymer coated liposomes such as poloxamer, polysorbate 80, carboxymethyl chitosan, and dextran derivatives [65-69]. While the possibility of coating liposomes with these polymers has been reported, few papers have dealt with the systematic evaluation of the physical stability of polymer coated liposomes. Moreover, contravening results have been also reported such as that polymer coated liposomes showed less stability than non-coated ones [65, 70].

In vivo stability of liposomes is also dependent on their charge. In serum, there are several proteins that are both positively and negatively charged. Liposomes with neutral charge are found to be more stable as they have much less electrostatic affinity towards proteins. [71].

Biological liposome stability plays important roles at various stages of drug delivery. However, liposomes are somewhat biologically unstable as a parenteral drug delivery system owing to their rapid uptake and clearance from circulation by cells of the mononuclear phagocytic system (MPS) located mainly in the liver and spleen [72, 73]. Biological stability of liposomes is dependent on the presence of agents such as proteins that interact with liposomes upon application to the subject and the administration route. There have been many strategies to enhance the biological stability of liposomes that improve the liposomal drug delivery in vivo and increase the circulation time in blood stream [74]. The complexation between polymers and liposomes has been studied as a way to increase the long-term stability of liposomes. Grafting hydrophilic polymers onto the head groups of phospholipids, or the addition of water soluble polymers containing several hydrophobic groups has been shown to increase the circulation time in vivo, as well as to inhibit liposome fusion [75-77]. These kinds of liposomes are called stealth liposome [78] or sterically stabilized liposomes [79]. The steric repulsion of these liposomes stabilizes the liposomes against aggregation. One of the most popular and successful methods to obtain long-circulating biologically stable liposomes is to coat the surface of the liposome with poly(ethylene glycol), PEG [80-84]. Although the PEG chemistry is successful in coating the liposome surface, alternative sterically protecting polymers are also under research. The candidate polymers should be biocompatible, soluble, hydrophilic and have highly flexible main chain for drug delivery. Some of these polymers given in the literature are synthetic polymers of vinyl series i.e. poly(vinyl pyrrolidone) (PVP) and poly(acrylamide) (PAA) [85, 86]. PVP has a similar history on pharmaceutical application to PEG [87, 88]. It shows high degree of biocompatibility and also acts as efficient steric protector for liposomes. It was found that the liposomal bilayers containing lipids with covalently attached to polyethylene glycol by which the membrane surface steric inhibits protein and cellular interactions with liposomes drastically prolonging the blood circulation time when injected in animals [89]. Doxil® is the liposomal doxorubicin available in the market which is stable for more than 18 months in the liquid state due to being stabilized by the usage of polyethylene glycol.

4. STERILIZATION OF LIPOSOMES

Pharmaceutical industry in general differentiates between two principally different approaches to ensure sterility of a parental product: terminal sterilization of the final product in its container (steam sterilization) and aseptical manufacturing. Terminal sterilization is the commonly used one because of its higher sterility assurance level achieved when compared with the aseptical methods. However, terminal sterilization is not applicable to many liposomal drug carrier formulations.

There are several sterilization methods; such as filtration, gamma irradiation, final steam sterilization, dry heat sterilization, ethylene oxide sterilization, and ultraviolet sterilization. Bearing in mind the susceptibility of liposomes to the previously mentioned physical and chemical degradation mechanisms, the conditions required in conventional sterilization techniques (except filtration) are rather concerning since they involve the usage of heat, radiation and/or chemical sterilizing agents. Therefore, identification of a suitable method for sterilization of liposome formulations is a major challenge.

Table 1. Summary of the Sterilization Techniques Applied on Liposomal Preparations.

Sterilization Technique	Advantage(s)	Disadvantage(s)	Convenience
Filtration	Low operation temperature	Applicable to liposomes lower than 200 nm in diameter Operation under aseptic conditions	Low
γ-irradiation	Moderate operation temperature Highest microbial death reliability	Large scale operation Risk of degradation of liposomes	High
Final steam sterilization	Low cost and convenient	Risk of degradation of liposomes	High
Dry heat	Low cost and convenient	Risk of degradation of liposomes	High
Ethylene oxide	Low operation temperature	Possible carcinogenic residues	Low
UV-sterilization	Low cost and convenient	Poor penetration into products Risk of degradation of liposomes	High

Filtration is the most suitable sterilization technique for the thermolabile liposomes since it does not include any form of heat or condition that can result in the degradation of liposomes or leakage of the encapsulated material. However, filtration has some drawbacks such as; being only applicable to the liposomes that are smaller than 200 nm in diameter and being an expensive method due to the equipment requiring to work under high pressure (25 kg/cm^2 and above). Additionally, this technique must be performed under aseptic conditions [90].

Filtration sterilization is relatively time-consuming and not efficient for the removal of viruses [91]. Studies have shown that polycarbonate membranes are less effective than hydrophobic Fluoropore membrane and cellulose acetate/surfactant-free membrane filtration units [91]. Although the limitations of filtration provoked researches on other sterilization methods, all resulted in the formation of degradation products via the previously mentioned degradation pathways. Filtration and the other methods are summarized according to their applicability on liposomal preparations in Table 1[92], given above.

5. CHARACTERIZATION OF LIPOSOMES

After preparation and before application, liposomes have to be characterized in order to ensure their in vitro and in vivo performance. Liposomal properties that are commonly discussed include lamellarity (the number of bilayers present in liposomes), diameter and size distribution, lipid composition and concentration determination, the encapsulant concentration and its encapsulation efficiency.

For the characterization of chemical properties, phospholipids can be quantitatively in terms of concentration either by Bartlett Assay or Stewart Assay. The phospholipid hydrolysis might be followed by HPLC where the column outflow can be monitored continuously by UV absorbance to obtain a quantitative record of the eluted components. Moreover, the phospholipid oxidation can also be followed by a number of techniques i.e., UV absorbance method, TBA method (2-thiobarbutiric acid) (for endoperoxides), iodometric method (for hydroperoxides) and GLC (gas-liquid chromatography) method [93].

The most direct method for determination of liposome size is the electron microscopy due to the possibility of viewing the liposomes individually and obtaining the exact information about the liposome population over the whole range of sizes [94]. As liposomes do not naturally create a contrast to be visible by electron microscopy, either cryo-TEM (Figure 2) should be used or staining of the liposome sample is required. Either way, it is a very time-consuming method and it requires equipments that may not always be immediately accessible. The other method for the determination of liposome size, dynamic light scattering [95, 96], is very simple and rapid to perform but it measures an average size of liposome bulk. More recently, atomic force microscopy is also used to determine the morphology, size and stability of liposomal structures. All these size determination methods are very expensive. If only an approximate size range is required, gel exclusion chromatography might be suitable.

Electrostatic stabilization of liposomes may be a desirable feature to prevent fusion. The surface charge on the liposomes is measured by zeta-potential measurements [98]. These measurements are useful in determination of the in vivo behavior of liposomes. Often zeta potential values <-25 mV or >+25 mV are considered stable [99]. However, as mentioned earlier, charged liposomes have the disadvantage of being unstable in biological conditions.

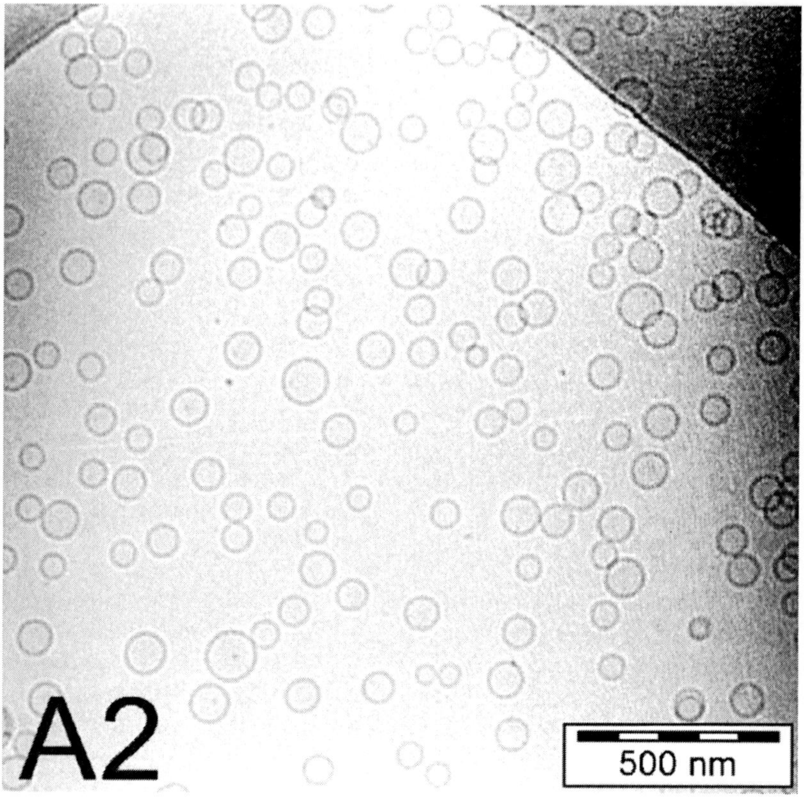

Adopted from Holzer, M., Barnert, S., Momm, J., Schubert, R., 2009. Preparative size exclusion chromatography combined with detergent removal as a versatile tool to prepare unilamellar and spherical liposomes of highly uniform size distribution. J. Chromatogr. A 1216, 5838–5848.

Figure 2. Cryo-TEM pictures of Size Exclusion Chromatography fractions eluted at 90 minutes and prepared from egg-phosphatidylcholine.

Residual solvent is very unacceptable for drug delivery applications, therefore residual solvent should be kept at a minimum in the formulations. Quantification of residual solvents as a result of preparation methods is done through gas chromatography (GC) [100-101] This is a very rapid and reliable method and most analytical and organic laboratories are equipped with a GC.

An important feature of liposomes is the existence of a temperature dependant, reversible phase transition, where the hydrocarbon chains of the phospholipid structures undergo a transformation from an ordered gel state to a more disordered fluid, liquid crystalline, state. This transition temperature is important in optimizing the storage conditions (i.e Temperature) to minimize fusion and drug leakage. These changes have been monitored by freeze fracture electron microscopy and much more easily by differential scanning calorimetry (DSC) [102-104, 93].

Entrapped volume is a crucial parameter that governs the morphology of liposomes. This internal volume is defined as the aqueous entrapped volume per unit quantity of lipids. The most promising way to determine the internal volume is to measure the quantity of water by replacing external medium (water) with a spectrophotometrically inert fluid (i.e. deuterium oxide) and then measuring water signal by NMR [93].

It is essential to measure the quantity of the encapsulated material inside liposomal structures before studying the behavior of this encapsulated material physically and biologically since the effects observed experimentally will be dose related. After the removal of the non-encapsulated material by the separation techniques the quantity of material remained can be assumed as 100% encapsulated. Minicolumn centrifugation and protamine aggregation methods are the general separation procedures that are commonly used [93].

Methods for determining the amount of material encapsulated within the liposomes typically rely on the destruction of the lipid bilayer and subsequent quantification of the released material [105]. In these measurements, the signal due to intact liposomes is typically monitored prior to bilayer disruption. The techniques used for this quantification depend on the nature of the encapsulant and include spectrophotometry [106, 107], fluorescence spectroscopy [108], enzyme-based methods [109] and electrochemical techniques. If a separation technique such as HPLC of field-flow fractionation (FFF) is applied, the percent encapsulation can be expressed as the ratio of the unencapsulated peak area to that of a reference standard of the same initial concentration [110, 111]. This method can be applied if the liposomes do not undergo any purification following preparation. Either technique serves to separate liposome encapsulated materials from those that remain in the extravesicular solution and hence can also be used to monitor the storage stability in terms of leakage or the effect of various disruptive conditions o the retention of encapsulants. Some authors have combined the size distribution and encapsulation efficiency determination in one assay by using FFF-MALS (multi angled light scattering) coupled to a concentration detector suitable for the encapsulant [112].

Since techniques used to separate free materials from liposome-encapsulated contents can potentially cause leakage of contents and, in some cases, ambiguity in the extent of separation, research using methods that do not rely on separation are of interest. Reported methods have included 1H NMR where free markers exhibited pH sensitive resonance shifts in the external medium versus encapsulated markers [113]; diffusion ordered 2D NMR which relied on differences in diffusion coefficients of entrapped and free marker molecules [114]; fluorescence methods where the signal from unencapsulated fluorophores was quenched by substances present in the external solution [115]; electron pin resonance (ESR) methods which rely on the signal broadening of unencapsulated markers by the addition of a membrane-impermeable agent [116, 117].

The drug release from liposomes can be followed by the usage of a well calibrated in vitro diffusion cell in order to predict pharmacokinetics and bioavailability of drug before expensive and time-consuming in vivo studies. For the determination of pharmacokinetic performance of liposomal formulations, dilution-induced drug release in buffer and plasma was employed and for the determination of drug bioavailability, another procedure is followed which involves the liposome degradation in the presence of mouse-liver lysosome lysate [93].

6. CLINICAL APPLICATIONS OF LIPOSOMES

New drug delivery systems such as liposomes are developed when the existing formulations are not satisfactory. Among all the nanomedicine platforms, liposomes have demonstrated one of the most established nanoplatforms with several FDA-approved formulations for cancer treatment, and had the greatest impact on oncology to date, because of their size, biocompatibility, biodegradability, hydrophobic and hydrophilic character, low toxicity and immunogenicity [118]. A vast of literature describes the feasibility of encapsulation of a wide range of drugs, including anti-cancer and antimicrobial agents, peptide hormones, enzymes, other proteins, vaccines and genetic materials, in the aqueous or lipid phases of liposomes which showed enhanced therapeutic activity and/or reduced toxicity in preclinical models and in humans when compared to their non-liposomal formulations.

Liposome applications in drug delivery depend, and are based on, physicochemical and colloidal characteristics such as composition, size, loading efficiency and the stability of the carrier, as well as their biological interactions between liposomes and cells. Based on these liposome properties, several modes of drug delivery can be listed: the major ones are enhanced drug solubilization (e.g. amphotericin B, minoxidil), protection of sensitive drug molecules (e.g. cytosine arabinose, DNA, RNA, antisense olgionucleotides, ribozymes), enhanced intracellular uptake (all agents, including antineoplastic agents, antibiotics and antivirals) and altered pharmacokinetics and biodistribution of the encapsulated drug.

Although lipid based formulations have advantages as drug carriers, drug-delivery systems based on unmodified liposomes are limited by their short blood circulation time, instability in vivo and lack of target selectivity [119, 120]. To increase accumulation of liposomal formulations in the desired cells and tissues, the use of targeted liposomes including surface-attached ligands such as; antibodies, folates, peptides and transferrin that are capable of recognizing and binding to the desired cells. Despite of some improvements in targeting efficiency by these immunoliposomes, the majority of these modified liposomes were still eliminated rapidly by the reticulo endothelial system, primarily in the liver [120]. Better target accumulations are expected if liposomes can be made to remain in the circulation long enough.

Schematic drawing of cytosolic delivery and organelle-specific targeting of drug loaded nanoparticles (i.e. most frequently liposomes) via receptor-mediated endocytosis is shown in Figure 3.

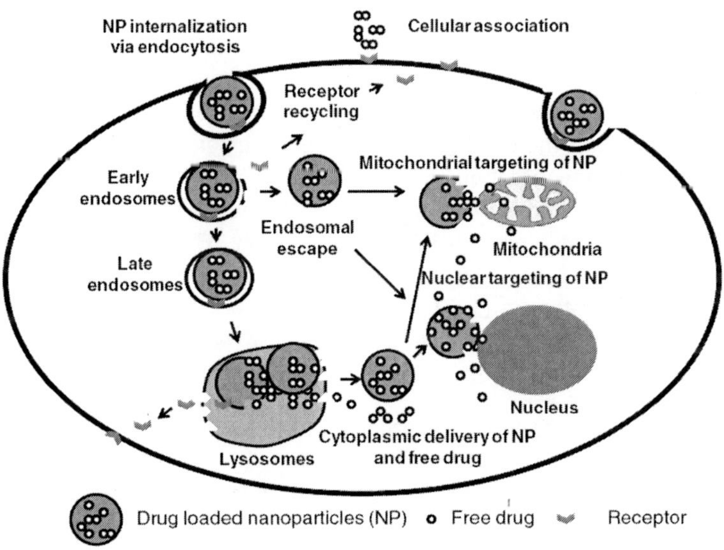

Figure 3. Schematic drawing of the cytosolic delivery and organelle-specific targeting of drug loaded nanoparticles via receptor-mediated endocytosis. After receptor mediated cell association with nanoparticles, the nanoparticles are engulfed in a vesicle known as an early endosome. Nanoparticles formulated with an endosome disrupting property disrupt the endosomes followed by cytoplasmic delivery. On the other hand, if nanoparticles are captured in early endosomes, theymaymake theirway to lysosomes as late endosomes where their degradation takes place. Only fraction of non-degraded drug released in the cytoplasm interacts with cellular organelles in a random fashion. However, cytosolic delivery of a fraction of organelle-targeted nanoparticles via endosomal escape or from lysosomes travel to the targeting organelles to deliver their therapeutic cargo [121].

Different methods have been suggested to achieve liposomes with high stability and long circulation times in vivo, including the surface coating of the liposomes with inert, biocompatible polymers such as PEG (stealth liposomes), which forms a protective layer over the liposome surface and slow down liposome recognition by opsonins and therefore subsequent clearance of liposomes [80, 84]. Long circulating liposomes are now being investigated in detail and are widely used in vitro and in vivo studies due their flexibility and also they found their place in the clinical applications. The flexibility allows a relatively small number of surface-grafted polymer molecules to create an impermeable layer over the liposome surface [122, 123]. Long-circulating liposomes demonstrate dose-dependent, non-saturable, log-linear kinetics and increased bioavailability [124].

The studies that attempt to combine the properties of long-circulating liposomes and immunoliposomes in one preparation place themselves in the literature as the further development in the liposomal formulations as drug carriers [125, 126]. In the early experiments, simple co-immobilization of an antibody and PEG on the surface of the same liposome has been performed despite the possibility of PEG creating steric hindrance for target recognition with the targeting moiety [125]. To achieve better selectivity of PEG-coated liposomes, it is advantageous to attach the targeting ligand via a PEG spacer arm, so that the ligand is extended outside the dense PEG brush which reduces steric hindrance of binding to the target [127]. The use of PEG-conjugated immunoliposomes for increasing drug carrying capacity of monoclonal antibody has been demonstrated [128]. In addition to costly monoclonal antibodies, common molecules such as folic acid, trensferrin and RGD peptides have also been studied for tumor targeting with enhanced selective uptakes [120].

Encouraging results of liposomal drugs in the treatment or prevention of a wide spectrum of diseases in experimental animals and in human, indicate that more liposome-based products for clinical and veterinary applications may be forthcoming. These could include treatment of eye and skin diseases in therapeutic applications, antimicrobial and anticancer therapy in clinical applications, metal chelation, enzyme and hormone replacement therapy, vaccine and diagnostic imaging, etc. Some of the liposome applications in terms of drug delivery are discussed below.

6.1. Ocular Applications

The eye is protected by three highly efficient mechanisms (a) an epithelial layer which is the barrier to penetration (b) tear flow (c) the blinking reflex. All these mechanisms are responsible for the poor drug penetration into the deeper layers of the cornea and the aqueous humor and for the rapid wash out of drugs from the corneal surface. Initially, in 1981 the enhanced efficiency of liposomes encapsulated idoxuridine in herpes simplex infected corneal lesions in rabbits was reported [129]. In 1985, it was concluded that ocular delivery of drugs can be either promoted or impeded by the use of liposome carriers, depending on the physicochemical properties of the drugs and the lipid mixture employed [130]. The use of mucoadhesive polymers, carbopol 934P and carbopol 1342 to retain liposomes at the cornea was proposed [131]. While precorneal retention times were indeed significantly enhanced under appropriate conditions, liposomes even in the presence of the mucoadhesive had migrated toward the conjuctival sac with very little activity remaining at the corneal surface.

6.2. Pulmonary Applications

Lung is a natural target for the delivery of therapeutic and prophylactic agents such as peptides and proteins. The past 15 years have been marked by intensive research efforts on pulmonary drug delivery not only for local therapy but also for systemic therapy as well as diagnostic purposes, primarily due to the several advantages the pulmonary route offers over other routes of drug administration. Drugs that undergo gastrointestinal degradation (such as proteins and peptides) are ideal candidates for pulmonary delivery.

Targeted drug delivery to the lungs has evolved to be one of the most widely investigated systemic or local drug delivery approaches. The use of drug delivery systems for the treatment of pulmonary diseases is increasing because of their potential for localized topical therapy in the lungs. This route also makes it possible to deposit drugs more site-specific at high concentrations within the diseased lung thereby reducing the overall amount of drug activity while reducing systemic side effects. To further exploit the other advantages presented by the lungs, as well as to overcome some challenges, scientists developed interests in particulate drug delivery systems for pulmonary administration, such as liposomes, micelles, nano-and micro-particles based on polymers.

The use of liposomes as drug carriers for pulmonary delivery has been reported for different kinds of therapeutics such as anti-microbial agents, cytotoxic drugs, antioxidants, anti-asthma compounds and recombinant genes for gene therapy in the treatment of cystic fibrosis.

Liposomes as carrier systems for pulmonary delivery offer several advantages over aerosol delivery of the corresponding non-encapsulated drug. Liposomes might be used to solubilize poorly soluble drugs, provide a pulmonary sustained release reservoir prolonging local and systemic therapeutic drug levels, facilitate intracellular delivery of drugs especially to alveolar macrophages, tumor cells or epithelial cells, prevent local irritation of lung tissue and reduce the drug's toxicity, target specific cell populations using surface bound ligands or antibodies and be absorbed across the epithelium to reach the systemic circulation intact [132].

Local delivery of medication to the lungs is highly desirable, especially in patients with specific pulmonary diseases such as cystic fibrosis, asthma, chronic pulmonary infections or lung cancer. The principal advantages include reduction of systemic side effects and application of higher doses of the medication at the site of drug action. Although simple inhalation devices and aerosols containing various drugs have been used since the early 19th century for the treatment of respiratory disorders, the past 15 years have been marked by intensive research efforts on pulmonary drug delivery not only for local therapy but also for systemic therapy as well as diagnostic purposes due to the several advantages the pulmonary route offers over other routes of drug administration. Lung is a natural target for the delivery of therapeutic and prophylactic agents such as peptides and proteins due to the large surface area available for absorption, the very thin absorption membrane and the elevated blood flow which rapidly distributes molecules throughout the body. Moreover, the lungs exhibit relatively low local metabolic activity, and unlike the oral route of drug administration, pulmonary inhalation is not subject to first pass metabolism [133].

Inhaled drug delivery devices can be divided into three principal categories: nebulizers, pressurized metered-dose inhalers and dry powder inhalers; each class presents unique strengths and weaknesses. A good delivery device has to generate an aerosol of suitable size and provide reproducible drug dosing. It must also protect the physical and chemical stability of the drug formulation.

For controlled delivery of drug to the lung, liposomes are one of the most extensively investigated systems in recent studies given that they can be prepared with phospholipids such as egg phosphatidylcholine (PC), distearoyl phosphatidylcholine (DSPC) and dipalmitoylphosphatidylcholine (DPPC) endogenous to the lung.

A significant disadvantage of many existing inhaled drugs is the relatively short duration of resultant clinical effects, which requires most medications to be inhaled at least twice daily. This often leads to poor patient compliance. A reduction in the frequency of dosing would be convenient, particularly for chronic diseases such as asthma. The advantages of such an approach include reduced dosing, increased effectiveness of rapidly cleared medicine and enhanced residence time at the target site for the treatment of infection. Many challenges exist in developing controlled release inhalation medicine, which is reflected in the fact that no commercial product exists. Cytotoxic agents, bronchodilators, anti-asthma drugs, antimicrobial and antiviral agents and drugs for systemic action, such as insulin and proteins are being investigated.

6.3. Cancer Therapy

The numerous anti-cancer agents that have a high cytotoxic effect on the tumor cells in vitro exhibit a remarkable decrease of the selective ant-tumor effect for in vivo procedures applicable in the clinical treatment. One of the significant limitations of the anti-cancer drugs is their low therapeutic index meaning that the dose required to produce an anti-tumor effect is toxic to normal tissues. The low therapeutic index of these drugs results from the inability to achieve therapeutic concentrations at the specific target sites, tumors. Further, it results from the non-specific toxicity to normal tissues such as bone marrow, renal, gastrointestinal tract, and cardiac tissue and also from the problems associated with a preparation of a suitable formulation of the drugs [134].

Many different liposome formulations of various anticancer agents were shown to be less toxic than the free drug so that most of the medical applications of liposomes that have reached the preclinical stage are in cancer treatment [135-137]. Entrapment of these drugs into liposomes resulted in increased circulation lifetime, enhanced deposition in the infected tissues, and protection from the drug metabolic degradation, altered tissue distribution of the drug, with its enhanced uptake in organs rich in mononuclear phagocytic cells (liver, spleen and bone marrow) and decreased uptake in the kidney, myocardium and brain. To target tumors, liposomes must be capable of leaving the blood and accessing the tumor. However, because of their size liposomes cannot normally undergo transcapillary passage. In spite of this, various studies have demonstrated the accumulation of liposomes in certain tumors in a higher concentration than found in normal tissues [138, 139]. Anthracyclines are drugs which stop the growth of dividing cells by intercalating into the DNA and therefore kill predominantly quickly dividing cells. These cells are not only in tumors but are also in hair, gastrointestinal mucosa, and blood cells; therefore, this class of drugs is very toxic. Many research efforts have been directed towards improving the safety profile of the anthracyclines cytotoxics, doxorubicin and daunorubicin, along with vincristine. Encapsulation of these drugs into the liposomes showed reduced cardiotoxicity, dermal toxicity and better survival of the experimental animals compared to the controls receiving free drugs [138]. Such beneficial effects of liposomal anthracyclines have been observed with a variety of liposome formulations regardless of their lipid composition and provided that lipids used high cholesterol concentration of phospholipids with high phase transition temperature are conducive to drug retention by the vesicles in the systemic circulation [45].

Active targeting of cancer drugs to the tumors is shown schematically in Figure 4.

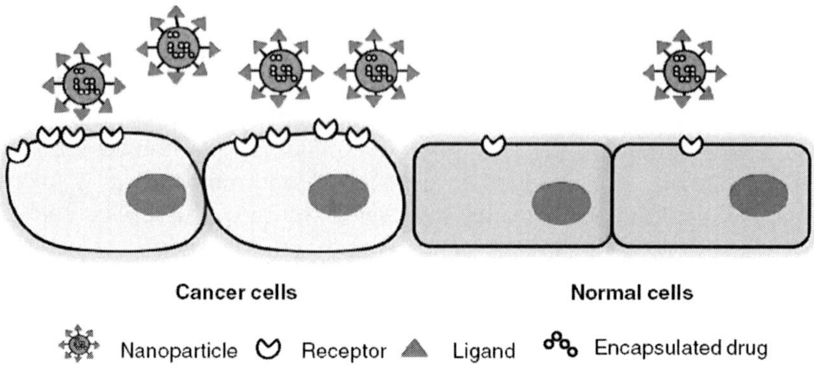

Figure 4. Representation of active targeting via receptors [121].

Currently several liposomal formulations are in the clinical practice containing different chemotherapeutics such as doxorubicin (Doxil1/Caelyx1), doxorubicin (Myocet1), daunorubicin (DaunoXome1) and cytarabine (DepoCyte1) for treating the ovarian cancer, AIDS related Kaposi's sarcoma, multiple myeloma, lymphomas, leukemia with meningeal spread. Several other liposomal chemotherapeutic drugs containing doxorubicin, annamycin, mitoxantrone, cisplatin, oxaliplatin, camptothecine, 9-nitro-20 (S)-camptothecin, irinotecan, lurtotecan, topotecan, paclitaxel, vincristine, vinorelbine and floxuridine are at the various stages of clinical trials [140].

Two liposomal formulations have been approved by the US Food and Drug Administration (FDA) and are commercially available for the treatment of AIDS-related Kaposi's sarcoma. Doxil, first liposomal drug approved by FDA and has been on the market since 1995, is a formulation of doxorubicin precipitated in sterically stabilized liposomes and has been on the market since 1995 [141], while DaunoXome, approved six months later than Doxil, is daunorubicin encapsulated in small liposomes with very strong and cohesive bilayers, which can be referred as mechanical stabilization [142].

DaunoXome is composed of small unilamellar vesicles containing distearoylphosphatidylcholine-cholesterol (2:1) with daunorubicin loaded by a pH gradient [137]. These liposomes are selectively stable in the circulation because they are small and their membrane is electrically neutral and mechanically very strong [142]. This reduces the charge-induced and hydrophobic binding of plasma components but does not protect against van der Waals adsorption. Also, uncharged liposomes are colloidally less stable than charged ones.

Doxil is a liquid suspension of 80-100 nm liposomes (2000PEG-distearoylphosphatidylethanolamine-hydrogenated-soya-bean phosphatidylcholine-cholesterol, 20 mM) loaded with doxorubicin HCl by ammonium sulfate gradient technique and additionally precipitation with encapsulated sulfate anions. These liposomes circulate in patients for several days, which increase their chances of extravasating at sites with a leaky vascular system. Their stability is due to their surface PEG coating as well as to their mechanically very stable bilayers [141, 142].

Cytarabine (Ara-C) is an effective hydrophilic chemotherapeutic agent used widely for the treatment of acute myelogenous leukaemia and lymphocytic leukeamia [143]. It has often been utilized in the combination chemotherapy, against solid tumors and leukaemias. Cytarabine is a cell cycle-dependent drug; hence, prolonged exposure of cells to cytotoxic concentrations is critical to achieve maximum cytotoxic activity. The toxicity of cytarabine is reduced if it is able to maintain an effective therapeutic level for a long period of time and, thus, it is a suitable candidate for administration in a controlled-release dosage form. Liposome encapsulated liposomes (DepoCytTM) are now commercially available.

Etoposide (VP-16-213) is another successful chemotherapeutic agents used for the treatment of human cancers. The drug is currently in its third decade of clinical use and is a front line therapy for a variety of malignancies, including leukaemias, lymphomas and several solid tumors [144]. It has a short biological half-life (3.6 h) with a terminal half-life of 1.5 h intravenously and a variable oral bioavailability ranging from 24% to 74%. Although intraperitoneal injection would result in initial high local tumor concentrations, prolonged exposure of tumor cells may not be possible [145].

The harmful and even destructive effect of cytotoxic drugs on healthy body cells makes it necessary to search for new delivery methods for drugs like cytarabine and etoposide. There are many articles describing the results of investigations of incorporation of cytarabine [146] and etoposide [147] into liposome. However, there is no information about their simultaneous incorporation, in spite of the fact that these two drugs have been used for more than 30 years.

Taxanes are complexes of diterpenoid natural products and semisynthetic analogs. Presently, these drugs belong to prominent anticancer agents used for combined chemotherapy [148]. Paclitaxel (PTX), the prototype of this class, emerges from a natural source [149]. This drug have been used for various cancers including ovarian, breast, head and neck, and non-small cell lung cancers [150].

The commercial PTX preparation (Taxol®) is formulated in the vehicle composed of Cremophor EL® (polyethoxylated castor oil used as a solubilizing surfactant) and dehydrated ethanol, which provides a homogenous preparation. However, some drawbacks have been reported for its clinical applications of this formulation such as severe hypersensitivity reactions, neurotoxicity and neutropenia [151, 152]. It was reported that these adverse effects associated with this formlation would be due to Cremophor EL rather than PTX itself [153]. PTX solubilized in Cremophor EL shows also an incompatibility with the polyvinyl chloride of the administration sets [152]. Furthermore, the short-term stability of PTX upon dilution with aqueous media can result in possible drug precipitation [154].

Special requirements regarding a proper filter device as well as appropriate containers and infusion bags for the storage and administration of the drug have to be fulfilled in order to overcome the problems of incompatibility and instability during the clinical application of Taxol®. Hence, the development of an improved delivery system for PTX is of high importance. Current approaches are focused mainly on the development of formulations that are devoid of Cremophor EL, investigation of the possibility of a large-scale preparation and a request for a longer-term stability. There are some promising possibilities to replace Taxol® by a less irritable preparation such as micelle formulations, water-soluble prodrug preparations, enzyme-activatable prodrug preparations conjugated with antibodies or albumin, parenteral emulsions, microspheres, cyclodextrins, and nanocrytals [155-162].

The preparation of an optimal PTX formulation requires important considerations such as the optimization of the liposomal composition, the balance of the PTX amount encapsulated in the liposomes and the stability of the prepared PTX liposomes during storage in aqueous media [163]. The main characteristics of PTX molecule are asymmetry, bulkiness, hydrophobicity, low solubility and tendency to crystallization in aqueous media. All these factors affect the final design and preparation of a suitable drug formulation.

Liposomes provide suitable environment enhancing the solubility of the hydrophobic nature PTX by associating the molecule within the membrane bilayers. Commonly prepared formulations of PTX with liposomes were able to encapsulate the highest achievable content of PTX, 3-4 mol% with stability for weeks to months whereas 4-5 mol% paclitaxel was stable in the time range of just several hours to a day, and 8% paclitaxel loading only resulted in 15 minutes of liposome stability. Generally, increasing the encapsulated amount of PTX causes a reduction in the stability of the liposomal-PTX formulation due to the crystallization of the drug molecule. Thereby, to achieve a high drug/lipid ratio while retaining the long-term physical-chemical stability, a freeze-drying method is employed to obtain a dry drug-lipid powder, which is rehydrated in an aqueous solution immediately before use [58]. The encapsulation of PTX into liposomes enhances the drug therapeutic efficacy, thus, the same therapeutic effect could be reached by a decreased PTX-dose. On the other hand, the maximum tolerated dose (MTD) of liposome-encapsulated PTX increased compared with the Taxol® [Straubinger, R.M. and S.V. Balasubramanian, Preparation and Characterization of Taxane-containing Liposomes, Methods Enzymol. 391 (2005) 97-117.]. [163].

Taxane liposomes have shown slower elimination, higher antitumor activity against various murine and human tumors and lower systemic toxic effect compared to Taxol® [58]. They have also shown antitumor effect in Taxol-resistant tumor models [164]. Abraxane®, the only nonliposomal preparation of PTX, (albumin nanoparticle-based PTX preparation) and Lipusu® (liposomal PTX approved by State FDA of China) have entered the field of clinical applications. LEP-ETU (NeoPharm) and EndoTAG®-1 (Medigene) have reached the phase II of the clinical trials. Generally, liposomes and protein nanoparticles represent a promising approach to the optimization of PTX delivery. Their commercialization is at the doorstep of modern drug delivery market.

7. NEW GENERATION LIPOSOMES

Liposomes made up of commonly used ester phospholipids such as phosphatidylcholine are referred as conventional liposomes. These structures are very attractive for encapsulation and drug delivery applications to entrap both hydrophilic and hydrophobic materials due to the presence of aqueous core part as well as the lipid bilayer. Up to this date, there are many formulations in the market and also in the clinical trials. However, none of them truly overcome their chemical and physical instability problems especially during the transfer to the site of action [120]. Various attempts like modification of the liposome surface with i.e. hydrophilic polyethylene glycol polymers, using cryoprotectants or incorporation of high amount of cholesterol into the bilayer have led to only limited success. Other than instability problems, liposomal drug vehicles show extensive leakage of water-soluble drugs during the passage through the gastrointestinal tract and they are heterogeneous in terms of size distribution. Therefore, scientists have been looking for new drug delivery formulations that could address these issues about liposomes, which lead to the so-called new generation of liposomes which will be summarized in this section.

Archaeosomes are liposomal formulations that are prepared with one or more lipids, mainly containing diether and/or tetraether linkages, found in archaeobacterial membrane [165]. These archaeobacterial lipids present unique features and higher stabilities to several conditions (high or low temperatures, high salinity, acidic media, anaerobic atmosphere, high pressure) over conventional liposomes [166]. The definition of archaeosomes also includes the use of synthetically derived lipids that have the properties of archaeobacterial ether lipids, that is, regularly branched phytanyl chains attached via ether bonds at sn-2,3 glycerol carbons [167]. The surprising stability of archaeosomes can be attributed to some properties brought by the archaeobacterial lipids' structure: (i) the ether linkages that are more stable than esters over a wide range of pH, and the branching methyl groups help both to reduce crystallization and permeability; (2) the stability towards oxidative degradation of these lipid membranes are provided by the fully saturated alkyl chains in the archaeobacterial lipids; (3) the unusual stereochemistry of the glycerol backbone ensures the resistance of the membrane to enzymatic attack; (4) the bipolar lipids span the membranes and enhance their stability properties [167, 168].

Archaeosomes can be prepared by using conventional procedures (hydration of a thin film followed by sonication or extrusion, detergent dialysis) at any temperature in the physiological range or lower, thus making it possible to encapsulate thermally labile compounds. Additionally, they can be prepared and stored in the presence oxygen without any degradation. According to the clinical experiments, in vivo and in vitro, these new drug delivery vehicles are not toxic. Thus, the biocompatibility and better stability of archaeosomes in numerous conditions offer advantages over conventional liposomes for their usage in biotechnology including vaccine and drug/gene delivery [167]. Consequently, they can be considered as better carriers than conventional liposomes, especially for protein and peptide delivery due to their high stability. Li et al. showed the superiority of archaeosomes over conventional liposomes in their study in which they used insulin as a model peptide for its oral delivery [169].

Another development aiming to enhance tissue targeting is virosomes in which the liposome surface is modified with fusogenic viral envelope proteins [170]. Virosomes have been used for the intracellular delivery of drugs and DNA [171, 172] as well as the basis of the newly developed vaccines which are very effective in the delivery of protein antigens to the immune system [173]. As a result, a whole set of virosomes-based vaccines have been developed for human and animal use. Special attention has been paid to the delivery of influenza vaccine using virosomes containing the spike proteins of influenza virus. Virosome-based vaccines were found to be highly immunogenic and well tolerated in children. A similar approach was used to prepare virosomal hepatitis A vaccine that elicited high antibody titres after primary and booster vaccination of infants and young children which was also confirmed for the healthy adults and elderly patients [174-176]. In general, virosomes can provide an excellent opportunity for the efficient delivery of both various antigens and many drugs, including nucleic acids, cytotoxic drugs and toxoids

[177, 178], although they might present certain problems associated with their stability, leakiness and immunogenicity.

Niosomes, exhibiting a similar behavior to liposomes, are the vesicles that are made up of nonionic surfactants (e.g. alkyl ethers and alkyl esters) and cholesterol. These structures are stable on their own and they increase the stability of the encapsulated drugs. No special conditions are needed for handling and storage of these surfactants. Niosomes improve the oral bioavailability of poorly absorbed drugs, and enhance skin penetration of drug. When compared with liposomes, their oral absorption is better due to the replacement of phospholipids with nonionic surfactants which are less susceptible to the action of bile salts, parenteral, as well as topical routes. These delivery systems are biodegradable, biocompatible and non-immunogenic. Niosomes improve the therapeutic performance of drug molecules by delaying the clearance from the circulation and protecting the drug from biological environment [179].

The transdermal delivery is one of the most important routes of drug administration. The main factor which limits the application of transdermal route for drug delivery is the permeation of drugs through the skin. Human skin has selective permeability for drugs. Lipophilic drugs can pass through the skin but the drugs which are hydrophilic in nature can not pass through. Water soluble drugs either show less or no permeation. To improve the permeation of drugs through the skin various mechanisms have been investigated, including use of chemical or physical enhancers, such as iontophoresis, sonophoresis, etc. Liposomes and niosomes are not suitable for transdermal delivery due to poor skin permeability, breaking of the system, aggregation, drug leakage, and fusion of vesicles [180].

A new type of carrier system, suitable for transdermal delivery, called transfersome has been proposed for the delivery of proteins and peptides like insulin, bovin, serum albumin, vaccines, etc. These systems are soft and malleable carriers that offer noninvasive delivery of drug into or across the deeper skin layers and/or the systemic circulation [181]. Transfersomes improve the site specificity while providing the safety of the drug. Transfersomes are the lipid supramolecular aggregates which make them very flexible. This flexibility as well as their good penetration ability causes them to be used in the effective delivery of non-steroidal anti-inflammatory agents like ibuprofen and diclofenac [182].

Alternatively, unlike classic liposomes [183, 184], that are known mainly to deliver drugs to the outer layers of skin, ethosomes can enhance permeation through the stratum corneum barrier [185-187]. Ethosomes, developed by Touitou in 1997, are the slight modification of well established drug carrier liposome, containing phospholipids, alcohol (ethanol or isopropyl alcohol) in relatively high concentration and water [188]. The size of these soft vesicles can vary from nanometers to microns [189-193]. The high concentration of ethanol makes the ethosomes unique. The ethanol in ethosomes causes disturbance in the skin lipid bilayer organization, hence when incorporated into a vesicle membrane, it enhances the vesicle's ability to penetrate the stratum corneum. Also, because of the high concentration of ethanol the lipid membrane is packed less tightly than conventional vesicles but has equivalent stability, allowing a more malleable structure and improves drug distribution ability in stratum corneum lipids. Ethosomes can be used for many purposes in drug delivery for the treatment of many diseases such as Minoxidil for baldness, testosterone as steroidal hormone, Trihexyphenidyl hydrochloride for Parkinson's disease, Zidovudine and Lamivudine as anti-HIV, Bacitracin as antibacterial, Erythromycin as antimicrobial, DNA for genetic disorders, Cannabidol in the treatment of rheumatoid arthiritis and many others [190, 192, 194-201].

Novasomes are the modified forms of liposomes [202] or a type of niosomes prepared from the mixture of monoester of polyoxyethylene fatty acids, cholesterol and free fatty acids with the diameter of 0.1-1.0 microns. They consist of two to seven bilayer shells that surround an unstructured space occupied by a large amorphous core of hydrophilic or hydrophobic materials [203]. The inner amorphous core can be loaded up to 80-85% with a medical drug and the surfaces of novasomes can be positive, negative or neutral.

Novasomes offer several advantages to the owners of the product such as: Both hydrophilic and hydrophobic products can be incorporated in the same formulation, drugs showing interactions can be incorporated in between bilayers to prevent incompatibility, they can be made site specific due to their surface charge characteristics, they can deliver a large volume of active ingredient, thus also reducing the frequency of application, and they have the ability of adhering skin or hair shafts which makes novasomes applicable in the cosmetic formulations [204].

Novasomes have extensive utilization in fields of foods, cosmetics, personal care, chemical, agrochemical and pharmaceuticals. The technology enhances absorption rate via topical delivery of pharmaceuticals and cosmeceuticals by utilizing non-phospholipid structures. Various FDA-regulated products such as human pharmaceuticals and vaccines can be developed by this technology [205, 206]. These nonionic vesicles composed of glyceryl dilaurate with cholesterol and polyoxyethylene-10-stearyl ether have been known to deliver greater amounts of cyclosporine into and through hairless mouse skin than phosphatidyl choline or ceramide based vesicles [206]. Among various liposomal formulations, novasomes appeared more effective when delivered under non-occluded conditions from a finite dose [206]. Various vaccines based on novasomes have been licensed for the immunization of fowl against

Newcastle disease virus and avian rheovirus [135]. Some of the novasome-based vaccines against bacterial and viral infections have been developed such as small pox vaccine while still many are under development [207]. Novasomes inactivate viruses such as orthomyxoviruses, paramyxoviruses, coronaviruses and retroviruses, etc., by fusing with enveloped virus and that the nucleic acid of the virus denatures shortly after the fusion [208].

Although liposomes are like biomembranes, they are still foreign objects of the body. Therefore, liposomes are known by the mononuclear phagocytic system (MPS) after contact with plasma proteins. Accordingly, liposomes are cleared from the blood stream. For more than two decades, various PEG derivatives have been used to stabilize for increasing efficiency in drug or gene delivery. Most 'stabilized' liposomes, the so-called stealth liposomes [78], or cryptosomes [84], contain a certain percentage of PEG-derivatized phospholipids, which reduce the uptake by MPS, thereof prolonging the circulation times and making available abundant time for these liposomes to leak from the circulation through the leaky endothelium. Unlike, conventional liposomes, PEG-liposomes do not show dose dependent blood clearance kinetics [209]. Vesicles containing PEG-conjugated lipids at various concentrations, molecular weights, or various sizes of PEG-containing vesicles were reported to have different circulation times [81, 84, 210-212]. These kind of liposomal systems are generally used in the ligand-mediated drug targeting [213]. This stealth principle has been used to develop the successful doxorubicin-loaded liposome product that is presently available in the market as Doxil (Janssen Biotech, Inc., Horsham, USA) or Caelyx (Schering-Plough Corporation, Kenilworth, USA) for the treatment of solid tumors.

Cryptosomes is a liposomal composition for targeted delivery of drugs. The composition comprises poloxamer molecules and liposomes encapsulating one or more delivery agents. Poloxamers are polyethylene oxide (PEO)-polypropylene oxide (PPO)-polyethylene oxide tri-block co-polymers of different molecular weights. The hydrophobic PPO group in the middle links the two hydrophilic PEO groups. The hydrophilic PEO groups of a poloxamer, on either side of the central PPO unit, can provide steric protection to a bilayer surface. The amphiphilic nature of the poloxamers makes them extremely useful in various applications as emulsifiers and stabilizers. It is considered that the central PPO unit, being hydrophobic, would tend to push into the bilayer interior serving as an anchor. Dislodging the poloxamer molecule from the bilayer is achieved by reducing its hydrophobicity which is achieved by decreasing the temperature. In an aqueous medium, poloxamers stay as individual molecules at temperatures below their critical micelle temperature (CMT), but at temperatures above the CMT, they form micelles due to their amphiphilic nature. In the presence of lipid bilayers, some poloxamer molecules would partition into the bilayers as well as forming micelles with other poloxamer units. If the temperature again goes below the CMT, the poloxamer molecules lose their amphiphilic nature and disassociate from the lipid bilayer or micelle [179].

Emulsome, having the characteristics of both liposomes and emulsions, is a novel lipoidal vesicular system with an internal solid fat core surrounded by phospholipid bilayer. Emulsomes comprise a hydrophobic core (composed of solid fates instead of oils) as in standard oil-in-water emulsions, but the core is surrounded and stabilized by one or more envelopes of phospholipid bilayers as in liposomes allowing water insoluble drugs in the solution form without requiring any surface active agent or co-solvent. Emulsomes differ from liposomes since their internal core is a lipid, whereas the internal core in liposomes is an aqueous compartment. The drug loading is generally followed by sonication to produce emulsomes of smaller size [214]. These systems are often prepared by melt expression or emulsion solvent diffusive extraction. The lipid assembly of emulsomes, stabilized by cholesterol and soya lecithin (5-10% by weight), has features that are intermediate between liposomes and oil-in-water emulsions droplets. Emulsomes provide the advantages of improved hydrophobic drug loading in the internal solid lipid core and the ability of encapsulating water-soluble medicaments in the aqueous compartments of surrounding phospholipid layers.

Beside the other vesicular formulations, emulsomes are much stabilized and nano range vesicles. It is a new emerging delivery system and therefore could play a fundamental function in the effective treatment of life-threatening viral infections and fungal infections such as hepatitis, HIV, Epstein-Barr virus, leishmaniasis, etc. appear promising for the treatment of visceral leishmaniasis specifically and hepato-splenic candidiasis [214-216]. Emulsomes could be utilized in order to improve oral controlled delivery of drug, vaccine, and biomacromolecules. It is due to the fact that they are nano sized in range and could be utilized for the intravenous route. The common application areas of emulsomes are drug targeting, anti-neoplastic treatment, leishmaniasis (a disease in which a parasite of the genus Leishmania invades the cells of the liver and spleen) treatment, and biotechnology. Moreover, emulsomes could represent a more economical alternative to current commercial lipid formulations for the treatment of viral infections and fungal infections. Emulsomes provide a controlled and sustain release of drug. In comparison to the liposomes, emulsomes provide a prolong release of drug up to 24 hours, whereas liposomes have shown release up to 6 hours [217-219]. Emulsomes are nano size range in comparison to other vesicular delivery system such as niosomes and ethosomes. Due to the reduced size (10-250 nm) they can be used to enhance bioavailability to drug and as the best carrier for the intravenous drug delivery as well as oral drug delivery.

The lipid core of emulsomes may contain one or more anti-oxidants which are generally α-tocopherol or its derivatives that are the members of Vitamin-E family. The presence of anti-oxidants reduces the formation of oxidative degradation products of unsaturated lipids such as peroxides. The need of anti-oxidant can be prevented by the usage of saturated fatty acids during the preparation of the lipid core [220]. In the formation of emulsomes, like in the case of liposomes, cholesterol is essential component for the system that influences the stability of emulsomal systems and plays an important role in the drug encapsulation [221-224].

The most important advantage of emulsomes is their ability to protect the encapsulated drug from harsh gastric environment of stomach before oral administration because the drug is inside the triglyceride lipid core which can be supported that the gastric pH and the gastric enzymes are unable to hydrolyze triglycerides. Also, they resist development of multi drug resistance, often associated with over expression of a cell membrane glycoprotein, which cause efflux of the drug from the cytoplasm and results in an ineffective drug concentration inside the cellular compartment [225].

The development of emulsomes, however, is still largely empirical, and in vitro models that are predictive of oral bioavailability enhancement are lacking. There is a need for in vitro methods for predicting the dynamic changes involving the drug in the gut in order to monitor the solubilization state of the drug in vivo. Attention also needs to be paid to the interactions between lipid systems and the pharmacologically active substance. The characteristics of various lipid formulations also need to be understood, so that guidelines can be established that allow identification of suitable candidate formulations at an early stage. Future research should involve human bioavailability studies as well as more basic studies on the mechanisms of action of this fascinating and diverse group of formulations.

Unilamellar vesicles or liposomes are commonly used as simple cell models and as drug delivery vehicles to follow the release kinetics of lipophilic drugs that require compartmental models in its therapeutics and triggers. The localization of the drug at the site of action, rate of achieving the therapeutic index and circulation lifetime are the key parameters for a liposome. Lately, their arises a need for a multi-compartment structure consisting of drug-loaded liposomes encapsulated within another bilayer, is a promising drug carrier with better retention and stability due to prevention enzymes or proteins reaching the interior bilayers. A vesosome is a more or less heterogeneous, aggregated, large lipid bilayer enclosing multiple, smaller liposomes that offer a second barrier of protection for interior compartments and can also serve as the anchor for active targeting components [226, 76]. The multi-compartment structure of vesosome can also allow for independent optimization of the interior compartments and exterior bilayer; however, just the bilayer-within-a-bilayer structure of the vesosome is sufficient to increase drug retention from minutes to hours [227, 228].

In nature, eukaryotes increased their ability to optimize their response to their surroundings by developing multiple compartments, each of which has a distinct bilayer membrane, usually of quite varied composition and physical structure. Mimicking this natural progression to nested bilayer compartments led to the development of the vesosome, or vesicles deliberately trapped within another vesicle. The vesosome has distinct inner compartments separated from the external membrane; each compartment can encapsulate different materials and have different bilayer compositions. In addition, while it has proven difficult to encapsulate anything larger than molecular solutions within lipid bilayers by conventional vesicle self-assembly, the vesosome construction process lends itself to trapping colloidal particles and biological macromolecules relatively efficiently [229, 230]. The nested bilayer compartments of the vesosome provide a degree of freedom for optimization not possible with a single membrane enclosed compartment and a more realistic approximation of higher order biological organization.

The vesosome structure could be used to deliver a cocktail of antibiotics or antimicrobials to sites at a fixed ratio; such mixtures have been shown to act synergistically when delivered in a single liposome [231]. Such multi-drug formulations may be useful to avoid inducing pathogen resistance to a single drug.

As vesosomes are simply liposomes within liposomes, it should be possible to directly translate the extensive body of research on liposome drug delivery to the vesosome with only minor changes, and perhaps significant major improvements. The vesosome is created by simply self-assembly steps very similar to those used in making conventional unilamellar liposomes [229]. An important question is whether such additional effort in developing new structures will provide a therapeutic benefit over direct injection of the free drug or drug delivery by conventional unilamellar liposomes. The most obvious potential application for the vesosome is for drugs that have already shown increased efficacy by delivery with conventional liposomes. As an example, ciprofloxacin (cipro), a synthetic bactericidal fluoroquinolone antibiotic with broad spectrum efficacy, is released much more quickly from unilamellar liposomes in serum relative to saline [232, 233]. Conventional pH-loaded liposomes can retain essentially all encapsulated ciprofloxacin when stored in buffer for 12 weeks at 21 0C and 8 weeks at 37 0C [234, 235]. Although liposomal cipro has shown increased efficacy due to prolonged residence of cipro in the blood (free cipro is cleared in minutes), the half-life of release from the liposomes was only 1 hour, yet the liposomes themselves circulated for more than 24 hours [232, 235]. A second example is vincristine, a naturally occurring dimeric catharanthus alkaloid that has been used extensively as an antitumor agent since 1960's. The therapeutic activity of vincristine is dictated by the duration of therapeutic concentrations at the tumor site [236, 238, 239]. However, conventional liposomes, while offering improved bioavailability, also cannot encapsulate vincristine for sufficient time to give optimal results [234, 236, 237]. Future work will determine if multiple compartment structures like vesosome give sufficient enhancement of small drug entrapment to lead to new therapeutics.

Genetics play an increasingly important role in medicine and is used routinely to diagnose diseases and to understand malfunctions at the molecular level. The active approach of trying to amend genetic defects or insufficiencies is a logical next step. Major elements in the successful advance of gene therapy are identification of the disease and target cells, tissues and organs as well as construction of appropriate gene vectors, effective gene transfer and expression in the targeted cells. Many inherited diseases follow the Mendelian inheritance pattern in which the cause is due to a single genetic defect. Because the existing therapeutic treatments of such diseases are in most cases very limited, it is hoped that by transfecting appropriate cells with the correct gene or by adding a missing one, the disease could be alleviated. Examples of such potential treatments are for cystic fibrosis, hemophilia, sickle cell anemia or hypercholesterimia and mutant tumor suppressor genes.

The aim of gene therapy is to deliver DNA, RNA or antisense sequences to appropriate cells in order to alleviate symptoms or prevent the occurrence of a particular disease, i.e. repair the defect and also its cause. The major approaches to gene therapy include gene replacement, addition of genes for production of natural toxins, stimulation of the immune system or over expression of highly immunogenenic genes for immune self-attack and sensitization of cells to other treatments.

Recently, the studies on gene delivery into eukaryotic cells by the use of non-viral-lipid-based macromolecular delivery systems have been experiencing a growing interest owing to the appearance of clinical protocols for gene therapy. Although the efficiency and specificity of such non-viral delivery systems are not yet very high, some of the problems concerning transfection methods are being successfully solved. To date, the transfection mediators that ensure effective and directed gene delivery into various cells have been created. Transfection of plasmid DNA is closely connected to the problem of condensation of its molecule since the plasmid is too large (13-15 kb) to effectively overcome the cellular membrane barrier. Besides, free DNA has to be protected from destruction by endogenous nucleases. Lastly, it is necessary to neutralize the negative charge on DNA.

Genosomes are the artificial functional complexes for functional gene or DNA delivery to cell [238]. For the production of genosomes, cationic phospholipids were found to be more suitable because they possess high biodegradability and stability in the blood stream. Gene delivery is a vast area of research and a detailed summary of work in that field is beyond the scope of this chapter.

New generation liposomes and their features are summarized in Table 2.

Table 2. New generation liposomes and their features.

Type	Main constituent	Advantage
Liposomes	Phospholipids	
Archaesomes	One or more lipids containing diether linkages	High stability at several conditions
Niosomes	Non-ionic surfactant and cholesterol	Less prone to action of bile salts
Novasomes	Monoester of polyoxyethylene fatty acids, cholesterol and free fatty acids. Two to seven bilayer shells	High loading of drugs
Transfersomes	Lipid supramolecular aggregates	More flexible hence better transdermal delivery
Ethosomes	Phospholipids and alcohol in relatively high concentration	More distruptive in the skin lipid bilayer organization hence better transdermal delivery
Virosomes	Lipids surface modified with fusogenic viral envelope proteins	Intracellular delivery of antigens, drugs and DNA
Cryptosomes	Phospholipids and polaxamers or PEG	More stable
Emulsomes	Internal solid fat core surrounded by phospholipid bilayer	Better for encapsulation of hydrophobic drugs
Vesesomes	Multilamellar liposomes	Multidrug formulations are possible
Genosomes	Complex of cationic phospholipids and a functional gene or DNA	Suitable for gene delivery

Extensively motivated by the need to increase the stability and bioavailability of drugs, and to reduce their side effects by targeting to the site of action, research in new drug delivery vehicles has taken giant steps. Liposomes and their derivatives, so called new generation liposomes, present a vast area in this field where several advances have already been achieved as summarized in this chapter. However, still further research is required to overcome the limitations faced today in terms of prolonged stability, drug loading and active targeting.

8. CONCLUSION

In the last decade from the concept of clinical utility of liposomes to their recognized position in mainstream of drug delivery systems, the path has been long and winding. The liposome systems have been explored in the clinic for applications as diverse as sites of infection and imaging, for vaccine, gene delivery and small molecular drugs, for treatment of infections and for cancer treatment, for lung disease and for skin conditions etc. Several liposomal formulations are already on the market, while quite a few are still in the pipeline for treatment of diseases. Conventional techniques for liposome preparation and size reduction remain popular as these are simple to implement and do not require sophisticated equipment. However, not all laboratory scale techniques are easy to scale-up for industrial liposome production. Many conventional methods, for preparing small and large unilamellar vesicles, involve use of either water miscible/immiscible organic solvents or detergent molecules. The need for improvements in the design and stability of liposomal diagnostic and therapeutic systems will continue to motivate innovative and efficient routes to their production.

REFERENCES

1. Bangham A.D., editor. The Liposome Letters. Academic Press; 1983.

2. Bangham A.D, Standish M.M, Watkins J.C. Diffusion of Univalent Ions Across the Lamellae of Swollen Phospholipids. Journal of Molecular Biology 1965;13 238-252.

3. Gregoriadis G, Florene A.T. Liposomes in Drug Delivery: Clinical, Diagnostic and Opthalmic Potential. Drugs 1993;45 15-28.

4. Van Rooijen N, van Nieuwmegen R. Liposomes in Immunology: Multilammellar Phosphatidylcholine Liposome as a Simple Biodegradable and Harmless Adjuvant without any Immunogenic Activity of its Own. Immunology Community 1980;9 243-356.

5. Campbell P.I. Toxicity of Some Charged Lipids Used in Liposome Preparations. Cytobios 1983;37 (1983) 21-26.

6. Grislain L, Couvreur P, Lenaerts V, Roland M, Depreg-Decampeneere D, Speiser P. Pharmacokinetics and Distribution of a Biodegradable Drug-carrier. International Journal of Pharmacology 1983;15 335-338.

7. Illum L, Gones P.D.E, Kreuker J, Daldwin R.W, Davis D.D. Adsorption of Monoclonal Antibodies to Polyhexylcyanoacrylate Nanoparticles and Subsequent Immunospecific Binding to Tumor Cells. International Journal of Pharmacology 1983;17 65-69.

8. Hashida M, Takahashi Y, Muranishi S, Sezaki H. An Application of Water in Oil and Gelatin Mirosphere in Oil Emulsions to Specific Delivery of Anticancer Agents into Stomach Lymphatics. Journal of Pharmacokinetics and Biopharmacetics 1977;5 241-144.

9. Mizushima Y, Hamano T, Yokohama K. Use of a Lipid Emulsion as a Novel Carrier for Corticosteriods. Journal of Pharmacology and Pharmacotherapeutics 1982;34 49-53.

10. Gregoriadis G, Ryman B.E. Liposomes as Carriers of Enzymes or Drugs: A New Approach to the Treatment of Storage Diseases. Biochemcal Journal 1971;124 58P.

11. Gregoriadis G. Drug Entrapment in Liposomes. FEBS Letters 1973;36 292-296.

12. Gregoradis G. The Carrier Potential of Liposomes in Biology and Medicine. Part 1,The New England Journal of Medicine 1976;295 704-710.

13. Gregoradis G. The Carrier Potential of Liposomes in Biology and Medicine. Part 2, The New England Journal of Medicine 1976;295 765-770.

14. Lasic D.D, Papahadjopoulos D. Liposomes Revisited. Science 1995;267 1275-1276.

15. Noble G. T, Stefanick, J. F, Ashley, J. D, Kiziltepe, T, Bilgicer, B. Ligand-targeted Liposome Design: Challenges and Fundamental Considerations. Trends in Biotechnology 2014;32 32-45.

16. Hofheinz R.D, Gnad-Vogt S.U, Beyer U, Hochhaus A. Liposomal Encapsulated Anticancer Drugs. Anticancer Drugs 2005;16 691-707.

17. Kulkarni S.B, Betageri G.V, Singh M. Factors Affecting Microencapsulation of Drugs in Liposomes. Journal of Microencapsulation 1995;12 229-246.

18. Koudelka S, Masek J, Neuzil J, Turanek J. Lyophilized Liposome-based Formulations of Alpha-Tocopheryl Succinate: Preparation and Physico-chemical Characterisation. Journal of Pharmaceutical Sciences 2010; 99 2434-2443.

19. Kobayashi T, Tsukagoshi S, Sakurai Y. Enhancement of the Cancer Chemotherapeutic Effect of Cytosine Arabinoside Entrapped in Liposomes on Mouse Leukemia L-1210., Gann 1975;66 719-720.

20. Mayhew E, Papahadjopoulos D, Rustum Y.M, Dave C. Inhibition of Tumor Cell Growth in vitro and in vivo by 1-β-D-arabinofuranosylcytosine Entrapped within Phospholipid Vesicles. Cancer Research 1976;36 4406-4411.

21. Lopez-Berestein G, Fainstein R, Hopfer R, Mehta K, Sullivan M.P, Keating M, Rosenblum, M.G, Mehta R, Luna M, Hersh E.M, Reuben J, Juliano R.L, Bodey G.P. Liposomal Amphotericin B for the Treatment of Systemic fungal Infections in Patients with Cancer: A Preliminary Study. Journal of Infectious Diseases 1985;151 704-710.

22. Gabizon A, Peretz T, Sulkes A, Amselem S, Ben-Yosef R, Ben-baruch N, Catane R, Biran S, Barenholz Y. Systemic Administration of Doxorubicin-containing Liposomes in Cancer Patients: A Phase I Study. European Journal of Cancer and Clinical Oncology 1989;25 1795-1803.

23. Lasic DD. Liposomes: From Physics to Applications. Elsevier; 1993.

24. Gomez-Hens A, Fernandez-Romero J. M. Analytical Methods for the Control of Liposomal Delivery Systems. Trends in Analytical Chemistry 2006;25 167-178.

25. Mozafari M.R, Johnson C, Hatziantoniou S, Demetzos C. Nanoliposomes and Their Applications in Food Nanotechnology. Journal of Liposome Research 2008;18 309-327.

26. Dua J.S, Rana A.C, Bhandari A.K. Liposome: Methods of Preparation and Applications. International Journal of Pharmaceutical Studies and Research 2012;3(2) 14-20.

27. Roger R.C. New Chapter 1 Introduction, Liposomes: A Practical Approach, Edited by R. R. C. New, IRL Press at Oxford University press, 1990.

28. Shashi K., Satinder K, Bharat P. A Complete Review on Liposomes. International Research Journal of Pharmacy 2012;3(7) 10-16.

29. Rickwood D, Hames BD. Liposomes: A Practical Approach. IRL Press; 1994.

30. Mayer L.D, Hope M.J, Cullis P.R, Janoff A.S. Solute Distributions and Trapping Efficiencies Observed in Freeze-thawed Multilamellar Vesicles. Biochimica et Biophysica Acta 1985;817 193-196.

31. Imperial Chemical Industries Ltd, 1978, Belgian Patent 866697.

32. Gregoriadis G. Liposome Technology. CRC Press, Boca Raton, Volume I, II and III, 1984.

33. Huang C. Studies on Phosphatidylcholine Vesicles. Formation and Physical Characteristics. Biochemistry 1969;8(1) 344-352.

34. Olson F, Hunt C.A, Szoka F.C, Vail W, Mayhew E, Paphadjopoulos D. Preparations of Liposomes of Defined Size Distribution by Extrusion Through Polycarbonate Membranes. Biochimica Biophysica Acta, 1980, 610, 559.

35. Pick U. Liposomes with a Large Trapping Capacity Prepared by Freezing and Thawing of Sonicated Phospholpid Mixtures. Archives of Biochemistry and Biophysics 1981;212 18194.

36. Ohsawa T, Miura H, Harada K. Improvement of Encapsulation Efficiency of Water-soluble Drugs in Liposomes Formed by Freeze-thawing Method. Chemical & Pharmaceutical Bulletin 1985;33(9) 3945-3952.

37. Liu L, Yonetaini T. Preparation and Characterization of Liposome-encapsulated hemoglobin by a Freeze-thaw Method. Journal of Microencapsulation 1994;11(4) 409-421.

38. Batzri S, Korn E.D. Single Bilayer Liposomes Prepared without Sonication. Biochimica et Biophysica Acta 1976;298 1015-1019.

39. Deamer D.W, Bangham A.D. Large Volume Liposomes by an Ether Vaporization Method. Biochimica et Biophysica Acta 1976;443 629-634.

40. Deamer D.W. Preparation and Properties of Ether-Injection Liposomes. Annals of the New York Academy of Sciences 1978;308 250-258.

41. Lasic D.D. Novel Applications of Liposomes. Trends in Biotechnology 1998;16 307-321.

42. Szoka Jr. F, Papahadjopoulos P. Proceedings of the National Academy of Sciences 1978;60 4194-4198.

43. Jain N. K. Controlled and Novel Drug Delivery. CBS Publisher, pp. 304-326.

44. Clerc S. Barenholz Y. Loading of Amphiphatic Weak Acids into Liposomes in Response to Transmembrane Calcium Acetate Gradients. Biochimica et Biophysica Acta 1995;1240 257-265.

45. Mayer L.D, Tai L.C, Bally M.B, Mitilenes G.N, Ginsberg R.S, Cullis P.R. Characterization of Liposomal Systems Containing Doxorubicin Entrapped in Response to pH Gradients. Biochimica et Biophysica Acta 1990;1025 143-151.

46. Mayhew E.G, Lasic D, Babbar S, Martin F.J. Pharmacokinetics and Antitumor Activity of Epirubicin Encapsulated in Long-circulating Liposomes Incorporating a Polyethylene Glycol-derivatized Phospholipid. International Journal of Cancer 1992;51 302-309.

47. Mayer L.D, Bally M.B, Hope M.J, Cullis P.R. Uptake of Neoplastic Agents into Large Unilamellar Vesicles in Response to a Membrane Potential. Journal of Biological Chemistry 1985;260 802-808.

48. Mayer L.D, Bally M.B, Hope M.J, Cullis P.R. Uptake of Antineoplastic Agents into Large Unilamellar Vesicles in Response to a Membrane Potential. Biochimica et Biophysica Acta 1985;816 294-302.

49. Bressler N.M. In Response to: Verteporfin Therapy of Subfoveal Choroidal Neovascularization in Age-related Macular Degeneration: Two Year Results of a Randomized Clinical Trial Including Lesions with Occult with No Classic Choroidal Neovascularization-Verteporfin in Photodynamic Therapy Report 2. American Journal Of Ophthalmology 2002;133 168.

50. Lambelet P, Löliger J. The Fate of Antioxidant Radicals During Lipid Autooxidation. I. The Tocopherol Radicals. Chemistry and Physics of Lipids 1984;35 185.

51. Kates M, Kushwaha S.C. (1976), In Lipids. Paoletti, R. et al. (eds), Raven Press, NY, Vol. 1: Biochemistry, p. 267.

52. Lasic D.D, Stuart M.C.A, Guol Fredeik P.M. Transmembrane Gradient Driven Phase Transitions within Vesicles: Lessons for Drug Delivery. Biochimica et Biophysica Acta 1995;12139 145-154.

53. Anchordoquy T.J, Carpenter J.F, Kroll D.J. Maintenance of Transfection Rates and Physical Characterization of Lipid/DNA Complexes After Freeze-drying and Rehydration. Archives of Biochemistry and Biophysics 1997;348 199-206.

54. Li B, Li S, Tan Y, Stolz D.B, Watkins S.C, Block L.H, Huang L. Lyophilization of Cationic Lipid-protamine-DNA (LPD) Complexes. Journal of Pharmaceutical Sciences 2000;89 355-364.

55. Molina M.C, Armstrong T.K, Zhang Y, Patel M.M, Lentz Y.K, Anchordoquy T.J. The Stability of Lyophilized Lipid/DNA Complexes During Prolonged Storage. Journal of Pharmaceutical Science 2004;93 2259-2273.

56. Bendas G, Wilhelm F, Richter W. Synthetic Glycolipids as Membrane Bound Cryoprotectants in the Freeze-drying Process of Liposomes. Biochimica et Biophysica Acta-Biomemembranes 1988;939 327-334.

57. Molina M.C, Allison S.D, Anchordoquy T.J, Maintenance of Non-Viral Vector Particle Size During the Freezing Step of the Lyophilization Process is Insufficient for Preservation of Activity: Insight from Other Structural Indications. Journal of Pharmaceutical Science.2001;90 1445-1455.

58. Sharma A, Mayhew E, Bolcsak L, Cavanaugh C, Harmon P, Janoff A, Bernacki R.J. Activity of Paclitaxel Liposome Formulations Against Human Ovarian Tumor Xenografts. International Journal of Cancer 1997;71 103-107.

59. Straubinger R, Sharma A, Mayhew E. Taxol Formulation. US Patent 5415869, 16 May, 1995.

60. http://www.avantilipids.com/index.php?view=items&cid=5&id=8&option=com_quickfaq&Itemid=385

61. Sospedra P, Nagy I.B, Haro I, Mestres C, Hudecz F, Reig F. Physicocehmical Behavior of Polylysine-[HAV-VPS Peptide] Constructs at the Air-water Interface. Langmuir 1999;15 5111-5117.

62. Zoonens M, Reshetnyak Y.K, Engelman D.M. Bilayer Interactions of pHLIP, a Peptide that can Deliver Drugs and Target Tumors. Biophyscal Journal 2008;95 225-235.

63. Coulon A, Berkane E, Sautereau A.M, Urech K, Rouge P, Lopez A. Modes of Membrane Interaction of a Natural Cysteine-rich sPeptide:Viscotoxin A3. Biochimica et Biophysica Acta-Biomembranes 2002;1559 145-159.

64. Sunamoto J, Iwamoto K, Takada M, Yuzuriha T, Katayama K. Improved Drug Delivery to Target Specific Organs Using Liposomes Coated with Polysaccharides. Polymer Science and Technology. 1983;23 157-168.

65. Jamshaid M, Farr S.J, Kearney P, Kellaway I.W. Polyoxamer Sorption on Liposomes: Comparison with Polystyrene latex and Influence on Solute Efflux. International Journal of Pharmaceutics 1998;48 125-131.

66. Kronberg B, Dahiman A, Carifors J, Karlsson J, Artursson P. Preparation and Evaluation of Sterically Stabilized Liposomes: Colloidal Stability, Serum Stability, Macrophage Uptake, and Toxicity. Journal of Pharmaceutical Sciences 1990;79 667-671.

67. Dong C, Rogers J.A. Polymer-coated Liposomes: Stability and Release of ASA from Carboxymethyl Chitin-coated Liposomes. Journal of Controlled Release 1991;17 217-224.

68. Alamelu S, Rao K.P. Studies on the Carboxymethyl Chitosan-containing Liposomes for Their Stability and Controlled Release of Dapson. Journal of Microencapsulation 1991;8 505-515.

69. Elferink M.G.L, de Wit J.G, Veld J.G, Int R.A, Driessen A.J.M, Ringdorf H, Konings W.N. The Stability and Functional Properties of Proteoliposomes Mixed with Dextran Derivatives Bearing Hydrophobic Anchor Groups. Biochimica et Biophysica Acta 1992;1106 23-30.

70. O'Connor C.J, Wallace R.G, Iwamoto K, Taguchi T, Sunamoto J. Bile Salt Damage of Egg Phosphatidylcholine Liposomes. Biochimica et Biophysica Acta 1985;817 95-102.

71. Hernandex-Caselles T, Villalain J, Gomez-Fernandez J.C. Influence of Liposome Charge and Composition on Their Interaction with Human Blood Serum Proteins Molecular and Cellular Biochemistry 1993;120(2) 119-126.

72. Beaumier P.L, Hwang K.J. Effects of Liposome Size on the Degradation of Bovine Brain Sphingomyelin/Cholesterol Liposomes in the Mouse Liver. Biochimica et Biophysica Acta 1983;731 23-30.

73. Alving C.R, Wassef N.M. Complement-dependent Phagocytosis of Liposomes: Suppression by Stealth Liposomes. Journal of Liposome Research 1992;2 383-395.

74. Simoes S, Moreira J.N, Fronseca C. On the Formulation of pH Sensitive Liposomes with Long Circulating Time. Advances Drug Delivery Reviews 2004;56 947-965.

75. Trubetskoy V.S, Torchillin V.P. Use of Polyoxyethylene-lipid Conjugates as Long-circulating Carriers for Delivery of Therapeutic and Diagnostic Agents. Advance Drug Delivery Reviews 1995;16 311-320.

76. Barenholtz, Y. Liposome Application: Problems and Prospects. Current Opinion in Colloid and Interface Science 2001;6 66-77.

77. Hwang M.L, Prud'homme R.K, Kohn J, Thomas J.L. Stabilization of Phosphatidyleserine/Phosphatidylethanolamine Liposomes with Hydrophilic Polymers Having Multple 'Sticky Feet'. Langmuir 2001;17 7713-7716.

78. Woodle M.C, Lasic D.D. Sterically Stabilized Liposomes. Biochimica et Biophysica Acta 1992;1113 171-199.

79. Woodle M.C. Controlling Liposome Blood Clearance by Surface Grafted Polymers. Advanced Drug Delivery Reviews 1998;32 139-152.

80. Klibanov A.L, Maruyama K, Torchillin V.P, Huang L. Amphiphatic Polyethyleneglycols Effectively Prolong the Circulation Time of Liposomes. FEBS Letters 1990;268 235-237.

81. Mori A, Klibanov A.L, Torchillin V.P, Huang L. Influence of Steric Barrier Activity of Amphiphatic poly(ethyleneglycol) and Ganglioside GM1 on the Circulation Time of Liposomes and on the Target Binding of Immunoliposomes in vivo. FEBS Letters 1991;284 263-266.

82. Allen T.M, Mehra T, Hansen C, Chin Y.C. Stealth Liposomes: An Improved Sustained Release System for 1-β-D-arabinofuranosylcytosine. Cancer Research 1992;52 2431-2439.

83. Gabizon A, Papahadjopoulos D. The Role of Surface Charge and Hydrophilic Head Groups on Liposome Clearance in vivo. Biochimica et Biophysica Acta 1992;1103 94-100.

84. Blume G, Cevc G. Molecular Mechanism of the Lipid Vesicle Longevity in vivo. Biochimica et Biophysica Acta 1993;1146 157-168.

85. Torchillin V.P, Shtilman M.I, Trubetskoy V.S, Whiteman K, Milstein A.M. Amphiphilic Vinyl Polymers Effectively Prolong Liposome Circulation Time in vivo. Biochimica et Biophysica Acta 1994;1195 181-184.

86. Torchillin V.P, Trubetskoy V.S, Whiteman K, Caliceti P, Ferruti P, Veronese F.M. New Synthetic Amphiphilic Polymers for Steric Protection of Liposomes in vivo. Journal of Pharmaeutical Science 1995;84 1049-1053.

87. Dreschler H. Indication to prescription of Blood and Blood Substitutes in Operative Medicine. Journal of Medical Laboratory and Diagnosis (Stuttg.) 1974;27 115-121.

88. Kramer S.A. Effect of Povidone-Iodine on Wound Healing: A Review. Journal of Vascular Nursing 1999;17 17-23.

89. Allen T.M, Hansen C, Martin F, Redemann C, yau-Young A. Liposome Containing Synthetic Lipid Derivatives of Poly(ethylene Glycol) Show Prolonged Circulation Half-lives in vivo. Biochimica et Biophysica Acta 1991; 1066 29.

90. Lukyanov A.N, Torchillin V.P. Autoclaving of Liposomes. Journal of Microencapsulation 1994;11 669-672.

91. Meure L.A, Foster N.R, Dehghani F. Conventional and Dense Gas Techniques for the Production of Liposomes: A Review. AAPS Pharm SciTech 2008;9 798-809.

92. Toh M.R, Chiu G.N.C. Liposomes as Sterile Preparations and Limitations of Sterilization Techniques in Liposomal Manufacturing. Asian Journal of Pharmaceutical Science XXX, 2013;E1-E8.

93. Jain NK. Controlled and Novel Drug Delivery. CBS Publisher, 304-326.

94. Ho R.J.Y, Rouse B.T, Huang L. Target-sensitive Immunoliposomes-Preparation and Characterization. Biochemical 1986;25 5500-5506.

95. Lodge T.P, Han C.C, Akcasu A.Z. Temperature Dependene of Dynamic Light Scattering in the Intermediate Momentum Transfer Region. Macromolecules 1983;16 1180-1183.

96. Ostrowsky N. Liposome Size Measurements by Photon Correlation Spectroscopy. Chemistry and Physics of Lipids 1993;64, 45-56.

97. Strömstedt A.A, Wessman P, Ringstad L, Edwards K, Malmsten M. Effect of Lipid Headgroup Composition on the Interaction between Melittin and Lipid Bilayers. Journal of Colloid and Interface Science 2007;311 59–69.

98. du Plessis J, Ramachandran C, Weiner N, Muller D. The Influence of Lipid Composition and Lamellarity of Liposomes on the Physical Stability of Liposomes upon Storage. International Journal of Pharmaceutics 1996;127 273-278.

99. Labhasetwar V, Mohan M.S, Dorle A.K. A study on Zeta Potential and Dielectric Constant of Liposomes. Journal of Microencapsulation 1994;11(6)663-668.

100. Vemuri S, Rhodes C. Preparation and Characterization of Liposomes as Therapeutic Delivery Systems: A Review. Pharmacetica Acta Helvtiae 1995;70 95-111.

101. Sullivan J.C, Budge S.M, Timmins A. Rapid Method for Determination of Residual tert-butanol in Liposomes Using Solid-phase Microextraction and Gas Chromatography. Journal of Chromatographic Science 2010;48(4) 289-93.

102. Biltonen R, Lichtenberg D. The Use of Differential Scanning Calorimetry as a Tool to Characterize Liposome Preparations. Chemistry and Physics of Lipids 1993;64 129-142.

103. Ohtake S, Schebor C, Palecek S, de Pablo J. Effect of Sugar-phosphate Mixtures on the Stability of DPPC Membranes in Dehydrates Systems. Cryobiology 2004;48 81-89.

104. Schofield M, Jenski L, Dumaual A, Stillwell A. Cholesterol versus Cholesterol Sulfate-Effects on Properties of Phospholipid-bilayers Containing Docosahexaenoic Acid. Chemistry and Physcs of Lipids 1998;95 23-36.

105. Buboltz J, Feigenson G. A Novel Strategy for the Preparation of Liposomes: Rapid Solvent Exchange. Biochimica et Biophysica Acta 1999;1417 232-245.

106. Manosroi A, Kongkaneramit L, Manosroi J. Characterization of Amphotericin B Liposome Forulations. Drug Development and Industrial Pharmacy 2004;30 535-543.

107. Sezer A, Bas A, Akbuga J. Encapsulation of Enrofloxacin in Liposome Preparation and in vitro Characterization of LUV. Journal of Liposome Research 2004;14 77-86.

108. Guo W, Ahmad A, Khan S, Dahhani F, Wang Y, Ahmad I. Determination by Liquid Chromatography with Fluorescence Detection of Total 7-ethyl-10-hydroxy-camptothecin (SN-38) in Beagle Dog Plasma After Intravenous Administration of Liposome-based SN-38 (LE-SN38). Journal of Chromatography B 2003;791 85-92.

109. Ramaldes G, Deverre J, Grognet J, Puisieux F, Fattal E. Use of an Enzyme Immunoassay for the Evaluation of Entrapment Efficiency and in vitro Stability in Intestinal Fluids of Liposomal Bovine Serum Albumin. International Journal of Pharmaceutics 1996;143 1-11.

110. Moon M, Giddings J. Size Distributions of Liposomes by Flow Field-Flow Fractionation. Journal of Pharmaceutical and Biomedical Analysis 1993;11 911-920.

111. Teshima M, Kawakami S, Nishida K, Nakamura J, Skaeda T, Terazono H, Kitahara T, Nakashima M, Sasaki H. Prednisolone Retention in Integrated Liposomes by Chemical Approach and Pharmaceutical Approach. Journal of Controlled Release 2004;97 211-218.

112. Arifin D, Palmer A. Determination of Size Distribution and Encapsulation Efficiency of Liposome Encapsulated Hemoglobin Blood

Substitutes Using Asymmetric Flow Field-Flow Fractionation Coupled with Multi-angle Light Scattering. Biotechnology Progress 2003;19 1798-1811.

113. Zhang X, Patel A, de Graaf R, Behar K. Determination of Liposomal Encapsulation Efficiency Using Proton NMR Spectroscopy. Chemistry and Physics of Lipids 2004;127 113-120.

114. Hinton D, Johnson C. Simultaneous Measurement of Vesicle Diffusion Coefficients and Trapping Efficiencies by Means of Diffusion Ordered 2D NMR Spectroscopy. Chemistry and Physics of Lipids 1994;69 175-178.

115. Oku N, Kendall D, MacDonald R. A Simple Procedure for the Determination of the Trapped Volume of Liposomes. Biochimica et Biophysica Acta 1982;691 332-340.

116. Mehlhorn R, Candau P, Packer L. Measurement of Volumes and Electrochemical Gradients with Spin Probes in Membrane Vesicles. Methods in Enzymology 1982;88 751-772.

117. Vistnes A, Puskin J. A Spin Label Method for Measuring Internal Volumes in Liposomes or Cells, Applied to Ca-dependent Fusion of Negatively Charged Vesicles. Biochimica et Biophysica Acta 1981;644 244-250.

118. Muthu M.S, Singh S. Targeted Nanomedicines: Effective Treatment Modalities for Cancer, AIDS and Brain Disorders. Nanomedicine-UK 2009;4 105-118.

119. Wang X, Wang Y, Chen Z.G, Shin D.M. Advances of Cancer Therapy by Nanotechnology. Cancer Research and Treatment 2009;41 1-11.

120. Torchilin V.P. Recent Advances with Liposomes as Pharmaceutical Carriers. Nature Reviews Drug Discovery 2005;4 145-160.

121. Biswas S, Torchilin V. P. Nanopreparations for Organelle-specific Delivery in Cancer. Advanced Drug Delivery Reviews 2013;66C 26-41.

122. Torchilin V.P, Omelyanenko V.G, Papisov M.I, Bogdanov A.A, Trubetskoy V.S, Herron J.N, Gentry C.A. Poly(ethylene glycol) on the Liposome Surface: on the Mechanism of Polymer-coated Liposome Longevity. Biochimica et Biophysica Acta 1994;1195 11-20.

123. Torchilin V.P, Trubetskoy V.S. Which Polymers can Make Nanoparticulate Drug Carriers Long-circulating? Advance Drug Delivery Reviews 1995;16 141-155.

124. Allen T.M, Hansen C. Pharmacokinetics of Stealth versus Conventional Liposomes: Effect of Dose. Biochimica et Biophysica Acta 1991;1068 133-141.

125. Torchilin V.P, Klibanov A.L, Huang L, O'Donnell S, Nossiff N.D, Khaw B.A. Targeted Accumulation of Polyethylene glycol-coated Immunoliposomes in Infracted Rabbit Myocardium. FASEB Journal 1992;6 2716-2719.

126. Blume G, Cevc G, Crommelin M.D, Bakker-Woudenberg I.A, Kluft C, Storm G. Specific Targeting with Poly(ethylene glycol)-modified Liposomes: Coupling of Homing Devices to the Ends of Polymeric Chains Combines Effective Target Binding with Long Circulation Times. Biochimica et Biophysica Acta 1993;1149 180-184.

127. Torchilin V.P, Levchenco T.S, Lukyanov A.N, Khaw B.A, Klibanov A.L, Rammohan R, Samokhin G.P, Whiteman K.R. p-Nitrophenylcarbonyl-PEG-PE-liposomes: Fast and Simple Attachment of Specific Ligands, Including Monoclonal Antibodies, to Distal Ends of PEG Chains via p-Nitrophenylcarbonyl Groups. Bochimica et Biophysica Acta 2001;1511 397-411.

128. Huwyler J, Wu D.F, Pardridge W.M. Brain Drug Delivery of Small Molecules Using Immunoliposomes. Proceeding of the National Academy of Sciences USA 1996;93 14164-14169.

129. Smolin G, Okumoto M, Feller S, Condon D. Idoxuridine Liposome Therapy for Herpes Simplex Keratisis. American Journal of Opthalmology 1981; 91 220-225.

130. Lee V.H, Urrea P.T, Smith R.E, Schanzlin D.J. Ocular Drug Bioavailability from Topically Applied Liposomes. Survey of Opthalmology 1985;29 335-348.

131. Davies N.M, Fair S.J, Hadgraft J, Kellaway I.W. Evaluation of Mucoadhesive Polymers in Ocular Drug Delivery. II. Polymer Coated Vesicles. Pharmaceutical Research 1992;9 1137-1142.

132. Gaspar M.M, Bakowsky U, Ehrhardt C. Inhaled Liposomes-Current Strategies and Future Challenges. Journal of Biomedical Nanotechnology 2008;4 1-13.

133. Adjei AL, Gupta PK. Inhalation Delivery of Therapeutic Peptides and Proteins. Marcel Dekker Inc., New York, Basel, Hong Kong;1997.

134. Sharma A, Sharma U.S. Liposomes in Drug Delivery: Progress and Limitations. International Journal of Pharmaceutics 1997;154 123-140.

135. Gregoriadis G. Engineering Liposomes for Drug Delivery: Progress and Problems. Trends in Biotechnology 1995;13 527-537.

136. Gregoriadis G., editor. Liposomes as Drug Carriers. J. Wiley;1988.

137. Lasic, DD. and Papahadjopoulos D. Medical Applications of Liposomes. Elsevier;1988.

138. Gregoriadis G. Overview of Liposomes. Journal of Antimicrobial Chemotherapy 1991; 28 39-48.

139. Gregoriadis G, Florence A.T. Liposomes and Cancer Therapy. Cancer Cells 1991;4 144-146.

140. Slingerland M, Guchelaar H.J, Gelderblom H. Liposomal Drug Formulations in Cancer Therapy: 15 Years along the Road. Drug Discovery Today 2012;17 160-6.

141. Lasic D.D. Doxorubicin in Sterically Stabilized Liposomes. Nature 1996;380 561-562.

142. Lasic D.D, Nedham D. The Stealth Liposome: A Prototypical Biomaterial. Chemical Reviews 1995;95 2601-2628.

143. Gahrton G. Treatment of Acute Leukemia—Advances in Chemotherapy, Immunotherapy, and Bone Marrow Transplantation. Advances in cancer Research 1983;40 255-329.

144. Hande K.R. Etoposide: Four Decades of Development of a Topoisomerase II Inhibitor. European Journal of Cancer 1998;34 1514-1521.

145. Reddy L.H, Adhikari J.S, Dwarakanath B.S.R, Sharma R.K. Tumoricidal Effects of Etoposide Incorporated into Solid Lipid Nanoparticles After Intraperitoneal Administration in Dalton's Lymphoma Bearing Mice. AAPS Journal 2006;8 E254-E262.

146. Hamada A, Kawaguchi T, Nakano M. Clinical Pharmacokinetics of Cytarabine Formulations. Clinical Pharmacokinetics 2002;41 705-718.

147. Sengupta S, Tyagi P. Encapsulation in Cationic Liposomes Enhances Antitumor Efficacy and Reduces the Toxicity of Etoposide, a Topo-isomerase Inhibitor II. Pharmacology 2001;62 163-171.

148. Michaud L.B, Valero V, Hortobagyi G. Risks and Benefits of Taxanes in Breast and Ovarian Cancer. Drug Safety 2000;23 401-428.

149. Wani M.C, Taylor H.L, Wall M.E, Coggon P, McPhail A.T. Plant Antitumor Agents 6. Isolation and Structure of Taxol, a Novel Antileukemic and Antitumor Agent from Taxus Brevifolia. Journal of American Chemical Society 1971;93 2325-2327.

150. Rowinsky E.K, Donehower R.C. Drug Therapy-Paclitaxel (Taxol). The New England Journal of Medicine 1995;332 1004-1014.

151. Lorenz W, Reimann H.J, Schmal A, Schult H, Lang S, Ohmann C, Weber D, Kapp B, Luben L, Doenicke A. Histamine Release in Dogs by Cremophor EL and its derivatives: Oxyethylated Oleic Acid is the Most Effective Constituent. Agent Actions 1977;7 63-67.

152. Dye D, Watkins J. Suspected Anaphylactic Reaction to Cremophor EL. British Medical Journal 1980;280, 1353.

153. Weiss R.B, Donehower R.C, Wiernik P.H, Ohnuma T, Gralla R.J, Trump D.L, Jr. Baker J.R, Van Echo D.A, Von Hoff D.D, Leyland-Jones B. Hypersensitivity reactions from Taxol. Journal of Clinical Oncology 1990;8 1263-1268.

154. Xu Q.Y, Trissel L.A, Martinez J.F. Stability of Paclitaxel in 5% Dextrose Injection or 0.9% Sodium Chloride Injection at 4, 22 or 32 Degrees C. American Journal of Hospital Pharmacy 1994;51 3058-3060.

155. Lee S.C, Kim C, Kwon I.C, Chung H, Jeong S.Y. Polymeric Micelles of Poly(2-ethyl-2-oxazoline)-block-poly(epsilon-caprolactone) Copolymer as a Carrier of Paclitaxel. Journal of Controlled Release 2003;89 437-446.

156. Feng X, Yuan Y.J, Wu J.C. Synthesis and Evaluation of Water-soluble Paclitaxel Prodrugs. Bioorganic and Medicinal Chemistry Letters 2002;12 3301-3303.

157. Dosio F, Arpicco S, Brusa P, Stella B, Catel L. Poly(ethylene glycol) Human Serum Albumin-Paclitaxel Conjugates: Preparation, Characterization and Pharmacokinetics. Journal of Controlled Release 2001;76 107-117.

158. Liu C.H, Strobl J.S, Bane S, Schilling J.K, McCracken M, Chatterjee S.K, Rahim-Bata R, Kingston D.G.I. Design, Synthesis and Bioactivities of Steroid-linked Taxol Analogues as Potential Targeted Drugs for Prostate and Breast Cancer. Journal of Natural Products 2004;67 152-159.

159. Lundberg B.B, Risovic V, Ramaswamy M, Wasan K.M. A Lipophilic Paclitaxel Derivative Incorporated in a Lipid Emulsion for Parenteral Administration. Journal of Controlled Release 2003;86 93-100.

160. Ruan G, Feng S.S. Preparation and Characterization of Poly(lactic acid)-poly(ethylene glycol)-poly(lactic acid) (PLA-PEG-PLA) Microspheres for Controlled Release of Paclitaxel. Biomaterials 2003;24 5037-5044.

161. Sharma U.S, Balasubramanian S.V, Straubinger R.M. Pharmaceutical and Physical Properties of Paclitaxel (Taxol) Complexes with Cyclodextrins. Journal of Pharmaceutical Sciences 1995;84 1223-1230.

162. Merisko-Liversidge E, Sarpotdar P, Bruno J, Hajj S, Wei L, Peltier N, Rake J, Shaw J.M, Pugh S, Polin L, Jones J, Corbett T, Cooper E, Liversidge G.G. Formulation and Antitumor Activity Evaluation of Nanocrystalline Suspensions of Poorly Soluble Anticancer Drugs. Pharmaceutical Research 1996;13 272-278.

163. Straubinger R.M, Balasubramanian S.V. Preparation and Characterization of Taxane-containing Liposomes. Methods in Enzymology 2005;391 97-117.

164. Sharma A, Mayhew E, Straubinger R.M. Antitumor effect of Taxol-containing liposomes in a Taxol-resistant murine tumor model. Cancer Research 1993;53 5877–5881.

165. Patel G.B, Agnew B.J, Deschatelets L, Fleming L.P, Sprott G.D. In vitro Assessment of Archaeosome Stability for Developing Oral Delivery Systems. International Journal of Pharmaceutics 2000;194 39-49, 2000.

166. Sprott G.D. Structures of Archaeobacterial Membrane Lipids. Journal of Bioenergetics and Biomembranes 1992;24 555-566.

167. Patel G. B, Sprott G.D. Archaeobacterial Ether Lipid Liposomes (Archaeosomes) as Novel Vaccine and Drug Delivery Systems. Critical Reviews in Biotechnology 1999;19 317-357.

168. Jacquemet A, Barbeau J, Lemiegre L, Benvegnu T. Archaeal Tetraether Bipolar Lipids: Structure, Function and Applications. Biochimie 2009;91 711-717.

169. Li Z, Chen J, Sun W, Xu Y. Investigation of Archaeosomes as Carriers for Oral Delivery of Peptides. Biochemical and Biophysical Research Communications 2010;394 412-417.

170. Kaneda Y. Virosomes: Evolution of the Liposome as a Targeted Drug Delivery System. Advances Drug Delivery Reviews 2000;43 197-205.

171. Sarkar D.P, Ramani K, Tyagi S.K. Targeted Gene Delivery by Virosomes. Methods in Molecular Biology 2002;199 163-173.

172. Cusi M.G, Terrosi C, Savellini G.G, Genova G.D, Zurbriggen R, Correale P. Efficient Delivery of DNA to Dendritic Cells Mediated by Influenza Virosomes. Vaccine 2004;22 735-739.

173. Bungener L, Huckriede A, Wilschut J, Daemen T. Delivery of Protein Antigens to the Immune System by Fusion-active Virosomes: A Comparison with Liposomes and ISCOMS. Bioscience Reports 2002;22 323-338.

174. Huckriede A, Bungener L, Daemen T, Wilschut J. Influenza Virosomes in Vaccine Development. Methods in Enzymology 2003;373 74-91.

175. Herzog C, Metcalfe I.C, Schaad U.B. Virosome Influenza Vaccine in Children. Vaccine 20 2002;5 B24-B28.

176. Usonis V, Bakasenas V, Valentelis R, Katiliene G, Vidzeniene D, Herzog C. Antibody Titres after Primary and Booster Vaccination of Infants and Young Children with a Virosomal Hepatitis A. Vaccine Infection 2004;32 191-198.

177. Gluck R, Moser C, Metcalfe I.C. Influenza Virosomes as an Efficient System for Adjuvanted Vaccine Delivery. Expert Opinion in Biological Therapy 2004; 4 1139-1145.

178. Moser C, Metcalfe I.C, Viret J.F. Virosomal Adjuvanted Antigen Delivery Systems. Expert Reviews of Vaccines 2003;2 189-196.

179. Gangwar M, Singh R, Goel R.K, Nath G. Recent Advances in Various Emerging Vesicular Systems: An Overview. Asian Pacific Journal of Tropical Biomedicine 2012 1176-1188.

180. Garg B.J, Saraswat A, Bhatia A, Katare O.P. Topical Treatment in Vitiligo and the Potential Uses of New Drug Delivery Systems. Indian Journal of Dermatology Venereology and Leprology 2010;76 231-238.

181. Jain S, Mishra D, Kuksal A, Tiwary A.K, Jain N.K. Vesicular Approach for Drug Delivery into or across the Skin: Current Status and Future Prospects" Available from: http://priory.com/pharmol/Manuscript-Jain.htm

182. Jain S, Jaio N, Bhadra D, Tiwary A.K, Jain N.K. Delivery of Nonsteroidal Anti-inflammatory Agents like Diclofenac. Current Drug Delivery 2005;2 223-227.

183. Size determination of liposomes, Liposomes-A practical approach, edited by RRC New (Oxford University Press, NewYork) 1990, 154.

184. Heeremans J.L.M, Gerristen H.R, Meusen S.P, Mijnheer F.W, Gangaram R.S, Panday G, Prevost R, Kluft C, Crommelin D.J.A. The Preparation of Tissue Type Plasminogen Activator (t- PA) Containing Liposomes: Entrapment Efficacy and Ultracentrifugation Damage. Journal of Drug Targeting 1995; 3 301-306.

185. Preparation of liposomes and size determination, Liposomes-A practical approach, edited by RRC New (Oxford University Press, New York) 1990, 36.

186. Touitou E, Dayan N, Levi-Schaffer F, Piliponsky A.Novel lipid vesicular system for enhanced delivery. Journal of Lipid Research 1998; 8 113-114.

187. Asbill C.S, El-Kattan A.F, Michniak B. Enhancement of Transdermal Drug Delivery: Chemical and Physical Approaches. Critical Reviews in Therapeutic Drug Carrier Systems 2000;17 621-658.

188. Touitou E. Inventor. "Composition of Applying Active Substance to or through the Skin" U.S. Patent 5 540 934. July 20, 1996.

189. Patel S. Ethosomes: A promising tool for transdermal delivery of drug. Pharma Info.Net 2007;5(3).

190. Touitou E, Dayan N, Bergelson L, Godin B, Eliaz M. Ethosomes Novel Vesicular Carriers for Enhanced Delivery: Characterization and Skin Penetration Properties, Journal of Controlled Release 2000;65 403-418.

191. Touitou E, inventor. Composition of applying active substance to or through the skin. US patent 5 716 638. October 2, 1998.

192. Touitou E, Godin B, Dayan N, Weiss C, Piliponsky A, Levi-Schaffer F. Intracellular Delivery Mediated by an Ethosomal Carrier. Biomaterials 2001;22 3053-3059.

193. Jain S, Umamaheshwari R.B, Bhadra D, Jain N.K. Ethosomes: a Novel Vesicular Carrier for Enhanced Transdermal Delivery of an anti-HIV Agent, Indian Journal of Pharmaceutical Science 2004;66 72-81.

194. Bhalaria M.K, Naik S, Misra A.N. Ethosomes:A Novel Delivery System for Antifungal Drugs in the Treatment of Topical Fungal Diseases, Indian Journal of Experimental Biology 2009;47 368-375.

195. Guo J, Ping Q, Sun G, Jiao C. Lecithin Vesicular Carriers for Transdermal Delivery ofCyclosporine A. International Journal of Pharmaceutics 2000;194(2) 201-207.

196. Touitou E, Godin B, Dayan N, Vaisman B. Intracellular Delivery by Cationic Ethosoms not Containing Positively Charged Phospholipids: Characterization and Intracellular Delivery Properties. Proceedings of the 6th PAT & 4th ICRS InternationalSymposium, Eilat, Israel.2001.

197. Lodzki M, Godin B, Rakou L, Mechoulam R, Gallily R, Touitou E. Cannabidiol- Transdermal Delivery and Anti-inflammatory Effects in a Murine Model. Journal of Controlled Release 2003;93 377-387.

198. Horwitz E, Pisanty S,Czerninsky R, Helser M, Eliav E, Touitou E.A Clinical Evaluation of a Novel Liposomal Carrier for Acyclovir in the Topical Treatments of Recurrent Herpes Labialis.Oral Surgery Oral Pathology Oral Radiology Endodontology 1999;88 700-05.

199. Dkeidek I, Touitou E. Transdermal Absorption of Polypeptides. AAPS Pharmaceutical Science 1999;1 202-210.

200. Paolino D, Lucania G, Mardente D, Alhaique F, Fresta M. Ethosomes for Skin Delivery of Ammonium Glycyrrhizinate: In vitro Percutaneous Permeation through Human Skin and in vivo Anti-inflammatory Activity on Human Volunteers. Journal of Controlled Release 2005;106 99-110

201. Dubey V, Mishra D, Dutta T, Nahar M, Saraf D.K, Jain N.K. Dermal and Transdermal Delivery of an Anti-psoriatic Agent via Ethanolic Liposomes, Journal of Controlled Release 2007;123148–154.

202. Lasic, DD. Liposomes and Niosomes. In: Surfactants in Cosmetics, Eds., M.M. Rieger and L.D. Rhein, Marcel Dekker: New York, 1997. p: 263-283.

203. Pinsky, M.A, 2010. "Materials and Methods for Delivering Antioxidants into the Skin" U.S. Patent 20,100,098,752.

204. Mills, R, Mathur R, Lawrence N. 2007.Mahonia aquifolim extract, Extraction process and pharmaceutical composition containing the same.U.S. Patent 20,070,148,226.

205. Wallach, D.F.H, Mathur R, Redziniak G.J.M, Tranchant J.F. Some Properties of N-acyl Sarcosinate Lipid Vesicles. Journal of the Society of Cosmetic Chemists 1992;43(2) 113-118.

206. Williams AC.Transdermal and Topical Drug Delivery from Theory to Clinical Practice. Pharmaceutical Press: United Kingdom;2003

207. Frézard F. Liposomes: From Biophysics to the Design of Peptide Vaccines. Brazilian Journal of Medical and Biological Research 1999;32(2) 181-189.

208. Varanelli C, Kumar S, Wallach D.F.H. 1996. Method of Inhibiting Viral Reproduction Using Non-phospholipid, Paucilamellar Liposomes.U.S. Patent 5,561,062.

209. Desai N.P, Hubbell J.A. Solution Technique to Incorporate Polyethylene Oxide and Other Water-Soluble Polymers into Surfaces of Polymeric Biomaterials. Biomaterails 1991;12 144-153.

210. Klibanov A.L, Maruyama, Beckerleg A.M, Torchilin V.P, Huang L. Activity of Amphipathic Polyethyleneglycol 5000 to Prolong the Circulation Time of Liposomes Depends on the Liposome Size and is Unfavorable for Immunoliposome Binding to Target. Biochimica et BiophysicaActa 1991;1062 142–148.

211. Maruyama K., Yuda T, Okamoto A, Ishikura C, Kojima S, Iwatsuru M. Effect of Molecular Weight in Amphiphatic Polyethyleneglycol on Prolonging the Circulation Time of Large Unilamellar Liposomes. Chemical and Pharmaceutical Bulletin 1991;39(6) 1620-1622.

212. Allen T.M, Hansen C, Martin F, Redemenn C, Yau-Young A. Liposomes Containing Synthetic Lipid Derivatives of Poly(ethylene glycol) Show Prolonged Circulation Half-lives in vivo. Biochimica et Biophysica Acta 1991;1066 29-36.

213. Cevc G.G. Drug-carrier and Stability Properties of the Long-lived Lipid Vesicles Cryptosomes, in vitro and in vivo. Journal of Liposome Research 1992;2 355-68.

214. Vyas S.P, Subhedar R, Jain S. Development and Characterization of Emulsomes for Sustained and Targeted Delivery of an Antiviral Agent to Liver. Journal of Pharmacology and Pharmacotherapeutics 2006;58 321-6.

215. Paliwal R, Paliwal S.R, Mishra N, Mehta A, Vyas S.P. Engineered Chylomicron Mimicking Carrier Emulsome for Lymph Targeted Oral

Delivery of Methotrexat. International Journal of Pharmaceutics 2009;380 181-8.

216. VanCott T.C, Kaminski R.W, Mascola J.R, Kalyanaraman V.S, Wassef N.M, Alving C.R. HIV-1 Neutralizing Antibodies in the Genital and Respiratory Tracts of Mice Intranasally Immunized with Oligomeric gp160. Journal of Immunology 1998;160 2000-12.

217. Schwarz C, Mehnert W, Lucks J.S, Muller R.H. Solid Lipid Nanoparticles (SLNs) for Controlled Drug Delivery: I. Production, Characterization and Sterilization. Journal of Controlled Release 1994;30 83-96.

218. Vyas S.P, Gupta S, Dube A. Antileishmanial Efficacy of Amphotericin B Bearing Emulsomes Against Experimental Visceral Leishmaniasis. Journal of Drug Targeting 2007;15 437-44.

219. Gupta S, Vyas S.P. Development and Characterization of Amphotericin B Bearing Emulsomes for Passive and Active Macrophage Targeting. Journal of Drug Targeting 2006;15 206-17.

220. Solid Fat Nanoemulsions As Drug Delivery Vehicles-Patent 5576016. Available from: http://www.docstoc.com/docs/48874511/Solid-Fat-Nanoemulsions-As-Drug-Delivery-Vehicles-Patent-5576016.

221. Barry B.W. Novel Mechanisms and Devices to Enable Successful Transdermal Drug Delivery. European Journal of Pharmaceutical Sciences 2001;14 101-14.

222. Devaraj G.N, Parakh S.R, Devraj R, Apte S.S, Rao B.R, Rambhau D. Release Studies on Niosomes Containing Fatty Alcohols as Bilayer Stabilizers Instead of Cholesterol. Journal of Colloid and Interface Science 2002;251 360-365.

223. Kirby C, Clarke J, Gregoriadis G. Effect of Cholesterol Content of Small Unilamellar Liposomes on Their Stability in vivo and in vitro. Biochemical Journal 1980;186 591-8.

224. Harasym T.O, Cullis P.R, Bally M.B. Intratumor Distribution of Doxorubicin Following I.V. Administration of Drug Encapsulated in Egg Phosphatidylcholine Cholesterol Liposomes. Cancer Chemotherapy Pharmacology 1997;40 309-17.

225. Gill B, Singh J, Sharma V, Hari Kumar S.L. Emulsomes: An Emerging Vesicular Drug Delivery System. Asian Journal of Pharmaceutics2012;6 87-94.

226. Bangham A.D, Standish M.M, Watkins J.C. Diffusion of Univalent Ions across the Lamellae of Swollen Phospholipids. Journal of Molecular Biology 1965;13 238-252.

227. Allen T.M. Liposomal Drug Delivery. Current Opinion in Colloid and Interface Science 1996;1: 645-652.

228. Gabizon A, Papahadjopoulos D. Liposome Formulations with Prolonged Circulation Time in Blood and Enhanced Uptake by Tumors. Proceedings of the National Academy of Sciences 1988;85 6949-6953.

229. Kisak E, Coldren B, Zasadzinski J.A. Nanocompartments Enclosing Vesicles, Colloids, and Macromolecules via Interdigitated Lipid Bilayers. Langmuir 2002;18 284-288.

230. Evans, C.A, Zasadzinski J.A. Encapsulating Vesicles and Colloids in Cochelate Cylinders. Langmuir 2003;193109-3113.

231. Schiffelers R.M, Storm G, ten Kate M.T, Stearne-Cullen L.E.T., Hollander J.G., Verbrugh H.A, Bakker-Woudenberg I. Journal of Liposome Research 2002;12 122-129.

232. Maurer N, Wong K.F, Hope M.J, Cullis P.R. Anomalous Solubility Behavior of the Antibiotic Ciprofloxacin Encapsulated in Liposomes: a H-NMR Study. Biochimica Biophysica Acta 1998;1374 9-20.

233. Maurer-Spurej E, Wong K.F, Maurer N, Fenske D.B, Cullis P.R. Factor Influencing Uptake and Retention of Amino-containing Drugs in Large Unilamellar Vesicles Exhibiting Transmembrane pH Gradient. Biochimica Biophysica Acta 1999;1416 1-10.

234. Webb, M.S., N.L. Boman, D.J. Wiseman, D. Saxon, K. Sutton, K.F. Wong, P. Logan and M.J. Hope. Antibacteria Efficacy Against an in vivo Salmonella Typhimurium Infection Model and Pharmacokinetics of a Liposomal Ciprofloxacin Formulation. Journal of Antimicrobial Agents and Chemotherapy 1998;42 45-52.

235. Bakker-Woudenberg I, ten Kate M.T, Guo L, Working P, Mouton J.W. Improved Efficacy of Ciprofloxacin Administered in Polyethylene Glycol-coated Liposomes for Treatment of Klebsiella Pneumoniae Pneumonia in Rats. Journal of Antimicrobial Agents and Chemotherapy 2001;45 1487-1492.

236. Embree, L, Gelmon K, Tolcher A, Hudon N, Heggie J, Dedhar C, Logan P, Bally M.B, Mayer L.D. Pharmacokinetic Behavior of Vincristine Sulfate Following Administration of Vincristine Sulfate Liposome Injection. Cancer Chemotherapy and Pharmacology 1998;41 347-352.

237. Krishna R, Webb M.S, St. Onge G, Mayer L.D. Liposomal and Nonliposomal Drug Pharmacokinetics After Administration of Liposome-Encapsulated Vincristine and Their Contribution to Drug Tissue Distribution Properties. Journal of Pharmacology and Experimental Therapeutics 2001;298 1206-1212.

238. Alatorre-Meda M, Gonzales –Perez A, Rodriguez J.R. DNA Metafectene Pro-Complexation: A Physical Chemistry Study. Physical Chemistry Chemical Physics 2010;12 7464-7472.

Chapter 9

Application of NMR Relaxometry to Study Nanostructured Poly(vinyl alcohol)/MMT/ Cephalexin Materials for Use in Drug Delivery Systems

Antonio de Pádua Castelo Branco Cunha, Maria Inês Bruno Tavares, Emerson Oliveira da Silva

Instituto de Macromoléculas Professora Eloisa Mano da Universidade Federal do Rio de Janeiro, CT, Bloco J, Cidade Universitária, Ilha do Fundão, Rio de Janeiro, Brazil

ABSTRACT

Polymers containing nanoparticles dispersed and distributed in the matrix can be used for control of drug release. In this work, hydrophilic matrix systems were prepared using poly(vinyl alcohol) and unmodified clay containing the same amount of cephalexin. The materials were obtained through in situ polymerization and were characterized by the conventional technique of FTIR and NMR relaxometry, through determination of proton spin-lattice relaxation time, in order to understand the molecular behavior of the new materials. The NMR relaxometry data showed that the new materials containing low quantities of clay (0.25% and 0.75%) and the same amount of cephalexin (0.5 g) had very good dispersion and distribution of the clay and drug in the polymer matrix. The combination of clay and cephalexin formed a more homogenous material with a narrow domain curve and low relaxation values. The material containing 0.25% clay presented a mixed morphology, with part exfoliated and part intercalated, as could be seen from the relaxation domain distribution, which was larger than that for material with 0.75% clay.

Keywords: Polymer, Relaxometry, NMR, Nanotechnology

1. INTRODUCTION

The generation of nanostructured systems for application in the pharmaceutical industry has been a subject of many studies around the world, particularly to develop drug delivery systems [1] - [3] .

Many types of matrices are used in drug delivery systems. If the polymer matrix is insoluble, an inert matrix will be formed, with a porous structure, from where the drug can be dispersed, but the material needs to have the same apparent surface area during the dissolution and diffusion to control these factors [1] . Therefore, the properties of hydrophobic matrices will depend on both the drug and excipient used for determination of the release mechanism, which can occur by erosion or diffusion through the pores. However, if the matrix formulation contains a hydrophilic polymer, it can provide an appropriate combination of swelling dissolution or erosion mechanisms. The predominance of one of these mechanisms invariably depends on the properties of the polymer used in the system, among which poly(vinyl alcohol) (PVAL) stands out. In this work we prepared a hydrophilic nanostructured system using poly(vinyl alcohol), because this polymer had very good characteristics for use as a hydrophilic matrix for delivery of hydrophilic drugs like cephalexin.

Poly(vinyl alcohol) is a water-soluble synthetic polymer that is used in papermakers, textiles, and a variety of coatings. It is resistant to oil, grease and solvents. It also has high tensile strength and flexibility, as well as high oxygen and aroma barrier properties. However, these properties are dependent on humidity. In other words, with higher humidity more water is absorbed. The water, which acts as a plasticizer, then reduces the material's tensile strength, but increases its elongation and tear strength. PVA has a melting point of 230°C [4] .

Cefalexin is a semi synthetic cephalosporin antibiotic for oral administration. It is indicated for the treatment of respiratory tract infections; otitis media; skin and soft tissue infections; bone and joint infections; genito-uri- nary infections, including acute prostatitis; and dental infections. Cefalexin is active against the following organisms in vitro: β-haemolytic streptococci; staphylococci, including coagulase-positive, coagulase-negative and penicillinase-producing strains; Streptococcus pneumoniae; Escherichia coli; Proteus mirabilis; Klebsiella species; Haemophilus influenzae; and Branhamella catarrhalis. Most strains of enterococci (Streptococcus faecalis) and a few strains of staphylococci are resistant to cefalexin. The drug is inactive against most strains of enterobacteria, morganella morganii, pr. Vulgaris, Colstridium difficule, and the following species: legionella, campylobacter, pseudomonas or herellea species. When tested by in vitro methods, staphylococci exhibit cross-resis- tance between cefalexin and methicillin-type antibiotics [5] .

The main objective of this work was to prepare hydrophilic matrix systems using poly(vinyl alcohol) and unmodified clay and cephalexin. The second objective was to evaluate the interaction among the components and the dispersion and distribution of clay and cephalexin in the polymer matrix, focusing on the characterization of the new materials, especially from nuclear magnetic resonance (NMR) relaxometry.

NMR relaxometry is chosen because it involves measurement of proton relaxation times, which are sensitive to changes in molecular mobility. As a consequence, proton spin-lattice relaxation time indicates the morphologies of the material, such as intercalated and exfoliated structures in the case of clay nanoparticles [6] - [10] . Generally speaking, the decrease in the proton spin-lattice relaxation time comes from the clay lamellae's exfoliation because the presence of paramagnetic metals in the presence of clay structure interferes in the near proton relaxation mechanism. The contrary effect in proton relaxation time is expected for the samples containing polymer chains intercalated in the clay lamellae because of the restriction of their molecular mobility [7] - [12] .

2. EXPERIMENTAL

2.1. Sample Preparation

The PVAL/clay nanocomposites were prepared by in situ polymerization, with varied clay content (0.25%, 0.75%, 1.0%, 1.5% and 3.0%). The drug was also added in the in situ polymerization. The PVAL/clay/cepha- lexin nanocomposites containing the five different amounts of clay and with the same cephalexin content were obtained.

2.2. FTIR Measurements

The infrared spectra of the nanomaterial films were recorded with a Varian Excalibur 3100 FTIR spectrometer with Pike Technologies MIRacle ATR accessory, with 100 scans, resolution of 4 cm^{-1}, from 400 to 4000 cm^{-1} wavelength.

2.3. NMR Relaxometry

All NMR relaxation measurements were carried out with a Maran Ultra 23 Spectrometer (Oxford Instruments, UK), operating at 23 MHz (for protons) and equipped with an 18 Nm NMR tube. Proton spin- lattice relaxation times with a time constant (T_1H) were determined by inversion-recovery (recycle delay-180°-t-90° acquisition data) pulse sequence. The temperature was 27°C and the range of t varied from 0.1 to 10.000 ms, with a recycle delay of 5 s. The 90° pulse was automatically calibrated and the relaxation values were obtained by fitting with WINFIT, while the domain distribution was obtained by the WINDXP software, which comes with the spectrometer.

3. RESULTS AND DISCUSSION

3.1. FTIR Analysis

Figure 1 shows the structure of cephalexin. The major absorption bands in the FITR cephalexin spectrum are observed at about 3500 cm^{-1}, attributed to the hydroxyl groups; 3000 cm^{-1}, related to the methyl group, and an intense band between 1800 - 1700 cm^{-1}, corresponding to the carbonyl group from the beta lactam ring.

Figures 2-6 show the FTIR spectra of the PVAL/Clay/cephalexin systems containing different amount of clay, but the same amount of cephalexin. These samples present characteristics of both PVAL and cephalexin compounds, the peak located at 3420 cm^{-1} is associated with the hydroxyl group of PVAL. The presence of wide bands corresponding to axial deformation of OH (alcohol) located in the range of 3550 - 3200 cm^{-1}indicates the presence of hydrogen bonding, while the absence of strong absorption in the 3650 - 3584 cm^{-1} range is characteristic of free OH indicates a high concentration of intermolecular linked hydroxyl. The absorption with broad band between 3300 - 2500 cm^{-1}, characteristic of axial deformation of OH free carboxylic acid (cephalexin), is present in the spectra. We also noted absence of an aliphatic C=O absorption band between 1750 - 1753 cm^{-1}. The interpretation of the spectra indicates there was negligible interaction between the polymer matrix and drug (cephalexin).

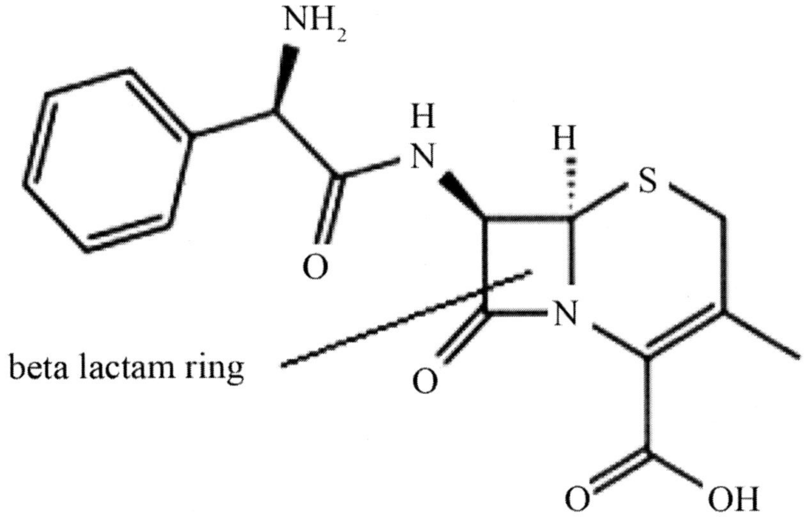

Figure 1. Structure of cephalexin.

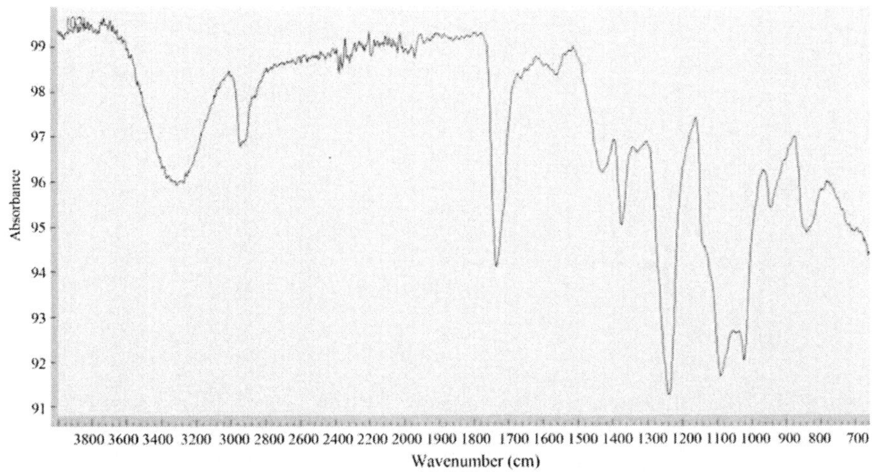

Figure 2. FTIR spectrum of the system formed by PVAL/Clay/cephalexin containing 0.25% clay and 0.5 g of cephalexin.

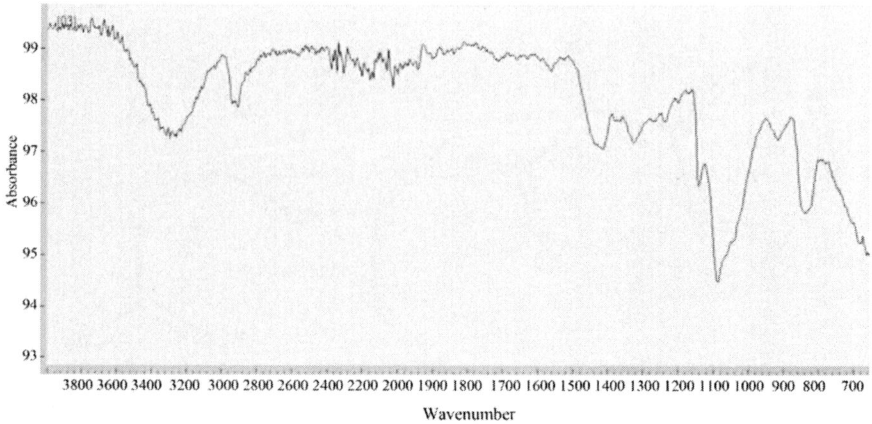

Figure 3. FTIR spectrum of the system formed by PVAL/Clay/cephalexin containing 0.75% clay and 0.5 g of cephalexin.

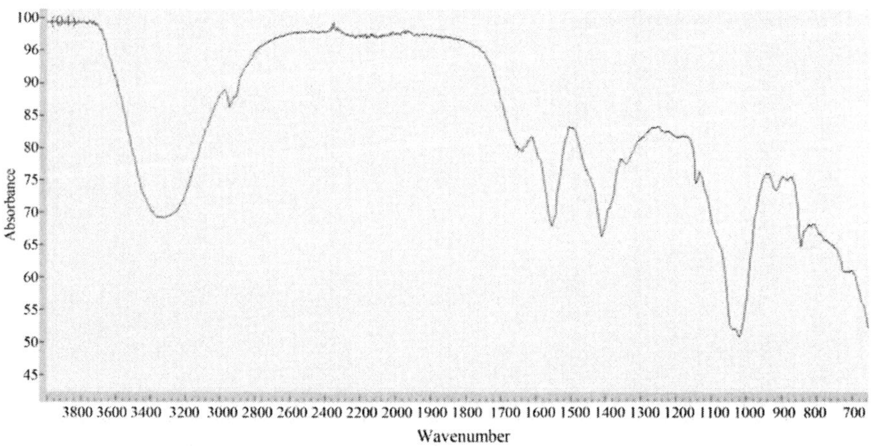

Figure 4.FTIR spectrum of the system formed by PVAL/Clay/cephalexin containing 1.0% clay and 0.5 g of cephalexin.

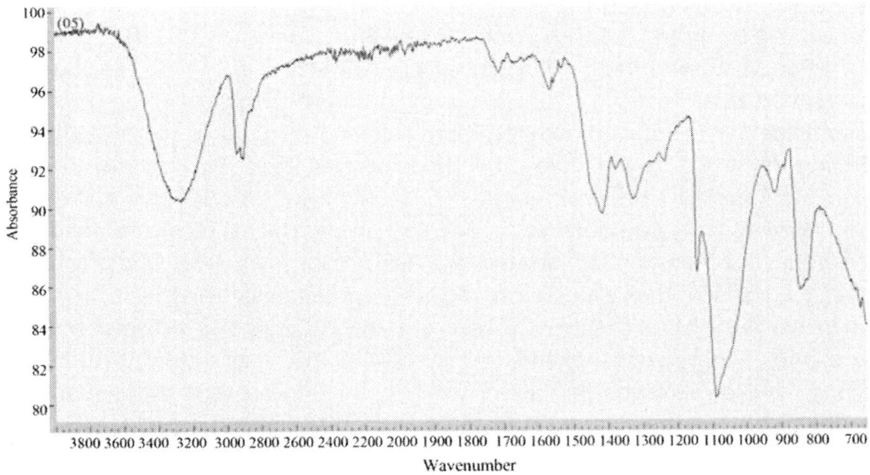

Figure 5. FTIR spectrum of the system formed by PVAL/Clay/cephalexin containing 1.5% clay and 0.5 g of cephalexin.

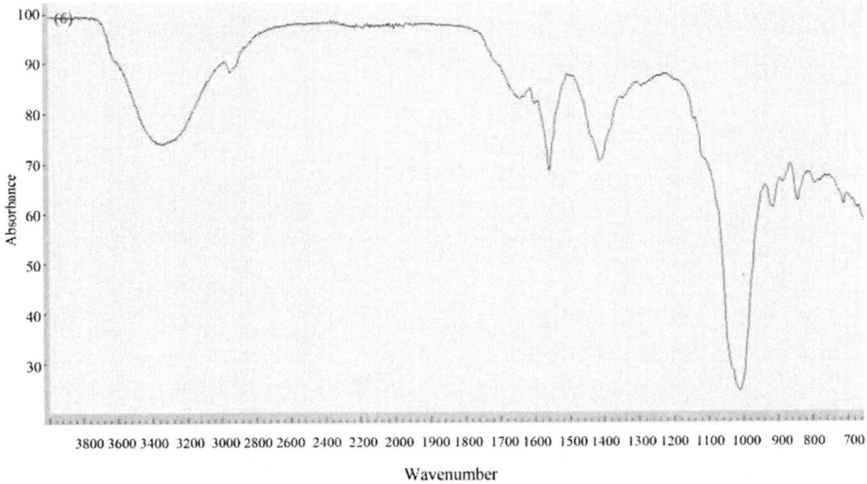

Figure 6. FTIR spectrum of the system formed by PVAL/Clay/cephalexin containing 3.0% clay and 0.5 g of cephalexin.

3.2. NMR Relaxometry Measurements

Table 1 shows the proton spin-lattice relaxation data of the PVAL/Clay/cephalexin systems. It can be seen that the increase clay concentration from 0.25% to 3.0% caused the samples to present particular behavior. The proton relaxation times decreased very quickly with the addition of only 0.25%, revealing formation of a mixed nanostructured material containing part exfoliated and part intercalated. The addition of 0.75% caused greater decrease in the relaxation time, derived from the increase in the exfoliated part in the new material. This behavior comes from the more exfoliated domain, which causes an increase in the chains' molecular mobility, since they are free to move around between the clay lamellae. As the amount of clay increased, the relaxation time showed a tendency to remain the same or increase slightly. The results revealed that all samples presented good exfoliation. Therefore, the addition of only 0.25% clay caused a dramatic change in the relaxation parameter, while a small increase in the quantity to 0.75% caused another decrease in this parameter, showing that both systems underwent changes in the PVAL/Clay/cephalexin chains' molecular mobility, because of the better dispersion and distribution of clay in the polymer matrix. Therefore, addition of 0.25% clay promoted a substantial change in the PVAL/Clay/cephalexin organization, while addition of 0.75% clay generated materials with higher proportion of exfoliation. The decrease in the relaxation times is related to the freedom of movement of the chains between clay lamellae, and only exfoliation of clay makes this possible. This behavior has already been seen for other systems [6] - [10] corroborating the data obtained for the system analyzed here.

Table 1. T_1H values for the PVAL/Clay/cephalexin systems.

PVAL/Clay/Cephalexin Systems	T_1H (ms) ± 2%
PVAL	247
PVAL/0.25/0.5g	**110**↓
PVAL/0.75/0.5g	**93**↓
PVAL/1.0/0.5g	96
PVAL/1.5/0.5g	95
PVAL/3.0/0.5g	96

We also can say that the relaxation time data support the behavior observed in the Fourier-transform infrared spectra.

The domain curve distribution of relaxation parameters determined for the PVAL/Clay/cephalexin systems are seen in Figure 7. From the behavior of these curves, we can obtain information on the samples' homogeneity.

In Figure 7, the polymer itself showed a narrow domain distribution curve, which is in accordance with the chains' organization, since its molecular organization is high. As the clay and drug were added in the polymerization process, the new materials presented different molecular organization due to the new intermolecular interactions. The addition of 0.25 clay caused a large change in the molecular organization due to the wideness of the domain curve baseline; this amount of clay caused some heterogeneity in the polymer nanostructure organization, probably due to the formation of a mixture of systems containing part exfoliated and part intercalated in the clay structures. The addition of 0.75% clay produced a narrower domain curve than with 0.25% clay, indicating that in this proportion a more homogenous domain was formed, probably a major quantity of exfoliated clay lamellae occurred. With the addition of 1.0% and 1.5% clay, the domain curves show the same behavior and are wider than with 0.75% clay added, suggesting a more heterogeneous mix of systems was formed. With addition of 3% clay an even more heterogeneous system was formed than with 1% and 1.5%. The behavior of domain curves distribution corroborates with the relaxation time results.

Figure 8 shows the behavior of the proton spin-lattice relaxation time with increasing clay content. There was a deep decrease in the value of relaxation time for the smallest amount of clay (0.25%), followed by another decrease after the addition of 0.75%, after which the values remained the same with increase of clay content up to 3%. This behavior shows that there is a dependence with relaxation data and clay proportion up to 0.75% of clay addition, for the others quantity no influence in this parameter was observed.

The MNR relaxometry was very effective in analyzing the PVAL/Clay/cephalexin systems; making it a good alternative technique to evaluate polymer/nanoparticles systems, since it allows observing the sample in various modes and the results obtained can explain the molecular dynamics of the sample and indicate the organization mode. This technique can also support the data obtained from other techniques commonly used to evaluate nanomaterials, and therefore gives a good response regarding dispersion and distribution of nanoparticles.

4. CONCLUSIONS

A series of nanocomposite materials composed of layers of montmorillonite (MMT) clay can be prepared by dispersion in PVAL, via in situ polymerization of vinyl acetate monomer, followed by hydrolysis with NaOH solution. The system investigated shows a marked degree of exfoliation, which demonstrates the possibility of controlling drug delivery by varying the clay content, since the insertion alters the degree of crystallinity of

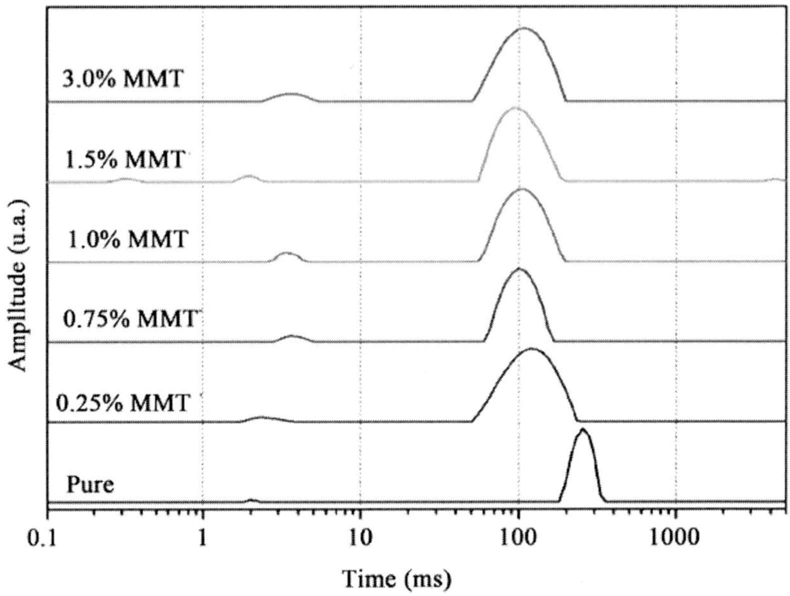

Figure 7. T_1H relaxation domain curves.

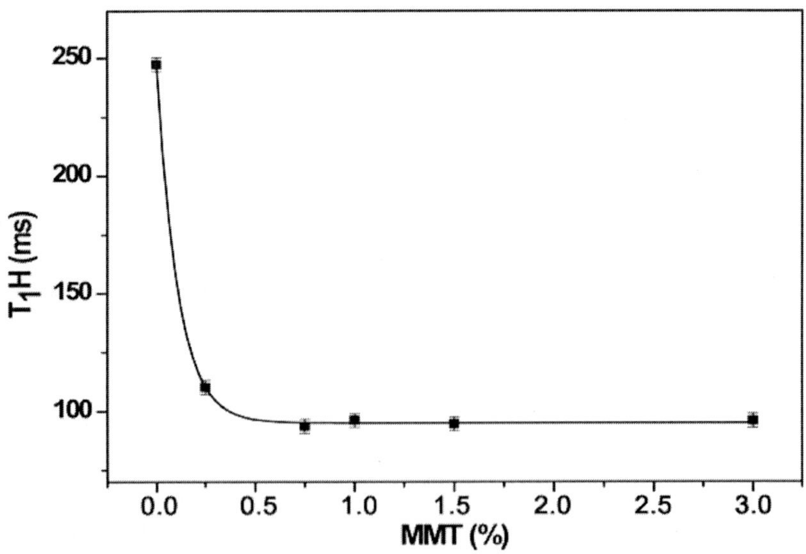

Figure 8. The behavior of T_1H values versus clay quantity.

PVAL, while there is little interaction of the drug with the polymer matrix, meaning it is possible to modulate the rate of delivery according to the structural arrangement.

The relaxation measurements provide relevant information—a profound structural modification in the polymer matrix is observed for the samples containing 0.25% clay in PVAL.

ACKNOWLEDGEMENTS

We are grateful to CAPES, CNPq and FAPERJ for supporting this study.

REFERENCES

1. Ansel, H.C., Popovich, N.G. and Allen, L.V. (2007) Formas farmacêuticas com velocidade controlada e sistemas de liberacao de fármacos. In: Farmacotécnica: formas farmacêuticas e sistemas de liberacao de fármacos, Chapter 9, Premier, Sao Paulo, 283-300.

2. Chan, J.M., Valencia, P.M., Zang, L., Langer, R. and Farokhzad, O.C. (2010) Polymeric Nanoparticles for Drug Delivery. Methods in Molecular Biology, 624, 163-175.

3. Kawashima, Y. (2001) Nanoparticulate Systems for Improved Drug Delivery. Advanced Drug Delivery Reviews, 47, 1-2. Filho, J.C.D. and Gomes, A.S. (2011) Hybrid Membranes of PVA for Direct Ethanol Fuel Cells (DEFCs) Applications. International Journal of Hydrogen Energy, 37, 6246-6252.

4. Molokhia, A.M. (1984) Res Commun Chem Pathol Pharmacol, 45,

5. dos Santos Almeida, A., Tavares, M.I.B., de Silva, E.O., Cucinelli Neto, R.P. and Moreira, L.A. (2012) Development of Hybrid Nanocomposites Based on PLLA and Low-Field NMR Characterization. Polymer Testing, 31, 267-275.

6. 7. Brito, L.M., Chávez, F.V., Tavares, M.I.B. and Sebastiao, P.J.O. (2013) Molecular Dynamic Evaluation of Starch-PLA Blends Nanocomposite with Organoclay by Proton NMR Relaxometry. Polymer Testing, 32, 1181-1185.

7. Monteiro, M.S.S.B., Chávez, F.V., Sebastiao, P.J. and Tavares, M.I.B. (2013) 1H NMR Relaxometry and X-Ray Study of PCL/Nevirapine Hybrids. Polymer Testing, 32, 553-566.

8. Brito, L.M. and Tavares, M.I.B. (2012) Evaluation of the Influence of Nanoparticles' Shapes on the Formation of Poly(lactic acid) Nanocomposites Obtained Employing the Solution Method. Journal of Nanoscience and Nanotechnology, 12, 4508-4513.

9. Vanderhart, D.L., Asano, A. and Gilman, J.W. (2001) Solid-State NMR Investigation of Paramagnetic Nylon-6 Clay Nanocomposites. 1. Crystallinity, Morphology, and the Direct Influence of Fe3+ on Nuclear Spins. Chemistry of Materials, 13, 3781-3795.

10. Cunha, A.P.C.B., Tavares, M.I.B., Silva, E.O. and Zaioncz, S.J. (2015) The Effect of Montmorillonite Clay on the Crystallinity of Poly(vinyl alcohol) Nanocomposites Obtained by Solution Intercalation and in Situ Polymerization. Journal of Nanoscience and Nanotechnology, 15, 2814-2820

11. Iulianelli, G.C.V., Sebastiao, P.J.O., Tavares, M.I.B. and dos Santos, F.A. (2015) Influence of Organoclay Structure on Nanostructured Materials Based on Eva. Materials Sciences and Applications, 6, 860-868.

Chapter 10

Pharmacokinetic Properties and Safety of Cadmium-Containing Quantum Dots as Drug Delivery Systems

Lourdes Rodriguez-Fragoso[1], Ivonne Gutiérrez-Sancha[1], Patricia Rodríguez-Fragoso[2], Anahí Rodríguez-López[1] and Jorge Reyes-Esparza[1]

[1] *Facultad de Farmacia, Universidad Autónoma del Estado de Morelos, Morelos, Mexico*

[2] *Departamento de Física, CINVESTAV-I.P.N Apartado, México*

1. INTRODUCTION

The pharmaceutical industry's current challenge to serve public health needs by has become increasingly difficult due to obstacles that slow down the process of identifying and developing new treatments of unmet medical diseases. There are many auspicious new therapies that have progressed into clinical trials in recent years; they include treatments for cancer, inflammation, neurodegenerative and psychiatric disorders, anti-infective respiratory and metabolic disorders, but their development has failed for a number of reasons. Overcoming these obstacles incurs tremendous costs and takes a lot of time; new therapies must then be identified get successfully issued into the marketplace. In response, government, academic and pharmaceutical industry researchers are looking for new ways to approach the discovery of new medicines and technologies that will not only combat illness but also improve the quality of life, a most important outcome of expensive new treatments. Counterbalancing this important goal are efforts to innovate in the face of increasing public pressure to control costs and increase the speed with which new medicines arrive on the marketplace.

For a few years now, nanotechnology has emerged as an area of science and technology that is leading us to a new industrial revolution. Nanotechnology is defined as scientific and technological development at the atomic and molecular levels, in the range of about 1-100 nm, to obtain a fundamental understanding of phenomena and materials on a nanoscale and to create and use structures, devices and systems that have novel properties and functions due to their size. The most interesting aspect of nanotechnology is its ability to work with materials of small size that, however, can change radically on a physical and chemical level at this scale: electrical conductivity, color, resistance or elasticity, among other properties, behave differently than they do in volumetric material. The emergence of nanotechnology in the health sciences has led to a new discipline called nanomedicine, the main objective of which is the development of tools to diagnose, prevent and treat diseases when they are still not very advanced or incipient [1].

Nanomedicine includes three main areas: nanodiagnosis, nanotherapy and regenerative medicine [2]. Their main goals are explained in the following paragraphs:

a) The purpose of nanodiagnosis is to identify diseases in their initial stages at the cellular or molecular level and, ideally, down to the level of a single cell, using contrast nanodevices and systems [3]. Early identification would lead to immediate application of appropriate treatment, increasing the probability of healing. Nanosystem diagnostics can be used *in vitro* or *in vivo*. *In vivo* diagnosis normally requires that devices penetrate the human body to identify and (ideally) quantify the presence of specific pathogen or cancer cells, for example. This entails a number of problems associated with the biocompatibility of the material of the device, as well as sophisticated design to ensure effectiveness and minimize side effects. Meanwhile, the *in vitro* diagnosis provides greater design flexibility of design because it can be applied to very small samples of body fluids or tissue from which specific detection can be performed (pathogens or genetic defects, for example) in a very short time with high precision and sensitivity [4]. Because of these fundamental differences, *in vitro* detection using nanoscale devices is expected to reach the market faster and consolidate more easily than *in vivo*methods. There are two main areas of work: images and nanosystems and biosensors. These systems rely on the use of nanoparticles, semiconductors, or magnetic metals, such as contrast agents for *in vivo*labeling. These new systems can increase sensitivity and give better contrast in imaging techniques. One of the first proposed nanoparticle systems was the identification of tumor cells. In the case of nanodiagnostics, the main testing devices being developed are nanobiosensors, devices capable of detecting in real time without the need for fluorescent or radioactive markers and with high sensitivity and selectivity all kinds of chemical and biological substances [5].

b) The aim of nanotherapy is to drive nanosystems containing recognition elements to act or transport and release drugs exclusively in cells or affected areas in order to achieve a more effective treatment, minimizing side effects [6]. Approximately 40% of the novel new molecules (NNMs) selected for full-scale development based on their safety and efficacy data fail to reach the clinical development phase due to poor biopharmaceutical properties, which translate into poor bioavailability and undesirable pharmacokinetic properties. Several nanotechnology-based products, including Doxil® (doxorubicin HCl liposome injection) and Abraxane® (paclitaxel protein-bound particles for injectable suspension) are already on the market [7, 8]. In addition, Baxter and Elan are promoting Nanoedge® dispersion technology and NanoCrystal® technologies respectively, so as to improve the biopharmaceutical properties of orally administered therapeutic agents [9]. Nanotechnology can play an important role in the development of proper formulations that address the drug delivery issues related to NNMs with poor biopharmaceutical properties, such as poor solubility, poor permeability across the intestinal epithelium, enzymatic or nonenzymatic degradation/metabolism, complexation with chelating ligands or metal cations, intestinal efflux, and poor transport properties. Additionally, nanotechnology can also achieve desirable pharmacokinetic and toxicological properties that aid in the accelerated development of the NNM. Nanoparticulate drug delivery systems are being used to alter the drug's biopharmaceutics and pharmacokinetics such as drug absorption, distribution, metabolism, and elimination [10]. Examples of nanoscale delivery systems include polymeric nanoparticles, liposomes, nanoemulsions, micelles, and dendrimers.

A number of nano-delivery systems are designed to encapsulate the drug in carriers (e.g., liposomes, micelles, polymeric nanoparticles, and dendrimers), which masks the unfavorable biopharmaceutical properties of the molecule and replaces them with the properties of the materials used to make the nano-delivery system. These approaches were used for a number of poorly soluble NNMs in aqueous phase or easily degraded and metabolized NNMs. Another approach involves the covalent conjugation of the molecules with carrier and targeting moieties (e.g., polymer-drug conjugate, antibody-drug conjugates, solubilizers-drug conjugates, etc.) that override the drug's poor biopharmaceutical properties and improve the pharmacokinetics and biodistribution. This approach was used for site-specific or targeted delivery to alter the pharmacokinetics of the drug by increasing the plasma elimination half-life, preventing degradation or metabolism of the drug in the systemic circulation, and possibly altering the organ and subcellular distribution of the drug, thus alleviating unwanted toxicity due to nonspecific distribution, improving patient compliance and providing favorable clinical outcomes [11]. Advances in nanomedicine are also applied for site-specific drug and gene delivery strategies, especially for the treatment of cancer and other life-threatening diseases [12, 13]. The nanotechnology approach, although expensive and time consuming, can significantly assist in the accelerated development of NNMs with adequate druglike properties and can assist the pharmaceutical companies in adding more lead molecules to their pipeline. One of the major challenges in this process is the development of "nanotherapies", specifically those targeting diseased tissues and organs while avoiding damage to surrounding healthy cells and, thus, the dreaded side effects of current treatments.

c) Regenerative medicine aims to repair or replace damaged tissues and organs using nanotechnology tools [14]. Regenerative nanomedicine deals with the repair or replacement of damaged or diseased tissues and organs by applying methods derived from gene therapy, cell therapy, chemical dosage and bio-regenerative tissue engineering, stimulating the human body's very own repair mechanisms [15]. The main contributions of nanotechnology to regenerative medicine are related to the production of new materials and support systems, the use of embryonic and adult stem cells, and the production of bioactive molecules that serve as signals for cell differentiation [16]. Nanotechnology can play a dominant role in tissue engineering by facilitating new materials and techniques that allow fro more efficient tissue integration and the ability to generate microenvironment parts that are particularly conducive to tissue regeneration. The main difficulty lies in finding suitable materials that allow for the fabrication of structures that remain active while the affected organ regenerates the damaged area [17]. Some of the materials that are being used include carbon nanotubes, the nanoparticles as hydroxyapatite or zirconia particles, biodegradable polymer nanofibers, nanocomposites, etc. One of the greatest achievements is the development of biomaterials with the ability to mimic the extracellular matrix, forming a real support identical to what appears naturally in cells and on which stem cells can be grown for subsequent implant in patients to repair or replace damaged organs.

The enormous advances in nanotechnology during the past decades have allowed for substantial developments in the field of health sciences. The systems and methods described are only selected examples of the enormous activity that is taking place in thousands of laboratories around the world to improve health and quality of life across the whole of society. In the present chapter, we discuss the pharmacokinetic properties and safety of cadmium-containing quantum dots as tools for diagnosis and drug delivery systems.

2. QUANTUM DOTS IN MEDICAL SCIENCE

Quantum dots (QDs) have aroused much interest in recent years, especially in view of their potential applications in biology and medicine [18]. This heterogeneous class of engineered nanoparticles that are both semiconductors and fluorophores is rapidly emerging as an important type of nanoparticles with numerous potential applications in medicine [19]. QDs are semiconductor inorganic nanomaterials ranging from 1–10 nm. They contain elements found in groups II–IV (e.g., CdSe, CdTe, CdS, and ZnSe) or III–V (eg, InP and InAs) of the periodic table. QDs have fluorescent properties that offer superior features to conventional organic dyes, including high quantum yield, broad absorption, and narrow emission spectra (Figure 1). QDs are more photostable than conventional fluorophores; e.g., it has been reported that, under the same excitation conditions, 90% of the fluorescence of a normal organic dye fades within 1 minute, whereas the fluorescence of QDs remains intact even after 30 minute or more [20].

(a)

(b)

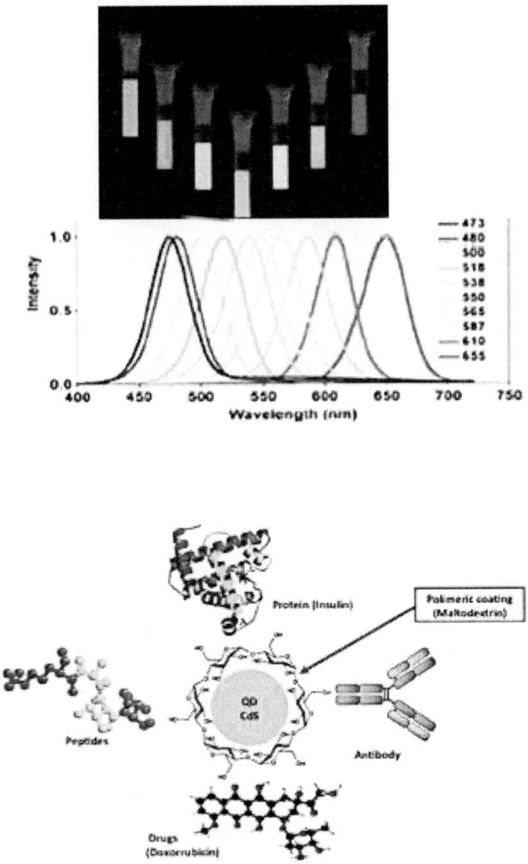

Figure 1. Spectrum and basic structure of quantum dots. (a) Emission spectra of quantum dots; (b) Schematic structure of quantum dots and conjugation to biomolecules.

In terms of their basic structure, QDs consist of an inorganic core, an inorganic shell and aqueous organic coating. The size of the inorganic core determines the wavelength (color) of light emitted following excitation (Figure 1). The inorganic shell is responsible for increasing the photostability and luminescent properties of the QDs [21]. The photo stability of the inorganic shell has allowed QDs to be used as probes for imaging cells and tissues over long spans of time. While there are many useful features to QDs, there are also a number of issues related to their structure and function [22]. One of the most problematic is a phenomenon known as “blinking”. This is the term used to describe the alternation between the light-emitting and –non-emitting state of the QD. This factor limits the number of photons that can be detected in a given time period and it also contributes to unpredictable photon arrival times. It has been proposed that this feature of QDs could be suppressed by “passivating” the QDs’ surface with thiol moieties, polymers, or by using the QDs in free suspension. A standard nomenclature is generally utilized to describe the component parts of various QDs: Core/Shell or Core/Shell-Conjugate. For example, a QD with a cadmium-sulfide core and a maltodextrin shell which has been protein conjugated would be designated as CdS/protein [23]. As fluorescent particles, quantum dots can be detected and tracked with the same approach developed for organic fluorophores. All the technical development has been directly transposed to QD imaging and tracking. Biomedical applications exploit the fluorescent properties of QDs, particularly their advantage over traditional organic dyes for both diagnostic and clinical applications. The *in vitro* biomedical and diagnostic applications of QDs include such techniques as the multicolor fluorescent labeling of cell surface molecules and cellular proteins in microscopy and other applications, detection of pathogens and toxins, DNA and RNA technologies, and fluorescence resonance energy transfer. QDs are also being explored for use in whole-body *in vivo* imaging of normal and tumor tissues. QDs may also find use in therapeutic applications such as targeted drug delivery, photodynamic therapy, and drug discovery [24].

3. CADMIUM-CONTAINING QUANTUM DOTS

Different results by various research groups indicate that cadmium (in group III–V) is extremely toxic if allowed to leach into the environment and this material also has DNA-damaging properties [25]. Other studies have shown that using cadmium in the cellular environment may lead to the formation of reactive oxygen species, resulting in cell death [26, 27]. The stability of groups III–V is known to be due to the presence of covalent rather than ionic bonding. The most optically suitable emitting ‘core’ materials have been cadmium-based materials. Cadmium selenide, Cadmium sulfide or Cadmium telluride particles provided bright emission across the visible and near infrared regions of the electromagnetic spectrum [28]. Questions have arisen regarding the suitability of cadmium-containing materials as biological labels. Other problematic factors include the suitability of the capping agents, the retention of particles over a certain size, biological magnification and, importantly, the breakdown and decomposition products of these inorganic materials. QDs are notoriously labile and the identity and ultimate destination of the inorganic decomposition products remains unclear. Despite this, cadmium-containing quantum dots provide a genuine advance in medical imaging and the numerous problems involving these particles are almost immediately dispelled if one wishes to image and explore fixed cells [29, 30].

Cadmium, which is the main component in the majority of quantum dots, is known to be acutely and chronically toxic to cells and organisms. In cells, it is taken into calcium membrane channels, where it accumulates [31]. Cadmium inhibits the synthesis of DNA, RNA and proteins, as well as breaking up DNA strands and mutating chromosomes [32]. On a cellular level, cadmium induces oxidative stress by depletion of endogenous antioxidants such as glutathione [33], as well as mitochondrial damage [34]. Cadmium nanoparticles exposure can lead to disturbances in cellular homeostatic mechanisms, resulting either in adaptive cellular responses or cell death. Cell death can occur either through an abrupt process named necrosis or a tightly regulated or programmed process (apoptosis and autophagy) [35]. Its toxicity is mainly associated with liver and kidney injury, osteoporosis and neurological dysfunctions at the level of living organisms. The toxic ions are commonly thought to be released from quantum dots when the surface of the nanoparticle is oxidized and early reports on the inclusion of simple quantum dots in bacteria support this [36]

Protecting the core can, to some degree, control toxicity related to cadmium leakage. However, the change in the physicochemical and structural properties of engineered quantum dots could be responsible for a number of material interactions that could also have toxicological effects [37, 38]. However, encapsulation is not simple and it has been reported that quantum dots have displayed toxicity even with well-protected cores. Recently, polymers that can act as coordination sites for cadmium ion aggregation have protected semiconductor nanoparticles. CdS nanoparticles protected with starch and, in particular, amylose, form a wide range of inclusion complexes for numerous guest molecules [39]. Soluble starch added during the synthesis has been used as a capping agent in the synthesis of CdS and CdSe nanoparticles, resulting in well-controlled and uniform particle sizes of cadmium-rich nanoparticles [40]. Early studies attempted to quantitatively determine values for the onset of cytotoxicity in CdSe and CdSe/ZnS quantum dots, either coated with mercaptopropionic acid (MPA), embedded in a silica shell or embedded in an amphiphilic polymer shell [41]. They found that the majority of the nanoparticles were ingested into the cells and were stored in vesicles around the nucleus, irrespective of the surface coating. We have previously synthesized CdS nanoparticles coated with maltodextrin polymer, and our results revealed that CdS-MD nanoparticles produced distinct dose-dependent effects (Figure 2) [42]. It is clear from this and other studies that the surface coating is related to the toxicity experienced by cells, which affects the level of toxic material released from the nanoparticles. Other studies have shown that different cell types have varying thresholds for quantum dot-induced toxicity.

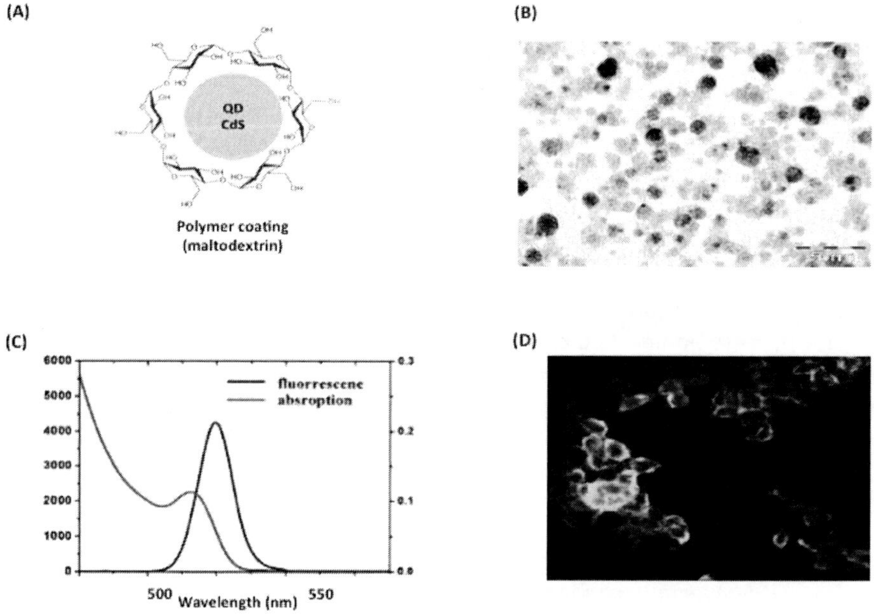

Figure 2. CdS/maltodextrin quantum dots. (a) Schematic structure of CdS/maltodextrin quantum dots; (b) Characterization of different sized CdS/MD quantum dots using TEM; (c) Spectra of CdS/MD quantum dots, the maximum luminescence of which is a wavelength of 520 nm (CdS/MD520); (d) HepG2 cells observed under fluorescent microscopy at (x40) magnification.

4. BIOCOMPATIBILITY AND FUNCTIONALIZATION OF CADMIUM-CONTAINING QUANTUM DOTS

Biocompatibility is a word that is used extensively in biomaterials science. The incorporation of QDs into biological systems often requires strategies for the manipulation of the ligands bound to the surface of the QDs surface in order to make them water-soluble and biocompatible, compatible with living tissue or a living system by not being toxic, injurious, or physiologically reactive [43]. QDs must be rendered water-soluble through the modification of their surface in preparation for biological applications. An ideal water-soluble ligand should meet the following requirements: (1) provide QDs with stability and solubility in biological buffers; (2) maintain a high resistance to photobleaching and other photophysical properties in aqueous media; (3) have functional groups which are able to conjugate to biomolecules; (4) minimize overall hydrodynamic size. The stability of QDs in water can be obtained through either a complete ligand exchange procedure, or through steric stabilization where the native hydrophobic surface is coated with amphiphilic molecules and/or polymers [44, 45].

QDs have been adapted to the desired application by conjugation to a recognition moiety, e.g., antibodies, peptides, oligonucleotides or aptamers, or by coating with streptavidin. Several functionalizations have been adapted to the shell layer coating the core, making the core/shell QDs most adaptable for biological applications [46]. In order to suitably functionalize the QDs, there are several methods that have been successfully used for conjugation of QDs to the desired biomolecules. These include electrostatic attraction, covalent linkage, adsorption, and mercapto (-SH) exchange [47]. The choice depends on the features of the biomolecule of interest; for example, thiol-containing biomolecules can be conjugated to QDs via mercapto exchange. In contrast, simple small molecules such as oligonucleotides and various serum albumins were found to readily adsorb non-specifically to the surface of water-soluble QDs. The factors affecting the adsorption are pH, ionic strength, temperature, and surface charge of the molecules [48]. There are three primary ways to target a biocompatible and functional quantum dot: with antibodies, with peptides, or with small molecules. The simplest labeling strategy uses antibodies; the most complicated is that of small molecules, as this approach usually requires more synthetic chemistry. Each approach has its advantages and disadvantages, and no approach is a universal solution.

Chemical conjugation of antibodies to semiconductor QDs is attractive because the proteins of interest can be visualized. For conjugation of QDs to antibodies, the orientation of the antibody on the QD is important given its functionality as a targeting moiety. The conjugation strategy contributes to the control of antibody orientation. For example, the use of biotinylated antibodies and streptavidin-coated QDs provides no control over the orientation of the antibody on the surface of the QD owing to the presence of multiple biotinylation sites on the antibody. Antibody-quantum dot conjugates have been used in a myriad of applications [49, 50]. An immunoassay for the detection of hepatitis B surface antigen [51] conjugated CdTe/CdS QDs to anti-hepatitis B surface antigen antibodies using protein G as a linking bridge, instead of covalently linking the QDs to the antibodies. Other studies developed a microplate immunoassay for detection of the cardiovascular marker C-reactive protein in 104 serum samples, with a limit of quantification of 0.19 μg/l within 1.5 h [52]. A multiplex immunoassay for the simultaneous detection of staphylococcal enterotoxin B and chicken IgY (IgG) in the same well of a 96-well microtiter plate was also undertaken [53]. A multiplex fluoroimmunoassay for the detection of lung cancer markers—neuron specific enolase (NSE) and carcinoembryonic antigen (CEA) in human serum—was recently developed [54]. A wide selection of antibody-quantum dot conjugates is also commercially available. Disadvantages to this approach include the availability of antibodies, their selectivity and affinity, and the increased hydrodynamic radius of the quantum dot conjugate. Nonetheless, antibody-QD conjugates are often the method of choice and make up much of the QDs in biology literature.

Peptides can also be conjugated to QDs in a direct approach by linking to thiol-rich domains. A direct binding approach was used to bioactivate and solubilize QDs with phytochelatin-related peptides [55]. Peptide-functionalized quantum dots have been successfully used for targeting cellular proteins such as growth factor receptors, G protein-coupled receptors, integrins, and ion channels [56, 57]. In particular, ~30-50 arginine-glycine-aspartatic acid (RGD) peptides have been conjugated to NIR quantum dots to specifically target αvβ3 integrins in mouse tumor neovasculature *in vivo* [58], while other studies have relied on high-affinity peptide neurotoxin quantum dot nanoconjugates to image endogenous proteins in living cells and *ex vivo* tissue [59]. Overall, peptide-quantum dot nanoconjugates offer distinct advantages over antibody-mediated targeting, and their potential as biological probes is being actively explored. On the other hand, a single QD can be conjugated to multiple protein molecules, which can be similar or different depending on the intended application. Approximately 15-20 maltose binding proteins, a 44-kDa protein measuring 3 × 4 × 6.5 nm, can be attached to a single 6-nm QD [60]. Because of their brightness and photostability, water-stabilized QDs have been used to track many receptor-mediated endocytic trafficking events in live cells using fluorescence microscopy [61]. For example, QDs conjugated to EGF have been used to track the dimerization of the EGF receptor (EGFR) and its ability to elicit downstream signal transduction events [62]. Biotinylated α-bungarotoxin was bound to streptavidin-conjugated QDs to characterize the assembly dynamics of acetylcholine receptor clusters in postsynaptic membranes [63]. Recently, high-resolution imaging methods in the nanometer range have been developed to image the membrane transport and dynamics of tumor cell proteins during metastasis in living mice using antibody-conjugated QDs [64]. This technology can also be applied to detecting cancer cells in sentinel lymph nodes in whole animals using QDs conjugated to tumor-specific molecules [65]. One can envision several ligand-conjugated quantum dots, with each ligand conjugated to a different size (color) quantum dot, allowing a multiplexed fluorescent assay for drug discovery.

Different schemes have been developed to conjugate ssDNA and dsDNA to the surface of QDs. DNA-QD conjugates retain the selectivity of DNA and the photophysical properties of QDs, allowing detection of single or multiple DNA targets. DNA–QD conjugates require solubility in water, stability under physiological conditions and minimal nonspecific DNA binding to the QD surface. The thiol-modified oligonucleotide can be conjugated to QDs in a direct ligand exchange approach (native cap exchange) where the oligonucleotide displaces the surface-bound mercaptopropionic acid and yields aqueous stable and strongly fluorescent oligonucleotide bound QDs [66]. Applications of QDs include*in vitro* diagnostics, imaging and therapeutics. QDs are used as labels in immunoassays, immunohistochemical staining, cellular imaging and multiplex diagnostics.

5. CADMIUM-CONTAINING QUANTUM DOTS AS A PLATFORM FOR NANOPARTICLE DRUG DELIVERY VEHICLE DESIGN

Recently, there has been an explosion in the development of nanoparticle-based drug delivery vehicles composed of lipids, polymers, carbon materials, and even hybrid combinations of those materials tailored not only for the dramatic improvement of the pharmacological properties of existing drugs, but also for enabling the delivery of new classes of potent anti-cancer drugs for gene therapy and immunotherapy [67, 68]. With QDs, a combination of unique physical, chemical, and optical properties facilitates in-depth study of nanocarrier interactions with biological systems through real-time monitoring of QDs biodistribution, intracellular uptake, drug release, and long-term nanocarrier fate. At the same time, compact size and compatibility with a variety of surface modification strategies enables substitution of virtually any QD core with a QD within single-nanoparticle drug delivery vehicles, or incorporation of QD tags within larger multicomponent vehicles. The combination of superior brightness and resistance to photo-degradation represents another set of QD properties that highly useful for long-term nanocarrier tracking.

The great interest in engineering NP-based drug delivery vehicles is driven by the powerful capability of nanocarriers to completely redefine the pharmacokinetic properties of virtually any drug, ranging from small-molecule therapeutics to large proteins and DNA plasmids. Encapsulation of the drug within the nanoparticles keeps it shielded from the biological environment until the moment of carrier degradation and drug release, thus minimizing non-specific and potentially adverse interactions en route to the target [69].

A few reports have appeared recently regarding this ambitious goal. It has previously conjugated captopril, an antihypertensive drug, to the QD surface and studied its pharmacodynamics and pharmacokinetics in stroke-prone spontaneously hypertensive rats [70]. The results show that the administered QD-captopril conjugates are capable of decreasing rat blood pressure to the same extent as the captopril alone in the first 30 min, but the therapeutic effect of QD-captopril disappears after 60 min. It is unclear whether the therapeutic effect results from the QD-captopril conjugates or captopril molecules detached from the QD surface. Another piece of interesting work was previously reported, wherein a targeting functionality was added to QDs by linking them with RNA aptamers (A10) that specifically bind to prostate specific membrane antigen (PSMA) [71]. Doxorubicin, a DNA-interacting drug widely used in chemotherapy, was immobilized onto QDs by intercalation within the A10 RNA aptamer [72]. Another study reported the ability of nanoconjugates of CdSe/CdS/ZnS and doxorubicin (Dox) to target alveolar macrophages, cells that play a critical role in the pathogenesis of inflammatory lung injuries. The results demonstrated that nanoparticle platforms can provide targeted macrophage-selective therapy for the treatment of pulmonary disease [73]. This was previously reported regarding siRNA delivery using QDs as delivery vehicles [74].

QDs already play an important role in fundamental biology and *in vitro* disease diagnostics and prognostics. Their unique structural and surface properties, such as their tunable and uniform size, flexible drug-linking and doping mechanisms, large surface-to-volume ratio and wide spectrum of surface reactive groups have enabled a new avenue of research: targeted and traceable drug delivery. However, high-quality QDs are mainly made with heavy metals, like cadmium, whose long-term toxicity is currently largely unknown. Despite this limitation, QDs have been applied to cells and small animals as drug carriers, serving as an outstanding discovery tool for drug screening and validation, and as prototype materials for drug carrier engineering [75]. One primary challenge of drug delivery is maintaining a useful concentration of the drug in the targeted tissue while preventing toxicity.

6. PHARMACOKINETICS OF CADMIUM-CONTAINING QUANTUM DOTS

Nanoparticle-based drug delivery is on its way to overcoming the fundamental limitations of simple free drug formulations, providing means to change their pharmacological properties and also understand their biological fate in great detail. Among many contrast agents for studying nanoparticle-based drug delivery vehicles, QDs are particularly suitable. Their unique amalgamation of useful features, such as small size, versatile surface chemistry, and exquisite optical properties make them an ideal platform for the comprehensive characterization of nanoparticle-based drug delivery vehicle behavior across single-cell to whole organism levels. In this new field, QDs have already made substantial contributions, enabling dynamic monitoring of nanocarrier cell uptake, intracellular distribution, circulation half-times, and biodistribution. Early on, the design of QDs drug delivery vehicles was governed by the intrinsically poor pharmacokinetic (PK) properties of conventional drugs. Low drug solubility, rapid metabolism and clearance and, most importantly, a lack of selectivity, regularly lead to therapeutic failure by causing severe systemic toxicity in healthy tissues, thus prohibiting the dose escalation necessary to eliminate tumor cells. Incorporating these drugs into nanocarriers offers an exciting opportunity to redefine the PK properties, improving therapeutic efficacy and reducing side effects.

When we utilize a nanopharmaceutical, it is important to realize that, in contrast to delivering a drug that is an organic molecule, we are delivering something of a discrete entity in a nanoparticle-comprised of atomic scale parts. Due to the quantum effects and electronic interactions that predominate at the nanoscale, we need to alter the way in which we think about pharmacological parameters in order to adapt to nanoscience. Nanopharmacology is further complicated by the need to establish the behavior of nanoparticles such as QDs within the traditional pharmacological parameters of absorption, distribution, metabolism and excretion (ADME). Nanoconstructs, in many cases, have limited metabolism and excretion and persist in biological systems; this becomes particularly important when toxic atoms such as cadmium are involved. The pharmacological parameters of the behavior of cadmium-containing quantum dots in biological systems is currently still under investigation. Dosing parameters, absorption, distribution, metabolism and excretion require considerable further study, since we have little information on these parameters at this point.

The first factor we need to establish before we study the pharmacokinetics parameter is the dose. Adequate estimates of QDs exposure during treatments such as cancer therapy must be in place so that both pharmacological and toxicological studies can be conducted within a physiologically relevant dose range. Importantly, how does cadmium content relate to dose? To date, these parameters have not been rigorously addressed. Dose metrics of QDs have been reported in terms of mg/kg (or mg/ml for *in vitro* studies) or on a molar basis, and this will no doubt need refinement. Given that a QD, or any other nanoparticle, is an engineered entity or "mini-reactor", dose via mass or molar number may be an inappropriate descriptor. The length and extent of QDs tissue retention is an important parameter for dosing considerations, since repeated doses may induce systemic accumulation, contributing to potential toxicity. Furthermore, persistence of QDs in tissues demands long-term studies to accurately assess risk. Therefore, the dose is another parameter that requires consideration.

The second factor to establish is the route of administration. This, along with the risks for exposure and possible toxicity should be addressed cautiously to ensure experimental and clinical safety. Moreover, an understanding of possible interactions of QDs within human tissues may shed light on the prevention of health risks in the laboratory and daily exposure to QDs. To date, research has established that various nanoparticles can enter an organism through skin, inhalation, oral delivery, and parenteral administration. Intravenous injection is a major route for drug administration. It has been reported that intravenously injected QDs may accumulate in unintended tissues, which implies that the potential toxicity might result from a failure to clear them from the body [76]. The possibility of tissue uptake of QDs via ingestion following exposure has also been proposed in animal and cell culture models. Skin is another important portal of entry for nanoparticles as potential route of systemic drug administration.

The abilities of nanoagents to penetrate the skin barrier are debatable. Some studies indicate that NP penetrate skin barrier under skin lesions, UV sunburn or ultrasound [77]. The potential beneficial and/or side effects of intradermally accumulated NP primarily depend on their localization in the tissues. It is also important to elucidate further migration pathways of particles, as this would determine their pharmacokinetic properties and systemic distribution in the organism. Topically applied QDs were reported to accumulate in the dermis and muscles [78]; however, a more detailed localization of particles has not been described. Other studies reported that the majority of the intradermally injected QDs remained at the injection site and a minority of QDs migrated into lymph nodes, highlighting QDs advantages for lym-phatic imaging [79, 80]. However, high retention of QDs at the injection site raises concerns about long-term physiological effects. There is a lack of in-depth analyses of QDs localization and migration pathways in the dermis. It was recently reported that the subcutaneous injection of CdSe/ZnS coated with mPEG-5000 polymer into the CDF1 of mice showed that basement membrane and dense connective tissue fibers limited the diffusion of QDs in the dermis [81]. Negligible QDs penetration into the epidermis, hair follicles, sebaceous and sweat glands, nerves and blood vessels was also observed. However, low permeation of QDs through the tissues could result in slow clearance and raises the risks of potential immune, inflammatory and cytotoxic responses.

The cornea is another common route of drug administration and also an important route of nanoparticle exposure in occupational scenarios and daily life. However, the possibility of QDs penetration into the cornea has not been discussed before. It has been previously demonstrated that specific QDs influence corneal stromal cell viability up to a significant magnitude of 50% in a relatively low concentration (5-20 nM) and under a short exposure period (24-48 h) [82]. QDs can also be retained in the cornea up to 26 days in an *in vivo* mouse model. Therefore, since corneal stromal cells are crucial for the maintenance of the health and transparency of the cornea, potential QDs cytotoxicity due to bioaccumulation is a major concern given the potential threat to corneal health.

Absorption via tissues and biological fluids is generally the first hurdle to be met and this is, of course, dependent on route of delivery. Currently, the most important route of delivery for QDs appears to be systemic distribution through parenteral delivery [83]. Nanoparticles are considered to absorb more effectively into the respiratory, skin, and gastrointestinal systems than micron-sized particles because of their unique physicochemical properties, such as their size and surface modifications [84]. For example, instillation of 5 nm QDs shows faster translocation to other organs than in the case of 27 nm QDs [85]. In addition, a recent study showed that nanoparticles were only translocated into the circulation system when administered into the lung; their absorption rate varied, depending on their surface properties [86]. When different sizes of polystyrene QDs were administered orally to rats, the absorption of 50–100 nm polystyrene QDs was about 250-fold higher than the absorption of larger microparticles (500 nm, 1, and 10 µm) [87]. Oral administration of different sizes of colloidal gold particles to mice showed size-dependent absorption [88]. Regarding surface modification, positively charged particles show better absorption than neutral or negatively charged particles [89]. However, in a recent study using gold nanoparticles, negatively charged particles showed higher absorption rates than positively charged particles [90]. Therefore, no general rule can be made about absorption from these results and further studies on the impact of surface modification on gastrointestinal absorption are required. Studying the kinetics of nanoparticles is an important issue in nanotechnology.

Regarding distribution, one of the first elements that parenteral delivered QD will encounter is the environment of the blood. Here, we have little to no information about blood/QD interactions. Plasma half-life is no doubt related to surface coating and addition of biological targeting ligands, if any. For example, PEG coating was reported to increase plasma half-life [91]. In the case of oxide nanoparticles, many are coated with endogenous plasma proteins immediately upon entry into the circulatory system and this appears to enhance tissue delivery. However, the interactions between QDs and plasma proteins are unknown. Immune responses may also be triggered at this level, as reviewed by [92], but the precise interactions of QDs at this level have not been examined. Recently, some studies have investigated the *in vivo* biodistribution of QDs [93-95]. All of the reports in the literature unanimously conclude that QDs show a preference for deposition in organs and tissues and that they do not remain circulating in the bloodstream [96]. Real-time imaging of live animals treated with the hyaluronic acid (HA)-conjugated QDs showed that the luminescence of NIR QDs could be detected for up to 2 months [97]. Others reported that QDs coated using an amphiphilic poly(acrylic acid) polymer remain fluorescent after at least four months *in vivo* [98].

Organ-selective biodistribution and elimination routes of synthesized QDs coated with 3-mercaptopropionic acid (QD MPA) and commercially available Qtracker 705 nontargeted quantum dots with poly(ethylene glycol) coating (QD PEG) were recently compared after intravenous injection to mice. QDs were deposited mainly in liver, spleen, kidney and lymph nodes [99]. Another study observed that, in the murine model, quantum dots (CdSe 100 pmol/kg) administered by intravenous injection mainly accumulated in the red pulps of the spleen, portal areas of the liver, and adrenal glands of the kidney within 1 h. It is believed that quantum dots do not degrade, as evidenced by the intensity of the fluorescence in the fluorescence spectrum image and comparable intensity profile of Cd [100]. One consistent theme in the existing literature is that QDs are eventually taken up by the reticuloendothelial system, including the liver, spleen, and lymphatic system [101]. On the other hand, it has been found that aqQDs are initially accumulated in liver after short-time (0.5- 4h) post-injection, and then are increasingly absorbed by kidney during long-time (15 – 80 days) blood circulation. Moreover, size-dependent biodistribution is obviously observed: aqQDs with larger sizes are more quickly accumulated in the spleen [102]. We have recently found that after i.p. injection, the CdS/Maltodextrin quantum dots mainly accumulated in the liver, kidney, spleen, thymus, intestine, lung and brain (Figure 3). The pharmacokinetics studies showed the presence of CdS/Maltodextrin in kidney 30 min after administration; at 18 h, the presence of quantum dots in kidney was more abundant. However, the amount of CdS/Maltodextrin quantum dots in liver was lower than in kidney, and the maximal presence was at 3 h. Our results suggest that the transition of CdS/Maltodextrin quantum dots via the liver is very fast, and the main route of elimination is renal (Figure 4).

The blood–brain barrier (BBB), is a critical interface and acts as a physical and metabolic barrier between the CNS and the peripheral circulation that serves to regulate and protect the microenvironment of the brain. The primary function of the normal BBB is to establish and maintain homeostasis in the CNS [103]. Under normal physiological conditions, BBB prevents transport of bacteria, large molecules, and most small molecules into the brain. To be BBB permeable, molecules need to be lipid soluble and less than 400 Da in size. There are more than 7000 drugs in the comprehensive medicinal chemistry database, and only 5% of these drugs can be used to treat the CNS diseases. In

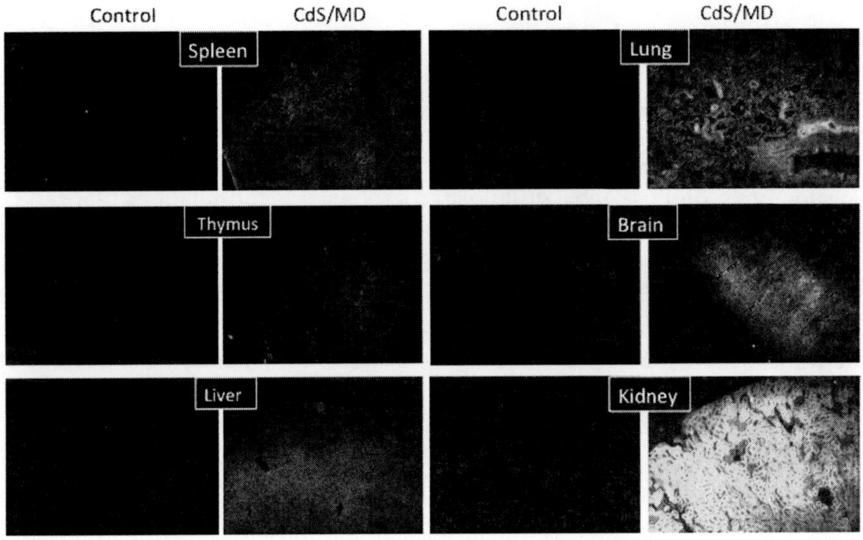

Figure 3. Biodistribution of CdS/Maltodextrin in Wistar rats. Tissue distribution of CdS/maltodextrin quantum dots after i.p. administration of 10 μg during 8 days. Quantum dots were observed in all analyzed tissues, including brain. The maximal observed presence of quantum dots was in lung and kidney.

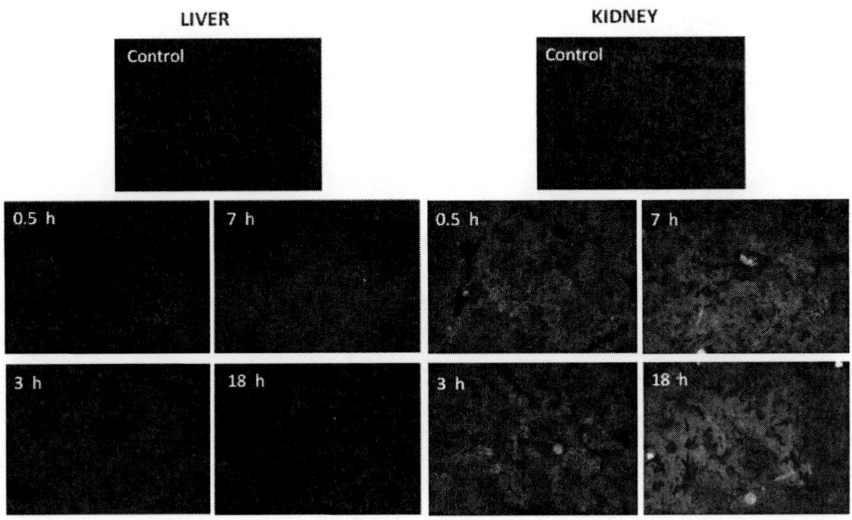

Figure 4. Biokinetics of excretion of CdS/maltodextrin quantum dots after a single i.p. administration of 10 μg in kidney and liver.

a related study, 12% of all drugs are shown to be active in the CNS, but only 1% of all drugs are active in the brain for diseases other than affective disorders [104]. The importance of developing new approaches to brain drug development is illustrated by considering the limitations of the existing brain drug delivery strategies. Therefore, there is great interest in nanomedicine to develop optimized traceable drug-loaded nanoparticle formulations that can be safely used to facilitate drugs across the BBB for treating brain diseases and, at the same time, visualizing the distribution profile of the nanoparticles in the brain. The use of QDs bioconjugates as efficient targeted probes for transmigration across the BBB has been previously demonstrated [105]. Since the transferrin receptor protein is highly localized on the endothelial surface of the brain, transferrin (Tf) was selected to trigger receptor-mediated transport across the BBB. It was discovered that the migration rate of Tf-conjugated QDs crossing the *in vitro* BBB is both concentration-and time-dependent [106]. It was recently demonstrated that the QDs-Tf-Saquinavir nanoformulation increases the drug solubility, enhancing systemic bioavailability, while the excellent optical properties of QDs also visualize the distribution and accumulation of nanoplexes in brain [107]. Such primary results offer a basis for the development of novel QDs with targeting molecules and drugs, which could enhance drug delivery efficacy across the BBB and facilitate the uptake of the QD-drugs in the brain. Despite the encouraging results on the use of QDs for drug delivery across the BBB, there is still serious concern regarding QDs toxicity *in vivo,* which mainly originates from the intrinsic, potentially toxic nature of the semiconductor materials themselves.

On the other hand, the placental barrier protects the embryo from various chemical agents and other foreign substances in the body. However, the passage of xenobiotic molecules through the placental barrier is not completely prevented, and drugs may affect fetal cell proliferation, embryonic growth, and organ formation [108]. Knowledge regarding embryotoxicity is of great importance because it is a necessary part of the toxicological profile that must be established for any new biologically active substance relevant to human safety. There are many studies in this field [109-111], but the detailed effects of NPs still pose many questions. A decrease in embryonic weight after QDs injection on the sixth day of embryogenesis (CdSe/ZnS QDs, 9.6%; CdT QDs, 6.2%) has been reported, and no embryotoxic or teratogenic effects were observed at any stage of embryogenesis [112]. Others have shown that NPs (nSP and TiO2s 70 nm and 35 nm in diameter, respectively) can cross the placental barrier in pregnant mice and cause neurotoxicity in their offspring [113]. They showed that the NPs were found in the placenta, fetal liver, and fetal brain. Other authors argue that some NPs (CdSe and CdTe/CdS) in different sizes, at different dosages, and with different outer capping materials can increase the rate of early-stage blastocyst death in mice and can be potentially transferred across the placenta to the fetus [109, 114]. These studies show that NPs can enter the embryo through the placenta, which is a natural barrier for a large variety of organic substances with diverse molecular structures. The NPs, which appear in the maternal body during pregnancy, can cross the placental barrier and may even cause developmental deformities. Recently, we demonstrated that CdS-MD nanoparticles were embryotoxics in a chicken embryo model (Figure 5) [42]. The nature of the observed abnormalities suggests that these effects could be directly associated with concentration. Therefore, according to the observed effects, the prolonged accumulation of quantum dots in the maternal organism may increase the risk of adverse effects on embryo development.

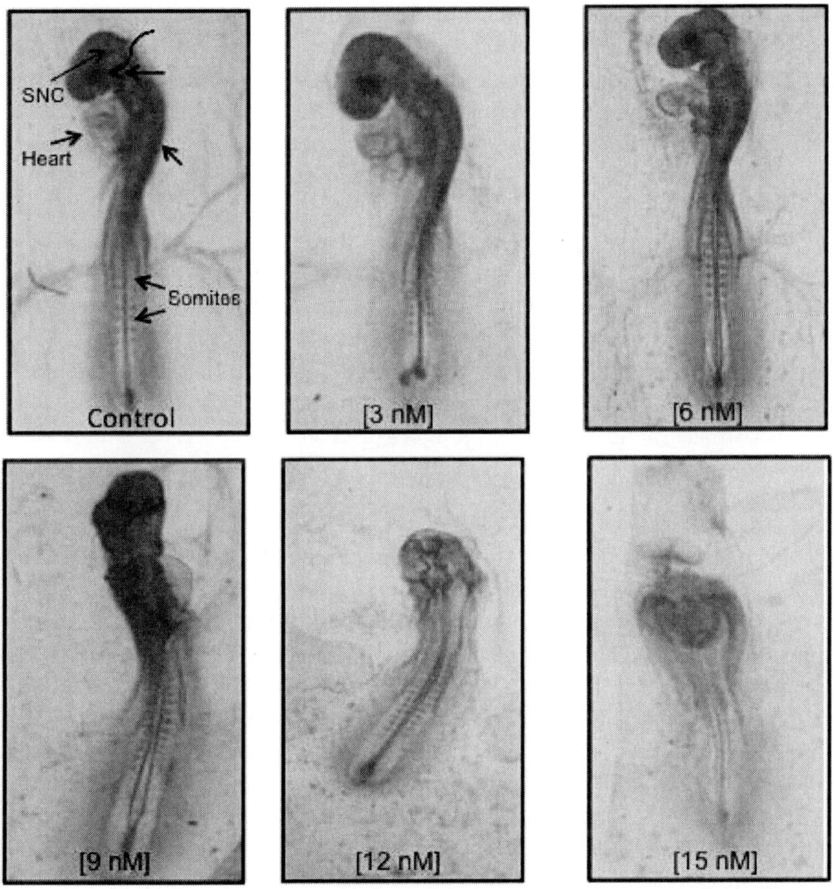

Figure 5. Photographs of 72 h-old chick embryos treated with CdS/Maltodextrin. Observed alterations were dose dependent.

The liver is know to have a high capacity to metabolize and degenerate a multitude of xenobiotics. The binding of proteins plays a key role in delivering xenobiotics from plasma into the liver. In addition, the reticuloendothelial system (RES) can phagocytose particles larger than 100 nm and then transport the particles into the liver in vivo. Metabolism of QDs is yet another understudied aspect of cadmium QDs. The QD cores do not appear to be subject to extensive enzymatic metabolism, but shells and coatings are. The extent of metabolism of the shell and coating becomes critical for toxicity, since they shield the more toxic CdSe or CdTe cores from the intracellular environment. Rather than metabolism per se, degradation of the shell and coatings within the biological environment appear to be more important. QD shells and coatings appear to degrade under photolytic and oxidative conditions, yet we know little about the degradation products or their biological effects, which may regulate release of toxic cadmium cores. The behavior of nanoparticles *in vivo* depend on properties such as the nanosize (surface area and size distribution), chemical composition (purity, crystallinity, electronic property, etc.), surface structure (surface reactivity, surface groups, inorganic or organic coatings, etc.), solubility, shape, and aggregation [115]. It has been suggested that the metabolic paths of QD nanoparticles are closely correlated to their aggregation states, and three metabolic paths were disclosed after intravenous injection: 1) the QDs that maintained their original nanosize without binding *in vivo*were rapidly excreted via the kidney; 2) some QDs binding to proteins were translocated to the liver and were excreted with feces; 3) a small fraction of the QDs aggregated to larger particles and were retained in liver tissue for a long time [116].

Several studies suggest that the kidneys can remove QDs that are less than 5 nm. It has been observed that, after i.v. administration of CdSe/ZnS-QDs, only 10% and 40% of the injected dose was found in the kidney and liver respectively, suggesting that only a fraction of the total QDs dose passed through this route [117]. Another study quantitatively detected the excretion of QDs in mice feces and urine after i.v. injection of CDSe QDs. The speed of excretion was quicker via feces, and the peak (0.214 ng of Cd) occurred 6–12 h postexposure. The excretion from urine was relatively delayed, and the peak (0.174 ng of Cd) was 24–36 h post-exposure [118]. The elimination of silica-coated CdSe QDs (~5.5 nm) from the body via feces and urine occurred in its totality after 5 days. Yet many reports propose that a portion of the administered QD dose may not be excreted and remains in the tissues. The extent of excretion and the extent of persistence in tissues take on added importance when one considers the potential delivery of QD as a cancer-targeting drug. More comprehensive studies of potential excretion will therefore be critical to QD development as a nanopharmaceutical.

Numerous studies have addressed the cellular level, but these are often difficult to compare due to varied dosing parameters and lack of physicochemical particle characterization. In general, it appears that most QDs examined found ready uptake at the cellular level, primarily via endocytic mechanisms, which depends upon the surface ligands coated over the QD surface [119, 23]. It has been reported that CdSe QDs and CdTe QDs that enter the cell, are visible at the cell surface and in the cytoplasm after a short time. QDs are likely to bind to the cell surface due to their interaction with cell surface glycoproteins and glycolipids [66]. Employing red-and green-emitting cationic QDs, it was found that the CdTe QD distribution was in part dependent on nanoparticle size. In the murine microglial N9 cell line, red cationic QDs (5 nm) were distributed throughout the cytoplasm. In contrast, green and also positively charged QDs (2 nm) were often found in the nucleus of N9 cells upon 1 h of QD exposure [120]. It has been shown that green QDs coated with tri-metoxysilylprolyl urea and acetate groups bind with high affinity in the cell nucleus of mouse 3T3 fibroblasts [121]. In human mammary epithelial tumor cells (MDA-MB-231) green-emitting CdSe/ZnS/SiO2 QDs were packaged in large vesicles found in the perinuclear region [23]. Confocal images have showed that MPA-coated QDs were distributed inside the cytoplasmic region of cells. In contrast, GA/TOPO-coated QDs were not found inside cells. These results indicate that cellular uptake of QDs depends upon the hydrodynamic size of the QDs as well as surface coating material [122]. These results strongly suggest that surface coatings can improve cytocompatibility and, consequently, decrease toxicity. Previous studies have shown that long-term exposure of surface coated QDs to their bioenvironment can destabilize the binding strength of the surface molecules, which in turn can yield unprotected QDs inside or outside the cells [123]. Therefore, the stability and binding strength of surface molecules over the QD surface define the cytocompatibility of the QDs and hence their cytotoxicity. Thus, according to previous studies: (1) the surface coating strategy could improve the cytocompatibility of QDs, (2) surface molecules could determine the intracellular uptake and consequent cytotoxicity of QDs, and (3) intracellular uptake of QDs could depend on their hydrodynamic size.

7. STRATEGIES FOR SAFE DRUG DELIVERY USING CADMIUM-CONTAINING QUANTUM DOTS

Discussion regarding the toxicity of cadmium-containing QDs can be somewhat confusing because of the diversity QDs being synthesized. Besides and as we have mentioned before, we have to consider that not all QDs are alike. Each individual type of QD possesses its own unique physicochemical properties, which in turn determine its potential toxicity or lack thereof [124]. In general, there are discrepancies in the current literature regarding the toxicity of QDs and these can be attributed to several factors: the lack of toxicology-based studies, the variety of QD dosage/exposure concentrations reported in the literature, and the widely varying physicochemical properties of individual QDs.

Up to date, toxicity studies have been conducted on a variety of both human and non-human cells and cell lines; research has been focused on *in vitro* assays of cytotoxicity [125-131]. *In vitro* studies are very important and can serve as background data to inform the design of *in vivo* studies but, on their own, they provide an insufficient basis for a complete risk assessment. Administration of QDs in animal models has revealed that QDs induce: (1) accumulation of QDs in specific organs [23, 132,133], (2) excretion in urine, bilis and feces [134], (3) toxicity in selective organs [135], (4) embryotoxicity [109, 111], and (5) oxidative damage [136-138]. Importantly, and a potential source of confusion in assessing QD toxicity, the latter depends on multiple factors derived from both individual QD physicochemical properties and environmental conditions: QD size, charge, concentration, outer coating bioactivity (capping material, functional groups), and oxidative, photolytic, and mechanical stability have each been shown to be determining toxicity factors. Therefore, all these aspects should be extended to examine alternate QD formulations, compositions, and shapes to help facilitate any future generalizations regarding size thresholds in the regulatory context. There are only a few studies specifically designed for toxicological assessment (e.g., dose, duration, frequency of exposure, mechanisms of action). Many of the studies, from which QD toxicity information is derived, it has been cited in reference to it were performed by nanotechnology researchers rather than toxicologists or health scientists. It is therefore difficult to extrapolate the results of such studies in order to reach any conclusions regarding the health and safety of QDs. Nonetheless, these studies may provide important insights that will be useful in guiding the eventual design of standardized toxicity tests and protocols.

The wealth of data accumulated from QD toxicity studies is an invaluable asset that should be exploited to design appropriate methodologies to further assess the toxicity of novel QDs. Researchers often neglect to carry out a comprehensive characterization of QDs prior to using them. In our opinion, this step is absolutely necessary, especially before any toxicity screening is started, precisely because the exact property or properties of QDs responsible for said toxicity are still poorly understood. This omission is one of the reasons behind the current state of confusion surrounding this issue. As epigenetic changes may lead to long-term reprogramming of gene expression long after the initial insult has been removed, results from "nanoepigenetic" assessments may have important implications on the future use of new nanomaterials in bioimaging and therapeutic applications. They should be evaluated early in the development of new QDs as well as QD-based devices and clinical tools. Future QD toxicity studies should be standardized and systematized because methodological variability in the current body of literature makes it difficult to compare and contrast results. We advocate the following steps for consistent, comparable toxicology data: (a) standardize dose metrics, (b) characterize QD uptake concentration, (c) identify *in vitro* models that reflect how the QDs QDs interact with cells *in vivo*, and (d) use multiple assays to determine sublethal toxicity and biocompatibility. Proceeding without careful evaluation of these critical areas will blunt the progress of nanomedicine and place human health at risk. However, judicious further research into these areas will undoubtedly contribute to development of nanopharmaceuticals for cancer treatment and drug delivery that have minimal to low risk and can highly benefit public health.

8. CONCLUSION

Cadmium-containing QDs are leading the way toward new preparations that can overcome the fundamental limitations of simple free drug formulations, providing the means to change their pharmacological properties and also understand their biological fate in great detail. However, ADME properties depend on multiple factors derived from both inherent physicochemical properties and environmental conditions. The findings also suggest that, under certain conditions, QDs may pose risks to human health, as determined by rodent animal models and *in vitro* cell cultures. This review outlined the unique features that make QDs an ideal platform for nanocarrier design and discussed how this model has been applied to study vehicle behavior for diverse drug delivery applications. However, it is clear that to make such a goal feasible and relatively risk-free for human beings, more extensive pharmacological and toxicological research of QDs are needed.

REFERENCES

1. Fortina P., Kricka LJ., Surrey S., Grodzinski P. Nanobiotechnology: the promise and reality of new approaches to molecular recognition. Trends in biotechnology. 2006. p168-173.

2. Moghimi SM., Hunter AC., Murray JC. Nanomedicine: current status and future prospects. FASEB J. 2005. p311-330

3. Rosenblum LT., Kosaka N., Mitsunaga M., Choyke PL., Kobayashi H. *In vivo* molecular imaging using nanomaterials: general *in vivo* characteristics of nano-sized reagents and applications for cancer diagnosis. Molecular membrane biology. 2010. p274-285

4. Aswathy RG., Yoshida Y., Maekawa T., Kumar DS. Near-infrared quantum dots for deep tissue imaging. Analytical and bioanalytical chemistry. 2010. p1417-1435

5. Madani SY., Shabani F., Dwek MV., Seifalian AM. Conjugation of quantum dots on carbon nanotubes for medical diagnosis and treatmen. International journal of nanomedicine. 2013. p941-950.

6. Jain KK., The role of nanobiotechnology in drug discovery. Drug Discovery Today. 2005. p1435-442.

7. Tejada-Berges T., Granai CO., Gordinier M., Gajewski W. Caelyx/Doxil for the treatment of metastatic ovarian and breast cancer. Expert review of anticancer therapy. 2002. p143-150

8. Gradishar WJ. Albumin-bound paclitaxel: A next-generation taxane. Expert opinion on pharmacotherapy. 2006. p1041-1053

9. Mo°schwitzer J., Muller RH. New method for the effective production of ultrafine drug nanocrystals. Journal of nanoscience and nanotechnology. 2006. p3145-3153

10. Schek RM., Hollister SJ., Krebsbach PH. Delivery and protection of adenoviruses using biocompatible hydrogels for localized gene therapy. Molecular therapy: the journal of the American Society of Gene Therapy. 2004. p130-138

11. Duncan R., Spreafico F. Polymer conjugates. Pharmacokinetic considerations for design and development. Clinical pharmacokinetics. 1994. p290-306.

12. LaVan DA., Lynn DM., Langer R. Moving smaller in drug discovery and delivery. Nature Reviews Drug Discovery. 2002. p77-84.

13. Duncan R. The dawning era of polymer therapeutics. Nature Reviews Drug Discovery. 2003. p347-360.

14. De Mel A., Oh JT., Ramesh B., Seifalian AM. Biofunctionalized quantum dots for live monitoring of stem cells: applications in regenerative medicine. Regenerative medicine. 2012. p335-347.

15. Grattoni A., Tasciotti E., Fine D., Fernandez-Moure J.S., Sakamoto J., Hu Y., Weiner B., Ferrari M., Parazynski S. Nanotechnologies and regenerative medical approaches for space and terrestrial medicine. Aviation, space, and environmental medicine. 2012. p1025-1036.

16. Kingham E., Oreffo RO. Embryonic and induced pluripotent stem cells: understanding, creating, and exploiting the nano-niche for regenerative medicine. ACS Nano. 2013. p1867-1881.

17. Anto VE., Gomes ME., Mano JF., Reis R.L. From nano-to macro-scale: nanotechnology approaches for spatially controlled delivery of bioactive factors for bone and cartilage engineering. Nanomedicine (Lond). 2012. p1045-1066.

18. Yaghini E., Seifalian AM., MacRobert AJ. Quantum dots and their potential biomedical applications in photosensitization for photodynamic therapy. Nanomedicine (Lond). 2009. p353-363

19. Mansur HS. Quantum dots and nanocomposites. Wiley Interdisciplinary Reviews: Nanomedicine and Nanobiotechnology. 2010. p113-129.

20. Ghasemi Y., Peymani P., Afifi S. Quantum dot: magic nanoparticle for imaging, detection and targeting. Acta Biomedica. 2009. p156-165.

21. Bruchez M., Moronne M., Gin P., Weiss S., Alivisatos P. The use of nanocrystals in biological detection. Nature Biotechnology. 2004. p47-52.

22. Baker M. Nanotechnology imaging probes: smaller and more stable. Nature Methods. 2010. p957-962.

23. Smith AM., Duan H., Mohs AM., Nie S. Bioconjugated quantum dots for *in vivo* molecular and cellular imaging. Advanced Drug Delivery reviews. 2008. p1226-1240.

24. Geszke-Moritz M., Moritz M. Quantum dots as versatile probes in medical sciences: synthesis, modification and properties. Materials Science and Engineering: C. 2013. p1008-1021.

25. Derfus AM., Chan WCW., Bhatia SA. Probing the cytotoxicity of semiconductor quantum dots. Nano Letters. 2004. p4-11.

26. Bottrill M., Green M. Some aspects of quantum dot toxicity. Chemical Communications, 2011. p7039-7050

27. Rzigalinski BA., Strobl JS. Cadmium-containing nanoparticles: perspectives on pharmacology and toxicology of quantum dots. Toxicology and applied pharmacology. 2009. p280-288

28. Chan WCW., Maxwell DJ., Gao X., Bailey RE., Han M., Nie S. Luminescent quantum dots for multiplexed biological detection and imaging. Current Opinion in Biotechnology. 2002. p40-46.

29. Piotrowska H., Geszke-Moritz M., Murias M., Balan L., Moritz M., Lulek, J., Schneider R. Thioglycerol-capped Mn-doped ZnS quantum dot bioconjugates as efficient two-photon fluorescent nano-probes for bioimaging. Journal of Materials Chemistry B. 2013. p698-706.

30. Rzigalinski BA., Meehan K., Davis RM., Xu Y., Miles WC., Cohen CA. Radical Nanomedicine. Nanomedicine. 2006. p339–412.

31. Li KG., Chen JT., Bai SS., Wen X., Song SY., Yu Q., Wang YQ. Intracellular oxidative stress and cadmium ions release induce cytotoxicity of unmodified cadmium sulfide quantum dots. Toxicology in Vitro. 2009. p1007-1013.

32. Nan C., Yao H, Yuanyuan S, Xiaoming L., Qing H., Haifeng W., Xiangzhi Z., Renzhong T., Chunhai F. The cytotoxicity of cadmium-based quantum dots. Biomaterials. 2012. p1238-1244.

33. Mailander V., Landfester K. Interaction of nanoparticles with cells. Biomacromolecules. 2009. p2379-2400.

34. Godt J., Scheidig F., Grosse-Siestrup C., Esche V., Brandenburg P., Reich A., Groneberg DA., The Toxicity of Cadmium and Resulting Hazards for Human Health. Journal of Occupational Medicine and Toxicology. 2006. p1-6.

35. Shiohara A., Hoshino A., Hanaki K., Suzuki K., Yamamoto K. On the cyto-toxicity caused by quantum dots. Microbiology and Immunology. 2004. p669–675.

36. Kloepfer JA., Mielke RE., Wong MS., Nealson KH., Stucky G., Nadeau JL. Quantum dots as strain-and metabolism-specific microbiological labels. Applied and environmental microbiology. 2003. p4205-4213.

37. Ipe BI., Lehnig M., Niemeyer CM. On the Generation of Free Radical Species from Quantum Dots. Small. 2005. p706-709.

38. Choi AO., Brown SE., Szyf M., Maysinger D. Quantum Dot-Induced Epigenetic and Genotoxic Changes in Human Breast Cancer Cells. Journal of Molecular Medicine, 2008. p291-302

39. Raveendran P., Fu J., Wallen S. Completely “green” synthesis and stabilization of metal nanoparticles. Journal of the American Chemical Society. 2003. p13940-13941

40. Rodriguez P., Muñoz N., San-Martın E., Gonzalez de la Cruz G., Tomas SA., Zelaya A. Synthesis and spectral properties of starch capped CdS nanoparticles in aqueous solution. Journal of crystal growth. 2008. p160-164.

41. Hossain Z., Huq F. Studies on the interaction between Cd(2+) ions and nucleobases and nucleotides. J Inorg Biochem 2002. p97-105.

42. Rodríguez-Fragoso P., Reyes-Esparza J., León-Buitimea A., Rodríguez-Fragoso L. Synthesis, characterization and toxicological evaluation of maltodextrin capped cadmium sulfide nanoparticles in human cell lines and chicken embryos. Journal of Nanobiotechnology 2012. p1-11.

43. Williams DF. On the mechanisms of biocompatibility. Biomaterials. 2008. p2941-2953

44. Zhang Y., Clapp A. Overview of Stabilizing Ligands for Biocompatible Quantum Dot Nanocrystals. Sensor 2011. p11036-11055.

45. Smith AM., Nie S. Semiconductor nanocrystals: structure, properties, and band gap engineering. Accounts of Chemical Research. 2010. p190-200.

46. Sandra J., Jerry C., Oleg K., James R., Tomlinson ID., Biocompatible Quantum Dots for Biological Applications. Chemistry Biology Journal. 201. p10-24

47. Lin Z., Su X., Mu Y., Jin Q. Methods for labeling quantum dots to biomolecules. Journal of nanoscience and nanotechnology. 2004. p641-645.

48. Clarke SJ., Hollmann CA., Aldaye FA., Nadeau JL. Effect of ligand density on the spectral, physical, and biological characteristics of CdSe/ZnS quantum dots. Bioconjugate Chemistry. 2008. p562-568

49. Lyer G., Xu J., Weiss S. Single-step conjugation of antibodies to quantum dots for labelling cell surface receptors in mammalian cells. Methods in Molecular Biology. 2011. p553-563

50. Tamer MS., Azzazy HM., Mansour MM., Kazmierczak SC. Quantum Dots: Heralding a Brighter Future for Clinical Diagnostics. Nanomedicine. 2012. p1755-1769

51. Zeng Q., Zhang Y., Song K., Kong X., Aalders MC., Zhang H. Enhancement of sensitivity and specificity of the fluoroimmunoassay of hepatitis B virus surface antigen through "flexible" coupling between quantum dots and antibody. Talanta. 2009. p307-312

52. Luo Y., Zhang B., Chen M., Jiang T., Zhou D., Huang J., Fu W. Sensitive and rapid quantification of C-reactive protein using quantum dot-labeled microplate immunoassay. Journal of Translational Medicine. 2012. p10-24.

53. Sapsford KE., Spindel S., Jennings T., Tao G., Triulzi RC., Algar WR., Medintz, IL. Optimizing two-color semiconductor nanocrystal immunoassays in single well microtiter plate formats. Sensors. 2011. p7879-7891

54. Cao Z., Li H., Lau C., Zhang Y. Cross-talk-free simultaneous fluoroimmunoassay of two biomarkers based on dual-color quantum dots. Analytica chimica acta 2011. p44-50

55. Pinaud F., King D., Moore HP., Weiss S. Bioactivation and cell targeting of semiconductor CdSe/ZnS nanocrystals with phytochelatin-related peptides. Journal of the American Chemical Society. 2004. p6115-6123.

56. Cai W., Shin DW., Chen K., Gheysens O., Cao Q., Wang SX., Gambhir SS., Chen X. Peptide-labeled near-infrared quantum dots for imaging tumor vasculature in living subjects. Nano Letters. 2006. p669-676

57. Orndorff RL., Rosenthal SJ. Neurotoxin quantum dot conjugates detect endogenous targets expressed in live cancer cells. Nano Letters. 2009. p2589-2599

58. Chopra A. ZW800-1, a zwitterionic near-infrared fluorophore, and its cyclic RGD peptide derivative cyclo-(RGDyK)-ZW800-1. Molecular Imaging and Contrast Agent Database (MICAD) [Internet]. Bethesda (MD): National Center for Biotechnology Information (US). 2004-2013.

59. Orndorff RL., Warnement MR., Mason JN., Blakely RD., Rosenthal SJ. Quantum dot *ex vivo* labeling of neuromuscular synapses. Nano Letters. 2008. p780-785

60. Medintz IL., Uyeda HT., Goldman ER., Mattoussi H. Quantum dot bioconjugates for imaging, labelling and sensing. *Natute Materials.* 2005. p435-446

61. Bharali DJ., Lucey DW., Jayakumar H., Pudavar HE., Prasad PN. Folate-receptor-mediated delivery of InP quantum dots for bioimaging using confocal and two-photon microscopy. Journal of the American Chemical Society. 2005. p11364-11371.

62. Danglot L., Chaineau M., Dahan M., Gendron MC., Boggetto N., Perez F., Galli T. Role of TI-VAMP and CD82 in EGFR cell-surface dynamics and signaling. Journal Cell Science. 2010. p723-735.

63. Geng L., Zhang HL., Peng H. The formation of acetylcholine receptor clusters visualized with quantum dots. BMC Neuroscience. 2009. P10-80.

64. Gonda K., Watanabe TM., Ohuchi N., Higuchi H. *In vivo* nano-imaging of membrane dynamics in metastatic tumor cells using quantum dots. The Journal of biological chemistry. 2010. p2750-2757.

65. Hikage M., Gonda K., Takeda M., Kamei T., Kobayashi M., Kumasaka M., Ohuchi N. Nano-imaging of the lymph network structure with quantum dots. Nanotechnology. 2010. p185103-185111.

66. Parak WJ., Gerion D., Zanchet D., Woerz AS., Pellegrino T., Micheel C., Alivisatos AP. Conjugation of DNA to silanized colloidal semiconductor nanocrystalline quantum dots. Chemistry of Materials. 2002. p2113-2119.

67. Wang AZ., Langer R., Farokhzad OC. Nanoparticle delivery of cancer drugs. Annual review of medicine. 2012. p185-198.

68. Weng KC., Noble CO., Papahadjopoulos-Sternberg B., Chen FF., Drummond DC., Kirpotin DB., Park JW. Targeted tumor cell internalization and imaging of multifunctional quantum dot-conjugated immunoliposomes *in vitro* and *in vivo*. Nano letters, 2008. p2851-2857.

69. Dey NS., RAO M. Quantum dot: Novel carrier for drug delivery. International Journal of Research in Pharmaceutical and Biomedical Sciences. 2011. p448-458.

70. Manabe N., Hoshino A., Liang YQ., Goto T., Kato N., Yamamoto S. Quantum dot as a drug tracer *in vivo*. NanoBioscience, IEEE Transactions on. 2006. p263-267

71. Bagalkot V., Zhang L., Levy-Nissenbaum E., Jon S., Kantoff PW., Langer R., Farokhzad OC. Quantum dot-aptamer conjugates for synchronous cancer imaging, therapy, and sensing of drug delivery based on bi-fluorescence resonance energy transfer. Nano Letters. 2007. p3065-3070

72. Levy-Nissenbaum E., Radovic-Moreno AF., Wang AZ. Langer R., Farokhzad OC. Nanotechnology and aptamers: applications in drug delivery. Trends in Biotechnology. 2008. p442-449

73. Chakravarthy KV., Davidson BA., Helinski JD., Ding H., Law WC., Yong KT., Knight PR. Doxorubicin-conjugated quantum dots to target alveolar macrophages and inflammation. Nanomedicine: Nanotechnology, Biology, and Medicine. 2011. p88-96

74. Derfus AM., Chen AA., Min DH., Ruoslahti E., Bhatia SN. Targeted quantum dot conjugates for siRNA delivery. Bioconjugate chemistry. 2007. p1391-1396.

75. Lifeng Q., Xiaohu G. Emerging application of quantum dots for drug delivery and therapy. Expert Opinion on Drug Delivery. 2008. p263-267.

76. Fischer HC., Liu LC., Pang KS., Chan, WCW. Pharmacokinetics of nanoscale quantum dots: In vivo distribution, sequestration, and clearance in the rat. Advanced Functional Materials. 2006. p1299-1305.

77. Kulvietis V., Zurauskas E., Rotomskis R. Distribution of polyethylene glycol coated quantum dots in mice skin Experimengtal Dermatology. 2013. P141-159.

78. Seto JE., Polat BE., Lopez RF., Blankschtein D., Langer R. Effects of ultrasound and sodium lauryl sulfate on the transdermal delivery of hydrophilic permeants: Comparative *in vitro* studies with full-thickness and split-thickness pig and human skin. Journal of controlled release: official journal of the Controlled Release Society. 2010. p26-32

79. Robe A., Pic E., Lassalle HP., Bezdetnaya L., Guillemin F., Marchal F. Quantum dots in axillary lymph node mapping: biodistribution study in healthy mice. BMC Cancer 2008. p111-120.

80. Kosaka N., Ogawa M., Sato N., Choyke PL., Kobayashi H. *In vivo* real-time, multicolor, quantum dot lymphatic imaging. The Journal of investigative dermatology. 2009. p2818-2822.

81. Kulvietis V., Zurauskas E., Rotomskis R. Distribution of polyethylene glycol coated quantum dots in mice skin. Experimental Dermatology, 2013. p141-159

82. Tsung-Rong K., Chia-Feng L., Sung-Jan L., Chen-Yuan D., Chia-Chun C., Hsin-Yuan T. Studies of Intracorneal Distribution and Cytotoxicity of Quantum Dots: Risk Assessment of Eye Exposure. ChemIcal Research in toxicology. 2011. p253-261

83. Schipper ML., Iyer G., Koh AL., Cheng Z., Ebenstein Y., Aharoni A., Keren S., Bentolila LA., Li J., Rao J., Chen X., Banin U., Wu AM., Sinclair

R., Weiss S., Gambhir SS. Particle size, surface coating, and PEGylation influence the biodistribution of quantum dots in living mice. Small. 2009. p126-134.

84. Fubini B., Ghiazza M., Fenoglio I. Physico-chemical features of engineered nanoparticles relevant to their toxicity. Nanotoxicology. 2010. p347-363

85. Choi HS., Ashitate Y., Lee JH., Kim SH., Matsui A., Insin N., Bawendi MG., Semmler-Behnke M., Frangioni JV., Tsuda A. Rapid translocation of nanoparticles from the lung airspaces to the body. Nature biotechnology. 2010. p1300-1303.

86. Kreyling WG., Semmler-Behnke M., Takenaka S., Moller W. Differences in the Biokinetics of Inhaled Nano-versus Micrometer-Sized Particles. Accounts of chemical research. 2013. p714-722.

87. Jani P., Halbert GW., Langridge J., Florence AT. Nanoparticle uptake by the rat gastrointestinal mucosa: quantitation and particle size dependency. The Journal of pharmacy and pharmacology. 1990. p821-826.

88. Hillyer JF., Albrecht RM. Gastrointestinal persorption and tissue distribution of differently sized colloidal gold nanoparticles. Journal of pharmaceutical sciences. 2001. p1927-1936.

89. Florence AT: Nanoparticle uptake by the oral route: fulfilling its potential? Drug Discovery Today: Technologies 2005. p75-81.

90. Schleh C., Semmler-Behnke M., Lipka J., Wenk A., Hirn S., Schaffler M., Schmid G., Simon U., Kreyling WG. Size and surface charge of gold nanoparticles determine absorption across intestinal barriers and accumulation in secondary target organs after oral administration. Nanotoxicology. 2012. p36-46.

91. Klement P., Du YJ., Berry L., Andrew M., Chan AKC. Blood-compatible biomaterials by surface coating with a novel antithrombin–heparin covalent complex. Biomaterials. 2002. p527-535.

92. Dobrovolskaia M.A., Mcneil S.E. Immunological properties of engineered nanomaterials. Nature nanotechnology. 2007. p469-478.

93. Fischer HC., Liu L., Pang KS., Chan WCW. Pharmacokinetics of Nanoscale Quantum Dots: *In Vivo* Distribution, Sequestration, and Clearance in the Rat. Advanced Functional Materials. 2006. p1299-1305.

94. Gopee NV., Roberts DW., Webb P., Cozart CR., Siitonen PH., Warbritton AR., Yu WW., Colvin VL., Walker NJ., Howard PC. Migration of intradermally injected quantum dots to sentinel organs in mice. Toxicology Science. 2007. p249-257.

95. Yang RS., Chang LW., Wu JP., Tsai MH., Wang HJ., Kuo YC., Yeh TK., Yang CS., Lin P., Persistent tissue kinetics and redistribution of nanoparticles, quantum dot 705, in mice: ICP-MS quantitative assessment. Environmental health perspectives. 2007. p1339-1343.

96. Pelley, JL., Daar AS., Saner MA. State of academic knowledge on toxicity and biological fate of quantum dots. Toxicological Sciences. 2009. p276-296.

97. Kim J., Kim KS., Jiang G., Kang H., Kim S., Kim BS., Park MH., Hahn, SK. *In vivo* real-time bioimaging of hyaluronic acid derivatives using quantum dots. Biopolymers. 2008. p1144-1153.

98. Ballou B., Lagerholm BC., Ernst LA., Bruchez MP., Waggoner AS. Noninvasive imaging of quantum dots in mice. Bioconjugate chemistry. 2004. p79-86.

99. Salykina YF., Zherdeva VV., Dezhurov SV., Wakstein MS., Shirmanova MV., Zagaynova EV., Savitsky AP. Biodistribution and clearance of quantum dots in small animals. In Sartov Fall Meeting. International Society for Optics and Photonics. 2010. p799908-799908.

100. TsingHai W., HuiAn H., YiKong H., ChiShiun C., YuhChang S., ChuFang W. The in vivo biodistribution and fate of CdSe quantum dots in the murine model: a laser ablation inductively coupled plasma mass spectrometry study. Analytical and bioanalytical chemistry. 2012. p3025-3036.

101. Wu X., Tian F., Zhao JX., Wu M. Evaluating pharmacokinetics and toxicity of luminescent quantum dots. Expert Opinion on Drug Metabolism & Toxicology. 2013. p1265-1277.

102. Su Y., Peng F., Jiang Z., Zhong Y., Lu Y., Jiang X., Huang Q., Fan C., Lee ST., He Y. *In vivo* distribution, pharmacokinetics, and toxicity of aqueous synthesized cadmium-containing quantum dots. Biomaterials. 2011. p5855-5862.

103. Weiss N., Miller F., Cazaubon S., Couraud PO. The blood–brain barrier in brain homeostasis and neurological diseases. Biochimica et biophysica acta. 2009. p842-857.

104. Lipinski, CA. Drug-like properties and the causes of poor solubility and poor permeability. Journal of pharmacological and toxicological methods. 2000. p235-249.

105. Kato S., Itoh K., Yaoi T., Tozawa T., Yoshikawa Y., Yasui H., Kanamura N., Hoshino A., Manabe N., Yamamoto K., Fushiki S. Organ distribution of quantum dots after intraperitoneal administration, with special reference to area-specific distribution in the brain. Nanotechnology. 2010. p335103-335110

106. Xu G., Yog KT., Roy I., Mahajan SD., Ding H., Schwartz, SA., Prasad PN. Bioconjugated quantum rods as targeted probes for efficient transmigration across an *in vitro* blood-brain barrier. Bioconjugate chemistry. 2008. p1179-1185.

107. Xu G., Mahajan S., Roy I., Yong KT. Theranostic quantum dots for crossing blood–brain barrier *in vitro* and providing therapy of HIV-associated encephalopathy. Frontier in Pharmacology. 2013. p1-8

108. Brendel K, Duhamel RC, Shepard TH. Embryotoxic drugs. Biological research in pregnancy and perinatology. 1985. p1-54.

109. Chan WH., Shiao NH. Cytotoxic effect of CdSe quantum dots on mouse embryonic development. Acta Pharmacologica. 2008. p259-266

110. Chu M., Wu Q., Yang H., Yuan R., Hou S., Yang Y., Sheng L. Transfer of quantum dots from pregnant mice to pups across the placental barrier. Small. 2010. p670-678.

111. Wick P., Malek A., Manser P., Meili D., Maeder-Althaus X., Diener L. Barrier capacity of human placenta for nano-sized materials. Environmental Health Perspectives. 2010. p432-436.

112. Žalgevičienė V., Kulvietis V., Bulotienė D., Didžiapetrienė J., & Rotomskis R. The effect of nanoparticles in Rats During Critical periods of pregnancy. Medicina (Kaunas). 2012. p256-64.

113. Yamashita K., Yoshioka Y., Higashisaka K., Mimura K., Morishita Y., Nozaki MI. Silica and titanium dioxide nanoparticles cause pregnancy complications in mice. Nature Nanotechnology. 2011. p321-328.

114. Wick P., Malek A., Manser P., Meili D., Maeder-Althaus X., Diener L. Barrier capacity of human placenta for nano-sized materials. Environmental Health Perspective. 2010. p432-436.

115. Nel A., Xia T., Madler L., Li N. Toxic potential of materials at the nanolevel. Science. 2006. p622-627.

116. Chen Z., Chen H., Meng H., Xing G., Gao X., Sun B., Fang X. Biodistribution and metabolic paths of silica coated CdSeS quantum dots. Toxicology and Applied Pharmacology. 2008. p364-371

117. Yang RS., Chang LW., Wu JP., Tsai MH., Wang HJ., Kuo YC., Yeh TK., Yang CS., Lin P. Persistent tissue kinetics and redistribution of nanoparticles, quantum dot 705, in mice: ICP-MS quantitative assessment. Environmental Health Perspectives. 2007. p1339-1343.

118. Vibin M., Vinayakan R., John A., Raji V., Rejiya CS., Abraham A. Biokinetics and In vivo Distribution Behaviours of Silica-Coated Cadmium Selenide Quantum Dots. Biological trace element research. 2011. p213-222

119. Hoshino A., Fujioka K., Oku T., Suga M., Sasaki T., Ohta M., Yasuhara K., Suzuki K., Yamamoto K. Physicochemical properties and cellular toxicity of nanocrystal quantum dots depend on their surface modifications. Nano Letters. 2004. p2163-2169.

120. Lovrić J., Bazzi HS., Cuie Y., Fortin GR., Winnik FM., Maysinger D. Differences in subcellular distribution and toxicity of Green and red emitting CdTe quantum dots. Journal of Molecular Medicine. 2005. p377-385

121. Mahto, SK., Park C., Yoon TH., &-Rhee SW. Assessment of cytocompatibility of surface-modified CdSe/ZnSe quantum dots for BALB/3T3 fibroblast cells. Toxicology *in vitro*. 2010. p1070-1077.

122. Zhang B., Wang X., Liu F., Cheng Y., Shi D. Effective reduction of nonspecific binding by surface engineering of quantum dots with bovine serum albumin for cell-targeted imaging. Langmuir. 2012. p16605-16613.

123. Cho SJ., Maysinger D., Jain M., Röder B., Hackbarth S., Winnik FM. Long-term exposure to CdTe quantum dots causes functional impairments in live cells. Langmuir. 2007. p1974-1980.

124. Yuan T., Songling H., Hongmei L., Xin C., Li-Huang L., Jianxiang Z. The role of surface chemistry in determining *in vivo* biodistribution. Biomaterials. 2013. p8741-8755.

125. Zheng X., Tian J., Weng L., Wu L., Jin Q., Zhao J., Wang L.. Cytotoxicity of cadmium-containing quantum dots based on a study using a microfluidic chip. Nanotechnology. 2012. p055102-055111.

126. Ryman-Rasmussen J. P., Riviere J. E., Monteiro-Riviere N. A. Surface Coatings Determine Cytotoxicity and Irritation Potential of Quantum

Dot Nanoparticles in Epidermal Keratinocytes. Journal of Investigative Dermatology. 2007. p143-153.

127. Chen N., He Y., Su Y., Li X., Huang Q., Wang H., Fan C. The cytotoxicity of cadmium-based quantum dots. Biomaterials. 2012. p1238-1244.

128. Su Y., Hu M., Fan C., He Y., Li Q., Li W., Huang Q. The cytotoxicity of CdTe quantum dots and the relative contributions from released cadmium ions and nanoparticle properties. Biomaterials. 2010. p4829-4834.

129. Soenen SJ., Demeester J., De Smedt SC., Braeckmans K. The cytotoxic effects of polymer-coated quantum dots and restrictions for live cell applications. Biomaterials. 2012. p4882-4888.

130. Bao YJ., Li JJ., Wang YT., Yu L., Lou L., Du WJ., Zhu JZ. Probing cytotoxicity of CdSe and CdSe/CdS quantum dots. Chinese Chemical Letters. 2011. p843-846.

131. Li S., Wang Y., Wang H., Bai Y., Liang G., Wang Y., Xiao Z. MicroRNAs as participants in cytotoxicity of CdTe quantum dots in NIH/3T3 cells. Biomaterials. 2011. p3807-3814.

132. Roberts JR., Antonini JM., Porter DW., Chapman RS., Scabilloni JF., Young SH., Mercer RR. Lung toxicity and biodistribution of Cd/Se-ZnS quantum dots with different surface functionalgroups after pulmonary exposure in rats. Particle and Fibre Toxicology. 2013. p1-17.

133. Yang RH., Chang LW., Wu JP., Tsai MH., Wang HJ., Kuo YC., Yeh TK., Yang CS., Lin P. Persistent tissue kinetics and redistribution of nanoparticles, quantum dot705, in mice: ICP-MS quantitative assessment. Environmental health perspectives. 2007. p1339-1343.

134. Fischer H., Liu L., Pang KS., Chan W. Pharmacokinetics of nanoscale quantum dots: *in vivo* distribution, sequestration, and clearance in the rat. Advanced Functional Materials. 2006. p1299-1305.

135. Geys J., Nemmar A., Verbeken E., Smolders E., Ratoi M., Hoylaerts MF., Hoet PH. Acute Toxicity and Prothrombotic Effects of Quantum Dots: Impact of Surface Charge. Environmental Health Perspectives. 2008. p1607-1613.

136. Gagné F., Auclair J., Turcotte P., Fournier M., Gagnon C., Sauve S., Blaise C. Ecotoxicity of CdTe quantum dots to freshwater mussels: Impacts on immune system, oxidative stress and genotoxicity. Aquatic Toxicology. 2008. p333-340.

137. Wiecinski PN., Metz KM., King-Heiden TC., Louis KM., Mangham AN., Hamers RJ., Pedersen JA. Toxicity of Oxidatively Degraded Quantum Dots to Developing Zebrafish (Danio rerio). Environmental science & technology. 2013. p9132-9139.

138. Li KG., Chen JT., Bai SS., Wen X., Song SY., Yu Q., Wang YQ. Intracellular oxidative stress and cadmium ions release induce cytotoxicity of unmodified cadmium sulfide quantum dots. Toxicology in Vitro. 2009. p1007-1013.

Index